Start Competitive Programming!:
Ace the USACO Bronze Competition

Zachi Baharav and Daniel Zingaro

Start Competitive Programming!: Ace the USACO Bronze Competition

Zachi Baharav and Daniel Zingaro

Contents

Part IV. Appendix 381

Letter to the student

Congratulations!! This book will take your computer science experience to the next level. Not only will you learn all that you need to ace the USACO Bronze level, but you will be doing this while discovering the joy of exploring questions and solving them. You took the first step, opened the door, and now come join us along the road.

Maybe you've never tried a USACO problem, or maybe you've taken a programming course and wanted to strengthen up, or maybe you've tried a USACO competition before and didn't make it to silver yet. This book will help you recognize typical types of problems. We will guide you through a systematic analysis process that will help you explore problems and arrive at an algorithm.

Practice is the most important ingredient for succeeding at the Bronze level. The book gives you many practice problems carefully selected to lead you on a successful path. Each question is accompanied with hints and directions, and a detailed solution is available on the book's web site.

So, settle in, start reading, and solve problems! And if you have any questions, ask away on the book's forum. I am looking forward to see the new ways in which you solve the problems!

—Coach B.

Letter to the parent

Training and participating in USACO competitions is a great step toward enjoying and learning computer science. It goes far beyond merely programming and algorithms: Training for USACO teaches you the art of exploring, solving, and enjoying complex questions!

Perhaps your kids have shown some interest in competitive programming, problem solving, or improving their programming skill. Or perhaps you'd like to introduce your kids to this material and see if it catches their interest.

This book is a great first step into the world of solving problems with a computational focus. It conveys in a friendly way the joy of investigating questions and then coding the solution. The setting of the book is a school club, where the students ask clarifying questions, suggest alternative solutions, and make mistakes. The welcoming club setting allows the reader to feel at home in this class and join the exploration process.

Way too often I have parents approach me with the question "How long does it take to reach platinum?" This book opens the door and starts your learner on the road, and I hope it will enrich their experience in Computer Science. It teaches them all they need to ace the Bronze, and instills good habits for solving complex problems.

Congratulations on starting the journey. I hope it will be the start of a joyous and enriching experience for your learner for many years to come.

—Coach B.

Letter to the trained professional

You're a professional programmer. But do you ever feel (secretly, perhaps) that your problem-solving skill isn't all that great?

I was there. I finished college without ever competing in any math or coding events. Every so often I looked at a few coding competition puzzles—I was curious!—but they always looked so tricky and specialized to me. Nothing I could easily solve. Okay, nothing I could solve. Period. Fast forward a few (15+) years: I graduated with a Ph.D., worked as a researcher in the industry, and was doing fairly complicated algorithmic and programming work. Yet, whenever I looked at these competitive programming problems, I continued to be confounded.

Then, I found my calling as a teacher in high school. Working with students who wanted coaching for these competitions, I decided the time had come for me to crack this. With all my college education, I should be able to actually solve these! Or at least, that's what I needed to tell myself.

I sat down and studied as many of these kinds of problems as I could. I tried solving them myself. I looked at other people's solutions. And slowly but surely, I began to demystify them.

Turns out many of these problems don't call for higher level math or learning new algorithms. And, I can admit now that the problems aren't phrased to trick or confuse you.

You likely already know much of what you need in order to solve and code these problems. All that is required is to be able to "talk the language", and to understand that these problems require your genuine interest in trying to explore new things.

This book is designed to help you use your existing programming knowledge to solve problems.

Once you learn the language that these problems speak and understand how to go from the problem through to an algorithm and implementation, I think you will enjoy (yes, enjoy!) working on them.

So sit back, relax, and enjoy the journey: You already know all the rules and algorithms. This book will help you re-discover the joy of exploring problems, and the excitement of finding a solution. Good luck!

—Coach B.

Acknowledgments

We thank Mohsin Muzammil for help with book editing and markup.

Cover photo image credit Cristina Gottardi.

Part I. Preliminaries

Chapter 1. USACO Bronze

This chapter covers

- Essential facts about USACO Bronze level.
- What you need to know to pass Bronze.
- What you do *not* need to study to pass Bronze.
- Solving and submitting your first USACO problem.
- Practicing with this book.

A journey of a million miles starts with one step, and you are now taking this first step. Congratulations! This chapter will orient you to the USACO Bronze competition. Very soon, you'll be solving and submitting your first problem.

The chapter map is described in figure 1.1. We start in section 1.1 by answering frequently asked questions about USACO Bronze and introducing the team that will help us along the way. What do you need to know to pass Bronze? What do you NOT need to know? We will quickly address these very important questions.

In section 1.2, we solve, and submit, a USACO problem. We will get you used to this process, which you will repeat many times throughout the book.

In the final section, section 1.3, we'll consider a few suggestions on how to make the most of your time and effort as you practice with this book.

That's all you'll need to know to get started! Much later in this book, we'll delve into the logistics of the competition and explore advanced levels in more detail. Let's begin!

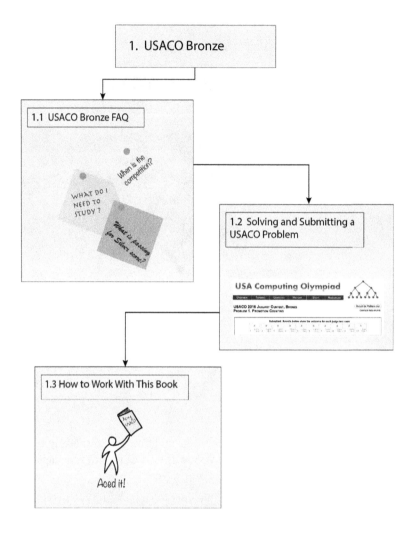

Figure 1.1 USACO Bronze chapter map. Answering common questions, submitting a USACO problem, and describing how to effectively use the book.

1.1. USACO Bronze FAQ

Coach B and four students are gathered in room 216, Tuesday, right after school. This is the first meeting of the USACO Bronze Club.

Coach B: Welcome to our first club meeting! I'm happy to see you all. I know you have many questions, and I will try to answer all of them. But my main goal for today is to get us solving and submitting a full problem to USACO!

Ryan: Yay! That would be awesome to dive right in. No icebreakers.

The team nods in agreement.

Coach B: Great minds think alike! So, here is what we'll do. Here's a pad of Post-it notes. Come on up here, all of you, and write your most pressing questions on the Post-its. Put those on the board, and as a team, try to group them into similar subjects. After about 5 minutes we'll reconvene. Sound like a good plan?

The team gives thumbs-up and nods. There's a flurry of motion as they scribble down questions, consult each other, and arrange and rearrange their Post-its on the board. As the room quiets, Coach B addresses the group.

Coach B: Good collection of questions! I will try and answer most of them. Oh, first, an introduction! I did say no icebreakers, but we do need to have a proper introduction. Let me start. My name is Dr. Zachi Baharav, and you can call me Coach B. As most of you know, I teach Math and Computer Science here at our high school, and I am also coaching two clubs: the Chess Club and the USACO club. I always learn from my students about new ways to solve problems, so I am really looking forward to what new things you'll come up with this year. Now, if we can go around, and just say your name, what grade you're in, and anything else you wish to share. Here, you can go first please, then go around in a circle.

Coach B gestures to Annie.

Annie: Hi, I'm Annie. I'm a ninth grader, a freshman, and I love puzzles and math. I did a programming camp over the summer and learned C++. I'm gonna take the Advanced Placement Computer Science course (AP-CS) next year. I heard good things about the USACO club from a friend who got to the Gold level in USACO, so I wanted to try it. Oh, I never did USACO or any coding competition. I did do the AMC, which is a math competition.

Coach B: Nice! Those are the American Mathematics Competitions, if you weren't aware. Next? Go ahead!

Ryan: Hi, I'm Ryan. A sophomore, tenth grader. Last year I had cross-country practice right when the club was meeting, so I couldn't join. This year, the time works. I'm taking AP-CS right now, and I know Python and Java. Python is my stronger language, though. Oh, and I am happy to try and learn C++. I heard it is not too different from Java.

Rachid: I'm Rachid. Also a freshman. Annie and I have 6 classes together, and now this club. I've been going to programming camps since 5th grade, so I've gotten fluent in C++ and Python. I actually tried USACO last year, but it was way too hard. I hope this year I can learn how to do it right.

Mei: Hi, I'm Mei. I'm a junior, eleventh grader. I never did programming camps or anything of sorts, but I took AP-CS last year and I really enjoyed it. This year I'm taking Data Structures. Coach B was my teacher last year, and he recommended I try this club, so here I am! I studied C++ over the summer with an online course, so I guess you can say I know Java and a little bit of C++. By the way, I'd never even heard about USACO before Coach B told me about it.

Coach B: Great! Thank you all. We have a mix of backgrounds, programming languages, and experience. All of you know at least one programming language and are comfortable using it, which is good—this is the only prerequisite for this club. Anyway, you're a good diverse mix, and I believe it will really help us see the problems from multiple angles. This is a key to getting better at solving these. And it should be fun working together as a team. Now let's tackle these questions you wrote down.

Coach B turns his attention to the board with the Post-its, shown in figure 1.2.

Coach B: I see that you've settled on a few basic clusters of questions that you all want to know. Thanks for not using the whole pad of Post-its!

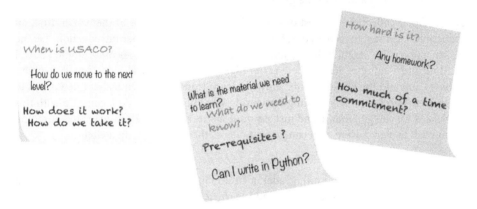

Figure 1.2 Questions about USACO, in three different groups, to be answered shortly.

Coach B: Let's look at the first group of questions, in yellow. You've agreed that you want to know when the competition is, and how it works. You want to know how to pass: how to get to the higher level. Perfect, yes, let's cover these basics. I'll add some bullet points here below the Post-its.

Coach B draws figure 1.3 on the board.

Coach B: We'll delve into this more as we get closer, but in short, the first contest is in December, and the last one is in March. You have four events, and you can go to all of them, or whichever ones you wish. Every new participant starts at the Bronze level. To be promoted to the Silver level, you need to pass one of the contests. Just one is enough.

When and how ?

When is USACO?

How do we move to the next level?

How does it work?
How do we take it?

- 4 competitions each season:
  December, January, February, US Open (in March)
- You can compete in any/all of the dates.
- Contests are usually 3 questions, in 4 hours, taken in one sitting. You can choose your start time within a window of a few given days.
- Take the contest from home, on your computer.
- We'll talk about more specifics later, when we address special "day-of" preparations.

Promotion

- You are at the Bronze level right now.
- If you pass, you reach Silver.

Passing
- If you get a perfect score, you are promoted automatically.
- If you get a partial score, you may get promoted, depending on a threshold determined after the contest is complete.

Figure 1.3 Common questions about the procedural aspects of the USACO Bronze competition.

While Coach B talks, pausing to write, the team scans the "When and how?" and "Promotion" boxes.

Ryan: Four hours? That's really long. Are there any breaks?

Coach B: Well, it's up to four hours. You may finish early, but yes, it might be up to four hours, and there's no official break. Once you start, your clock starts ticking. You have a little timer on the top of your competition page that shows how much time you have left, and it counts down from four hours to zero. You can't pause it. You're definitely welcome to get up from your chair and take a stretch, go and get some water, take a bathroom break, etc. But it's on your time.

Rachid: That sounds hard!

Coach B: Well, yes and no. You do have to stay focused for this amount of time. That's part of test-taking at high school and at these levels. But on the other hand, time flies when you're in the thick of solving a problem. You barely notice how the hours go by.

The team looks at each other. Four hours is definitely up there with the SAT and other big tests.

Coach B: Trust me, you can handle focusing for four hours! Now, the next group of your questions: let's see; they're about the content of the competition and the material we will need to know. Here, I'll jot everything down for you.

Coach B writes on the board, as in figure 1.4.

What am I tested on?

Bronze level focuses on three things:
1. **Problem solving skills** - Finding a solution to a problem.
2. **Algorithmic thinking** - Translating a solution into an algorithm.
3. **Fluency in coding** - Coding an algorithm without mistakes.

What do I need to study?

We will study these together:
- How to approach a problem and find a solution.
- How to convert a solution into an algorithm.
- How to code an algorithm correctly.

You do **NOT** have to study the following:
- **NO** specific algorithms, like sorting or searching.
- **NO** specific data-structures, like stacks, queues, graphs, or trees.
- **NO** specific coding techniques, like recursion or dynamic programming.

Figure 1.4 Material included in the USACO bronze level. The three main focus areas for Bronze level are: Problem solving skills; Algorithmic thinking; and Coding proficiency.

Coach B: I cannot emphasize it enough: The most important thing at the Bronze level is to be comfortable with solving problems. This is the main thing we will practice. Yes, you do need to know how to convert your solution to an algorithm, and you do need to code it afterwards. But by far the most critical requirement is to be able to read a problem, and try different methods until you find a solution.

The team looks a little confused.

Annie: Well, aren't all school tests always about solving problems?

Coach B: Not always. Some tests focus on your ability to memorize details or techniques. Here, let me put it another way. See how I've listed what you DON'T need to study? In earlier years, I had students dashing off to learn complicated algorithms, watching videos about graph algorithms and dynamic programming. Of course, everything you learn is helpful, but those fancy techniques just aren't the focus. The focus is solving problems. In other words: in terms of technique and programming, you all probably know enough to pass as-is. It's true that you *will* further improve your programming skills with practice, but that would be a bonus—a side effect, really. The main thing you'll learn here in the club will be how to solve problems.

The team members frown at each other.

Coach B: I see you're not convinced! But wait a couple of minutes, until we solve a real USACO problem. I think it will become clearer.

Ryan: So just to make sure, you're saying that I don't have to learn C++ for the competition, right?

Coach B: Absolutely right. You said your preferred language for coding is Python. Yep—you should be able to do well with it.

Ryan lets out a sigh of relief.

Mei: Just for the record, I'm still debating between Java and C++, but we'll see.

Coach B: Sounds good! Your last group of questions right here in figure 1.5 is focused on the time commitment.

How hard is it?
How much time and practice do I need?

- It's hard. Only about 10% of students who attempt it will pass Bronze. But it's definitely doable!

- To prepare fully, I recommend that you devote about 3 to 4 hours per week to practicing, for a period of three months.
- In these three months, you should solve 40 or more practice problems.
- Practice is the key: it exposes you to many types of problems and improves your coding.

Figure 1.5 Expected time commitment.

Coach B: We'll see for ourselves today what practice actually entails. But, in general, since we have about three months until the first contest, my experience is that you will need to devote at least 3 to 4 hours a week to practice on your own. It may take different amounts of time for different students, and that's totally okay. It's all about learning, and we all learn in different ways. Personally, I am usually slow on these in practice, as I like to reflect and think about problems a little deeper. Hopefully, you'll enjoy trying new problems, so it won't feel like school homework. Rather, it should feel like a challenge. I will emphasize it again when we talk in section 1.3 about practice, but it is really important not to get frustrated! The problems are not easy, and you'll need to take time to learn to solve them. But you'll have many ways to get hints and help. So, again: plan on dedicating at least 3 to 4 hours a week, and remember it is all about solving problems and coding them.

Rachid: What kind of hints and help? Like, is there an answer key?

Coach B: Yes, there is an answer key, and much more than that. We'll touch on it later today when we talk about how to practice. But, in short, for every problem you get assigned, you will have hints at various levels, and the full solution available. So you're never doomed to be stuck on any single problem.

The team relaxes in their seats, giving each other a few smiles.

Coach B: Alright, that's a good pause point! Let's take a five-minute bio-break, and then we'll come back and solve our first USACO problem!

Every section of this book will end with an epilogue, which adds perspective on what we just did. It helps us keep the larger picture in mind. And, every section will end with a vocabulary corner, where we'll explore some aspect of a relevant word.

EPILOGUE

In this section, we briefly answered the most common questions about USACO Bronze. Toward the end of the book, we will discuss in more detail the specifics of the test day, how to take the test, what to expect, and what will happen when you pass the Bronze level. If you're burning to know those specifics right now, go ahead and skip ahead to chapters 9 and 10. Otherwise, join us in solving and submitting a USACO problem in the next section.

 VOCABULARY Corner: **USACO, IOI,** and **OLYMPIAD.** USACO, which stands for **USA** Computing Olympiad, is the USA qualifying stage for selecting the team to represent the nation at the International Olympiad in Informatics (IOI). Both acronyms contain the word "Olympiad," which has its origins in Greek. Just like the "Olympics," it means "from Olympia" or "from Olympus." Olympia, a city in ancient Greece, hosted the original Olympic games every 4 years, a tradition that peaked around 500 B.C. The city, and its games, were named for Mount Olympus, the home of the mythic Greek gods. Thus, athletes in the original Olympic games were expected to perform epic, near-superhuman feats of strength. All this history of fame, myth, glory, and competition has influenced the word "Olympiad," meaning "a major national or international competition"—such as our own USA Computing Olympiad, where you'll rise to new heights, even under the pressure of performing, as your problem-solving abilities grow.

1.2. Solving and Submitting a USACO Problem

The team returns from their bio-break, stretching and grinning as they find their seats.

Coach B: As promised, let's solve and submit our first USACO problem! Please take out your laptops and go to http://www.usaco.org.

Coach B writes the URL on the board, and there's a little bustle as laptops come out and power up.

Ryan: Okay, we're at the site. Which problem are we going to do?

Coach B: First things first. You need an account, so you can log in and submit your work for verification, even when you're practicing and not competing. So, first, please follow the directions there to open an account with USACO. You will need to supply a working email address, and make sure it's one you can access right now, because that's how you'll activate your account.

The room is quiet as the students type and tap, setting up their accounts.

 TIP: You can use either your school email or your personal email. If you don't receive a confirmation email from USACO within a minute or so after registering, check your spam folder, and if it's not there either, you might need to try a different email address. At times, some email providers block messages from the USACO site.

Coach B: Okay, is everyone logged in? Great! Let's find our problem. Go into the contests tab on the top bar, and look for the 2015-2016 season. Within this season, go to the January 2016 contest. This is the page you should arrive at: http://usaco.org/index.php?page=jan16results

Now, scroll down on this page, until you see the heading for Bronze, as shown in figure 1.6. We will solve problem 1, "Promotion Counting."

🏆 USACO 2016 JANUARY CONTEST, BRONZE

The Bronze division had 1165 total participants, of whom 921 were pre-college students. We saw a large number of very high scores in the bronze contest this time around as well.

All competitors who scored 750 or higher on this contest are automatically promoted to the silver division -- to all who were promoted, congratulations! Detailed results for those promoted are <u>here</u>.

1 **Promotion Counting**
<u>View problem</u> | <u>Test data</u> | <u>Solution</u>

2 **Angry Cows**
<u>View problem</u> | <u>Test data</u> | <u>Solution</u>

3 **Mowing the Field**
<u>View problem</u> | <u>Test data</u> | <u>Solution</u>

Figure 1.6 Bronze event problems from the January 2016 competition.

Rachid: There's a solution already! That's cheating!

Coach B: Yes, there's a solution. And no, it's not cheating. We are not competing right now, we are practicing. The people at USACO are very considerate to publish a solution, often accompanied by a brief explanation. It is a great resource and we will talk later about how and when to use the given solution. For now, you are welcome to just click on "Solution" and see it's there.

Ryan: I clicked on "Test Data" and it downloaded a file to my laptop. Is that okay?

Coach B: Yes, USACO is a site you can trust, and these are the files that are used to test your solution. But let's not get too far ahead of ourselves. First, let's all go to the problem itself. Click on "View problem."

The students arrive at http://usaco.org/index.php?page=viewproblem2&cpid=591, and see something similar to figure 1.7.

Coach B: Please read the problem and we'll discuss it. I highly recommend you find and read it on the website rather than read it from my projection here. It is important that you know how to find the problem there.

Figure 1.7 The problem itself: 2016, January contest, Bronze level, problem 1. Please go to the website and read it there, as you will need to submit the problem on the site.

TIP: If you do not see the "Submit Solution" button at the bottom of the USACO problem page, this means you are not logged in. You need to go back to the USACO home screen, log in, and then navigate back to the problem.

As they finish reading the problem, the team members look up, not sure what to do next.

Coach B: Okay, seems like everyone's done reading. Does anyone want to explain the problem? Mei, maybe you want to try it?

Mei: Well, I don't know how to solve it.

Coach B: Oh, I didn't mean solving it. The first step is just to make sure we understand it, and that we can follow the sample case. USACO problems are very good at giving a sample input and sample output, and then even a short explanation. So, our first step is always visualizing the problem, and trying to follow the given example. Can you do that? Can you draw the sample input and output?

Mei: Oh, sure. I can try that.

Visualize it: Mei walks up to the board and draws figure 1.8.

Mei: On the left, I drew what's given, and on the right, I drew their solution.

Coach B: Looks great, thanks. I especially like how you noted the input and output. Our algorithm will take the input, and produce the desired output. Nice. Any questions or comments from the team?

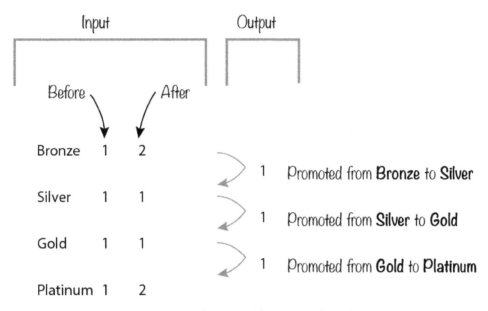

Figure 1.8 The sample input and the corresponding solution.

Ryan: I don't get something. I see that, for example, we had one cow in Gold before, and one after. So why do we say there was one cow promoted from Silver to Gold? I mean, the number of cows in Gold didn't change.

Mei: Well, the number of cows in Platinum did change. This means that one cow was promoted from Gold to Platinum. In that case, we need one cow to be promoted from Silver to Gold.

Ryan: But what if there was one cow promoted from Silver to Platinum directly?

Mei: Hmm... Let me think.

Rachid: Wait, the question says that a cow can be promoted multiple times. I think what it means is that if it moved from Silver to Platinum, we still count it as two promotions: from Silver to Gold, and from Gold to Platinum.

Coach B: Yes, I agree. Each promotion is counted once. You can't jump a level and go directly to Platinum. Does this make sense?

Rachid looks at his teammates, who shake their heads.

Rachid: Yeah, no questions, so we kind-of understand the problem, I think. And it's easy to see how the input they gave us leads to the output. But, solving it for the general case? Um, yeah, that's a whole other issue.

 TIP: One of the most useful methods we will use in this book is drawing out the problems and the test cases. It helps you understand the problem, clarify your perspective, and even get ideas for algorithms. You do not need to be an accomplished artist to draw these. All you need is to be able to symbolize, or illustrate, your ideas.

Coach B: Perfect. Usually, at this stage, we will try to understand the given solution a little deeper, and draw a few more test cases. Then we can look for an algorithm, and then code it. However, since our main goal today is to go through the process of submitting a solution on the site, let's take a shortcut. I'll go ahead and just give you a solution.

Annie: Wait, can I try something first? I think I have at least part of the solution.

Coach B: Of course! Here, the board is yours.

Annie draws figure 1.9.

Annie: We know that after the contest, there were 2 cows at the Platinum level. We also know that beforehand, there was only 1 cow at Platinum. That means that one cow had to be promoted from Gold to Platinum. So we solved the part asking how many were promoted to Platinum.

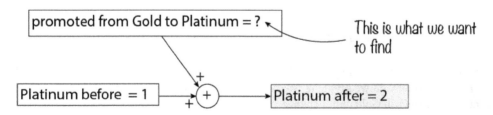

Figure 1.9 Finding the number of cows promoted from Gold to Platinum. Since there were 2 after, and only 1 before, it means one was promoted.

Ryan joins Annie at the board, reaching for the marker.

Ryan: Nice. Writing this drawing as a formula yields

```
platinum_after = platinum_before + promoted_platinum
```

Ryan: And since we know the values of `platinum_before` and `platinum_after`, we can calculate the number of cows promoted to platinum. And writing it in code form, it would be:

```
promoted_platinum = platinum_after - platinum_before;
```

Coach B: You two are on a roll!

Rachid: Oh, I get it. Thanks Annie and Ryan, that's nice. I think we can extend it also to the other parts of the question.

Rachid gets up to the board, takes the marker and draws figure 1.10.

Rachid: This is actually very similar to what Annie just did. I mean, the only difference is that some cows might be promoted out of the Gold level. In Annie's drawing, no cow can get promoted out of Platinum. But in our case, they can be promoted out of Gold, so we need to account for that.

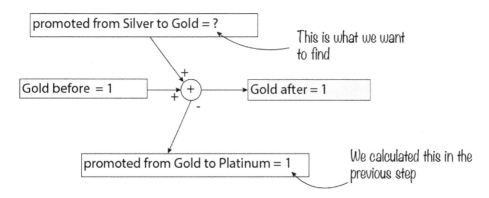

Figure 1.10 Finding the number of cows promoted from Silver to Gold.

Coach B: Nice drawings, Annie and Rachid. They tell the whole story. So, Rachid, in your case, we know there was one Gold before, and there's one Gold after. We already found that there was one promoted from Gold to Platinum, so that means we need to have one cow promoted to Gold. I think you've managed to solve two-thirds of the problem already: how many were promoted to Platinum, and how many to Gold.

Ryan: And I can write it in code as well. All I need is to translate the drawing. The drawing tells us that the number we will have in the Gold level after the contest is equal to the number of Gold level cows before the contest, plus those who were promoted to Gold during the contest, and minus those that were promoted from Gold to Platinum. So, as a formula, it is:

```
gold_after = gold_before + promoted_gold - promoted_platinum
```

Ryan: In this equation, the only unknown variable is `promoted_gold`, the number of cows promoted from Silver to Gold.

Ryan adds a new line to his code:

```
promoted_gold = gold_after - gold_before + promoted_platinum;
```

Coach B: The only thing left for us to find is then the number of promotions to Silver. Who can tackle that?

Mei: I can do that! Seems like we're going backward, though. We found the promotions to Platinum first, then Gold, and last is Silver. And I believe Silver is very much the same as Gold.

Rachid passes the marker to Mei, who draws figure 1.11.

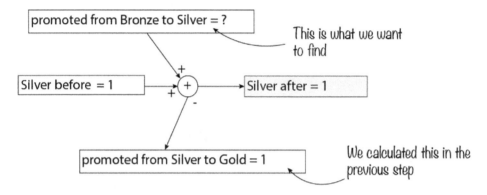

Figure 1.11 Finding the number of cows promoted from Bronze to Silver is very similar to the process of finding the promotions from Silver to Gold.

Ryan: And the code for that is almost exactly the same as before. Let me add one more line.

Ryan adds the last line to the board, which now looks as follows:

```
promoted_platinum = platinum_after - platinum_before;

promoted_gold = gold_after - gold_before + promoted_platinum;

promoted_silver = silver_after - silver_before + promoted_gold;
```

Coach B: Hmm. Yup: you got it! Perfect. We should also check corner cases, also known as edge cases, and step through the algorithm. Corner cases in this problem would be, for example, if some of the levels have zero cows in the "before" column, or zero in the "after" column. But today I want to make sure we get to submit it on the site, so let's move forward. I believe it does address all the edge cases, and we will get to check it on the real site. Let's see how to submit on the site!

The team shares high fives.

Coach B: Okay, let's finish it up. We just need to put the framework of code around it, and we can submit it!

ALGORITHM

Coach B: The next time we meet, we'll talk about common patterns that appear in competitive programming. That means dealing with input and output, dealing with multiple test cases, and so forth. For now, let me just write it with only a few comments. The only tricky part might be the two lines in the code that deal with the files. Just follow along for now and we'll cover this process soon. Oh, and pay attention to how I'm naming the code file as we save it. I'm not just calling it some random word, like "cows" or "USACO" or "practice." We want to be methodical about the file names. That way we can easily access them, and not clutter up our laptops!

TIP: Have a clear system in place for naming your files. During our practice, you will write code for many USACO problems. To keep yourself organized, so that you can easily access, study, upload, and share your files, it is a good idea to have a naming convention for them. Pick a system that's informative, easy to remember, and above all, consistent. The system I recommend using, and the one that we will follow throughout this book, is demonstrated below in figure 1.12.

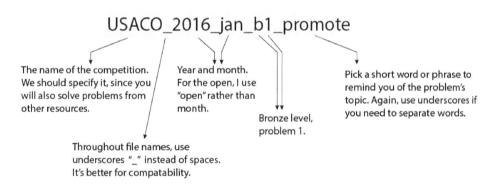

Figure 1.12 The naming convention for files, used throughout this book.

Coach B writes the code as in listing 1.1, and the team copies it down.

Coach B: Note that the problem clearly specifies the input and output files as "promote.in" and "promote.out," so these are the ones we use in the code.

TIP: Python—You can find the Python code for this problem in listing 1.3 and figure 1.14, as well as on the book's web resource page: http://www.usacoclub. com/.

Listing 1.1 USACO_2016_jan_b1_promote (C++ code, first version)

```cpp
1  #include <iostream>
2  using namespace std;
3
4  int main() {
5      freopen("promote.in", "r", stdin);  // Two lines dealing with files
6      freopen("promote.out", "w", stdout);
7
8      int bronze_before, bronze_after, silver_before, silver_after;
9      int gold_before, gold_after, platinum_before, platinum_after;
10
11     cin >> bronze_before >> bronze_after;
12     cin >> silver_before >> silver_after;
13     cin >> gold_before >> gold_after
14     cin >> platinum_before >> platinum_after;
15
16     int promoted_platinum, promoted_gold, promoted_silver;
17     promoted_platinum = platinum_after - platinum_before;
18     promoted_gold = gold_after - gold_before + promoted_platinum;
19     promoted_silver = silver_after - silver_before + promoted_gold;
20
21     cout << promoted_silver << "\n";
22     cout << promoted_gold << "\n";
23     cout << promoted_platinum << "\n";
24 }
```

Coach B: We will talk about it more next week, but I wanted to say something about variable names here as well. In competitions, you usually don't use such long and verbose variable names. Using such descriptive long variable names is useful when you have the time to write them. In competitions, time is of the essence. So, for example, instead of "bronze" you can use "b", and instead of "before" use "0". Thus, "bronze_before" would be converted into "b0", and "bronze_after" would be converted to "b1". The resulting code would look like listing 1.2. If you already copied the previous version, no need to copy this one.

Listing 1.2 USACO_2016_jan_b1_promote (C++ code, second version)

```
1   #include <iostream>
2   using namespace std;
3
4   int main() {
5       freopen("promote.in", "r", stdin);  // Two lines dealing with files
6       freopen("promote.out", "w", stdout);
7
8       // Naming convention for the variables:
9       // 'b' - Bronze, 's' - Silver, 'g' - Gold, 'p' - Platinum
10      // 0 - means before, 1 - means after, m - means promoted
11      // Examples:
12      // g0 - Number of Gold before.
13      // sm - Number promoted to Silver.
14
15      int b0, b1, s0, s1, g0, g1, p0, p1;
16      cin >> b0 >> b1 >> s0 >> s1 >> g0 >> g1 >> p0 >> p1;
17
18      int pm, gm, sm;
19      pm = p1 - p0;
20      gm = g1 - g0 + pm;
21      sm = s1 - s0 + gm;
22
23      cout << sm << "\n";
24      cout << gm << "\n";
25      cout << pm << "\n";
26  }
```

Coach B: Admittedly, some would say that this second version of the code is too cryptic. You will need to find the middle ground that keeps the code readable while making it easy for you to write it. As I said, we will discuss it in more detail in our next meeting.

The team looks at the two versions of the code, and appreciates the differences.

Coach B: Before submitting your program, it's always a good practice to run it on the sample case on your computer. Actually, this sample case is the first test case that will be tested when you submit your solution. To do this, we will need to create the file "promote.in" on your computer. Create a regular text file and name it "promote.in", and write the given input in it. You do not need to create a file "promote.out": The program itself will create it.

TIP: If you are using an IDE (integrated development environment) to compile and run your code, you will also need to make sure the program runs, or executes, in the same directory as the file "promote.in." You can usually access this setting in the project configuration settings.

Coach B: Ryan, I believe you are writing in Python, right? Anyone else? Okay, so, if you are writing in Python, please be patient with us for a second. We will cover Python right after the C++ section. For those who are writing in C++, figure 1.12 describes the progression on my machine. This is all done from the command line. Your environment might look different, and you might be working through an IDE. But you should be following similar steps.

TIP: If you are already familiar with running your solution on your machine but need guidance on submitting it to USACO, you can skip ahead to just before figure 1.15. If you are familiar with the submission process as well, you can jump ahead and verify that you obtain the same results as shown in figure 1.16, and continue reading from there.

Coach B: Listen carefully, as there are many details to follow:

1. Create the main program file, "USACO_2016_jan_b1_promote.cpp".
2. Create the input file "promote.in" and add the sample test case.
3. Run your program. In many IDEs there is a menu item, or a button, labeled "run". In the screenshots below, where the process is followed in the terminal rather than an IDE, the process is composed of two different steps:

a. Compile and link your program, to create an executable.

b. Run the executable, which will produce the output file "promote.out".

4. Examine the output file.

The team looks at figure 1.13, compares it to their screens, and progresses along.

Coach B: Seems like it's all running on your machines, and the created output file looks like the one indicated in the problem. Okay, then! You are ready to submit!

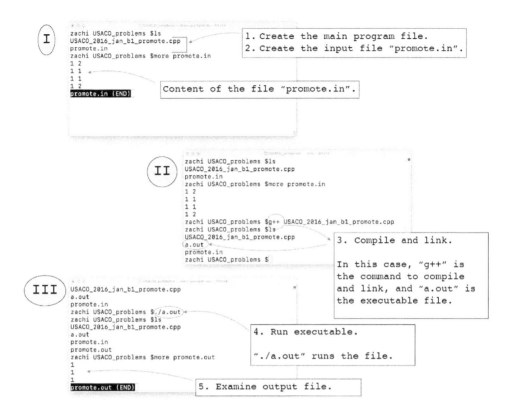

Figure 1.13 Running and testing your C++ program on your machine. Your specific screens might look different, especially if you are using an IDE. The principles should be the same.

Coach B: For those who write in Python, the process is very similar. Below is the code and the steps to follow. You can also see these illustrated in figure 1.14.

1. Create the main program file, "USACO_2016_jan_b1_promote.py".
2. Create the input file "promote.in" and add the sample test case.
3. Run the program, which will produce the output file "promote.out".
4. Examine the output file.

Listing 1.3 USACO_2016_jan_b1_promote (Python code)

```
1   f_in = open('promote.in', 'r')
2
3   b0, b1 = map(int, f_in.readline().split())
4   s0, s1 = map(int, f_in.readline().split())
5   g0, g1 = map(int, f_in.readline().split())
6   p0, p1 = map(int, f_in.readline().split())
7
8   pm = p1 - p0
9   gm = g1 - g0 + pm
10  sm = s1 - s0 + gm
11
12  f_out = open('promote.out', 'w')
13  str1 = str(sm) + '\n' + str(gm) + '\n' + str(pm) + '\n'
14  f_out.write(str1)
```

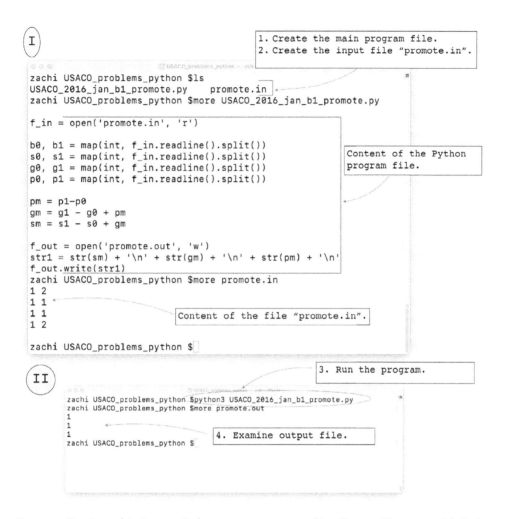

Figure 1.14 Running and testing your Python program on your machine. Your specific screens might look different, especially if you are using an IDE. The principles should be the same.

Coach B: Okay, if all runs well on your machine, it's time to submit. To submit, just go to the bottom of the page, select the appropriate language and version (for C++ I would recommend version 17, and for Python version 3.6.9 and above), choose the file, and hit the submit button.

This process is illustrated in figure 1.15.

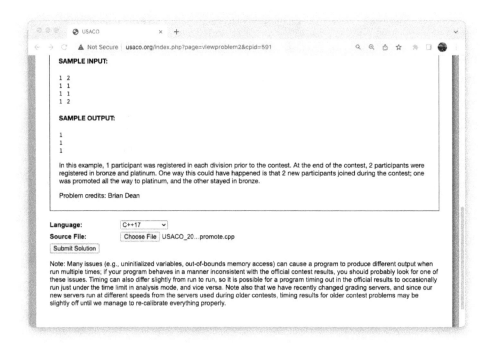

Figure 1.15 Submitting your solution. Select the language, choose the right file, and hit the "Submit Solution" button.

Coach B: And, a drum roll, please! If everything works well, you will get the highly satisfying "All green" result!

See figure 1.16.

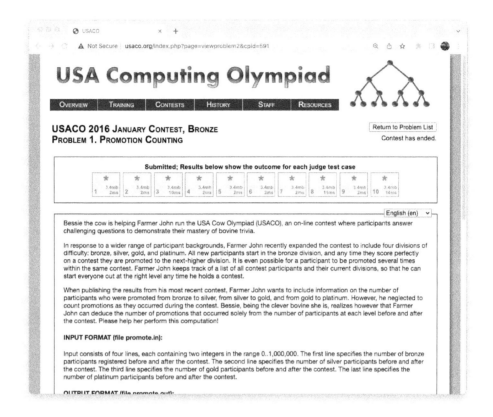

Figure 1.16 All test cases passed successfully, so you got the green light.

Coach B: Let's see, did it work for everybody?

The team nods.

Ryan: Yes! We did it!

Mei: Whoop!

TIP: If you were not able to submit your code successfully: Go to the book's resource page, and download the appropriate file (either .cpp or .py). Submit this file, and check if you get all green marks. This can be a starting point for your debugging. We will talk more about ways to debug your code in chapter 2.

Coach B: Amazing! Well done, everyone! Before we go, let's quickly run through what you should expect for future meetings, and how you should be practicing in between meetings.

EPILOGUE

We submitted our first USACO problem together! That's a big achievement. Well done! If the process seemed overwhelming to you, I assure you that with practice, it will become second nature to you. By the time you submit your 10th problem, it will be a breeze.

 VOCABULARY Corner: **C++** , pronounced "C plus plus," was created by the Danish computer scientist Bjarne Stroustrup around 1985. He created it as the successor of the C language, which itself derived from a language called B. These names really are the full names of the languages; they aren't abbreviations. C++ added many modern features, most notably classes, while still keeping C's advantages of efficiency and performance. C++ kept evolving through the years, and today is considered the prime language for programming competitions, thanks to its efficiency and its extensive library of data structures.

1.3. How to Work With This Book

Coach B: Okay, you've all gotten off to a great start! Just like we did today, at every meeting, we'll solve one or more USACO problems, and through the process we'll discover and learn new patterns. Your homework, too, will be to solve problems. Here's the general flow of how we'll get ready for the competition.

Figure 1.17 is projected on the board.

Coach B: We always start by reading the problem. A great place to start. We will get better at reading as time goes on, noticing various details and clues. That will come with time. Then comes the most important part, exploration!

Ryan: Are those a pencil and paper drawn next to it? I thought USACO is all online.

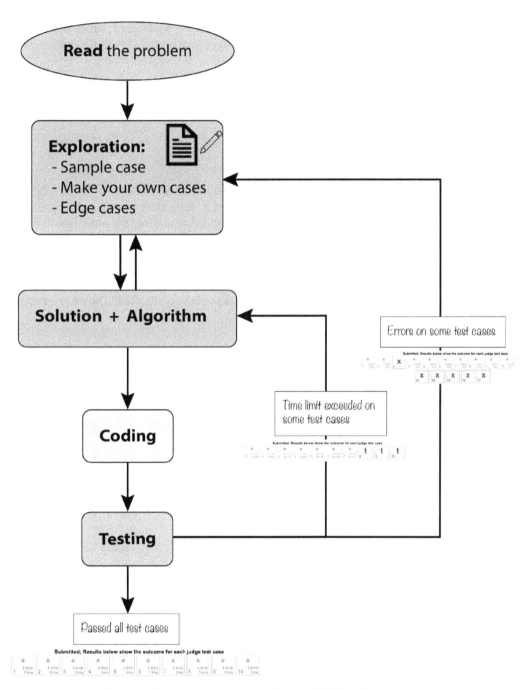

Figure 1.17 The typical procedure for solving a USACO problem.

Coach B: Correct on both counts, Ryan. USACO is all online, and these are paper and pencil indeed. We need tools for exploration and solving the problem, and for many people those tools are paper and pencil. In class, we will use the whiteboard, but at home, when you solve the practice problems, make sure you have your preferred tools for exploring and taking notes.

 TIP: Feel free to draw on the book, but be aware that usually you will need much more space than is available here.

Ryan: So is this for writing the code? I don't follow.

Coach B: Coding comes later. Exploration is just playing around with the problem, following the given sample cases, and trying to make sense of it. Remember when Mei drew the input sample case? And then when Annie and the rest joined in drawing the other cases? This is exactly what we are talking about.

Annie: Well, but sometimes we can just see the solution right away, right?

Coach B: I've been doing these problems for many years, and I still always draw them first. My daughter loves the phrase "Things always look perfect in your mind." Does it ever happen to you?

The team smiles.

Annie: Oh, I know what she means. I always have it before writing an essay or preparing a poster. Before I start, I know exactly how it will look and what I will write, and it's perfect in each and every way. It's only when I start actually putting things down on real paper that things start falling apart.

Coach B: Exactly, and that's very, very common. The point is that if you read the problem and immediately start coding it because you think you can clearly see the algorithm and solution in your head, you'll run into reality pretty hard. And it is much, much harder to go back to pencil and paper once you already have an idea and you've started coding it. So, this is the crucial part: you need to show discipline, work with pencil and paper first and make sure you understand the problem. That's what we mean by exploring the question.

 TIP: I recommend using looseleaf unlined paper and a simple pencil. No need for a special notebook. You want your notes to flow freely, without worrying about how they will look later on, or how organized they will be, or how to save space.

Mei: What are these double arrows between the two boxes? Right here, around "Exploration" and "Solution and Algorithm"?

Coach B: Those show movement in both directions! During exploration, we find some patterns and may find a solution, which we can convert to an algorithm we can code. However, more often than not, we discover something during this process which takes us back to exploring. For example, in the problem we just solved, when we write the algorithm we might wonder, "Will this algorithm work if we have zero cows promoted at all levels?"

To check it, we go back to pencil and paper, and verify. If it works, great. If not, we need to look for alternatives. This is called an iterative process. We go back and forth between these two steps until we are happy with the resulting algorithm, and then we move to coding.

Mei: Okay. So it means that for this whole process, exploration, solution, and algorithm, we use pencil and paper? No computer yet?

Coach B: Correct. Paper or the whiteboard. The point is, we work by hand.

Rachid: And then finally, the coding part?

Coach B: Yes, coding and submitting our solution to the problem so that our code can be tested. A clear and simple algorithm will make your coding easier. Then you can submit the code, and hopefully you get all green.

Annie: And if not...

Coach B: Back to the drawing board! We will talk more on debugging next week, but in general, there are different marks on your test-cases depending on the reason it failed. If you got the wrong answer for some cases, you probably missed these cases in your exploration. You need to go back to the exploration phase, and identify which cases you did not consider. On the other hand, if you didn't pass a test case because your program execution time was too slow, it probably means you used the wrong algorithm. As I said, we'll cover those in more detail next week, when we'll talk about debugging.

Ryan: You mentioned at the start of the meeting, in figure 1.4, about the three things the USACO Bronze tests. This was something like, if I remember correctly: find the solution to the problem; convert the solution to an algorithm; and then code it. I'm trying to see how it all fits together. Can you add those phases to this drawing?

Coach B: Excellent point, Ryan. Let me add that on.

Coach B adds to the drawing, and the result is shown in figure 1.18.

Coach B: Basically, we're working to build skills in these three main areas. The first is exploring the problem. We will solve selected problems in a specific order, and I'll scaffold them for you appropriately. Too often people just dive in head-first into random problems, and that can be frustrating for beginners. We do the USACO problems in a specific order. This should really help with developing the ability to explore the problems.

Coach B then points to the "Solution + Algorithm" block.

Coach B: The second area is filling your bag of tricks for solving these problems. As we explore the problems, we will see common patterns. For example, problems that require searching for the best value, or problems that involve geometry, or problems that involve modeling. We will learn to identify and group these problems together, and will secure these into our repertoire of problems we know how to solve. Last, we will also practice coding. We'll look at each other's coding so everyone can get feedback and exposure to different styles.

TIP: One of the best ways to improve your coding is seeing others' code, and comparing it to yours. You might like some of the things they did, and you might prefer some of the things you did. But reading a different code solution gives you a fuller appreciation and understanding of coding styles and techniques. Of course, sharing your own code and hearing others' comments on it is valuable as well! All the computer can do is give you a passing or failing score. But a human classmate, or coach, can examine your code and give you insights, ideas, and inspiration.

The team starts fidgeting. They are ready to be done for today.

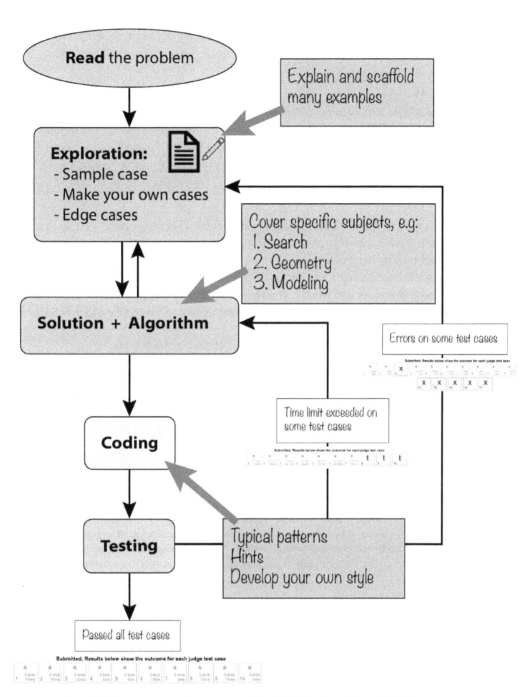

Figure 1.18 Focus on areas where your practice with the book can be most effective.

Coach B: Okay, I see you are ready to be done. You're so fidgety! But keep your focus going just a little longer—it's good practice for that four-hour exam! So here, I'll assign one problem as homework. You'll find it on the club's page. But let's talk about how to work on it.

The team sits up straighter, ready to take notes.

Coach B: The most important part: Don't get frustrated with the problem. There are plenty of hints available, and even the solution. There's a process I suggest you use to work on a problem, and—look how serious I am about it: I've turned it into a poster! Yes, go ahead and snap a photo of it, but I'll put it on the club's page as well.

The team points their phones at the poster, figure 1.19, while Coach B describes it.

Coach B: Okay, here's what I want you to do:

1. Prepare a few blank sheets of paper and a pencil. That's important!
2. Look at what time it is, and write the time at the top of a page.
3. Start reading the problem.
4. Draw the sample input and output case(s). Make sure you understand how they work.
5. Draw other cases if needed. If you see a possible solution, go to step 7.
6. If you are working for more than 20 minutes on this problem, take a look at the hints, or the full solution, and go to step 5.
7. Translate your solution to an algorithm. If needed, go back to step 5.
8. Code your algorithm, and test it on the sample case on your computer.
9. Submit your code for testing.
10. If it's not complete, start debugging, and go back to step 5 or 7.
11. When you've submitted it successfully, you're done!

Coach B: See? This way, no matter how hard the problem is, you won't get stuck spinning your wheels for too long. Any questions on this?

TIP: If you can't find a solution on your own, don't beat your head against the wall: instead, look at the solution file and descriptions. Try to understand it. See how the solution works, and how the code is structured. Then, put this file aside, and now that you understand what a solution looks like, go back to develop your own solution. If you need to, look again at the given solution until you get it right.

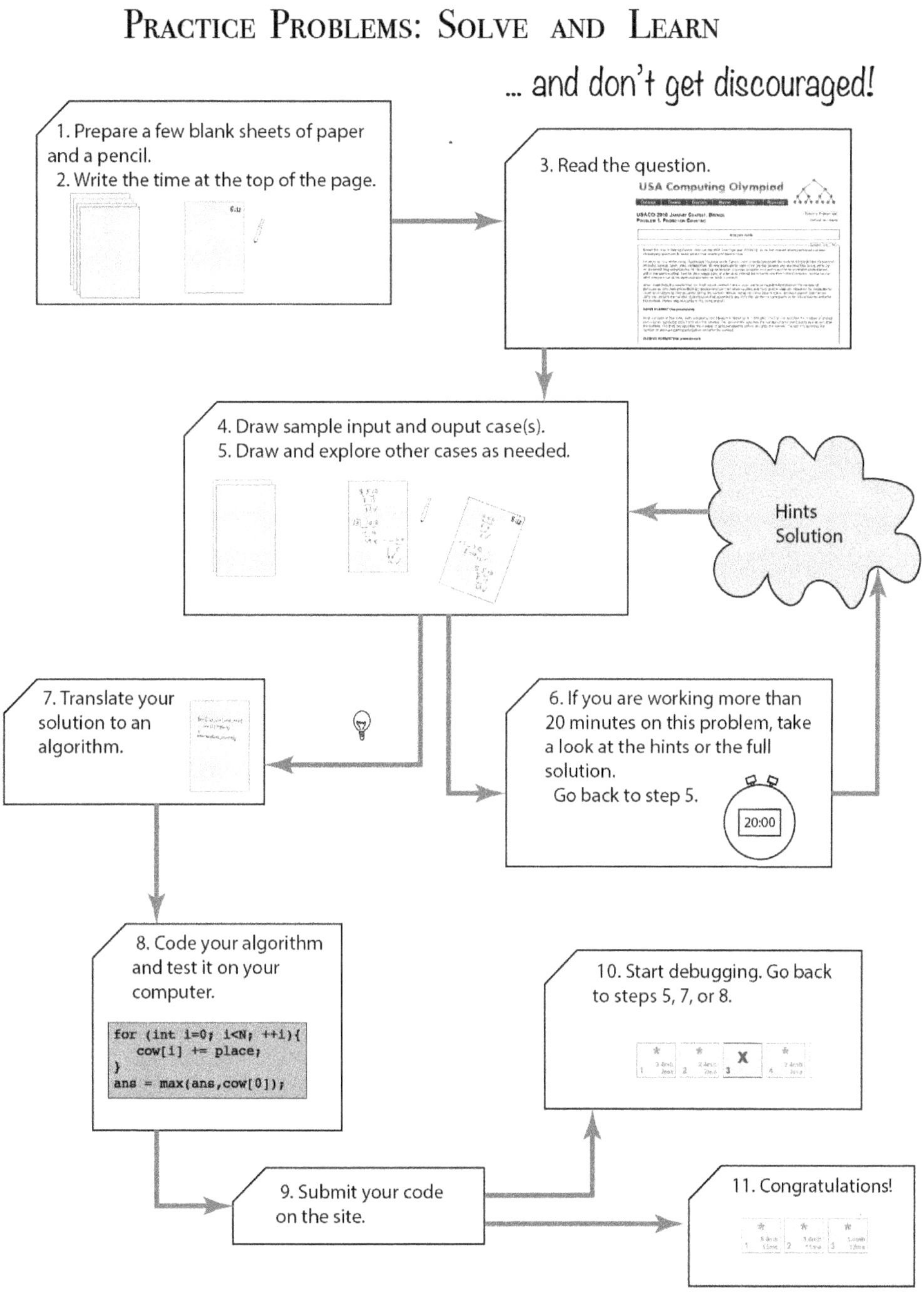

PRACTICE PROBLEMS: SOLVE AND LEARN

... and don't get discouraged!

Figure 1.19 Solving practice problems.

Annie: But it is okay for us to work on it longer than 20 minutes if needed, right? It's not a time limit?

Coach B: Definitely, but on the other hand, don't spend an hour trying to draw cases. There's a balance. Our goal is to learn and get better. Right now, getting stuck for too long on a problem is not beneficial. So, feel free to work on it for 30 minutes if you wish before you look at the hints or solution. But at some stage, solving more problems is perhaps even more valuable than solving any single problem on your own.

The team is starting to slump down in their seats again.

Coach B: Okay, that's enough damage for one day. I'm tired, too! And we did solve and submit a full problem! That's a milestone! I will put one problem as practice for next week. Try and work on it, use the hints and whatever is needed, and if you need help, just find me mid-week or bring your question for next week. Remember, don't get frustrated with any single problem. See you next week! Thank you.

TIP: If you are serious about earning a Bronze, be sure to work through the practice problems that are assigned to the club in each chapter yourself! Reading this book allows you to observe first-hand the process for developing correct algorithms and programs that solve each of the types of problems you will face in the competition, but is no substitute for solving numerous practice problems of each type independently.

EPILOGUE

You should carry two main takeaways from this section. First, use a pencil and paper. A lot. This is the sure way to get into the habit of analyzing a problem and exploring it. Second, don't get frustrated when trying to solve a practice problem. Follow the steps, and feel free to use the hints and solution. You are training yourself in an entirely new skill. The hints and the solutions are your training wheels. They'll get you moving.

VOCABULARY Corner: **ITERATIVE PROCESS**. Iterative processes are those that involve repeating certain steps as many times as necessary. The word "iterative" comes from the Latin *iterare*, meaning "to repeat: to do something again." In programming, and in problem-solving processes in general, we often describe processes as "iterative" rather than "repetitive" to emphasize that there's a good reason for the repetition! It's not a sign of failure, but rather of incremental progress, when we move forward to a new iteration. Sometimes the best way to step forward, toward a solution, is to step backward, to refine your method.

PRACTICE PROBLEMS

Hints and full solutions to the problems can be found on the club's page: http://www.usacoclub.com

1. USACO 2019 February Bronze Problem 1: Sleepy Cow Herding

   http://usaco.org/index.php?page=viewproblem2&cpid=915

a. Draw a few test cases, ones that you make on your own.

b. There are only three possible answers for the minimum number of moves possible: 0, 1, or 2. Make sure your made-up test cases explore all three of these possible outcomes.

c. This is a logic problem disguised in geometry's clothing. There's no need to calculate any distances.

d. Hint: The inputs are the coordinates of the three cows, and your code will be much simpler if you put these in sorted order first.

e. Hint: If 'a' is the smallest coordinate, 'b' is the middle, and 'c' is the largest, we can write the logic part of the problem as:

```
// Algorithm
if (c - a == 2) {
    ans_min = 0;
} else {
    if (c - b == 2 || b - a == 2) {
        ans_min = 1;
    } else {
        ans_min = 2;   // we can always do it in 2
    }
}
ans_max = max(c - b - 1, b - a - 1);
```

ON THE CLUB'S PAGE:

Note from Coach B: Two extra practice problems

The following two problems are from two different sites: https://www.cses.fi/ and https://codeforces.com/. These are great resources for practice problems and competitions. Because this book is focused on USACO competition, we use mainly USACO problems. However, you have many options to practice more and with different styles of problems. If you need help navigating or submitting on these sites, see the details on the club's page.

1. CSES, Introductory problems: Weird Algorithm

   https://cses.fi/problemset/task/1068

   a. A straightforward implementation of an algorithm.

   b. Hint: the value of n can get very large. Even larger than the maximum integer. You will need to use "long long" for the variable n. (This is just in C++. In Python you do not have to worry about this).

2. Codeforces, Round #839 (Div. 3) Problem A: A+B?

   https://codeforces.com/problemset/problem/1772/A

   a. Evaluate an input expression.

1.4. Summary

- **USACO Bronze** focuses on:

  - **Problem-solving skills** – Understanding a problem and finding a solution.
  - **Algorithmic thinking** – Translating a solution to an algorithm.
  - **Fluency in coding** – Coding the algorithm without mistakes.

- **Solve problems** using the prescribed process:

  - **Read** the problem.
  - **Explore** the problem using pencil and paper. These are your essential tools.
  - Look for a pattern, leading to a **solution**.
  - Translate this into an **algorithm**.
  - **Code** and try the sample case on your machine.
  - **Submit your code for testing**, and go back to the drawing board if needed.

- **Don't get frustrated** by a problem.

  - Make sure you devote at least 20 minutes to exploring the problem on your own.
  - Beyond that, take advantage of the hints and/or the full solution. It's a learning process.

- **Improve your coding** by reading others' code and comparing theirs to yours, and by sharing your code and receiving feedback from others.

Chapter 2. Solving and Coding: Competition Specifics

This chapter covers

- A problem-solving process for solving USACO problems: Reading, Visualizing, and Coding.
- Coding form and style as appropriate for a USACO timed competition.
- Checking and debugging your program, in practice and in the competition.

Now that you've learned how to submit a USACO problem, let's focus on optimizing your performance during practice and in the competition. We'll elaborate on the systematic approach to solving USACO problems described in the previous chapter. This approach will aid you in discovering the solution and coding it accurately and efficiently. Additionally, we will cover the essential steps to verify and debug your code. Because you're entering a coding competition, with distinct characteristics, we'll be focusing on how to optimize our time and performance for this particular setting.

In this chapter, we will explain the three primary characteristics that are most relevant for USACO Bronze. The first is time pressure, which is strictly enforced in USACO competitions and impacts the entire problem-solving and coding process. You'll work more efficiently under this time constraint by developing a structured approach and becoming familiar with typical coding patterns.

The second characteristic is the goal and scope of your solution and code. Your code's sole purpose is to solve the given problem, and it only needs to function within the competition's time constraints. Your code is limited in size and complexity and will be used by you alone. As a result, for example, you don't need to comment your code to make it easier for others to understand. Writing comments takes time, and since no one else will read your code, you can save time by omitting them.

The third defining characteristic of competition coding is obvious yet critical: You, and you alone, are responsible for solving and coding the problem. It's not a team project, and you are not permitted to seek assistance from other individuals or resources, such as Internet forums or books. USACO does have one exception to that rule, and it is that you are allowed to consult sources describing the syntax or library functions of your programming language. Other than this exception, the competition is a solitary endeavor consisting of just you and the problem. One of the subtler impacts of working solo is that you might develop tunnel vision, where you become fixated on one particular approach and fail to consider other viable ones. We will address this issue in both practice and competition settings. These three characteristics—working within a time limit, creating a one-off solution, and doing it all on our own—shape our approach to competing at the Bronze level.

Based on these characteristics, we will delve more deeply into the problem-solving process, along with guidelines for coding and debugging.

The chapter map is described in figure 2.1. We start with the very first step of every USACO problem: reading the problem and analyzing it to find a solution. Section 2.1 serves as an introduction to the process, which consists of three main parts: reading the problem, visualizing it, and developing an algorithm. The subsequent section, section 2.2, covers the coding phase, including form, style, and common coding patterns found in USACO Bronze. Next, since it's possible that your code will fail to pass all the test cases, section 2.3 explains debugging, highlighting the differences between debugging during practice and in a competition. Finally, section 2.4 focuses on using solutions as an essential practice tool. Solutions can provide hints when you are stuck and enable you to compare and reflect when you have your own solutions. This section helps you utilize solutions to improve your skills.

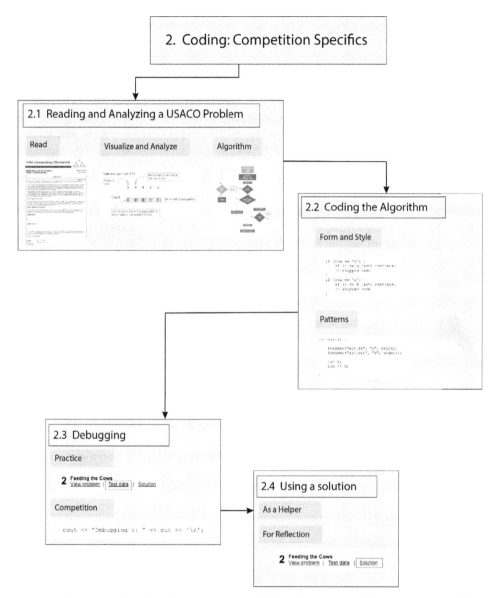

Figure 2.1 Competition Specifics chapter map. We will follow the process of solving a USACO problem, exploring the unique characteristics of competition problem-solving.

2.1. Reading and Analyzing a USACO Problem

The team gathers in the room, excited for their first real practice for USACO.

Coach B: Happy Tuesday! It's great to see all of you here for more USACO practice. Last time, we covered some general information and even submitted our first USACO problem together. This time we will go a little deeper into the process of solving a problem. We already did it last week, but today we're going to focus on how to do it right.

Ryan: Right? Didn't we get all green lights on the test cases last time?

Coach B: Yes, you're correct, but that's not what I meant by "do it right." I meant doing the problem in a way that will give you an edge in the competition. You can gain an advantage in a few ways, like learning how to solve some parts of the problem faster by using common coding patterns. Since USACO is a timed competition, every minute counts, and solving faster will give you an advantage. Another way to gain an advantage is by developing a process for solving problems.

Rachid: A process? Wouldn't this just slow us down?

Coach B: USACO isn't just about speed. You need to find the correct solution as well. We'll explore how following a process can help you arrive at the right answer and aid you in debugging your algorithm. But first, let's put this discussion in the context of a real USACO problem! Who's up for a challenge?

The team cheers.

> *TIP*: Although following a structured problem-solving process is not mandatory, it's a valuable tool to have and can serve as a fallback when shortcuts don't work out. I highly recommend following the suggested process here. However, if you read the problem and immediately see a solution, feel free to skip the process. If your solution works, that's fantastic! But if it doesn't, you can always come back to the process for guidance. With experience, you'll learn when it's appropriate to skip parts of the process.

Coach B: Let's get started by logging into your USACO accounts. Is everyone logged in? Excellent! Our problem is from the 2022-2023 season, from the December competition, and it's Problem 2: Feeding the Cows. I will display the problem statement on the board, but please make sure to locate it on your browser as well, as you'll need to submit your solution there. Here's the URL.

He writes it on the board: http://usaco.org/index.php?page=viewproblem2&cpid=1252.

Coach B: Please read the problem. Once you've finished, we can discuss it together.

The team settles in, reading the problem on the board, as in figures 2.2 and 2.3.

USA Computing Olympiad

| OVERVIEW | TRAINING | CONTESTS | HISTORY | STAFF | RESOURCES |

USACO 2022 DECEMBER CONTEST, BRONZE
PROBLEM 2. FEEDING THE COWS

Return to Problem List
Contest has ended.

Analysis mode

English (en) ∨

Farmer John has N ($1 \le N \le 10^5$) cows, the breed of each being either a Guernsey or a Holstein. They have lined up horizontally with the cows occupying positions labeled from $1 \ldots N$.

Since all the cows are hungry, FJ decides to plant grassy patches on some of the positions $1 \ldots N$. Guernseys and Holsteins prefer different types of grass, so if Farmer John decides to plant grass at some location, he must choose to planting either Guernsey-preferred grass or Holstein-preferred grass --- he cannot plant both at the same location. Each patch of grass planted can feed an unlimited number of cows of the appropriate breed.

Each cow is willing to move a maximum of K ($0 \le K \le N - 1$) positions to reach a patch. Find the minimum number of patches needed to feed all the cows. Also, print a configuration of patches that uses the minimum amount of patches needed to feed the cows. Any configuration that satisfies the above conditions will be considered correct.

INPUT FORMAT (input arrives from the terminal / stdin):

Each input contains T test cases, each describing an arrangement of cows. The first line of input contains T ($1 \le T \le 10$). Each of the T test cases follow.

Each test case starts with a line containing N and K. The next line will contain a string of length N, where each character denotes the breed of the ith cow (G meaning Guernsey and H meaning Holstein).

OUTPUT FORMAT (print output to the terminal / stdout):

For each of the T test cases, please write two lines of output. For the first line, print the minimum number of patches needed to feed the cows. For the second line, print a string of length N that describes a configuration that feeds all the cows with the minimum number of patches. The ith character, describing the ith position, should be a '.' if there is no patch, a 'G' if there is a patch that feeds Guernseys, and a 'H' if it feeds Holsteins. Any valid configuration will be accepted.

Figure 2.2 The first part of the problem: 2022, December contest, Bronze level, Problem 2: Feeding the Cows.

SAMPLE INPUT:

```
6
5 0
GHHGG
5 1
GHHGG
5 2
GHHGG
5 3
GHHGG
5 4
GHHGG
2 1
GH
```

SAMPLE OUTPUT:

```
5
GHHGG
3
.GH.G
2
..GH.
2
...GH
2
...HG
2
HG
```

Note that for some test cases, there are multiple acceptable configurations that manage to feed all cows while using the minimum number of patches. For example, in the fourth test case, another acceptable answer would be:

```
.GH..
```

This corresponds to placing a patch feeding Guernseys on the 2nd position and a patch feeding Holsteins on the third position. This uses the optimal number of patches and ensures that all cows are within 3 positions of a patch they prefer.

SCORING:

- Inputs 2 through 4 have $N \leq 10$.
- Inputs 5 through 8 have $N \leq 40$.
- Inputs 9 through 12 have $N \leq 10^5$.

Problem credits: Mythreya Dharani

Language: C ▼

Source File: Choose File   No file chosen

Submit Solution

Figure 2.3 The second part of the problem, describing sample test cases and the corresponding expected results.

2.1.1. Reading

The team reads the problem, and then looks up.

Coach B: Everyone done reading? Okay, good. Let's take a moment to discuss the importance of this initial step, the act of reading the problem. Due to the time constraint, you need to read the problem carefully, paying attention to details, but also quickly enough. Avoid getting stuck on specific details for too long, as the problem may become clearer later on or through examples. Remember, you can always go back to any part of the problem text if needed. The key is to acknowledge the presence of every detail during the first read-through, then investigate further if necessary.

TIP: USACO problems follow a well-defined structure consisting of a problem statement, followed by the input and output format descriptions. Additionally, a sample case is provided with its corresponding input and output. Sometimes, there may also be an explanation of the sample output.

Annie: It's funny you bring this up. When I first read the problem, I got stuck on the initial paragraph, because I didn't know whether gaps were allowed between the cows in the line. I even read that part twice and didn't figure it out. I eventually moved on and looked at the provided examples, and that's when I figured out that gaps aren't allowed. When I read the whole thing again, I realized the problem specified N cows positioned along the line from 1 to N, which effectively eliminated any possibility for gaps.

Coach B: That's a great example, Annie. It's important to keep in mind that USACO problems go through rigorous vetting processes. As a result, you can assume that the problem statement is correctly phrased, all the relevant information is included, and there is no ambiguity in the wording. If you don't grasp a concept immediately, don't panic—keep reading. Trust the problem to be well-formulated. Additionally, the included examples can be incredibly useful in providing context and clarifying any uncertainties.

Rachid: But the sample case was a little confusing for me. It seems like there were multiple test cases.

Coach B: You're absolutely right—this can be a bit confusing. There is one sample input, but the first line of it contains the number of test cases we will have. In this sample input, the first line is 6, which means we will have six test cases. Maybe it'll help if you think of this distinction between sample input and test cases: We have 1 sample input, and it contains 6 test cases. Does this help? To help clarify this, let's move onto the second step in our approach after reading the problem: visualizing the given example. In our case, this means picturing all six test cases provided and verifying if we can reproduce the correct output for each.

TIP: Visualizing the given example is a critical component of the problem-solving process. Many students believe that they can simply envision how it works in their head and do not need to sketch anything. However, two key points should be kept in mind. Firstly, things always appear clearer in your mind and tend to become more complicated and convoluted when communicated. I often use the expression "things look perfect in your head" to emphasize this point. In USACO, your algorithm needs to be functional in the real world and pass the test cases. It can't just work in your head, so it is critical to flesh it out. Secondly, visualizing the example helps to slow you down slightly. This is a timed competition, but taking a moment to contemplate the problem can be incredibly beneficial. It is time well spent, as it results in a much stronger algorithm.

2.1.2. Visualizing

Coach B: Visualizing the problem involves writing out the sample input in our own handwriting and adding annotations. This helps us understand the problem and how the input leads to the expected result. It's a crucial step in our process of solving the problem, and solving problems is at the heart of USACO Bronze. Would anyone like to volunteer to draw the first test case of the sample input? We have six in total.

 TIP: Some people describe USACO problems as "tricky." This term can suggest that the problems are designed to deceive you or mislead you. However, as you solve more problems and learn new techniques, you'll realize that there's nothing inherently tricky about these questions. Nobody is trying to confuse you or give you ambiguous input. On the contrary, everything is presented as clearly as possible. Your job is simply to navigate the problem carefully and pay close attention to details. This is precisely why visualizing the problem is such an important first step. By understanding the problem thoroughly, you've already overcome half the challenge of solving it.

Mei: You mean visualizing the case that starts with the line '5 0'?

Coach B: Yes, please. That's indeed the first case.

Coach B hands the marker to Mei, who approaches the board and draws figure 2.4.

Mei: In this first test case, the input line of '5 0' tells us there are five cows, and they are willing to move zero positions to get food. In other words, the cows are not willing to move at all from their original spot in order to get food. This means that each cow needs to have its own patch of grass. So that's what I drew.

Coach B: Very nicely done, Mei. You did an excellent job of presenting the input clearly, annotating everything, and using different markers to make it easy to understand. I think the first sample input is now very clear for anyone reading the problem. Do the rest of you agree with me?

The team nods in agreement, as Mei bobs a curtsy. The team smiles.

Coach B: So in the first test case, we need 5 patches of grass. You described one plausible arrangement for this, which matches the one given in the sample output. Actually, this is the only possible arrangement.

The team looks at the sample output, and everyone nods.

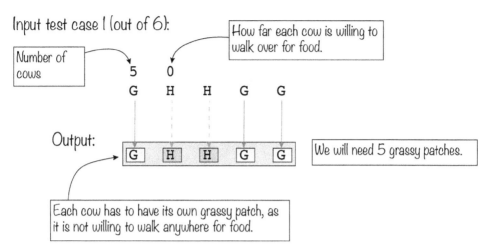

Figure 2.4 The first test case, with five cows who are not willing to move even a single position to the side to get food. Farmer John will need to plant five patches.

Coach B: Great job! We've completed one test case, and we have five more to go. Who would like to take on the second test case?

Rachid: Here, I can try.

Mei passes the marker to Rachid, and he draws figure 2.5.

Rachid: Based on the input line '5 1' in this scenario, we know that there are five cows and each cow is willing to move at most one position to reach food. This means that the two H cows and two G cows that are standing together can share the same patch, allowing us to feed all five cows using only three patches.

Annie: I get what you're saying, and it looks correct. But, the sample output from the problem is different.

Annie goes to the board and draws figure 2.6.

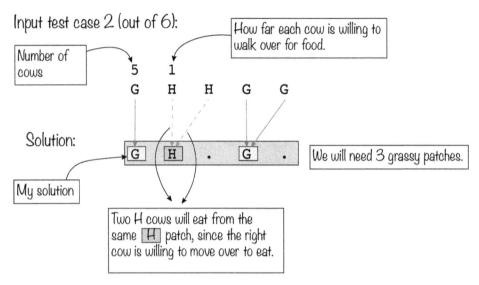

Figure 2.5 The second test case. Five cows, each willing to move at most one position over to reach her food.

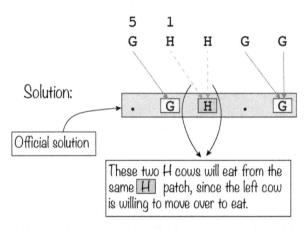

Figure 2.6 The second test case and the official output, given in the problem itself.

Coach B: Indeed, I understand your point. Rachid's approach and the official output both indicate that 3 patches are required, but their placement varies. It's intriguing. Does anyone have any insights as to why this might be?

The group is quiet for a moment.

Rachid: As far as I can see, both solutions work. And if I may say so myself, my solution makes more sense. Look: in the official solution, the first cow has to walk over to her patch of grass. In my solution, the first cow has her patch located right with her.

The team murmurs their agreement.

Coach B: Now we're grappling with this: why is there another solution? And why was that solution chosen to be the official one? Firstly, regarding the existence of multiple solutions, the problem itself offers several clues to indicate this likelihood.

Coach B grabs a red marker and circles three parts, as in figure 2.7.

USACO 2022 DECEMBER CONTEST, BRONZE
PROBLEM 2. FEEDING THE COWS

Return to Problem List

Contest has ended.

Analysis mode

English (en) ⌄

Farmer John has N ($1 \leq N \leq 10^5$) cows, the breed of each being either a Guernsey or a Holstein. They have lined up horizontally with the cows occupying positions labeled from $1 \ldots N$.

Since all the cows are hungry, FJ decides to plant grassy patches on some of the positions $1 \ldots N$. Guernseys and Holsteins prefer different types of grass, so if Farmer John decides to plant grass at some location, he must choose to planting either Guernsey-preferred grass or Holstein-preferred grass --- he cannot plant both at the same location. Each patch of grass planted can feed an unlimited number of cows of the appropriate breed.

Each cow is willing to move a maximum of K ($0 \leq K \leq N - 1$) positions to reach a patch. Find the minimum number of patches needed to feed all the cows. Also, print a configuration of patches that uses the minimum amount of patches needed to feed the cows. Any configuration that satisfies the above conditions will be considered correct.

INPUT FORMAT (input arrives from the terminal / stdin):

Each input contains T test cases, each describing an arrangement of cows. The first line of input contains T ($1 \leq T \leq 10$). Each of the T test cases follow.

Each test case starts with a line containing N and K. The next line will contain a string of length N, where each character denotes the breed of the ith cow (G meaning Guernsey and H meaning Holstein).

OUTPUT FORMAT (print output to the terminal / stdout):

For each of the T test cases, please write two lines of output. For the first line, print the minimum number of patches needed to feed the cows. For the second line, print a string of length N that describes a configuration that feeds all the cows with the minimum number of patches. The ith character, describing the ith position, should be a '.' if there is no patch, a 'G' if there is a patch that feeds Guernseys, and a 'H' if it feeds Holsteins. Any valid configuration will be accepted.

HG

Note that for some test cases, there are multiple acceptable configurations that manage to feed all cows while using the minimum number of patches. For example, in the fourth test case, another acceptable answer would be:

.GH..

This corresponds to placing a patch feeding Guernseys on the 2nd position and a patch feeding Holsteins on the third position. This uses the optimal number of patches and ensures that all cows are within 3 positions of a patch they prefer.

SCORING:

- Inputs 2 through 4 have N $\leq$ 10.
- Inputs 5 through 8 have N $\leq$ 40.
- Inputs 9 through 12 have N $\leq 10^5$.

Problem credits: Mythreya Dharani

Language: C   ⌄
Source File: Choose File   No file chosen
Submit Solution

Figure 2.7 Three different places where the problem hints that there is more than one possible solution.

Coach B: See what I've circled? "Any configuration that satisfies," "Any valid configuration," and "multiple acceptable configurations." All indicate there might be more than one configuration possible. One out of many. Now, as to why they chose to show a specific solution: Any thoughts on that?

Rachid: Maybe they want to trick us?

The team laughs.

Coach B: I would give them the benefit of the doubt, or even more than that, I would say they genuinely want you to succeed in solving the problem. They might choose different solutions so as not to expose a pattern that will give away the right algorithm. But this is not the case usually, and this time in particular, it's not the case. So, any other thoughts why they chose that specific solution?

Ryan: Yes, actually. Here's what I'm seeing. For the first cow, it appears as though they put the patch of grass as far away as the cow can walk. This is strange.

Annie: However it does make sense when you come to think of it. We want to feed as many cows as possible with this patch of grass. And we know the first cow is willing to walk one position over. So it makes perfect sense to put the patch as far as we can from that cow, and then it may feed other cows farther away. In this case, there's no other cow that can benefit from this, but there might be in other situations.

Coach B: Great observations, Ryan and Annie. I believe you got the idea. Can you now try and complete the other test cases for us? You can do it as a team.

The team joins Rachid and Annie at the board, and after a few minutes of discussion, ends up drawing figure 2.8.

Annie: Tada! We're done.

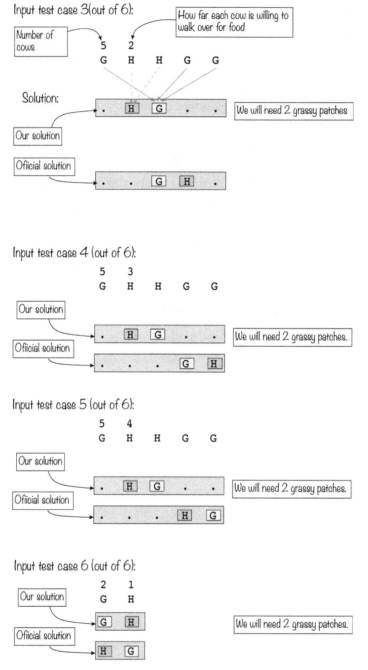

Figure 2.8 Test cases 3 through 6. For each, both the team's result and the official results are shown.

Coach B: This was quite swift. It seems that your solution rarely, if ever, aligns exactly with the official one. Why is that?

Rachid: But we did say that they don't have to match exactly. The number of patches required should be the same, but the specific configurations are allowed to differ, right?

Annie: Wait, don't answer yet, Coach. The truth is that we know how they arrived at their solutions, but we preferred ours. They tried to put the first patch as far away as possible from the first cow that requires it. While this might be a good idea in more complex scenarios, for all the test cases, our more intuitive solution worked equally well, so we stuck with it.

Coach B: Very well then. As long as you understand the reason for this disparity, we are good to go. Are you confident that you now fully comprehend the problem and have a notion of how to solve it?

The team nods affirmatively.

Coach B: Excellent. The next step is then to take your understanding of the problem and your idea for solving it... and translate it all into an algorithm.

2.1.3. Algorithm

Coach B: To describe the algorithm, we will use code snippets written in C++. I know some of you will be writing in Python, but fear not: the idea is that the code will be simple enough to comprehend even if you do not code in C++. Keep in mind, the sole purpose of the snippet is to describe an algorithm. So don't worry if you are not fluent in C++. Try to read the code, and see if you can follow. Implementing it, or writing the code as a program, is the next step that follows. Would anyone like to volunteer to write the algorithm?

Rachid: Sure, I can give it a try.

Coach B: Great. And keep in mind that when developing an algorithm, you don't need to be concerned with input/output or variable declarations. Your primary focus should be on writing code that accurately describes the algorithm itself.

 TIP: There are different ways to describe an algorithm. We will use C++ code, omitting peripheral things such as input/output or variable declarations. Other commonly used alternatives to describe an algorithm are flow charts and pseudo code. Flow charts provide a more visual representation of the algorithm but can be challenging to communicate if you're only using a text editor. On the other hand, pseudo code employs a generic code format. The problem with pseudo code is that it doesn't follow specific coding language rules and may cause confusion. If you feel more comfortable using a different method to describe an algorithm other than what we're using here, please continue using it. The key is to have a clear way of communicating your algorithm, even if it's only for your own use.

Rachid: First I'm just going to describe the code in words, because we developed it as a team, so I want to make sure I got it right. And, I am going to describe the idea from the official sample cases, in which they put the patch as far as possible. The algorithm begins by examining the input string of cows from left to right. For each cow, we check if there's a patch of grass nearby, within the allowed distance, that the cow can eat from. If not, we add a new patch as far to the right from the cow as possible. For instance, suppose the cow is located at position 0 and can move 2 spaces to reach a patch. In that case, we will place a patch at position 2. That'll make sure that all cows of the same type, up to position 4, will be covered by this patch. Does this all sound right?

The team gives nods of approval, and Rachid writes the code as in listing 2.1.

Listing 2.1 Feeding the Cows (Algorithm)

```
 1  string out(N, '.');
 2  int cnt = 0;
 3
 4  int g_last_covered = -1;  // Initially, no spot is covered
 5  int h_last_covered = -1;
 6
 7  for (int i = 0; i < N; ++i) {
 8      char cow;
 9      cow = str[i];
10
11      if (cow == 'G') {
12          if (i <= g_last_covered) continue;
13          cnt++;  // We need to put a new patch.
14          int new_loc = i + K;  // Try to put it as far as possible.
15          new_loc = min(new_loc, N - 1);
16          out[new_loc] = 'G';
17          g_last_covered = i + 2 * K;
18      }
19      if (cow == 'H') {  // Exactly as for 'G'
20          if (i <= h_last_covered) continue;
21          cnt++;
22          int new_loc = i + K;
23          new_loc = min(new_loc, N - 1);
24          out[new_loc] = 'H';
25          h_last_covered = i + 2 * K;
26      }
27  }
28
29  cout << cnt << "\n";
30  cout << out << "\n";
```

Coach B: Great work, Rachid. Your code is clear and easy to follow. Any questions before we proceed?

Ryan: I noticed you assigned `g_last_covered = i + 2 * K`. Shouldn't it be only one K away from the current position `i`, instead of `2 * K`?

Rachid: That's a good point, Ryan. Since the current cow is at position `i`, we place the patch at a distance of K from it, which brings us to `i + K`. This patch will then feed any cows of the same type up to K positions away from the patch, which brings us to `i + K + K`, or `i + 2 * K`. Does this explanation make sense?

Ryan: Oh, right. Yup, I get it now.

Coach B: It seems there are no other questions about the algorithm itself. This speaks a lot to how clearly you wrote it, Rachid. Well done. Let's move on and put it into a full code solution.

2.2. Coding Your Algorithm

Coach B: Before we dive into actual coding, let's get oriented. USACO, and coding competitions in general, have unique characteristics that can guide us through our code writing. I think these two new posters will help us. First, drum roll, please.

The team obliges, slapping their hands on their thighs in a quick rhythmic pattern, as the coach unfolds the poster as in figure 2.9.

Coach B: Here they are, the three main characteristics of the USACO coding competition. The first: Time pressure. Time pressure is a critical factor in competitions. USACO competitions are strictly timed, and you must submit your solution within the allotted time, usually 4 hours. Following a problem-solving process like ours will help you keep organized and solve the problems quickly and efficiently. We will demonstrate this process many times throughout our practices. As for coding itself, it is essential to move quickly through routine parts of your code, such as input and output, and utilize programming patterns efficiently for an edge. For Bronze level, common patterns include finding the maximum value in an array or using nested loops for two-dimensional arrays. We will cover these patterns today and in upcoming meetings.

 TIP: Following a problem-solving process is a time-saver. It does happen that students scan the problem too quickly, think they have the solution, and start coding it immediately, not following a process. It's great if this ends up working well, but usually it does not—and trying to correct things is harder and takes more time than doing them right the first time around. Get used to working methodically and carefully, and it'll pay great dividends in the end.

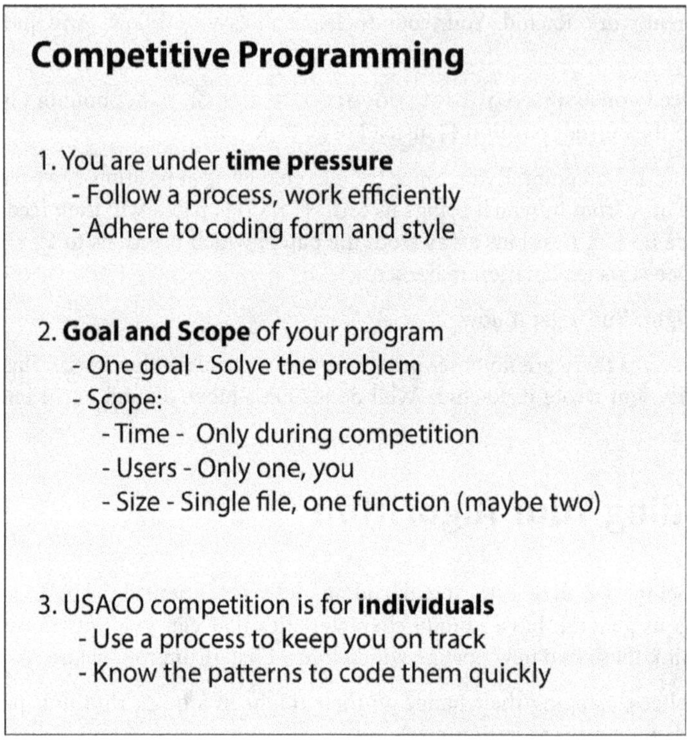

Competitive Programming

1. You are under **time pressure**
   - Follow a process, work efficiently
   - Adhere to coding form and style

2. **Goal and Scope** of your program
   - One goal - Solve the problem
   - Scope:
     - Time - Only during competition
     - Users - Only one, you
     - Size - Single file, one function (maybe two)

3. USACO competition is for **individuals**
   - Use a process to keep you on track
   - Know the patterns to code them quickly

Figure 2.9 The 3 tenets of competitive programming.

Rachid: Um, yeah: I am definitely one of those who jump right to a solution. I guess it works for simple things, but I get your point for USACO. There's always something tricky going on.

Coach B: Not tricky, remember? Detailed and hard, but not tricky.

Rachid: For me they feel tricky until I learn how to solve them.

Coach B: Okay, fair point. This is why we are here: to turn "tricky" into "interesting."

Rachid smiles.

Coach B: Now, for the second characteristic, Goal and Scope. The goal of your code is simply to solve all the test cases. It doesn't need to be the shortest code possible, nor easy to read, nor modular or extendable. It just needs to work, and work well. And this relates directly to the scope of your solution. In terms of time span, your code has served its purpose once the competition is done. You can contrast this with conventional commercial code, where your code for a game might be used for many years to come.

Annie: Oh, and in apps, too. The software in those things is used for many, many years.

Coach B: Correct. And this relates to the scope in terms of who will look at your code. In games, apps, even word processors, there is a big team involved, and more people join over time. Many people will be interacting with your code, expanding it, or adapting it for new devices. But in the competition, you are the sole person who will ever look at this code. That's a very big difference.

Mei: So, can I keep my code messy?

The team laughs.

Coach B: Not really, because you do need to make sure it works well, and messy code is hard to debug. But yes, you can disregard some of the conventional wisdom that holds for team projects.

Coach B points at the last item on the poster.

Coach B: We saw that the scope of your code is limited in terms of time and the number of people who will interact with it. One more aspect of the scope is the size of your program. Your program should be small. Granted, "small" is a relative term, so what we mean here is that it is not expected to be multiple functions and classes, spread over multiple files. You do need to write it in the span of a few hours at most. In Bronze level, everything can fit into one function, usually. Rarely do you need to use another function to make the code simpler. But for sure, if you find yourself defining multiple classes, you are probably on the wrong track.

 TIP: Keep It Simple. That's a principle we will follow throughout. It's important in algorithm development as well as in coding. Keeping codes simple makes them easier to verify, and to debug. Sometimes, you will first find a solution which is a little convoluted, and only later on will you find a way to simplify it. That's normal: you naturally understand the algorithm better as you work with it.

Coach B: The last characteristic is probably the clearest. The competition is an individual endeavor! No team to help, nor websites to consult. USACO does have one exception to that rule, and it is that you are allowed to consult sources describing the syntax or library functions of your programming language. But that's it: just syntax and libraries.

Ryan: And you have only yourself to blame if it doesn't work.

Coach B: Ha ha, true, but in the real world, diversity of minds is great for debugging: having someone looking over your shoulder and helping with a different perspective. Too often you get constrained by your own perception of how to solve the problem, and might therefore have tunnel vision, which means it's hard for you to consider other options for a solution. You might be unable to identify why your code fails for certain test cases, and there is no one else to help you find the flaw. We will address this issue, though. So don't worry.

 TIP: It is worth noting that some coding competitions do require teamwork. For example, ICPC, the International Collegiate Programming Contest, is a team competition. These competitions encourage team members to brainstorm solutions and collaborate on code. Diversity is also very beneficial for your practice. Seeing different solutions and coding methods is one of the best ways to improve your problem solving skills and programming.

Coach B: Have we all processed that pretty well? Good! Now let's move on to some practical "do"s-and-"don't"s of competitive programming. There are six of them.

Coach B unfolds the second poster, as in figure 2.10.

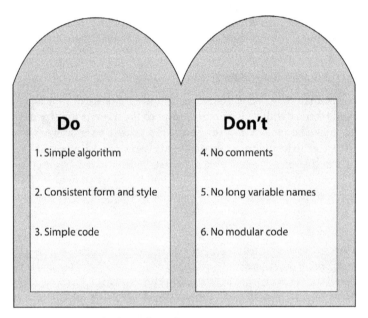

Do

1. Simple algorithm

2. Consistent form and style

3. Simple code

Don't

4. No comments

5. No long variable names

6. No modular code

Figure 2.10 "Do"s and "Don't"s for competitive programming.

Annie: I guess you want us to follow these as the 6 commandments?

Coach B: Eh, I wouldn't be quite so religious about them. Let's say, they're less like commandments, more like guidelines. You can bend these rules, if you need to.

Coach B points at the poster.

Coach B: I know we all want to get back to coding, so we'll just go briefly over these. Keep your algorithm simple, and keep your code simple. And regarding the form and style of your coding: keep that consistent. We'll come back to these principles again and again.

 TIP: Keep It simple. When you discover your code doesn't work correctly for a few cases, you may be tempted to make a quick fix, adding conditional statements to deal with these specific cases. Resist the temptation! Conditional statements tend to make the code appear more convoluted, moving you away from a simple, general solution to the problem. We need to keep things simple. Instead of adding conditional statements, you may reconsider your algorithm.

Coach B: As for the "Don't"s, these are much more cut and dry. Don't add extraneous comments, as you are the only one using the code. Of course, if it helps you to put a reminder at a specific point, go ahead and add a comment. But it takes time, so don't just add comments for the sake of posterity. There is no posterity!

Ryan: That's the polar opposite of what we are being taught in AP-CS!

Coach B: Yes, but this is competitive programming. You're coding as a single competitor, not a community. This is an important difference.

Annie: I actually like that. Writing the comments is a chore.

The team nods in agreement.

Coach B: Yes, a chore you can, and should, avoid! And the same goes for long variable names. On the one hand, you do need to have descriptive variable names. On the other, shorter is better. For example, consider the algorithm Rachid just wrote. I would say that "g_last_covered" is a bit too long of a name, but calling it "g" would be way too short and confusing. You might forget what "g" means. Maybe a name like "g_last" would be a good compromise? Striking the right balance will come with experience. But anyway, the big picture is this: a good code should be read and understood easily, with not too many comments, and clear variable names.

> *TIP:* The goldilocks principle for variable names: Not too long, not too short, just right. It's not uncommon for programmers to ponder "what is the right descriptive name?" for a few minutes. You do not have this luxury of spending time in a competition. A good short name is good enough. Don't agonize over it too long.

Coach B: The last of the "Don't"s is about modularity. Again, as you probably learned in AP-CS, good programming demands modular code. Meaning, you keep things more abstract and general, so they can be reused, or changed, relatively easily. For example, in our example we have only two types of cows, "G" and "H." Should we make the program easy to modify to handle three types of cows? If you are in AP-CS? Sure. But if you are in a USACO competition? No way! This program will never need to be modified to accommodate three types of cows. You should not add any complexity to your code in order to make it easily amenable to this change. Again, if it helps your coding to make any aspect more abstract and modular, go ahead and do it. But don't do it for the sake of writing modular programs, per se. Your score depends on your code's function, not its elegance.

> *TIP:* As you move to more advanced levels beyond Bronze, and use more advanced algorithms, it is often beneficial to use abstraction to simplify your code. You do it so you can use generic patterns on your specific data. For example, you may benefit from using a generic binary-search pattern by defining special comparators for the relevant problem. However, for USACO Bronze level, use as little abstraction as necessary.

TIP: A common CS adage is "Don't use magic numbers". This adage means that rather than using literal numbers in your code, like 2 or 10, called "magic numbers," you should assign these to variables (or constants) and then use the variable names instead. You don't necessarily need to toss this adage out the window for the competition, but use it judiciously. If some problem specifies that, for example, there are no more than 200 cows, and you are going to use this number only once in your program, feel free to use it explicitly as a magic number, rather than go through the trouble of defining a variable called max_-number_of_cows = 200, only to use that variable once. It's not an efficient use of your time.

The team gets antsy, moving in their seats.

Coach B: Alright, let's roll right into coding!

The team opens their laptops, and follows along as Coach B writes the code as in listing 2.2.

Listing 2.2 Feeding the Cows (First try)

```
1   #include <iostream>
2   using namespace std;
3
4   int main() {
5
6       int T;
7       cin >> T;
8
9       for (int t = 0; t < T; ++t) {
10          int N, K;
11          cin >> N >> K;
12          string str;
13          cin >> str;
14
15          string out(N, '.');
16          int cnt = 0;
17
18          int g_last = -1;
19          int h_last = -1;
20          char cow;
21          for (int i = 0; i < N; ++i) {
22              cow = str[i];
23              if (cow == 'G') {
24                  if (i <= g_last) continue;
```

```
25              cnt++;
26              int new_loc = i + K;
27              new_loc = min(new_loc, N - 1);
28              out[new_loc] = 'G';
29              g_last = i + 2 * K;
30          }
31          if (cow == 'H') {
32              if (i <= h_last) continue;
33              cnt++;
34              int new_loc = i + K;
35              new_loc = min(new_loc, N - 1);
36              out[new_loc] = 'H';
37              h_last = i + 2 * K;
38          }
39      }
40
41      cout << cnt << "\n";
42      cout << out << "\n";
43  }
44 }
```

Coach B waits for the team to catch up typing, and when everyone is done, he continues.

Coach B: Before we go into specifics, we need to get your seal of approval, Rachid: Does the main part of this code follow the algorithm you outlined?

The team scrutinizes the code, then nods.

Rachid: Yes. You shortened a few variable names, but otherwise, it's basically my algorithm.

Coach B: Great. So let's talk briefly about two aspects: form and style, and then about common coding patterns.

2.2.1. Form and Style

Coach B: Hopefully you can appreciate that the code looks organized; it looks consistent. This is the "Form" part of "Form and Style." For example, if you put no spaces between the end of a statement and the semicolon, then do it like that for *every* statement. Do this.

(Coach B projects on the board.)

```
1   int T;
2   cin >> T;
```

Coach B: And not this.

```
1   int T;
2   cin >> T ;
```

Coach B: For another example, keep the same spacing around logical operators. Do this.

```
1   if (cow == 'G') {
2       if (i <= g_last) continue;
3           // skipped code
4   }
5   if (cow == 'H') {
6       if (i <= h_last) continue;
7           // skipped code
8   }
```

Coach B: And not this.

```
1   if (cow == 'G') {
2       if (i<=g_last) continue;
3           // skipped code
4   }
5   if (cow=='H') {
6       if (i <= h_last) continue;
7           // skipped code
8   }
```

Coach B: These are small things, but they make a great impact, like keeping your room tidy or keeping your school notebook organized. For some of you, this consistency comes naturally. For others it's a conscious effort. But, in coding, it will help you immensely to get used to being consistent. And in truth, if you practice it in writing your code, it will become second nature. Guaranteed.

 TIP: The best way to practice good form is to go over your code after you are done, and adjust things as needed. It takes some extra time, which is okay during practice. By the time you get to the competition, the habit will be second-nature. If you are working with an IDE, many of those have the "reformat code" feature, which does exactly that: it keeps the form of your code consistent. If you do use this feature from time to time, pay attention to how it modifies your code. It will help you to be more consistent the next time.

Coach B: As for "Style," the second component of "Form and Style," this has more to do with how we actually structure the code itself. Whereas form is concerned with how we put spaces, indentations, and so on, style deals with where we put statements and declarations, and how we structurally organize the code. For example, some styles define all variables at the top, and use them in the code as needed. However, I'll always suggest that you define variables close to where they are used.

He writes on the board.

Coach B: Instead of doing this, defining all at the top:

```
1   int main() {
2
3       int T;
4       int t;
5       int N, K;
6       string str;
7       string out(N, '.');
8       int cnt = 0;
9       int g_last = -1;
10
11      cin >> T;
12      for (t = 0; t < T; ++t) {
13          cin >> N >> K;
14          cin >> str;
```

The style I use is as follows, where I define things closer to where they are used:

```
1   int main() {
2
3       int T;
4       cin >> T;
5
6       for (int t = 0; t < T; ++t) {
7           int N, K;
8           cin >> N >> K;
9           string str;
10          cin >> str;
11
12          string out(N, '.');
13          int cnt = 0;
```

```
14
15          int g_last = -1;
```

Mei: Okay, Coach, I don't mean to be rude, but are you sure this is important? I mean, I agree some code segments look nicer than others, but if all that matters in the competition is correctness, then why should we worry about this cosmetic stuff?

Coach B: Correctness is great, but it's not easy to get there. Keeping your form and style will actually help you write a correct code the first time around. For example, you'll avoid mismatched curly braces and other mishaps. And a well-structured code is easier for you to read. For example, you can see which operations are included in a loop, or what conditions apply to what cases. That's helpful whenever your code fails and you have to go back in and tweak it.

Mei nods slowly, pursing her lips.

Coach B: You don't look convinced! That's alright! All I ask is that when your code fails and you can't see why, take a step back, try to make your code a little more organized, and see if that helps. Doing things organized in the first place can save time, but better later than never.

Mei gives a thumbs-up.

2.2.2. Coding Patterns

Coach B: The next thing I want to mention about the code we wrote is the common patterns we used. These are code patterns that appear commonly in your program, and you should be comfortable moving through them without too much deliberation. I would consider these part of your technique. Not a thing you need to be creative about or spend time or thought over. For example, consider the pattern of file input and output.

Annie: Did I miss something? We didn't have any file handling in this example.

Coach B: Oh, you are absolutely right. In this example the input came from the standard input, the console, or in C++ language stdin, and the output went to the terminal as well, or in C++ language it is stdout. However, this was not always the case. In USACO problems prior to December 2020, input and output was done through files. Thus, you will use files often in your practices. So here is a common pattern I will be using for dealing with files.

He projects on the board:

```
1   #include <iostream>
2   using namespace std;
3
4   int main() {
5
6       freopen("art.in", "r", stdin);
7       freopen("art.out", "w", stdout);
8
9       int N;
10      cin >> N;
11  }
```

Coach B: All you need to know are the two lines with `freopen`, and you are all set. The rest of the program uses `cin` and `cout` as usual. This is what I mean by pattern: something you can use, mechanically, without much thinking.

Rachid: I learned to do this with `fstream`. Is this okay?

Coach B: Sure, but there are pros and cons for each of these methods. However, for the purpose of USACO competitions, these are both good. As long as you have a pattern to follow, and you don't agonize over it during the competition, you are good to go.

Rachid: Thanks. Your way actually seems simpler, so I'll try it out.

Coach B: Great! Now, another pattern is the one dealing with multiple test cases in each input sample. In our case, it is dealt with in the code like this.

```
1   int main() {
2
3       int T;
4       cin >> T;   // Input the number of test cases
5
6       for (int t = 0; t < T; ++t) {   // Loop over test cases
7           // Code here
8   }
```

Coach B: Again, there is no big revelation in this piece of code, but rather something you should be familiar with, used to, and not spend any brain cycles during competition trying to decipher. If you see a problem with multiple test cases per input, you simply need to loop over all these test cases.

Annie: Do we need to memorize all these?

Coach B: Oh, certainly not! You should be familiar with what is a common pattern, and by virtue of doing it so many times during practice, it will be committed to your memory.

Specifically, and I am saying it in full seriousness, I do not want anyone to go home today and memorize these patterns by heart. The important thing is to be cognizant of them, and ingrain them as you keep practicing.

The team gives an audible sigh of relief.

Coach B: Sorry if I scared you, I certainly didn't mean to. And, while we are on this point of recognizing and knowing patterns, there are many, many more patterns: looping over a two-dimensional array, or searching for a maximum value in a one-dimensional array, and so on. These are common patterns that come up time and again. As we'll practice, we'll accumulate more of these. Now, let's go to the next step, that of running our code.

Ryan: You mean submitting it to USACO?

Coach B: Almost. There is one more step we need to complete beforehand. Before submitting, we need to make sure the code works on the sample case, on our machine. Let's run our code on the sample input, and see what we get.

Coach B projects his result on the screen, as seen in figure 2.11.

TIP: When you cut and paste the input from the USACO website into your terminal, be sure to include the final carriage-return from the input. In other words, if your program seems to be stuck, it might be that you need to hit the return key one more time to signal the end of input.

```
zachi USACO_problems $
zachi USACO_problems $g++ USACO_2022_dec_b2_patches.cpp -o 2022_dec_b2_patches
zachi USACO_problems $./2022_dec_b2_patches
6
5 0
GHHGG
5 1
GHHGG
5 2
GHHGG
5 3
GHHGG
5 4
GHHGG
2 1
GH
5
GHHGG
3
.GH.G
2
..GH.
2
...GH
2
....H
2
.H
zachi USACO_problems $
```

Input: 6 test cases

Output: 6 test cases

Figure 2.11 Running our code on the sample input.

Coach B: Does the output look like what we expected? You can compare to the sample answer given in the problem itself.

Ryan: Yes, we're good. Well, wait a second, we're not! The last two cases don't match! We should have ended with "HG" in both, and we ended up with only one ".H" as the last two characters. What's going on?

Coach B: Hmm, a problem indeed. This brings us to the debugging phase. Hopefully, your code runs perfectly the first time around. But if this is not the case, you will need to debug it.

2.3. Debugging

Coach B: So here we are, debugging our code. In the best-case scenario, your code works perfectly from the get-go. However, if there is a problem, the second-best case is that your code fails on the sample input. This allows you to debug your program when you know both the input and the expected output.

Rachid: Can I use my IDE debugger for help?

Coach B: You are welcome to do that, Rachid. However, we will try and use print messages, as these will allow us a clearer look at what and how to debug. For the USACO Bronze, and in general for competitions, I prefer using print statements. But feel free to use your IDE's debugger if it is more convenient for you. First, I want you folks to consider the difference between debugging in practice and debugging during a real competition.

2.3.1. Debugging In Practice (when you have the expected solution)

Coach B: Debugging in practice means that you have both the input to your program, and the expected resulting output from your program. In our case the input is the sample input. Any ideas of what went wrong?

The team murmurs and looks puzzled.

Ryan: Um, we really don't know. Our algorithm seemed to work just fine.

The others nod, frowning.

 TIP: While you are practicing USACO problems, if your program fails on any test case, it may help to download the relevant input and the expected output. You do this by clicking on the "Test data" link on the contest page as is shown in figure 2.12. This will load all the tests, and their expected results, onto your computer. You can then examine the relevant case.

🏆 USACO 2022 December Contest, Bronze

The bronze division had 10226 total participants, of whom 8057 were pre-college students. All competitors who scored 750 or higher on this contest are automatically promoted to the silver division.

1 Cow College
View problem | Test data | Solution

2 Feeding the Cows
View problem | Test data | Solution

3 Reverse Engineering
View problem | Test data | Solution

Figure 2.12 Accessing the Test Data. You also have access to a sample solution.

Coach B: We can try and debug this in two ways. One way is to go through the code by hand, with the given input, and go step by step as if we were running the code to see what went wrong. There are cases when this might seem easier, and there are students who find this method faster and easier than what I am going to describe next.

Mei: In AP-CS, since we wrote our code on paper, this was our only way to check it. We learned to try and run it by hand, one line at a time, and see how it will perform.

Coach B: Yes, when you have only paper and pencil, this is your only resort. But we will try and use the power of our program. What we will do is add print statements in the code, and see if we get any insights from this. Any idea of what would be informative for us to print out?

Annie: How about printing the out string every time we modify it? This is the string we eventually print out, and it's apparently wrong in those two cases.

Coach B: Great idea, Annie. There are many different ways to debug a program, so it's okay if you came up with a different one. But let's try Annie's idea. Here, let me add a print statement in the code.

Coach B adds two lines to the code, as in listing 2.3.

Listing 2.3 Feeding the Cows (Debugging)

```
1  #include <iostream>
2  using namespace std;
3
4  int main() {
5
6      int T;
7      cin >> T;
8
9      for (int t = 0; t < T; ++t) {
10          int N, K;
11          cin >> N >> K;
12          string str;
13          cin >> str;
14
15          string out(N, '.');
16          int cnt = 0;
17
18          int g_last = -1;
19          int h_last = -1;
20          char cow;
21
22          cout << "\n\nDebugging Before Loop:: " << out << "\n";   // Debug
23
24          for (int i = 0; i < N; ++i) {
25              cow = str[i];
26              if (cow == 'G') {
27                  if (i <= g_last) continue;
```

```
28                     cnt++;
29                     int new_loc = i + K;
30                     new_loc = min(new_loc, N - 1);
31                     out[new_loc] = 'G';
32                     g_last = i + 2 * K;
33                 }
34             if (cow == 'H') {
35                     if (i <= h_last) continue;
36                     cnt++;
37                     int new_loc = i + K;
38                     new_loc = min(new_loc, N - 1);
39                     out[new_loc] = 'H';
40                     h_last = i + 2 * K;
41                 }
42
43             cout << "Debugging :: " << out << "\n";   // Debug
44         }
45
46     cout << cnt << "\n";
47     cout << out << "\n";
48 }
```

Coach B: To make it simpler, let's just run one of the test cases that failed. So our input would be like this.

1

5 4

GHHGG

Coach B: And the output should be...

2

...HG

The team copies the new code, and runs it in parallel with Coach B, who gets the results as in figure 2.13.

TIP: When adding a debugging printout, feel free to be loose and verbose, and give enough spaces and markers to make it very easy for you to read. These debug outputs are just for you, so they need to be as informative and readable as possible. No need to save on space, keep tight formatting, etc. You will remove all of these once the program works appropriately.

```
zachi USACO_problems $
zachi USACO_problems $g++ USACO_2022_dec_b2_patches.cpp -o 2022_dec_b2_patches
zachi USACO_problems $./2022_dec_b2_patches
1
5 4
GHHGG
Debugging Before Loop:: .....
Debugging :: ....G
Debugging :: ....H
2
....H
zachi USACO_problems $
```

Figure 2.13 Debugging printouts for the problem.

Coach B: Let's look at it carefully. Before starting the loop, our debugging output shows that the `out` string is all periods. Is this okay?

Mei: Yes, it is. This is what we have initialized the string for.

Coach B: Okay. And then it goes through the input string, the first cow is 'G', and our algorithm puts a patch as far as possible from it, which means 4 positions away. So this is how we got ". . . . G". Does everyone agree?

The team nods.

Coach B: And then the code reads the next cow on the input string, which is cow 'H', and tries to put the patch as far from it as possible. However, it cannot put it any further than the end of the out string, so our code placed an 'H' patch on top of our 'G' patch. Hmm, that's not good.

Annie: Oh, I got it. We need to check that a position is free before we put a patch there.

She heads to the board and picks up a marker.

Annie: We need to replace this part...

```
1   int new_loc = i + K;
2   new_loc = min(new_loc, N - 1);
3   out[new_loc] = 'G';
```

Annie: with this...

```
1   int new_loc = i + K;
2   new_loc = min(new_loc, N - 1);
3   if (out[new_loc] != '.') new_loc = max(0, N - 2);
4   // There are other ways to deal with the case of the position being
5   // occupied. Feel free to use other forms.
6   out[new_loc] = 'G';
```

Annie: And the same for the 'H' cows. It's just two more statements.

Coach B: Go ahead, let's try it.

Coach B and the students add the code, and the result appears as in figure 2.14.

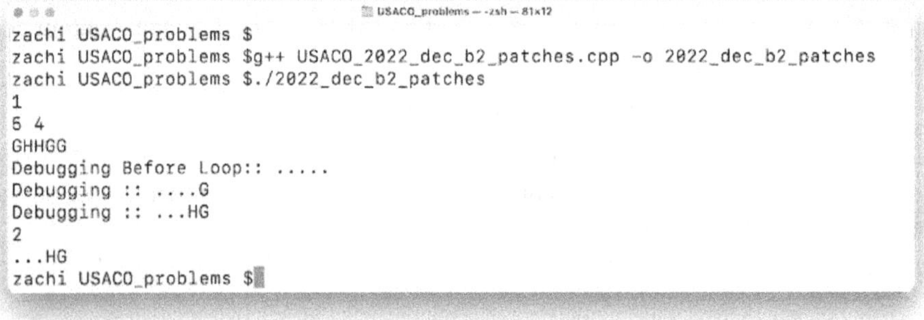

Figure 2.14 Debugging the output after adding the two lines as suggested by Annie.

The team cheers.

Annie: It worked! It produced the right result!

She high-fives her teammates.

Coach B: Excellent! Let's wrap it up then. Now, please comment out the debugging printouts, run it on the sample case once more to see if it really produces the right output, and then you can submit it on USACO.

The team hunches over their keyboards, racing to get to the all green-lights on USACO.

Annie: Got it. All green lights!

The rest of the team follows right behind with "All green!" exclamations.

Coach B: Great! You made it. Before we leave, I want to very briefly touch on two more things: how to debug in the actual competition, and how to use the given sample solution.

2.3.2. Debugging In The Competition

Coach B: If your program fails on the sample case, then it is exactly like the scenario we just examined. You have the test-case that was given as input to your code, and you also have the expected output. All you need to discover is the reason your actual output did not match the expected one. However, when your code fails on one of the other test cases, during the competition, the situation is very different. All you have then is a red flag by the USACO server telling you your program failed on a specific test-case. You **don't** know what the test-case was, nor do you know the expected output from this test case.

Rachid: So how can you debug anything? If you don't know what's wrong, how can you fix it?

Coach B: That's the dilemma. We don't have any concrete information on why things failed, so we just have to try and infer. I will mention a few ideas here, and we will see these in action later on. Some of these might be hard to perceive right now, but you'll encounter these for sure as you solve more problems. These are especially important because at competition time, you don't have anyone next to you to give suggestions or bring in different points of view.

The team looks a little disconcerted.

Coach B: Yes, it's surely not an easy situation to be in, but it will inevitably happen, and knowing how to deal with this will help a lot in competition time. Here, let me write these on the board.

 TIP: When your program fails some test cases, remember two positive things. The first is *partial credit.* You get credit for all the test cases you did pass. Hooray! The second is that you are moving forward. *You are not stuck.* You understood the problem at some level, and found a solution. Now, you need to make it better. But you are well beyond the starting square.

Coach B writes table 2.1 on the board.

Table 2.1 Debugging when your program fails during the competition

If your program fails on...	The likely diagnosis is...	The action you should take is...
Two or three test cases (e.g. test cases 3 and 7)	Missed special edge	Look for edge cases
Last few test cases (e.g. test cases 8 through 10)	Algorithm is not fast enough	Change algorithm (we will talk more about time-complexity next class)
All test cases other than the sample input	Something basic is wrong with the	Create a few more test cases of your own

If your program fails on...	The likely diagnosis is...	The action you should take is...
(first test case)	algorithm	

 TIP: USACO will give you informative indications on how your program performed on the test cases. The top-level indication is green for correct, and red for incorrect. Incorrect answers are further marked as follows: 'X' to denote incorrect result; 'T' to denote time limit exceeded; '!' to denote run-time error or memory limit exceeded; 'E' to denote empty output file; or 'M' to denote missing output file. If your program fails to compile, you will be shown the relevant error messages from the compiler.

Coach B: The first case we'll look at is when your program failed only a few test cases, scattered among the general test cases. This probably indicates your algorithm failed to deal with an edge case. Edge cases are cases that push to the limits one or more of the constraints given in the problem. For example, can you point to any edge cases in the problem we just solved?

The team pauses, looking back at the problem.

Annie: Maybe the case where there are cows only of one type?

Mei: Or the case when there is only one cow?

Ryan: Another could be when K = 0, when the cows can't move to a new position. We did solve for it, but it was still an edge case.

Coach B: Yes, all are great examples. So when your code fails on just a few cases, first of all you should feel good knowing that you are on the right track. Your algorithm works for most cases, and you will certainly get partial credit. Next, you should consider some edge cases, and see if your code handles them correctly. Does this make sense?

Rachid: Yeah, but how can we test those edge cases? I mean, if I suspect that a test case with only one cow broke my code, how do I verify it?

Coach B: There are two ways. The first is to simulate, by hand, how your code would run on such an input. Just like you do in AP-CS. The other way is to create your own input to simulate this case, and feed it to your program. For example, in our case, how would you simulate a case of all cows of the same type?

He hands a marker to Rachid, who approaches the board.

Rachid: I can give as an input something like this:

1

4 2

GGGG

Coach B: Perfect! One test case, with N = 4 and K = 2, and all four cows of the same type.

The team sighs in relief.

 TIP: One way to look for edge cases is to focus on the range limits on the variables given in the problem. For example, our most recent problem specified 0 <= K <= N - 1. Two natural edge cases would be when K = 0 and when K = N - 1.

Coach B: The second common case is when your program fails on the last few test cases. This will usually be accompanied by an indication your program failed on the time constraint. In other words, your program exceeded the allotted time, which means your algorithm is too slow. It is common for the USACO test cases to grow in complexity, and size of input, for the last few test cases. This failure means you need to speed up your algorithm. We will discuss this in detail at our next meeting. But, the really good news in this case is that you understood the problem correctly and found a correct algorithm to solve it. This algorithm is not fast enough, but it is still correct.

Ryan: What does that mean, "not fast enough but still correct?"

Coach B: Hold onto that question for one more week please, as this will be the subject of our next meeting. We will dedicate a whole meeting to this very thing.

Ryan: Sounds good.

Coach B: And the third common failure mode is when your program just fails on all test cases other than the first one. Does anyone know why it doesn't fail on the first one?

Mei: I think the first one is the same as the sample input, right?

Coach B: Yes, it is. And since we checked the sample input before we submitted our code, we know it works well. So unless we didn't check our code properly, we should always pass the first test case. However, if the program failed all other cases, it means we are missing something basic in our code. We didn't read the problem well enough, and are missing a basic fact. The best way is then to create some samples of your own, and run your program on these.

Rachid: If we create our own test cases, how do we know what is the expected output?

Coach B: That's a good question. The idea is that if you read the problem and created a simple test case, you should be able to determine on your own what the correct output is. Now, of course you might be wrong in determining that, because maybe you didn't understand the problem well enough. But in the competition, you are the only one you can rely on, so you're just trying your best.

Rachid: I hope I never need to debug during the competition. Sounds like searching in the dark.

Coach B: You are absolutely right, but as I said, this will most likely happen to all of us at some time, so thinking about it ahead, and preparing strategies, will help. And now, talking about strategies, I want to move to the last topic for today: how to use a given sample solution in your practice.

TIP: Once in a while you may run into a weird case where your program runs well on the sample input on your machine, yet fails to do even that on the USACO server. This is a relatively rare occurrence. USACO offers very good advice on this case, which appears at the bottom of the page for every problem: "Note: Many issues (e.g., uninitialized variables, out-of-bounds memory access) can cause a program to produce different output when run multiple times; if your program behaves in a manner inconsistent with the official contest results, you should probably look for one of these issues." For Bronze level, and writing in C++, the most common culprits are uninitialized variables.

2.4. Using a Solution

Coach B: Last but not least, let's touch on how you can use the given sample solution when you are practicing, or doing homework. Here, let's go again to the contest page, and let's see that you actually have a solution link there.

Coach B shares his screen, as in figure 2.15.

Coach B: Go ahead and click on this link, and take a quick look at the answer.

The team heads as instructed to http://www.usaco.org/current/data/sol_prob2_bronze_dec22.html.

Coach B: As you can see, and this is often the case, there's a short explanation, followed by sample code.

Rachid: There is actually code in C++, Java, and Python. Wow!

Coach B: True for this case, but often there's a solution in only one language.

 TIP: There is usually more than one way to solve a problem. And your solution might be different than the official one. If this is the case, it is a great exercise to understand the official solution as well, and see how it differs from yours. This will enrich your understanding of the problem and add to your toolbox of solution techniques.

☰ USACO 2022 December Contest, Bronze

The bronze division had 10226 total participants, of whom 8057 were pre-college students. All competitors who scored 750 or higher on this contest are automatically promoted to the silver division.

1 Cow College
View problem | Test data | Solution

2 Feeding the Cows
View problem | Test data | Solution

3 Reverse Engineering
View problem | Test data | Solution

Figure 2.15 The official solution and how to use it.

Coach B: Let me start by describing the *wrong* way to use a solution.

The team relaxes in their seats, ready for a moment of comic relief.

Coach B: Say you have a problem as homework. You read the problem, think about it for 2 minutes, and can't see a way out. You click on the solution, read the explanation, and it makes sense, but seems too complicated to code. You look at the code, and *now* you really get it: It is so simple! How come you didn't think about it earlier? You cut and paste the code into your file, submit it, and get all green lights: You did it!

The team laughs.

Mei: That's totally ridiculous! Do some people really do that?

Coach B: Oh, yes. Okay, I am happy we all had a good laugh. So here, help me out, what went wrong in this scenario? We mentioned it in the previous meeting when we discussed how to practice.

Ryan: To start with, we talked about spending some time on the problem before going to a solution. Two minutes seems too short. We should first wrestle with the problem for about 15 to 20 minutes.

Mei: And then, we should try and understand the solution. You don't learn a thing if you just copy and paste the code.

Coach B: I couldn't have said it better! You use the solution to understand the code, and then write it in your own way. You will notice the subtleties, and remember them better, if you write the code on your own.

Rachid fidgets with his hands, and Annie tries to hide a yawn.

Coach B: Okay, seems like you are ready to be done. We covered a lot today. Next time we'll dig a little deeper into USACO algorithms, and after that we'll dive into the actual problems. We are moving forward! I'll post one or two problems as homework for next time. Just to get you some practice. Thanks, and see you next time.

EPILOGUE

Competition coding is special in many aspects, from being strictly timed to being a fully individual endeavor. These aspects directly impact the way you should practice. As we move forward in this book, we will revisit these practice strategies again and again, especially as you tackle homework questions on your own.

VOCABULARY Corner: **DEBUGGING** We are all familiar with the term 'Debugging', which is, according to the Oxford dictionary, "the process of identifying and removing errors from computer hardware or software." But what do bugs have to do with software errors? The story goes back to the 1940's. Admiral Grace Hopper, a pioneer of computer programming, was working at Harvard University on one of the early computers used by the US Navy. These were large machines, with electrical wires stretching between electrical circuits. When one of her colleagues found a moth that impeded the operation of the computer, she coined the term 'debugging': Literally meaning 'taking the bugs out'. Real bugs. The term stayed, even though today's computers are made with one solid chip, and no real bug is likely to fit in there.

PRACTICE PROBLEMS

Hints and full solutions to the problems can be found on the club's page: http://www.usacoclub.com

1. USACO 2015 December Bronze Problem 1: Fence Painting

   http://usaco.org/index.php?page=viewproblem2&cpid=567

   We will revisit this problem when we learn about geometry problems. You are getting a preview of the subject by solving this problem.

   a. Note that the painted segments might overlap.

   b. Follow the problem-solving process we discussed:

   c. Read the problem.

   d. Visualize and analyze the sample cases.

   e. Search for an algorithm. If you need hints, try the club's page at http://www.usacoclub.com. You can also look at the official solution, which can be reached from the contest page: http://www.usaco.org/index.php?page=dec15results. Or directly: http://www.usaco.org/current/data/sol_paint_bronze_dec15.html

   f. Code the algorithm.

   g. Debug if needed. You can reach the test-cases from the contest page: http://www.usaco.org/index.php?page=dec15results

2. USACO 2024 January Bronze Problem 1: Majority Opinion

   http://usaco.org/index.php?page=viewproblem2&cpid=1371

Reading the problem and understanding the scenario can be rather confusing for this problem. However, the implementation is not so bad once you understand the concept. In the following, we will walk you through the solution.

a. If you have two adjacent cows with the same preference, you can start to form focus groups around these two cows, and convert all the others to have the same preference.

b. If you have two cows with the same preference, separated by only one other cow, you can create a focus group with these three, convert the middle cow, and you are in the same situation as in (a) above.

c. Consider groups greater than 3. In order to form a majority in such a group, you will always end up that either (a) or (b) above holds. Try it: draw a group of 5 (and then 6) cows, where you have 3 (or 4) cows with the same preference. Any arrangement will conform with either (a) or (b). This means that groups greater than 3 don't give us any new possibilities for converting cows. Therefore, we need to consider focus groups of only size 2 and 3.

d. Your algorithm should then go over the list of cows' preferences, and whenever either (a) or (b) occurs, this preference can become a majority.

e. As a final step, you need to trim duplicates from your findings in (d), and make sure the results are sorted.

2.5. Summary

- **Competitive programming** has three main characteristics that impact the way we practice and compete:

  - **Time Pressure** – You need to follow a problem-solving process and work efficiently. Code with proper form and style.
  - **Goal and Scope** – The sole goal of your program is to solve the problem. Your program will only be read by you, and should be simple and easy for you to handle.
  - **Individual** – Competition is a personal endeavor, and you should take advantage of common coding patterns to help you cruise through common parts.

- The "Do"s and "Don't"s of competitive programming:

  - **Do** Keep the Algorithm Simple. If the algorithm requires too many special cases, you should take a step back and reexamine it.
  - **Do** have consistent form and style. It will help you write a correct code.
  - **Do** Keep the Code Simple. In Bronze, all your code should fit within one, or at most two, functions.
  - **Don't** have long comments. Keep only comments that will help you in the process.
  - **Don't** have long variable names. Use good variable names that will help you remember what they are.

      – **Don't** put effort into making a modular code. Don't make your code especially easy for extension or abstraction. Keep it specific and relevant.

- Follow a **problem-solving process for solving a USACO problem**:

      – Read the problem.
      – Visualize the sample case. Draw it and compare the result to the one given.
      – Analyze the problem. Maybe use more sample cases.
      – Write an algorithm. Use a convenient form of pseudocode for this.
      – Code your algorithm. Keep to form and style to make sure it is a clear and correct translation of your algorithm.
      – Debug your algorithm if needed. Depending on how many, and which, test cases failed, the issue might be missed edge cases, a slow algorithm, or a misunderstanding of the problem.

- When **practicing**, you can use the **official solution** to help you with hints. Use it as a scaffold, not as a life-saving buoy.

Chapter 3. Complexity Analysis

This chapter covers

- Understanding why complexity analysis is important.
- Analyzing complexity using big O notation.
- Solving using an algorithm with improved time complexity.
- Reducing the space complexity of an algorithm.
- Recognizing the role of complexity analysis in Bronze-level problems.

Writing efficient algorithms is at the very heart of solving computer science problems. Granted, given a problem, the first step is to find a solution. However, in many practical cases, the next step is to check that this solution is feasible and useful. This is where complexity analysis comes in.

For example, consider the problem of finding the shortest route between two points on a map. You leave your home, get into the car, and want to find the way to a theater downtown. You enter the address in your GPS, and wait for the answer. Behind the scenes, an algorithm searches for a few plausible routes, and finds (say) 10 candidates. Then, the algorithm needs to choose the best one among these and present it to you. The algorithm weighs these routes according to traffic conditions, length of the route, speed limits, and other factors. Eventually, the algorithm presents you with one or two options, and you can start driving. The algorithm did a lot of work. But you haven't even noticed because the whole process took less than a second or two. If it had taken 10 minutes, you would have noticed, and complained.

So we have an algorithm that finds the best route between two points pretty fast if both points are within your city. That's great. In that case, there are only a handful of different options to choose from, and the algorithm completes within 2 seconds. What would happen if you wanted to travel from your home to a place 2000 miles away, in a different country? In this case, there are many more routes to consider. Would the algorithm now take 10 minutes to find the best route, or would it still be able to find it within a few seconds?

Complexity analysis deals with this issue exactly: how does the algorithm execution time change with the scaling of the problem size? In our example, complexity analysis will give us an insight into how much time it would take to analyze 100 or 1000 possible routes, given that it took 2 seconds to analyze 10 routes.

So far, we've focused on how much time an algorithm takes. We could also explore an algorithm's demand for space, or memory. For example, if considering each route requires you to save a full map and analyze it, then it wouldn't be a big issue if there are only 10 possible routes, and if the map is only of the neighborhood. However, if you have to consider 1000 routes, and each requires a map of the whole USA, then memory might become an issue.

We'll consider both time and memory as we introduce complexity analysis for the Bronze level in this chapter, as described in figure 3.1. We start in section 3.1 by introducing the big O notation, which is the notation used to analyze and communicate complexity. We then solve an example in section 3.2, and present two solutions with different time complexities. In section 3.3 we repeat the process for a problem concerned with space complexity.

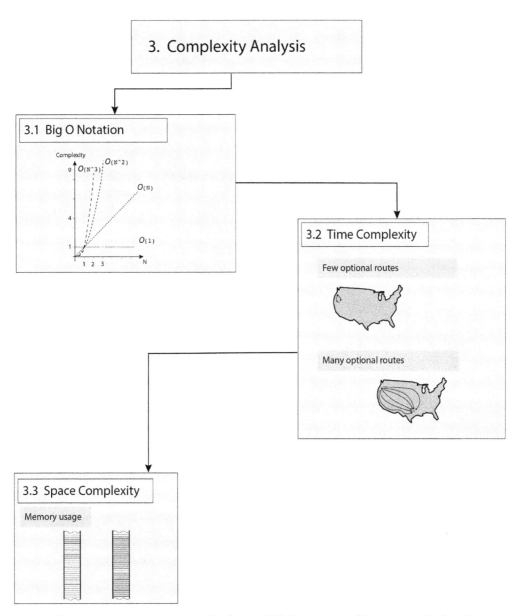

Figure 3.1 Complexity Analysis chapter map. We first establish the notation and language used to describe complexity. We then use this language to analyze examples involving time complexity and space complexity.

3.1. Big O Notation

The team gathers for a practice session, looking energized as they unpack their laptops.

Coach B: Happy Tuesday! Our subject today is complexity analysis. Although it is a very important subject in computer science (CS) and in the more advanced USACO levels, in USACO Bronze it takes only a back seat. The front seat in Bronze is reserved for the ability to solve the problem itself, which we'll spend most of our time on, starting from our next meeting. As this is the case, we will go pretty fast today through all the relevant complexity subjects for Bronze.

Ryan: So you mean we'll try to keep complexity analysis simple?

The team smiles. Coach B laughs.

Coach B: Yes, exactly. This is appropriate for Bronze. We will start with explaining the language used to describe complexity, and then consider two specific examples. So get comfortable and let your laptops rest for a little bit, because for the next 10 minutes we are going to learn a new language: the language of describing complexity in computer science.

The team closes their laptops and settles in for a short lecture.

Coach B: Let's say we have a program to find the largest among 10 numbers. The program simply goes over all the numbers and keeps the largest one. It takes this program 1 second to run. If we then want to run the same program over 100 numbers, about how much time do you think it would take?

Ryan: Ten times longer, so 10 seconds.

Coach B: Good. And if we had 1000 numbers?

Rachid: Again 10 times more numbers, so 100 seconds.

Coach B: Makes sense. So if this algorithm takes a certain time to run for, say, 1 number, then for N numbers it will take about N times that to run. This kind of algorithm, in which execution time changes approximately in equal proportion with the size of the input, is denoted as $O(N)$. That's the Big O notation.

The team nods in understanding as Coach B writes $O(N)$ on the board. That doesn't look too complicated.

TIP: Complexity analysis is concerned with how the execution time changes as the input size, N, gets larger. Complexity analysis is not concerned with the exact execution time itself. Specifically, it doesn't involve units of seconds or minutes. When you are calculating complexity in the Bronze level, focus on the big picture, and don't worry about making exact calculations.

Annie raises her hand, and Coach B nods for her to go ahead.

Annie: Just curious: you keep on saying "approximately" and "about" when you're describing the run time. Isn't the example we just did an exact case? I mean, if it took 1 second for 10 numbers, then it'll take exactly 10 seconds for 100 numbers, right?

Coach B: Very good question, Annie. When executing a program, there are many things happening, most "behind the scenes" as far as we are concerned. For example, let's say the numbers are read from a file. Reading from a file first requires your program to reach out to the operating system, get permission to access the file, and open the file. Only then can it read the numbers. This reaching out to the operating system is done only once per file, no matter if you need to read 10 numbers or 100. So this part will not take 10 times longer. And in general, there are many other "preparatory" operations that take place in the actual run of the algorithms. These don't necessarily scale in the same way. It's like how you don't necessarily have to pay extra shipping fees if you order five shirts instead of one. Does this make sense?

TIP: Do I need to measure the time of my algorithm? No! USACO does it for you. In USACO, all programs run on the same computer, with the same operating system and all other conditions the same, so you don't have to worry about the specifics of measuring time. The team at USACO takes care of that.

Annie: Makes perfect sense that the timing is not exact, but now I'm really confused. If this Big O notation is only approximate because of all these reasons, is it useful at all?

Coach B: Turns out, it is very useful! But you are raising a perfectly valid point. Big O notation should be handled with care if we want to use it to find specific execution times. But, it is a very valuable tool and a very good indicator of execution time when we work with large data. Going any deeper into it would be beyond the scope of Bronze, but let's look at a few more cases and see if the notation makes sense. Sound good?

Annie and the other team members nod.

TIP: You can always plug in numbers to get a feeling for how complexity changes with increasing input size. For an algorithm with a complexity of $O(N)$, doubling the input size from $N = 2$ to $N = 4$ will cause the output time to scale by two as well. For an algorithm with a complexity of $O(N^2)$, doubling the input size from $N = 2$ to $N = 4$ will cause the running time to change from $2^2 = 4$ to $4^2 = 16$, which is quadruple (multiplied by 4) the run time.

Coach B: Great! Now, say we want an algorithm to sum all the numbers in an array. What will be the complexity of this algorithm?

Mei: It would need to go over all the elements of the array and sum them up. So it's also $O(N)$.

Coach B: Yes, correct. And if we want an algorithm that will find the smallest element in the array, and then subtract it from all the elements of the array? What is the complexity of that?

There's a pause as the team considers this.

Annie: We'd need to go over all the elements of the array twice: once in order to find the minimum value in the array, and a second time in order to subtract it from all the elements. This means the complexity is $O(2N)$.

Coach B: Correct, but... the point is that in the Big O notation, we are not concerned with multiplicative, or additive, factors. Therefore, we omit the factor of 2, and just call it $O(N)$. This is another aspect of our approximations.

The team tries to digest this concept.

Rachid: Okay, so we... omit the factor 2. That's really stretching the meaning of "approximate."

Coach B: Yes, with Big O notation, we really are just focusing on the big, big picture. Now, next, assume we want an algorithm that will find the index of the first element equal to 15 in an array of length N. What would be the complexity of that?

Ryan: This looks different. If we're very lucky, the first element is equal to 15, and we're done. But, we might be very unlucky, and it's the last element which is equal to 15, in which case we need to go over all N elements. So I would say the complexity for this case depends on the values in the input.

Coach B: Good catch there, Ryan. Indeed, the execution time might be different depending on the input. However, we are going to think about complexity for the worst-case scenario. In this case, it means we need to assume the number we are looking for is, in fact, the last one. Hence, to find it we will need to go over all N elements, and the complexity here is again $O(N)$.

Ryan: This seems unfair, to assume always the worst case.

Coach B: I hear you Ryan, and indeed, there are complexity analysis methods aimed at average cases or other special settings. However, for many applications, including USACO, worst-case scenario is the way to go. Sorry.

 TIP: With complexity analysis, you should always consider the worst-case scenario: the one that maxes out the time or space that the algorithm would need. Often, if you can identify this worst case, then you've found an insight into how to improve the algorithm.

The team sighs. Complexity analysis is more ambiguous than they expected.

Coach B: No reason to be concerned. As you'll see, at the Bronze level, complexity analysis is limited to only a few typical scenarios. We're just taking a general view of the concept for now. We'll see an example shortly, but let's elaborate on complexity just a little more. So far, we considered only cases with $O(N)$. Let's see some other cases. I hope you are all familiar with the standard 6-sided die?

Reaching into his pocket, Coach B takes out a regular cube die, and the team lights up.

Ryan: Are we going to play?

Coach B: Well, maybe later. I have backgammon boards over there in the corner by the fish tank. But, are you familiar with other kinds of dice?

He takes out several more dice, with different shapes and colors, and more than 6 faces.

Ryan: Yeah, for sure. We play with these in Magic, the card game.

Annie: And in D&D.

Coach B: Great. So here is the question: assume we have two N-sided dice, and each side has a number written on it. You roll the two dice and add the numbers facing up. What are all the possible values you can get? It's okay if there are repetitions, but we do want to print all possible combinations.

Mei: That was our first example of nested loops in AP-CS! Exactly this problem! We did one loop that goes over all the possible values of the first die, and inside that, as a nested loop, we have another loop that goes over all the possible values of the second die.

Coach B: Can you write it down for us? I think it would be easier to see.

Mei goes to the board and writes the code as in listing 3.1.

Listing 3.1 Nested Loops for Two Dice

```
1  for (int i = 0; i < N; ++i) {   // Outer loop.
2      for (int j = 0; j < N; ++j) {   // Inner loop (nested loop).
3          int sum = die1[i] + die2[j];
4          cout << sum << "\n";
5      }
6  }
```

Coach B: Perfect. So, how many times do we execute the statement where we calculate the sum?

Mei: That would be N times for the outer loop, and each time we loop through that outer one, we go another N times in the inner loop. So, altogether, we have N times N, which is N^2.

Coach B: Yes, this algorithm has a complexity of $O(N^2)$. If we started with two 10-sided dice, and moved to 50-sided dice, then the complexity, or running time, would jump not by 5, but by 25. When we have an algorithm with complexity of $O(N^2)$, the increase in computation time as N increases is much more dramatic than in an $O(N)$ algorithm.

Ryan: Is there an $O(N^3)$ algorithm?

Coach B: Yes, and also $O(N^4)$, and so on. Any ideas for examples?

Annie: Say, if we have 3 dice, or four?

Coach B: Yes, very good, Annie. For each additional die we need one more nested loop, which requires going N times over all the values.

The team ponders this.

Coach B: Okay, last example. What is the complexity of an algorithm that gives you the first element of an array?

There's silence. The team frowns.

Mei: That's strange. Is that Big O of nothing? I mean, it doesn't depend on N at all.

Coach B: That's right. It's independent of N. But it does take some time, so we call it $O(1)$.

Ryan: But who needs that kind of algorithm? Is it relevant at all to Bronze?

Coach B: Here's an example. Say you have your address book, and you want to get the first name that's listed in the book. This is exactly the algorithm you need.

Ryan: Um... okay?

Coach B: Okay, let's say you need the 38th name in your address book. What is the complexity of getting this name from an array?

Ryan: Well, it would be 38 times the complexity, or time, taken to get the first element.

Coach B: Eh, this was a tricky question. In C++, and in many other languages, reaching any specific element in an array takes exactly the same amount of time, no matter its location. C++ does it by calculating the address in memory of the desired location, and bringing the information directly. Does it make more sense now?

Ryan nods half-heartedly.

Coach B: Yes, complexity is not a simple subject, but I believe we covered all we need for Bronze! And hopefully it will be clearer with the examples to follow. So let me summarize what we've seen so far with regard to complexity.

Coach B goes to the board, scribbling down the information in table 3.1.

Table 3.1 Complexities of different algorithms.

Complexity	Algorithm
$O(1)$	Retrieving the 38th element from an array
	Retrieving the first name from an address book
$O(N)$	Finding the maximum element in an array of length N
	Calculating the sum of all elements in an array of length N
	Finding the minimum element, and subtracting it from all other
	elements in the array of length N
$O(N^2)$	Finding all possible combinations of the sum from two N-sided dice
	using nested loops
$O(N^3)$	Finding all possible combinations of the sum from three N-sided dice

Coach B: This table not only summarizes the examples we saw so far, but it's also emphasizing the obvious: a complexity of $O(1)$ is better than a complexity of $O(N)$, which in turn is better than $O(N^2)$, and so on. Here, we can visualize it even better with a graph.

Coach B draws the graph as in figure 3.2.

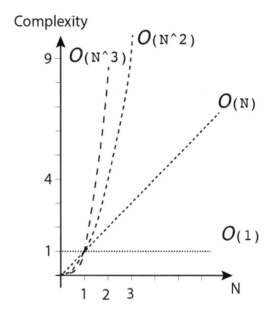

Figure 3.2 A graph demonstrating how different complexities change with increasing N. Note that it is common to denote an exponent using the caret.

Coach B: Check that out. Now it's even more apparent how different complexity levels behave with increasing N values.

Mei: Sorry, but I still don't get what it means for us when solving a problem?

Coach B: Let's look at the time aspect. We know that USACO problems have a running time limit. For C++ it is usually 2 seconds, and for Java and Python it is 4 seconds. Considering how many operations the grading computer can do in a second, a good rule of thumb is that if an algorithm is of complexity $O(N)$, then N has to be less than 10^7 in order to fit within the time limit.

Mei: Oh, so if the complexity is $O(N^2)$, then N has to be less than the square root of 10^7?

Coach B: Exactly! So just to round things up we can say that N has to be less than 10^4 in this case.

Ryan: And what if they change to a faster computer?

Coach B: Good point. We would then need to update the bounds on N I just gave you, or USACO might change the allotted running time for each program. But let's not confuse ourselves. For Bronze, there are actually only two things you need to remember: if $N > 10^4$, an algorithm of $O(N^2)$ will probably not fit in the time limit; if $N < 100$, almost any brute force method would work. Let's end with this, and try an example. How does this sound?

Coach B looks around, seeing the team nod with impatience.

Coach B: Good, then we're ready to move on! Let's dive right into an example of the use of complexity in USACO Bronze.

The team sighs, then cheers. They're ready for a real problem.

> *TIP*: When you read the problem, pay attention to the maximum size of the number of elements. If the maximum number of elements, or cases, is small, say $N < 100$, then almost any brute force method for a solution would work. If the number of elements is large, to the tune of $N > 10^4$, an algorithm of $O(N^2)$ will probably not fit in the time limit, and you might need to look for a simpler algorithm.

3.2. Time complexity

Coach B: Let's look at a specific example where time complexity comes into play. This time, it seems Bessie is visiting Washington, D.C. And as you can see, this problem is not from any past USACO event. Actually, most of the problems we will solve during the club are designed to highlight a specific aspect of a subject, and are not from USACO. The homework problems, on the other hand, are almost exclusively from USACO.

Problem 3.1: Exact Group Size

Bessie and her friends are excited to visit the Capitol Building, which houses the US Congress (the legislative arm of the US). The guided tour they are planning to take walks through the chambers of Congress and promises to be a very educational experience.

There are two lines for groups waiting to have the guided tour. Each line has N groups, and the group sizes are $a_1, a_2, \ldots, a_N$ and $b_1, b_2, \ldots, b_N$, respectively.

The first guided tour will take one group from each of the lines, and is planned for a total size of exactly K members.

Please help the tour organizers find two groups, one from each line, such that the total number of members is K.

Input Format

Three lines.

The first line contains two integers: N, K.

The next two lines contain N integers each, denoting the sizes of the different groups:

$a_1, a_2, \ldots, a_N$ and $b_1, b_2, \ldots, b_N$.

It is given that $a_1 < a_2 < a_3 < \ldots < a_N < 100$ and $b_1 < b_2 < b_3 < \ldots < b_N < 100$, and that N and K are positive and smaller than 10^6.

Output Format

One line with two numbers, the sizes of the two selected groups. You can print these in any order.

Sample Input

4 20

4 7 12 15

6 8 14 17

Sample Output

12 8

This is correct output because it takes a group of 12 from one of the lines and a group of 8 from the other line, and those two numbers add to 20.

SCORING:

- In test cases 2-5, N is less than 1000.
- In test cases 6-10, there are no additional constraints.

TIP: Refer back to the problem to understand all of the variables in the Input Format. For example, part of the Input Format here is "The first line contains two integers: N, K.$" Look back at the problem to figure out what N and K refer to! In this case, N is the number of groups in each line, and K is the combined group size that we want.

DISCUSSION

Coach B: Is the problem clear?

Ryan: What is the scoring thing at the bottom? What does it mean?

Coach B: Great question, and we will answer it shortly. Let's start solving the problem, and in a moment we'll get to the scoring thing. Any volunteers to draw the sample case?

Annie: I can try. It's not exactly a drawing that I have in mind, but let me show you what I mean.

Visualize it: Annie walks to the board and draws figure 3.3, including a rough sketch of the Capitol Building.

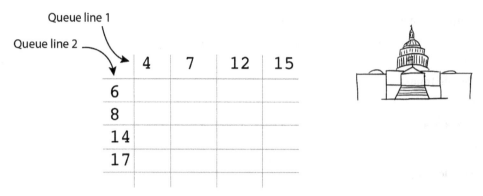

Figure 3.3 Setting up the sample problem, with two queue lines and different group sizes.

Ryan: Wow, that's a great drawing of the building, Annie.

Annie: Thanks. I remember it from our 5th grade trip to DC. And as for the problem... I just drew the group sizes in the two queue lines, and now I plan to fill in all the possible combinations of groups, and take the two that give the desired number, 20. Does this sound right?

The team nods in agreement and joins Annie to fill in the table as in figure 3.4.

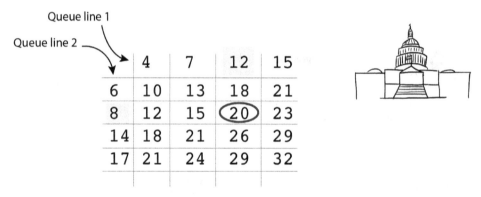

Figure 3.4 A filled-in table of all possible combinations of groups. Highlighted is the combination that yields an exact combined group size of 20.

Mei: There it is, the only combination that works is the two groups with 12 and 8 members.

Coach B: Looks very good. Can you translate it into an algorithm?

ALGORITHM (FIRST TRY)

Mei walks to the board and writes the code in listing 3.2.

Mei: The outer loop goes over all the groups in the first line, and the inner loop goes over all the groups in the second line. And inside the loops, we add them and check if this is the desired group size.

Listing 3.2 Exact Group Size: Brute Force

```
1  for (int i = 0; i < N; ++i) {  // Outer loop.
2      for (int j = 0; j < N; ++j) {  // Inner loop.
3          int sum = line1[i] + line2[j];
4          if (sum == K) {
5              cout << line1[i] << " " << line2[j] << "\n";
6              return 0;
7          }
8      }
9  }
```

Ryan: Classical nested loop structure. Nice!

Mei: Well, I did have to add a `return 0` from inside the loop, which is an uncommon thing to do. The reason is that we need to find and print only one pair, even if there are more pairs to be found. I could have used a flag to break out of the nested loops, but I thought this would be shorter.

Coach B: Agreed. It is uncommon, but it is beneficial and makes the code simpler in this case. So, I think it was a good decision. Well done!

Mei gives a thumbs up and heads back to her seat.

Coach B: Very nice analysis, Mei, and classic, indeed, Ryan. Recognizing patterns in coding is a great tool to have in your bag. So, taking advantage of this observation, can anyone say what is the time complexity of this algorithm?

Rachid: It should be $O(N^2)$, right? We had the nested loops pattern when going over all possible combinations of the two dice.

Coach B: Correct! So is it a good or bad complexity?

The team looks at each other, eyebrows raised.

Coach B: I know it's confusing. There's no direct answer to this question. An algorithm with complexity $O(N^2)$ might be the best there is for a certain problem, in which case it is as good as it gets. However, if there is an algorithm with a lower complexity for the same problem, then $O(N^2)$ is not that good.

Ryan: So how do we know if it's good or bad?

Coach B: In USACO problems, it is very simple: if you submit your code, and it fails on the time constraint, you know it's a bad complexity and you need to look for something better. As we will see, there are often hints in the problem that time complexity might be an issue. For our sample problem, as Ryan pointed out, there is a special note about the scoring. The note says that in test cases 2-5, N is less than 1000, and that in test cases 6-10, there are no additional constraints. In the problem it says that N is less than 10^6. This section about scoring is a clear indication of possible issues with time complexity. The cases where N is small, cases 2 through 5 (and also case 1, which is the sample case), will fit within the time constraint even with an inefficient algorithm. But in order to do well on the larger values of N, you will need to have a more efficient algorithm.

Ryan: So, in our problem, is $O(N^2)$ good enough?

Coach B: Sadly, not good enough for full credit. If you recall, we also mentioned that for an algorithm with complexity of $O(N^2)$ we need to have $N < 10^4$. And in our case, N can get up to 10^6. So, we still have work to do! Any ideas on how to make our algorithm faster?

He waits as the team thinks it over.

Coach B: I know, sometimes it's hard to find a different solution once you have one that works. Here's one way to try and get over this hurdle: Re-read the problem, and see if there's any information we haven't used yet.

The team looks at the problem again, trying to look for some new insights.

ALGORITHM (SECOND TRY)

Ryan: I can't find anything new. I think we followed it all.

Rachid: Well, almost. We never used the fact that the group sizes in the two lines are sorted from smaller to larger. I mean, it says $a_1 < a_2 < a_3 < \ldots < a_N$, which means they are sorted. I'm not sure we can actually use it to our benefit, because we just add all the combinations anyway.

Coach B: That's a great observation! Let me try and help here. Look, I'll draw the same two queue lines a little differently.

Coach B draws figure 3.5, where the two lines are next to each other, and have arrows on them.

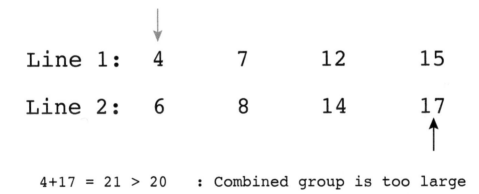

Figure 3.5 The two lines, and the group sizes. The arrows point at the two groups we currently consider joining. In our case, groups of size 4 and 17.

Coach B: Let's consider the first group from line 1, which is the smallest in line 1, and the last group from line 2, which is the largest in line 2. Everyone okay so far?

The team nods.

Coach B: If we add these two together, we get $4 + 17 = 21$. This is more than the required 20 members for the combined group. Can the group of 17 be paired with any of the other groups in line 1?

Annie: Not really. I mean, the group of size 4 was the smallest from line 1. So any other group will be larger, and will bring a result even larger than 21.

Coach B: Right. So we found out that the group of 17 cannot be paired with any other group, so we can skip it for sure.

Coach B adjusts the arrow on the second line, as in figure 3.6.

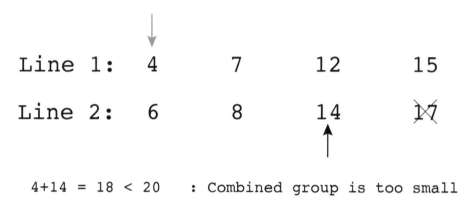

Figure 3.6 Since 17 is deemed to be too large to be added to any group, and we do not need to consider it anymore, we crossed it out. Now we are considering the groups of size 4 and 14.

Coach B: Now we have $4 + 14 = 18$, which is too small. What does this tell us?

Silence. The group holds still, thinking hard. You can hear the fish breathing in the back corner.

Coach B: Well, consider the group of size 4: is there any option for it to be part of our solution?

Mei: Oh, I think not. If we pair it with any other remaining group in line 2, the total size would be even smaller than what we got right now, 18. So no, it can't be part of the solution.

Coach B: Nice. So that means we do not need to consider the group of size 4 anymore. And you see, all this is because we know the groups in the two lines are sorted by size. So let me update the figure.

Coach B adjusts the arrows on the first line, as in the top of figure 3.7. He gestures to urge the group forward.

Coach B: Here, take the marker, and try to finish it up.

The group clusters by the board, with Annie taking the lead.

Annie: So now we have 7 and 14, and this ends up too large, so we can remove 14 from the possible groups.

Markers squeak softly as the group finishes up.

TIP: The two-pointer technique uses two indices into array(s), and moves these indices to point at progressive locations into the arrays. This is a common technique, and we will see it in action in more USACO Bronze problems.

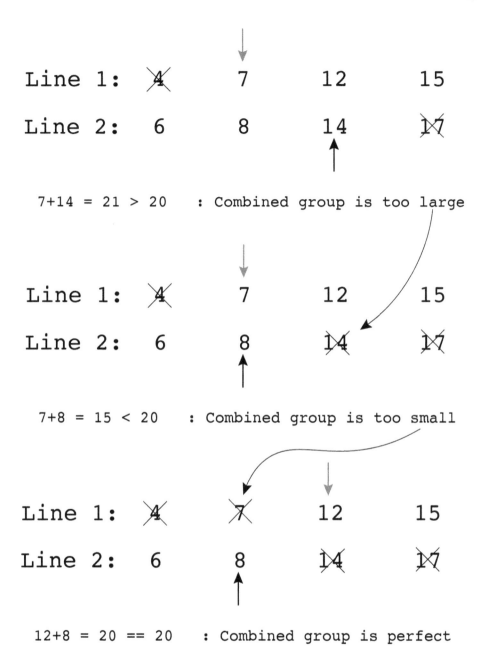

Figure 3.7 The next few steps as drawn on the board. In each step, the two arrows point at the presently considered two groups to join. We decide on which groups are not relevant anymore according to the resulting group size.

Coach B: Very nice. Well done!

The team smiles as they step back, looking at their work.

Coach B: Anyone willing to put it into an algorithm? No? No worries, we are just starting. Let me put it down in listing 3.3, but then one of you will need to explain it. Deal?

The team nods in relief.

Listing 3.3 Exact Group Size: Two Pointers Method

```
1   int i = 0;   // Index into first list.
2   int j = N - 1;   // Index into second list.
3
4   while (i < N && j >= 0) {   // Only one loop! No need for nested loops
5       int sum = line1[i] + line2[j];
6       // Three possible cases for the sum
7       if (sum == K) {   // sum is the size we want
8           cout << line1[i] << " " << line2[j] << "\n";
9           return 0;
10      }
11      if (sum > K) j--;   // Sum too large.
12      if (sum < K) i++;   // Sum too small.
13  }
```

Mei: I think I can explain the code. Your i and j variables are the two arrows we drew, and they're pointing to the two relevant groups on the two queue lines. Then, in each step of the loop, you check what the resulting group size is – this is the sum variable – and you update the arrows, which are i and j, accordingly, just as we did on the board.

Coach B: Yes. Now, here is the big question: what is the complexity of this new algorithm?

Ryan: The worst-case scenario is that we need to move the two arrows all the way to the other side. That means that we move each one of them N locations, so overall we perform the loop $2N$ times. So this is $O(2N)$.

Coach B: And as we said, we are not concerned with multiplicative factors, so this is just $O(N)$. Magic, isn't it? I mean, we had an $O(N^2)$ algorithm, and now we have a much simpler $O(N)$ algorithm. What just happened?

Annie: We traded in brain cycles for computer cycles.

The team laughs.

Coach B: Yes, we did that, and we used the fact the group sizes were sorted. That allowed us to use logic and cancel one group size every time: either from line 2 or line 1. So now, if we were to submit this, we would get a perfect score, even for the large N values!

The team cheers.

Coach B: Now, I think it is important to acknowledge that we had two perfectly valid solutions to the problem. But they had different time complexities, and therefore only one of them would pass all test cases.

The team settles back into their seats, looking at the solution.

Rachid: You know, Coach, I gotta say that the code looks really nice and simple, and straightforward. It's like you literally took our drawings and translated them into code. I'm sure that if I had to write it, it would be a mess. Like, the very same algorithm, but it would look all convoluted.

Coach B: Thanks, Rachid, and yes, I know exactly what you mean. Noticing nice code is the very first, and crucial, step in getting there. And I can't emphasize it enough: Look at your friends' code, look at the suggested solutions, look at any code you see, and you will learn something from each. Maybe you'll learn how you want your code to look... and maybe you'll learn how you *don't* want it to look. Both are important!

> *TIP*: Getting better at coding is important, so how do you do it? First, you need practice, which means writing more code. Second, you need to revisit your code after it works to solve the problem, so you can reflect on it, finding ways to make it cleaner. Third, you need to look at your friends' code, and get them to look at yours. Exchanging feedback with each other is invaluable; everyone gains by looking at their code together.

Coach B looks at his watch.

Coach B: Okay, we ran out of time, so maybe complexity can't be made that simple after all. Let's stop here. I will put only one or two problems on the club's page to help you fall in love with the subject. These are not easy problems, so remember to use the hints as needed. Next week, we'll look at space complexity.

The team looks concerned. Rachid draws in a dramatic breath.

Coach B: Oh, it is going to be much, much, simpler than today. You already have all the tools needed, like Big O notation, and besides, space complexity is a much less frequent guest in USACO Bronze problems. But we will need some brain power! So come ready. See you next week.

EPILOGUE

In this section, we put to good use our new language of describing complexity: Big O notation. The example problem asked us to find two groups that would add up to a specified size. The first solution considered all possible group combinations, and had a complexity of $O(N^2)$. By using the fact that the group sizes were sorted, we were able to devise an algorithm that had a complexity of only $O(N)$. That same problem led us to two algorithms, with different time complexities. It is important to remember that in USACO Bronze, the number one priority is finding a solution; only afterward do we search for a way to reduce the complexity. Thus, at the Bronze level, even with a non-optimal algorithm, you will earn partial credit. Moreover, you will have clear indications in the problem itself that complexity might be an issue. We will continue to highlight these indicators in the practice problems.

VOCABULARY Corner: **COMMODORE 64** Time and space constraints always had an important role in programming. Let's look as far as forty years back. The Commodore 64, aka the C64, was introduced in 1982, and is considered one of the icons of the early personal computer (PC) era. It was one of the first programmable, general-purpose computers, available to the consumer market. With 64KB of RAM memory, the reason for its name, the C64 worked at a clock speed of 1MHz and cost about $600. Compare that to a typical computer today, which has about 8GB of RAM (125,000 times more than the C64), and works at a speed of 3GHz (3,000 times faster). However, with increased computation power came an equal increase in the amount of data these machines need to process. Thus, complexity analysis remains as relevant today as it was back then. As long as we keep pushing the limits of what we can do with computers and algorithms, we'll keep relying on complexity analysis.

PRACTICE PROBLEMS

Hints and full solutions to the problems can be found on the club's page: http://www.usacoclub.com

Also, please note that we have just started our journey, and the problems in this section are not easy. If you find these too hard right now, feel free to skip these for now, and return to do these later on. In the next chapters we will focus on problem solving, which will help you a lot when re-visiting these problems later on.

1. CSES, Sorting and Searching: The Sum of Two Values

   https://cses.fi/problemset/task/1640

   a. This problem is very similar to the Exact Group Size problem.

   b. This problem works on only one vector.

   c. Since the array values are not sorted in this problem, we use a library function to sort the values. Please use the code given below if you need help using this library function.

   d. Hints:

   - Read the input into an array a.
   - Copy the input array to a new array b so we can still access the original unsorted data: copy(a, a + N, b);
   - Sort the input array: sort(a, a + N);
   - Use the two indices into the same array a, and proceed as we did in the sample problem.
   - Find the indices of the two numbers in the original array, now kept in b.

   e. Code (for main parts of the problem):

```
1       copy(a, a + n, b);
2       sort(a, a + n);
3
4       int i0 = 0;
5       int i1 = n - 1;
6       bool found = false;
7       while (i0 < i1) {
8           if (a[i0] + a[i1] > x) {
9               i1--;
10              continue;
11          }
12          if (a[i0] + a[i1] == x) {
13              found = true;
14              break;
15          }
16          if (a[i0] + a[i1] < x) {
17              i0++;
18              continue;
19          }
20      }
21
22      if (!found) {
23          cout << "IMPOSSIBLE";
24          exit(0);
25      }
26
27      int val1 = a[i0], id1 = -1;
28      int val2 = a[i1], id2 = -1;
29      for (int i = 0; i < n; ++i) {
30          if (id1 == -1 && b[i] == val1) id1 = i;
31          if (id2 == -1 && id1 != i && b[i] == val2) id2 = i;
32      }
33      cout << id1 + 1 << " " << id2 + 1;
```

2. USACO 2023 February Bronze Problem 1: Hungry Cow

   http://usaco.org/index.php?page=viewproblem2&cpid=1299

   a. Note how the problem specifies, at the very bottom:

   - Inputs 4-7: $T \leq 10^5$

- Inputs 8-13: No additional constraints.

b. This is a clear hint that either space or time complexity will be an issue for this problem. And moreover, the variable to watch for is T.

c. The straightforward way to solve this problem is to have a loop over the days, going from 1 to T, and verifying how many haybales Bessie will eat.

d. However, this solution requires doing T steps, and T can be very large ($T \leq 10^{14}$). This solution will give you credit for cases 1 through 7, but will fail for cases 8 through 13.

e. The alternative way is to loop over the number of haybales, and calculate how long they will sustain Bessie. In this case, your loop goes only over N cases, which is much smaller ($N \leq 10^5$).

f. Hint: Here is the suggested code, going over N :

```
long long t = 1;
long long ans = 0;

for (int i = 0; i < N; ++i) {
    long long d;
    long long b;

    cin >> d >> b;

    if (t <= d) t = d;
    if (T - t + 1 < b) b = T - t + 1;

    ans += b;
    t += b;
    if (t == T) break;
}
cout << ans << "\n";
```

3. USACO 2023 January Bronze Problem 1: Leaders

   http://usaco.org/index.php?page=viewproblem2&cpid=1275

   a. We will revisit this problem in chapter 7 in our study of Strings.

   b. Note how the problem specifies, at the very bottom:

   - Inputs 3-5: $N \leq 100$.
   - Inputs 6-10: $N \leq 3000$.

- Inputs 11-17: No additional constraints.

c. This is a clear hint that either space or time complexity will be an issue for this problem.

3.3. Space complexity

Coach B: Welcome back! Already, we're on our fourth meeting! Thanks for the email replies; it's good to know you've all done okay with the homework problems. That's great. We are warming up to those USACO problems, for sure. Next week we'll actually dive into specific common subjects in USACO Bronze. But today is still part of the introduction section, and we'll talk about space complexity.

The team settles in, smiling and stretching their fingers, ready for a new problem.

Annie: You did say last week, when we did the Big O notation and all about time complexity, that space complexity is going to be easier, right?

Coach B: I admit to that, and I really think it will be easier, but I guess you'll be the final judges of that. So, without further ado, let's look at a space complexity problem.

He projects the problem onto the whiteboard.

Problem 3.2: Missing Number

Bessie is looking forward to visiting the Smithsonian National Air and Space Museum. Her childhood dream was to be the first cow-astronaut sent on a mission in space. In the museum, Bessie notices a large wall with numbers written all over it, with a plaque below titled "Finding the missing parts." The plaque continues to describe the following problem.

Given $(N - 1)$ different numbers in the range 1 through N, inclusive, find the missing number.

Input Format

Two lines.

The first line contains one integer: $N, N \leq 10^6$.

The second line contains $(N - 1)$ different integers in the range 1 through N, inclusive.

Output Format

One line with one number, the number missing from the input.

Sample Input

8

2 1 8 6 7 4 3

Sample Output

5

==

DISCUSSION

Coach B: If anything, the problem is, at least, pretty short.

Ryan: So it has a small space complexity, right?

The team laughs. Rachid pretends to punch Ryan in the shoulder.

Coach B: Anyone want to share an idea for solving it?

Ryan: I can try. It seems pretty simple to me.

Visualize it: Ryan walks to the board and draws figure 3.8.

Ryan: I create an array to contain all the numbers from 1 through N. Initially all the array is full of zeros. Then, for every input number, I mark the respective location at the array as 1. Finally, I just go over the array and find the only place with a zero in it. That's the place of the missing number.

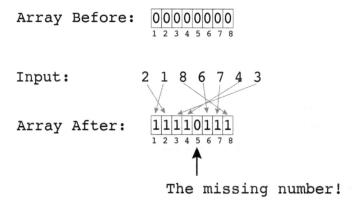

Figure 3.8 Finding the missing number in the input sequence.

Coach B: Looks good to me. Any questions? Comments?

Rachid: Maybe a comment. Ryan, why did you use an integer array? Rather than a boolean array? Because if you'd used a boolean array, all the zeros would be false, and the ones would be true.

Ryan: Hmm... yes, I guess I could have. The code would probably also be more readable then. Thanks, yes, good idea!

Coach B: Thanks Rachid, good point. Okay, even though this is not the main topic for today, let's review, and get this part out of the way: what is the time complexity of this algorithm?

Annie: We need to go over all the input numbers and mark the right places in the array, so that's $O(N)$, and then we need to go over the array and find the zero, which is another $O(N)$. Since $O(2N)$ is the same as $O(N)$, I would say this is $O(N)$.

Coach B: Correct! And any thoughts about what the space complexity of this algorithm might be? In other words, put it in terms of Big O notation, and say how much space we need for this algorithm.

Annie: Well, since we need an array of size N to store everything, I would say it is also $O(N)$.

Coach B: Correct again! And this is the first time we're looking at space complexity. Now, I'll ask a question similar to the one I asked when we were learning about time complexity: Is a space complexity of $O(N)$ good or bad? And the answer is, again, "it depends." If we have another algorithm which takes less space, then this is bad.

 TIP: The space allotted for your program on the USACO server is 256MB. This means $256*10^6$ Bytes. What does it mean in practice? It means you have a limit on the size of arrays (or lists in Python) that you can declare and use. As a good rule of thumb, if you need to store more than 10^7 integers in an array, you may need to find an alternative way to solve the problem.

Annie: But we can't really do better than this, can we? I mean, we do need to store the N numbers somewhere.

Coach B: You'll be surprised then. We *can* do better than that!

The team starts talking all at once, giving each other confused looks.

Coach B: Okay, okay. Here's a hint: What is the sum of all the numbers from 1 to N? Now, take 5 minutes to think this through, and let's see what you come up with.

The team looks even more confused with the given hint, but they get up and huddle by the board to try and make sense out of all this.

After 5 minutes, Coach B speaks up.

Coach B: That's a good effort, team. Listen up, and I'll explain how to solve this.

Annie: No, no, no, no, no, no. We're onto something. Hold on.

Another 5 minutes go by, with the team talking in hushed, excited voices.

Coach B: Have an answer?

Mei straightens up.

Mei: Yes, we think we do! Okay, here goes. To start with, we were really confused by the hint. Our first thought was to do a loop over all the values from 1 to N and add them up. But then Annie pointed out that there's a formula for that.

Annie: Yes, we learned it in the unit on Sequence and Series. The formula goes like this.

She gestures to the board, where she's written:

(sum of 1 to N) = $\frac{N \cdot (N+1)}{2}$.

Annie: So, for example, if we want to do the sum of the numbers from 1 to 8, it would be like this.

She points below.

(sum of 1 to 8) = $\frac{8 \cdot (8+1)}{2} = 36$.

Mei: But then again, if you don't remember the formula, we can just do a loop to calculate it.

> *TIP:* Carl Friedrich Gauss is considered one of the greatest mathematicians of all time. Legend has it that when he was still in primary school, the teacher gave the class an assignment to add up all the numbers from 1 to 100. After a few seconds, Gauss came with the correct answer, 5050. Amazed, the teacher asked him to explain. Gauss said that he simply noticed that $1 + 100 = 2 + 99 = 3 + 98 = \ldots = 101$. So, if you pair the numbers, you end up with 50 pairs, the sum of each being 101. Do the math, and $50 \times 101 = 5050$. If this story is true, then he certainly saved his classmates from a great deal of tedium. And the lesson for us? Don't be afraid to use mathematical formulas to save coding.

Coach B: Nice remembering the formula. It is always nice to have a closed form way to calculate something. And now, what did you do with this sum?

Mei: Yes, this was our next step. We couldn't understand why we needed this hint. Then Ryan came up with–actually, Ryan, you can tell it!

Ryan: Well, what I thought is that if we sum up all the numbers we get as input, we will almost reach this sum. We'll just be missing the number which is not there. That means, we just need to take the difference between the expected full sum and the sum we got from our input, and this difference is the missing number!

Coach B: That's the way! I knew you all were onto it! And how does it help us with the space complexity?

Ryan: We don't really need to have any array to store the numbers. For every new number, we just add it to the sum. So the space complexity is $O(0)$.

Coach B: Well, if you remember, when it is independent of the N in the problem, we actually denote it as $O(1)$. Great analysis, though: you cracked it. Isn't it amazing? We can solve the problem without storing any of the numbers, or without keeping an array to indicate if we had the number.

The team agrees.

Mei: It's a really surprising solution. At first, we didn't think we could do anything better than having the array of length N.

Coach B: Exactly. But we're not quite done yet. Anyone ready to wrap up this problem? It's just writing the algorithm.

Rachid: I'll take a crack at it.

ALGORITHM (FIRST TRY)

Rachid walks to the board and writes the code in listing 3.4.

Rachid: First, I calculated the total sum of the numbers from 1 to N using the formula, and then I calculated the sum of the given input numbers. The difference is the missing number.

Listing 3.4 Missing Number

```
1  // Formula to calculate sum of numbers 1-N
2  int sum_all = (N * (N + 1)) / 2;
3  int sum_input = 0;
4  for (int i = 0; i < N - 1; ++i) {
5      int t;
6      cin >> t;
7      sum_input += t;
8  }
9  int answer = sum_all - sum_input;
```

Ryan: Hold up. It seems like you have extra parentheses in the expression for the `sum_all` formula. Couldn't we write it with fewer parentheses, like `N * (N + 1) / 2`?

Rachid: Maybe, but I included my extra parentheses on purpose. We perform an integer division operation when we divide by two, so I wanted to be sure that this division happens last.

Coach B: I like it. It's called "defensive programming." Integer division bugs are really hard to find. It's best to try and avoid them. Any other thoughts or comments?

The team seems to be happy with the result of their work.

Coach B: Okay, so one more thing I wanted to bring up with regard to the code. The problem specifies that N can be as large as 10^6. What would be, approximately, the value of the total sum in that case?

Annie: Oh, I see. The total sum would be close to $\frac{10^6 \cdot (10^6 + 1)}{2}$, which is almost 10^{12}. That's too large for a variable of an integer type. An integer type can only hold up to about 10^9. So I guess we should use a variable of type long long?

Coach B: That's correct. Again, just a small detail, but it's the kind of thing that will prevent you from getting full credit. Your program would fail on large N values.

TIP: When an integer gets too big to fit into an `int` variable type, it is called an **overflow**. When your program fails for large values, and in the printout you see unexpected (possibly even negative) numbers, then that's your cue to look for a variable, or calculation, that overflows.

Coach B: Well, you see, you really cracked this problem much faster! You definitely are getting the hang of complexity analysis. That's great. Next week we'll start solving typical USACO problems, and as we move along, we will encounter complexity issues every so often. I think you are now well-equipped to deal with these.

The team looks happy.

Coach B: And look, we even finished early today. We've still got twenty minutes. So here, I'll post just one problem for you to do this week on your own, and you can tackle it right now. Then, have a free week. How about that?

Mei: We've got twenty minutes? Definitely, we can do it!

Coach B: That's the spirit. Let's go! I am here to help if needed. Otherwise, see you all next week.

EPILOGUE

The problem of the missing number has a direct solution that uses an array of size N to consider all the elements. This solution has a space complexity of $O(N)$. By instead determining the expected sum of elements, we developed an algorithm that does not require any storing of the input data, and has a space complexity of $O(1)$. Problems concerned with space complexity, at the Bronze level, are even more rare than those concerned with time complexity. Specifically, this problem would get full credit even if we do store all the N numbers. However, it is an important concept to keep in mind, and will become more important and relevant as you progress through the USACO levels. Similar to time complexity, we will see more examples in future chapters, and we will continue to highlight the appropriate indications given in the problems themselves, so you can recognize when to pay attention to complexity. Until then, let's keep in mind the big picture: in USACO Bronze, the emphasis is primarily on solving, and only secondarily on complexity.

 VOCABULARY Corner: **VIRTUAL MEMORY** As you consider issues of complexity, you might wonder: What happens when a computer needs more memory than it has available? It can resort to virtual memory! For example, the algorithm for finding routes on maps might need to cover a very large map but lack the space to store it. Virtual memory is a mechanism that allows the algorithm to act as if it has a much larger memory. It saves the maps in another place, for example on a remote machine, and fetches the relevant parts into memory as they are needed. Hence the name: the memory is located elsewhere. It's virtual.

PRACTICE PROBLEMS

Hints and full solutions to the problems can be found on the club's page: http://www.usacoclub.com

1. CSES, Introductory Problems: The Missing Number

   https://cses.fi/problemset/task/1083

   a. This is identical to the missing number problem. But now, you can submit and test it.

2. USACO 2020 December Bronze Problem 3: Stuck in a Rut

http://usaco.org/index.php?page=viewproblem2&cpid=1061

a. This is a very hard problem in the scale of Bronze. We will revisit it later, in chapter 6. I highly recommend solving it using a two dimensional array at this stage, and then come back for a more efficient algorithm after you have completed chapter 6.

b. Note how the problem specifies, at the very bottom:

- In test cases 2-5, all coordinates are at most 100.
- In test cases 6-10, there are no additional constraints.

c. This is a clear hint that either space or time complexity will be an issue for this problem.

d. The brute-force way to solve this problem would be to create a two-dimensional array that holds the whole relevant field.

- For cases 2-5 (and also case 1, which is the given sample case), an array size of 100×100 would suffice. An array of this size easily fits within the space constraints for a USACO problem.
- For cases 6-10, the array might be as large as $10^9 \times 10^9$. This will exceed the space constraints for the problem.

e. Remember: partial credit counts! Moreover, if you solve the problem in a manner that passes only for the first cases, then you understand the problem correctly, and you have a correct algorithm. The only trouble: it is not efficient enough! So now you can try and make it better.

f. Again, we will revisit this problem in chapter 6, so no need to solve it here. Just do your best to grapple with the element of complexity.

3.4. Summary

- **Complexity analysis** examines how computation time and required space change along with increased input size.
- **Big O** notation is used to classify algorithms according to their behavior as the input size grows.

  - $O(1)$ — Does not depend on the input's length, e.g., retrieving an element from an array.
  - $O(N)$ — Changes linearly with an increasing N, e.g., calculating the sum of all the elements in the input.
  - $O(N^2)$ — Grows as N^2, e.g., when using a nested loop to find all the possible sums of two dice.

- An algorithm can be correct and produce the right results, and yet be too slow in terms of its time complexity to fit within the time constraints.

    - This will cause failures in some of the test cases.
    - You need to modify the algorithm to achieve a better time complexity. For example, use the two-pointers technique.

- When time complexity is an issue in a Bronze level problem, there are often telling signs in the problem description itself. For example, you may see a statement that for some test cases the size of N is limited.
- **Space complexity** issues appear much less frequently in the Bronze level.

    - If space constraints cause a failure in some test cases, consider a solution that does not need to save all the input data, but rather processes it as it comes.

- Time and space complexity, which play a much more prominent role in the advanced USACO levels, are relatively rare concerns at the Bronze level.

Part II. Core Techniques

Chapter 4. Modeling and Simulation

This chapter covers

- Recognizing modeling problems in the context of USACO.
- Solving dynamic modeling problems described by a progression of steps.
- Solving static modeling problems described by a scenario and rules.
- Analyzing periodic modeling problems and using the appropriate tools for solving them.
- Accelerating the solutions of modeling problems.

Modeling problems are often referred to as simulation problems or implementation problems. These problems describe a process and ask a question related to the outcome of this process.

For example, consider a modeling problem where a cyclist adapts her speed in response to the terrain. When she pedals uphill, her speed is reduced by half every minute. When she pedals downhill, her speed triples every minute. Given a specific terrain and a starting speed, you are asked to simulate her speed along the ride and determine her finish time for a race.

At the Bronze level, solving modeling problems usually boils down to brute-force implementation of the procedure described in the problem. Thus, the main goal of the problem is to assess one's ability to understand the process, to pay attention to the fine details of implementation, and to demonstrate mastery of the programming language.

In this chapter, as described in Figure 4.1, we will cover different types of modeling problems, so you can identify them and simulate them effectively. The chapter opens with dynamic processes in section 4.1, where in each step of the simulation the state of the problem evolves. For example, in every step of the modeling, our cyclist is moving to a new part of the road.

We move next to dealing with a static process in section 4.2, where rules are applied to different settings. For example, suppose a problem describes the rules to assign clue-numbers to squares in a crossword puzzle. Your task is to apply the rules and assign clue-numbers for a given grid of black and white squares. As you can see, there is no time evolution in this process.

Section 4.3 then deals with periodic processes, where a part of the process repeats periodically. For example, a problem may describe the number of people arriving at a Ferris Wheel, and the capacity of each tub on the Ferris Wheel. Due to the nature of the wheel, the same tub will be at the bottom every full cycle. Modeling this problem has to take into account this periodicity.

We close the chapter in section 4.4 with ways to speed up the modeling. In certain modeling problems, a brute-force implementation may exceed the allotted execution time for some of the test cases. Although this issue is more common in the advanced USACO levels, it does occur at the Bronze level, and thus merits our attention.

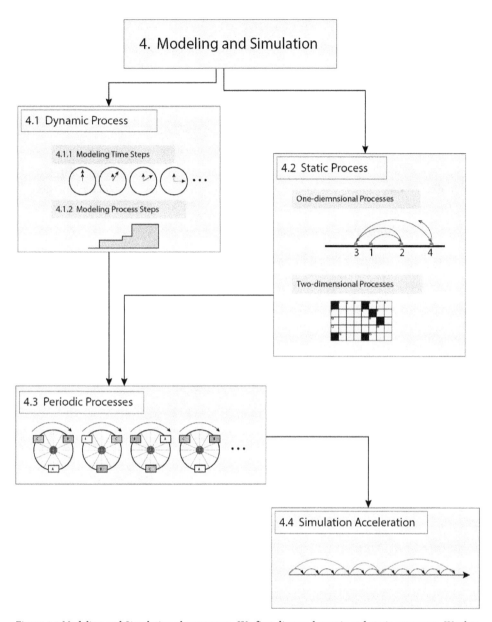

Figure 4.1 Modeling and Simulation chapter map. We first discuss dynamic and static processes. We then move to solutions for periodic problems and methods for accelerating modeling algorithms, which apply to both dynamic and static processes.

4.1. Modeling a Dynamic Process

We start our discussion of modeling problems with modeling of dynamic processes. These processes describe sequential steps, and after each step the state of the system may change. We will examine by examples what we mean by "state of the system," but for now it may suffice to think about it as the collection of the different variables that describe the system. Thus, to model the entire problem, we need to progress step by step and determine the evolution of the system's state, that is, the values of these different variables.

In our first example of a dynamic process, the evolution is described in terms of time steps; and in the second example, we investigate a dynamic process with no explicit time steps.

4.1.1. Modeling Time Steps

Coach B: Happy Tuesday! Seems like Bessie, Elsie, Farmer John, and the whole farm made it to New York City! The first problem takes place in Central Park. In this problem we have a process where the state changes every given time interval. Here, the time interval is one minute. But in other problems, this time interval might be a second, a minute, or even a year. Read the problem, and when you're done please come to the board to draw and discuss.

Problem 4.1: Walk Around The Lake

Bessie the cow misses her green pastures back home and invites her old friend Elsie for a walk around The Lake in Central Park. On arrival, Bessie discovers that Elsie did not wait for her to start walking and is already D meters away.

Bessie starts walking in the same direction, and for the next N minutes she is trying to catch up. During minute i, Bessie covers d_i meters, while her friend covers e_i meters.

Determine the first minute in which Bessie will not be behind Elsie.

Input Format

Three lines.

The first line contains two integers: D, N.

The second line contains N integers: $d_1, d_2, \ldots, d_N$.

The third line contains N integers: $e_1, e_2, \ldots, e_N$.

All integers are in the range $0 \ldots 100$.

Output Format

One number, the first minute Bessie will not be behind Elsie. If Bessie will not catch up within the first N minutes, output -1.

Sample Input

```
30 5
8 14 19 16 6
6 5 6 5 6
```

Sample Output

4

After 4 minutes, Bessie traveled $8 + 14 + 19 + 16 = 57$ meters from the starting point. During the same time, Elsie traveled $6 + 5 + 6 + 5 = 22$ meters. Keeping in mind Elsie had a 30 meter head start, she would be 52 meters from the starting point after 4 minutes. Since Bessie reached 57 meters, Bessie is ahead. A minute before, Bessie had covered only 41 meters and was behind Elsie.

DISCUSSION

The problem describes how the location of Bessie and her friend evolves over time. By simulating their location over time, we can determine if and when Bessie will reach Elsie. The "state of the system" in this problem is the location of the two cows, and this state is evolving over time. It has a clearly defined time step of one minute.

Visualize it: Annie walks to the board and starts drawing the problem following the sample input, as seen in figure 4.2.

Annie: Here's the initial state at $t = 0$. We'll follow the evolution of the state over time. During the first minute, Bessie covered 8 meters, which means her location at the end of the 1st minute will be 8 meters from the start. Her friend had a head start of 30 meters, and after the first minute–when she covered 6 meters–she'll be at 36 meters from the start. On the second minute Bessie covered 14 meters, so that brings her to a total of $8 + 14 = 22$ meters from the start... and so on.

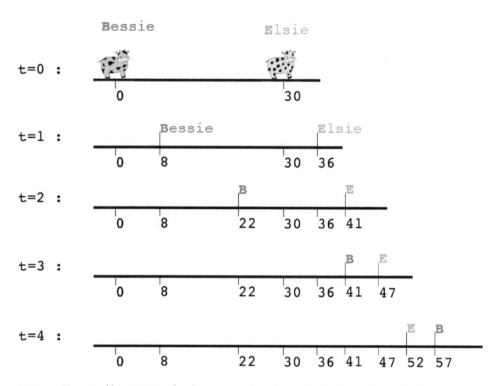

Figure 4.2 Two cows' locations simulated over time. Elsie, the cow in the blue outfit, starts 30 meters ahead of Bessie, who is in the red outfit. After 3 minutes Bessie still lags behind, but after 4 minutes Bessie is ahead by 5 meters.

Finished, Annie sets down her marker and turns to the group.

Annie: The problem asks us for the first minute Bessie will not be behind her friend. Therefore, we can keep simulating the process by calculating the locations of both Bessie and Elsie at every minute, until Bessie reaches or passes her friend, or until we reach the end of the given time steps. In this example, 4 minutes is the first time Bessie passes Elsie.

Coach B: Very well done, Annie. Any questions? Comments?

No one speaks up, all nod in agreement.

Coach B: Great. Any special cases we need to consider?

TIP: In modeling problems, all special cases are usually mentioned in the problem description explicitly, as the programmer needs to know how to handle these in the simulation.

Ryan: Here is one: If $D = 0$, it means Bessie and Elsie are starting together. Since Bessie is not behind at time $t = 0$, the output in this case should be 0. This was an easy special case.

Rachid: Right, and another case is maybe when Bessie never catches up. That means that after N time steps, Bessie is still behind. This case is mentioned specifically in the problem, and the output should then be -1. So this is again not a real worry.

Ryan: I just thought of something: What happens if Bessie catches up, but then falls behind again? We might need to search for multiple times of catching up.

Annie: That's true but I don't think we need to let that complicate things. Look at the wording of the problem: "Determine the first minute." This means we don't care what happens after that! We just need to find the first time Bessie catches up.

With no other special cases in mind, the group quiets.

Coach B: Okay, I think we got all the cases. Now, the algorithm for modeling problems is often a direct translation of the process description into code, with careful attention to details. Any volunteers to write it down for us?

ALGORITHM

Mei gets up to share her algorithm, as shown in listing 4.1.

Mei: The important part of the program is the `while` loop. We keep stepping through the time steps until one of two things happens: either we exhaust all time steps and we reach t=N; or Bessie reaches or passes her friend, so `dist_bessie >= dist_friend`. On second thought, these two events could happen together: Bessie can reach Elsie at the very last time step. At any rate, all these cases are handled correctly after the loop.

Listing 4.1 Walk Around The Lake

```
1   int dist_bessie = 0;
2   int dist_friend = D;
3   int t = 0;
4   while (t < N && dist_bessie < dist_friend) {
5       dist_bessie += bessie_covers_in_minute[t];
6       dist_friend += friend_covers_in_minute[t];
7       t++;
8   }
9   if (dist_bessie >= dist_friend)
10      answer = t;   // Loop ended because Bessie caught up.
11  else
12      answer = -1;  // Loop ended because we stepped through all N steps.
```

Coach B: Thanks, Mei. This is a very concise and clean code. Well done!

Coach B turns to the group.

Coach B: Any questions? Alright then. I guess this was a relatively simple problem for you all. Modeling problems tend to be simple in the sense that you just need to implement a given process. Two factors may make these problems a little more difficult, though: identifying the right variables to model the process, and understanding the given rules. You will see both of these issues come up in the practice problems. I will put some relevant modeling problems from USACO on the club's page. As usual, I will add hints and guides there, and please do use those as needed. Hints are there to get you rolling, and feel free to consult the solution to get unstuck. See you next week!

EPILOGUE

We considered a problem that covered the most intuitive modeling case, where each step in the process is a time interval. We solved it by progressing through the steps, which resembles progressing through time. These problems require attention to detail, careful programming, and in some cases, methods to accelerate through the time development. Acceleration methods are discussed in section 4.4.

 VOCABULARY Corner: **DYNAMICS** The word "dynamics" has its origins in Greek, where it means "force, power." In English, it first described the scientific study of bodies in motion. From there it expanded to describe general things in a state of change. For example, "group dynamics" refers to the change and evolution in the behavior of a group. And here in our modeling cases, dynamic processes are the ones in which changes occur as the process unfolds.

PRACTICE PROBLEMS

Hints and full solutions to the problems can be found on the club's page: http://www.usacoclub.com

1. USACO 2012 December Bronze Problem 1: Meet and Greet

   http://usaco.org/index.php?page=viewproblem2&cpid=205

   a. There is a maximum of one million time steps, so we have the space in memory to store all this data. We can create two arrays to store the location of each cow at every time step.

   b. *Visualize it:* What would the two arrays look like for the sample input? See figure 4.3.

   - Note that after time step 11, Bessie stays in the same spot. Elsie, on the other hand, keeps on moving, and eventually meets Bessie at location 3.
   - Note that while the two cows walk together from point 1 to point 3, we count it as only one "moo" when they first meet in this section of the road.

   c. After we store the location at each time step, we can go over these two arrays to compare the locations. Whenever Bessie and Elsie are at the same location (with the caveat below), they exchange one more moo.

   d. Watch out for the following cases:

- At the very end of the process, if the cows don't stop at the same time, it means that one cow kept walking around, while the other stayed in one place. They can still meet even if one cow is not moving!
- If both cows are walking together, they are at the same location, but do not necessarily need to keep exchanging moos. They need to exchange a moo only when they meet anew. One way to resolve this issue: Check if the cows are together in the current time step *and* that they were not together in the previous time step.

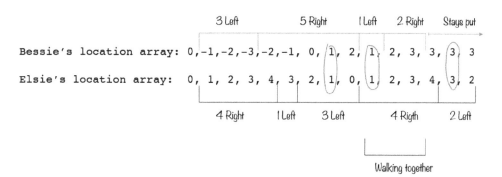

Figure 4.3 Values in the arrays according to the sample input. The green marks denote places the two cows will meet and greet.

2. USACO 2016 January Bronze Problem 3: Mowing the Field

   http://usaco.org/index.php?page=viewproblem2&cpid=593

   a. This is a two-dimensional setting, which requires the use of a 2D array.

   b. *Visualize it:* In figure 4.4, we've made a drawing of the problem with the given sample input. We can see that at times 7 and 17, FJ arrives at the same field, circled in the drawing. The time difference then is $17 - 7 = 10$ units. FJ also arrives at a previously visited field, albeit a different field than before, at times 2 and 26, also circled, this time yielding a time difference of 24. Since we need to take the minimum time difference, the answer is 10.

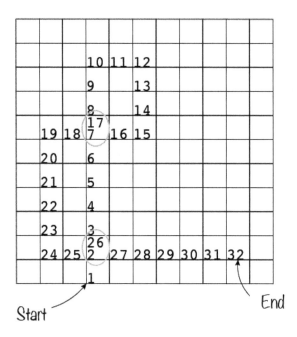

Figure 4.4 Drawing the sample input for Mowing the Field. Start by going north (up) 10 units of time, then going east (right) for two units, and so on.

3. USACO 2013 March Bronze Problem 1: Cow Race

   http://usaco.org/index.php?page=viewproblem2&cpid=259

   a. Each cow is given at most $1,000$ segments, each with an amount of time that does not exceed $1,000$ time units. Thus, the total possible time of running does not exceed $1,000 \times 1,000 = 1,000,000$. This is a small enough number that we can keep an array with all the time steps.

   b. *Visualize it:* The problem, with the sample input, is depicted in figure 4.5. Bessie initially moves at speed 1 for two time units. Then, she moves at a speed of 4 for one time unit, and so on. Her location is saved in the array. A similar process is done for Elsie. To find the answer, we scan the two arrays to determine the green encircled times, when a leadership change occurs.

   c. We can create two arrays of a length equal to the total number of time steps, that will contain the location of the two cows at each time unit.

   d. Finally, we step through the arrays, determining who is in the lead at any given moment, and whether this represents a switch in leadership.

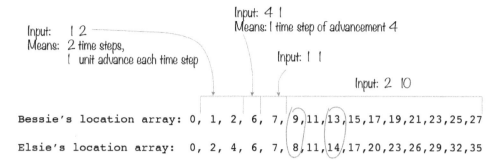

Figure 4.5 Cows' locations according to the sample input for Cow Race. At time 0, Bessie's location is 0 (the start). After one unit of time, her location is 1. After 3 units of time, her location is 6. The green marks denote the times when a transition occurs in leadership.

4. USACO 2020 Open Bronze Problem 3: Cowntact Tracing

   http://usaco.org/index.php?page=viewproblem2&cpid=1037

   a. This problem involves searching, which we will cover in more depth in the next chapter. Thus, you can try it now with the help of the hints below, or come back to it after reading the next chapter.

   b. We are searching for two parameters: which cow is "patient zero," and what the value of K is, where K is the number of hoof-shakes before a cow is recovered.

   c. This search can be implemented as a nested loop, followed by a simulation of the process, which means stepping through time and following the rules. At the end, we can check for a fit to the given end state.

```
// Outside loops are doing the search
for (int k = 0; k <= 251; ++k) {
    for (int cow0 = 1; cow0 <= N; ++cow0) {
        // Inside loop simulates the process
        for (int t = 1; t <= 250; ++t) {
            // your code here
        }
    }
}
```

4.1.2. Modeling Process Steps

We will now solve a modeling problem where no specific notion of time is considered. There is a sequence of steps, one after the other, which implies a time progression. However, no explicit notion of time is mentioned, and moreover, the time component is not of interest.

Coach B: Rise and shine! Welcome to the morning edition of our USACO club! With the spirit-week activities this afternoon, thank you all for being so flexible and changing the meeting time to before school. I hope you are all awake.

Annie: Awake and ready!

The team smiles.

Coach B: Let's go! Seems Bessie and Farmer John are still in New York City, and today Farmer John is puzzled by a street magician. Please read the problem, and we'll discuss it together.

Problem 4.2: Where Is The King?

Farmer John loves to play chess, and he is heading to Washington Park where he can play some fun chess games outdoors. It's a sunny day, and there is a magician showing a trick involving the king piece. The magician has N plastic cups arranged upside-down on the table. Under one of the cups is the king. The trick starts by the magician showing the audience under which cup the king is hidden: call it location K. The magician then shuffles the cups, takes a breath, shuffles them again, and continues to do so a total of M times. Everything was too fast to track, but Farmer John realizes the magician has been doing the exact same shuffling M times.

A shuffle is represented as a sequence of N integers, $a_1, a_2, \ldots, a_N$. Number a_i means that, after one shuffle is complete, the cup that had been in location i before the shuffle is now at location a_i.

Determine where the king is at the end of M shuffles.

Input Format

Two lines.

The first line contains three integers: N, M, K.

The second line contains N integers: $a_1, a_2, \ldots, a_N$.

All integers are in the range $1 \ldots 100$.

Output Format

One number, the location of the cup under which the king resides.

Sample Input

8 3 7

3 7 2 1 4 8 5 6

Sample Output

1

The King started at location 7. In each subsequent shuffle it moved as follows:

Start: $7 \rightarrow 5 \rightarrow 4 \rightarrow 1$:End

Thus, after three shuffles, it will be under the cup at location 1.

DISCUSSION

Coach B: The problem describes a process involving multiple shuffles, and each step of this process is one shuffle. We progress through the modeling by going from the first shuffle to the second shuffle, then to the third, and so on.

Ryan: I don't really get how the shuffling even works with these a_i items. Can we go over that first, please?

Coach B: That's really the crux of this problem. Understanding the process. Any volunteers?

Mei: I'll try. I can draw the cups, their location, and the king. Here goes.

Visualize it: Mei walks up to the whiteboard and draws figure 4.6. Coach B comes and adds circled letters on each cup.

Coach B: Let me add a cup-identifier to each cup. It will be useful for us when we try to track these.

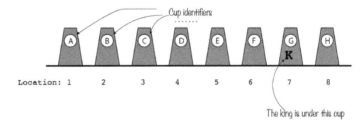

Figure 4.6 Eight cups on the table, before the first shuffle. The king is under cup G, at location 7.

 TIP: Use different identifiers for different variables to avoid confusion. Here, for example, rather than say "cup 1 at location 1," which will become confusing very soon, we can now say "cup A at location 1." It is immediately clear that A refers to the cup's name, and 1 refers to a location.

Mei: Now, I can also write the shuffling as it's described in the problem.

And Mei puts on the board figure 4.7.

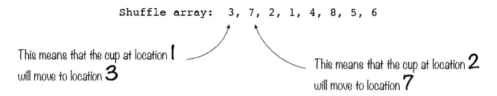

Figure 4.7 The shuffling as given in the problem, as a sequence of numbers.

Coach B: The key point to this problem is understanding how the shuffle is described, and how it is translated to the cup's locations. So take a careful look at the board (figure 4.7), and make sure you follow what it says.

Rachid: Let's see if I can do it with this drawing. According to the shuffling description, the cup at location 1 moves to a new location, 3. Here, is this correct? (And he augments the drawing as in figure 4.8.)

Ryan: Okay, so then the second cup goes to location 7, and so on. Is that right?

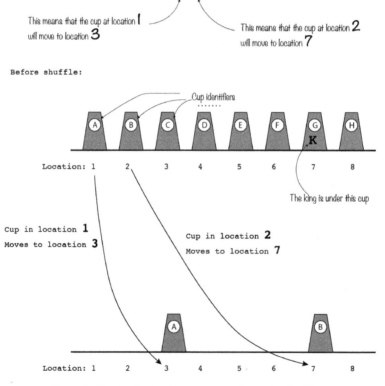

Figure 4.8 Moving the first two cups according to the shuffling.

Coach B: I think so. Seems like we figured out the shuffling. We still need to make sure we get the expected result. Ryan, can you finish it up?

Ryan stands up and heads to the board, but Rachid pipes up.

Rachid: But we only need to know where the king is, right? So why don't we follow only the cup with the king underneath it? Cup *G*?

Coach B: Sounds good to me! And it will also save Ryan some cups to draw. I will say, though, that when we get to the code, I want us to track all of the cups because that will be useful for the homework. Rachid, please remind me to come back to this before we wrap up. But for now... Ryan, can you just track the king?

Ryan erases the bottom part of the board, and adds three more arrows, as in figure 4.9.

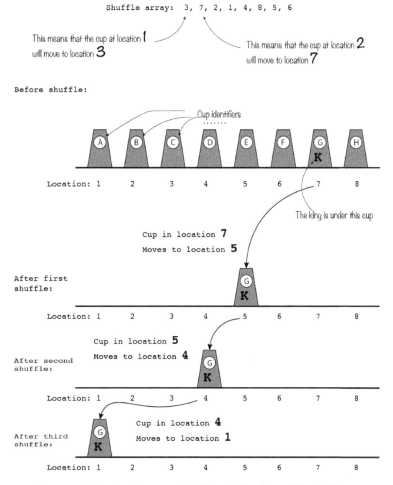

Figure 4.9 Following the cup with the King hidden through the shuffles.

Coach B: Yes, and we see the King is at location 1, which is indeed the expected answer. Great. Does the shuffling process make sense now? Good. We visualized the process, and we can see how it works. Another way to verify understanding is to write a code snippet. Do we have any brave soul who'll try and write it as code? Just the shuffling—not the whole solution.

ALGORITHM

Annie steps up and starts writing.

Annie: First I have the shuffling description stored in an array a[]. Then, I declare the arrays holding the cups' location before shuffling and after. So, for example, cups_old[5] will tell us which cup is in location 5.

```
1   int N = 8;
2   int a[N];     // {a_1, a_2, ..., a_n};
3   char cups_old[N];    // {'A', 'B', ..., 'H'};
4   char cups_new[N];
5
6   // Skipping input and initialization
7
8   for (int old_loc = 0; old_loc < N; old_loc++) {
9       int new_loc = a[old_loc];
10      cups_new[new_loc] = cups_old[old_loc];
11  }
```

Rachid: I think we can write the body of the loop more concisely. We use new_loc only once, so we can eliminate it.

Rachid walks to the board and writes:

```
1   for (int old_loc = 0; old_loc < N; old_loc++)
2       cups_new[ a[old_loc] ] = cups_old[old_loc];
```

Coach B: Nice. I have good news and bad news. Good news first? Both of these will work the same. It's mostly a matter of style, which way to leave it. Annie's code is more verbose and clearer, and Rachid's code is more concise, but might be hard to understand for the uninitiated reader.

Rachid: And the bad news?

Coach B: Well, both of these have a bug. Hint? It's not exactly in the loop. But it's related.

The team looks baffled. There are only declarations before the loop. And they all look perfectly okay!

Coach B: Okay, I'll help you find the bug. What is the first location in the problem?

Mei: We started with cup A at location 1.

Coach B: Right. Location 1. And the values that describe the shuffling, what values are these?

Mei: These are from 1 to N, and in our case, from 1 to 8.

Coach B: And we store everything in a C++ array. What is the first location in a C++ array?

Mei: C++ arrays start at zero. Oh, now I see! The array starts from zero, but all our indexing deals with locations 1 and beyond.

 TIP: Zero-indexed arrays can be confusing when mapping a problem into code. Watch out for these cases.

Ryan: Wait, but we can easily fix it! Rather than using a[old_loc], we should be using instead a[old_loc] - 1, because the array starts from zero. That's an easy fix. And then when we need to output the answer, we should add one back.

Mei: Or we can modify the array a[ ] just once, by subtracting one from each element in it, and then use zero indexing forever after.

Coach B: That would probably work, Ryan, and the same for your approach, Mei. But I would like to offer another option. At least for me, if I have to remember to add or subtract 1 every time I do an operation on the location, that's a sure way to make a mistake. I will surely forget to do it. There is another way of doing it. Here, I'll show you on the board.

Coach B writes down the new snippet of code, as in Listing 4.2.

Coach B: All the arrays are expanded by one, and the zero element is never accessed in our program. Our real interest in the arrays starts only from index 1.

Listing 4.2 **Where Is The King?**

```
1   int N = 8;
2   int a[N + 1];   // {0, a_1, a_2, ..., a_n};
3   char cups_old[N + 1];   // {' ', 'A', 'B', ..., 'H'};
4   char cups_new[N + 1];
5
6   // Skipping input and initialization
7
8   for (int old_loc = 1; old_loc <= N; ++old_loc) {
9       int new_loc = a[old_loc];
10      cups_new[new_loc] = cups_old[old_loc];
11  }
```

Coach B: One can argue it's a matter of style. Here, I did have to remember to add 1 to the array sizes. I like this option because it makes the code more readable and accessible to me. But, you are welcome to develop your own method and preference. Just remember to watch out for the zero-based arrays!

TIP: When you are correcting a bug in your code, try and make the correction as simple and basic as possible. Too many 'i f' statements or 'magic numbers' (like -1) would be confusing and error-prone.

Coach B: I see we're running out of time. Do we need to go over the full code for this, or can you complete it on your own from here?

Annie: We saw how to do one shuffle cycle. Now we just need to do it M times, right? We do need to copy at the end of every cycle the arrangement from cups_new to cups_old, but I think that's the only real tricky thing. After all, it's a modeling problem, so we just need to model the shuffling. Oh, and we have to figure out where the king is at the end. But I'm good with finishing this at home.

Everyone else nods in agreement.

TIP: Identifying the type of problem often helps you make connections to previous problems you solved, and thus helps conceive the algorithm.

Coach B: Great. So I'll put one note about special cases on the club's page, and also some practice problems. And remember, you can always find all the full solutions to these problems on the club's page.

Rachid: Oh oh, but what about my idea to track only the king? We can just figure out after each step where the king swaps to. We don't need to track the other cups.

Coach B: Ahh yes; thank you, Rachid. I'll put this simplified version of the code up there, too. But remember: for some of the homework, we are going to need to track everything, and now you all know how to do that. Great job, all.

On the club's page:

Note from Coach B: Special cases for the shuffling problem

I wanted to mention that there are two interesting special cases in this problem, but neither is impacting the way we will simulate the process or write our code. However, the insights afforded by these two special cases may prove beneficial when looking for a more efficient algorithm if we need to accelerate the execution time.

1. **Special shuffle arrangement**–There might be special shuffles that create interesting patterns. For example, consider cups F and H, at locations 6 and 8 respectively. According to the given shuffle, the cups in these two locations simply switch places

with each other every shuffle. Thus, on every even-shuffle, cup H will be in location 8, and on an odd-shuffle, cup F will be in location 8.

Similarly, we might encounter a shuffle that rotates among three cups, or one that keeps a cup staying in the same location.

2. **Periodic cycle**–All shuffles on a finite set of cups will lead to a periodic cycle, where the arrangement repeats an ordering we already had. But it could be a very long cycle. If the cycle is short, we might be able to use it to accelerate modeling.

As mentioned, we are not going to take advantage of either of the above insights for this problem. Since we are only dealing with M shuffles, and M is not more than 100, we will simulate the whole process directly.

EPILOGUE

This modeling problem involved stepping through a process, following sequential steps. However, there was no explicit stepping in time. Each shuffle could have taken 1 second for a fast magician, or 10 seconds for a magician-in-training. The important thing is that whenever one shuffle ended, we followed with another shuffle, and so on.

We noted that, to succeed in these problems, we absolutely had to attend to the details. Both when reading the description of the problem, as well as in designing the implementation and coding it.

VOCABULARY Corner: **PERMUTATION** A permutation is an arrangement of items in a certain order. For example, if you take a set of numbers $\{1, 2, 3\}$ and look for all possible ways to place them in order, then you're trying to find all the permutations. There are six permutations: 123, 132, 213, 231, 312, and 321. Permutations are common subjects in more advanced USACO levels; plus, they play an important role in group-theory and combinatorics. Even more broadly, the idea of permutations can be applied to wordplay. Permutation of words are called anagrams. Although most anagrams are gibberish, some are meaningful, offering a delight when you discover them. For example, an anagram of "listen" is "silent." Can you find a meaningful anagram for the name "Madam Curie"? (Marie Curie was the first woman to win a Nobel Prize, and the first person to win two of them, all for her research on radioactive materials. Sadly, she succumbed to a disease caused by those materials.) To play along, we use the polite version of her name, "Madam Curie." Do you give up? This researcher of radioactive materials, "Madam Curie," has an eerie anagram: "Radium came." Naturally, that anagram is just one of many possible permutations of the letters in her name. Try looking for these permutations in words: it's a fun way to keep your mind busy and practice analyzing chunks of data!

PRACTICE PROBLEMS

Hints and full solutions to the problems can be found on the club's page: http://www.usacoclub.com

1. USACO 2017 December Bronze Problem 2: The Bovine Shuffle

   http://usaco.org/index.php?page=viewproblem2&cpid=760

   a. Very similar to problem 4.2, Where Is The King?

   b. Two plausible ways to solve it:

   - We could simulate the shuffling, as we did from an initial state, but this time we'd find the correspondence between the cups and the final arrangement.
   - We could find the "unshuffling" formula by moving from the end backward, one step at a time. This can be an interesting exercise.

2. USACO 2017 Open Bronze Problem 1: The Lost Cow

   http://usaco.org/index.php?page=viewproblem2&cpid=735

   a. Visualize it: this is especially important for this problem. Make sure you get the same result as specified. You can see a drawing in figure 4.10.

   b. Modeling of the process:

   - The direction changes every iteration.
   - The step size, or the distance Farmer John walks from his original location, doubles every iteration.

   c. Consider a special case: $x == y$.

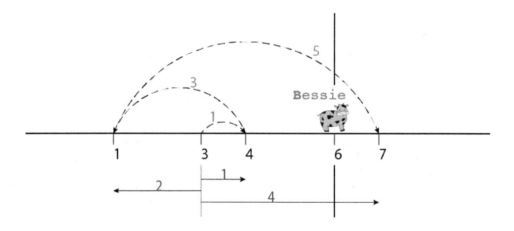

Total covered: $1 + 3 + 5 = 9$

Figure 4.10 Drawing the sample input for The Lost Cow. Starting from location x = 3 , Farmer John walks to 3 + 1 = 4, then to 3 - 2 = 1, and then he is aiming for 3 + 4 = 7, but luckily, he finds Bessie before that!

3. USACO 2017 February Bronze Problem 3: Why Did the Cow Cross the Road III

   http://usaco.org/index.php?page=viewproblem2&cpid=713

   a. This is a modeling of a process that involves time, but does not involve a fixed increment of time every step.

   b. No sorting is needed for a solution that receives full credit.

   c. Solution hint: Find the cow with the minimal arrival time who has not been served yet and serve her. The total time should then be updated to be:

   ```
   total_time = max(total_time, arrival_time) + service_time;
   ```

4. USACO 2019 January Bronze Problem 1: Shell Game

   http://usaco.org/index.php?page=viewproblem2&cpid=891

   a. You have three options for where the pebble could have been at the very beginning.

   b. For each one of the possible starting positions, you can simulate the ensuing game, and see how many times Bessie was correct.

5. USACO 2023 December Bronze Problem 1: Candy Cane Feast

   http://usaco.org/index.php?page=viewproblem2&cpid=1347

   a. Implement using double loop:

   - Outer loop - For each cane: Initialize height of the base of the cane to 0.
   - Inner loop - For each cow: Eat from the cane as much as you can, and then increase the height of the cow and the height of the base of the cane.

4.2. Modeling a Static Process

The next problem is a static modeling problem where no evolution occurs. These kinds of problems describe rules to determine a value, and then supplies various settings where you are asked to apply these rules. Like with all modeling problems, to solve this one, you must understand the given rules, consider special cases, and program carefully, with attention to details.

Coach B welcomes the team, and projects the following problem.

Problem 4.3: A Visit To The Mooseum

Bessie loves museums, especially ones featuring animals, and especially her favorite, dinosaurs. The next stop is therefore the Mooseum of Natural History, with dinosaurs galore! There are so many rooms, and to make her visit most enjoyable, she decides to visit only rooms that satisfy the following conditions:

1. She must visit every room that has a dinosaur in it.

2. She may visit one of the food-concession rooms of her choice for lunch.

3. She may visit any room which is adjacent to two or more dinosaur rooms.

The map of the museum is given as a two-dimensional square grid of rooms, with N rooms on a side, $1 \leq N \leq 100$. To consider two rooms adjacent, they must share a wall; each room has, at most, four adjacent rooms.

Help Bessie determine the minimum and maximum number of rooms she may visit.

Note: When Bessie moves through a room only to go from one place to another, those rooms are not counted as "visited", since she only passes through them briefly.

Input Format

$N + 1$ lines.

The first line contains one integer: N.

The next N lines describe the map of the museum. Each character represents a room. A '.' (dot) means a room that contains neither food nor dinosaurs. A D means a room with a dinosaur. An F is a food-concession room.

Output Format

Two integers, the minimum and the maximum number of rooms Bessie will visit.

Sample Input

```
5
..D..
.D..F
D...D
.F...
....D
```

Sample Output

```
5 11
```

Bessie will surely visit all 5 dinosaur rooms. Bessie can choose to visit either one of the F rooms, and then there are potentially 5 more rooms adjacent to two D rooms.

DISCUSSION

The problem describes a set of rules about which rooms Bessie must or may visit. The problem then gives a specific scenario, which is the map of the museum, for which you need to apply the rules. There is no time component to the problem, nor is there any specific sequence of steps to follow.

Coach B: As you can see, this is a different kind of modeling problem. Any thoughts?

Ryan: It looks like a straightforward problem. We just need to apply the rules.

Coach B: You know how Yogi Berra said "In theory there is no difference between theory and practice–in practice there is"? Well, I believe that applies here. In theory, you are absolutely right: We just need to follow the rules and we can solve the problem. In practice, however, following the rules might prove tricky. Here, can you please draw the sample input for us?

Visualize it: Ryan walks up to the board and draws figure 4.11.

Ryan: There are three rules in the problem. According to the first rule, Bessie must visit every dinosaur room, and there are 5 of those. The second rule states she visits up to one food-concession room, so I picked only one of those. The third rule talks about adjacent rooms to two dinosaur rooms. I marked all these, 5 in total. Therefore, the minimum number of rooms she will visit is the 5 dinosaur rooms, and the maximum number of rooms she may visit includes the 6 additional rooms: $5 + (1 + 5) = 11$.

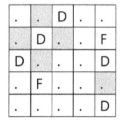

Dinosaur rooms
Bessie **must** visit

Food concession room
Bessie **may** visit

Adjacent rooms
Bessie **may** visit

Figure 4.11 Maps of the museum, highlighting the different rooms Bessie must visit or may visit.

Rachid: Yes, looks good. So, I guess the algorithm would be simply to count all these rooms and add them up. Simple.

Annie: I wonder why they gave two food-concession rooms. Maybe just to check we know to choose only one of them?

Coach B: Very good point. Maybe so. But is there any case where it will be important which one we choose?

Rachid: As long as we choose only one, I think we are fine.

Coach B: I'm not sure. What about a case when the food-concession room is adjacent to two dinosaur rooms?

Coach B steps to the board and draws figure 4.12.

Annie: Oh, I see the problem. In this case, this specific room may be visited either as a food concession room, or as a room adjacent to two dinosaur rooms. If we hadn't noticed that, we might have double-counted it!

Rachid: Wait, but we can choose the other food-concession room in that case, right?

Annie: And what if there is no other food-concession room?

Ryan: Or if all the food-concession rooms are adjacent to two dinosaur rooms? Because then, we couldn't just add a food-concession room to the total sum—it would be double-counting the same room.

Sample special case:

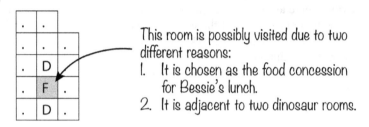

Figure 4.12 Demonstrating a special case of interest: a room that might be counted twice, Once as a food-concession room and once as a room adjacent to two dinosaur rooms.

Rachid ponders.

Rachid: Do they say in what order we should apply the rules?

Everyone looks at the problem more carefully. There's no sign of that.

Rachid: In that case, I don't know how we can decide why she visits the room. How do we continue?

Coach B: Okay, let's remember that the problem just asks about the minimum and maximum number of rooms Bessie will visit, and is not concerned with the reason for visiting any specific room. In this respect, all we need to know is whether there is a food concession room that might not be visited due to any of the other rules, as it can still be chosen as her lunch room. And if all the concession rooms can be visited due to the other rules, we should not double-count any of those.

Rachid, and the team, seem to be confused.

Coach B: Here, maybe if we try to write the algorithm things will become clearer.

 TIP: If you get stuck, try to go ahead and write an algorithm, even if you think it is not going to solve all cases, and see what exactly the faults are. That's assuming it won't take too long to write this algorithm, and that the algorithm isn't too complicated.

ALGORITHM

The algorithm in static modeling problems may often seem to be straightforward, but it does require careful attention to details. Rachid goes to the board and writes listing 4.3a, together with comments and help from his friends.

Rachid: Okay, here it is. I think it still has the double-counting problem.

Coach B: Let me see if I get how you've set it up. You implemented the rules. The first one is that if the room is a dinosaur room, she must visit it. Then, you check if this is a food concession room, and we consider only one of those. Last is checking for a room being an adjacent room. Nice work using that auxiliary two_adjacent_D function for determining this: it keeps the code much cleaner and clearer. We'll worry about writing that function later.

Coach B: So, the question is, is this going to double-count a room that is both an adjacent room and a food-concession room, or not?

The group thinks.

Listing 4.3.a A Visit to the Mooseum (a work-in-progress code)

```
1   char rooms[N][N];
2   int must_visit = 0;
3   int optional_visit = 0;
4   bool visited_food = false;
5   for (int row = 0; row < N; ++row) {
6       for (int col = 0; col < N; ++col) {
7           // <-- The structure of applying the rules will be modified!!
8           if (rooms[row][col] == 'D' )
9               // Dinosaur room
10              must_visit++;
11          if (rooms[row][col] == 'F' && !visited_food) {
12              // Food-concession room
13              optional_visit++;
14              visited_food = true;
15          }
16          if (two_adjacent_D(rooms, row, col))
17              // Adjacent room
18              optional_visit++;
19      }
20  }
```

Rachid: I think it will double-count in some cases. For example, if we have only one food-concession room that's also adjacent to two dinosaur rooms, it will count this room twice.

Coach B: Right! So... any suggestions for a fix?

Mei: How about if we add a check that it is not a food-concession room? We can add something like `rooms[row][col] != 'F'` for the adjacent rooms condition statement.

Coach B: Nice idea. Hold that thought, because there's another case we did not consider yet: What if a D room is adjacent to two other D rooms? Would we double-count it then?

Mei: Okay, so we can also add a `rooms[row][col] != 'D'` to the condition.

Coach B: I think we are starting to get entangled with too many conditionals. That's a tricky situation, like trying to cover a wound by crisscrossing it with Band-Aids. Here's another approach: Apply one rule at a time, and know that only one rule should be applied to each room. Otherwise, we might double-count a room. This way of applying one rule at a time will ensure no double-counting.

Coach B modifies the listing as is shown in listing 4.3.

Listing 4.3 A Visit To The Mooseum

```
1   char rooms[N][N];
2   int must_visit = 0;
3   int optional_visit = 0;
4   bool visited_food = false;
5   for (int row = 0; row < N; ++row) {
6       for (int col = 0; col < N; ++col) {
7           if (rooms[row][col] == 'D') {
8               // Dinosaur room
9               must_visit++;
10          } else {
11              if (rooms[row][col] != 'D'
12                  && two_adjacent_D(rooms, row, col)) {
13                  // Adjacent rooms
14                  optional_visit++;
15              }
16              else {
17                  if ( rooms[row][col] == 'F' && !visited_food ) {
18                      // Food-concession room
19                      visited_food = true;
20                      optional_visit++;
21                  }
22              }
23          }
24      }
25  }
```

Coach B: I'd like you to notice that we're handling adjacent rooms prior to food-concession rooms. Only if the room cannot count as an adjacent room do we use up our food-concession room on it.

Rachid: When you write it like this, we do not really need to check for rooms[row][col] != 'D' because it will not get there at all if this was a dinosaur room.

Coach B: Correct. We can remove it then.

Mei: And good thing we have only three rules. Otherwise, this if/else indentation would turn real weird.

Coach B: True. But we can also write it without all this if/else. Hint: Use the "continue" statement. Anyone want to try it?

Mei: Here, let me try.

Mei writes listing 4.4.

Listing 4.4 A Visit To The Mooseum

```
1   char rooms[N][N];
2   int must_visit = 0;
3   int optional_visit = 0;
4   bool visited_food = false;
5   for (int row = 0; row < N; ++row) {
6       for (int col = 0; col < N; ++col) {
7           if (rooms[row][col] == 'D' ) {
8               // Dinosaur room
9               must_visit++;
10              continue;
11          }
12          if (two_adjacent_D(rooms, row, col)) {
13              // Adjacent room
14              optional_visit++;
15              continue;
16          }
17          if (rooms[row][col] == 'F' && !visited_food) {
18              // Food-concession room
19              visited_food = true;
20              optional_visit++;
21              continue; // We do not really need this continue
22          }
23      }
24  }
```

Coach B: Very nice. I like that you put the last continue in as well: It is not really necessary, but it brings symmetry to the structure.

 TIP: Often there are multiple ways to express the same condition. Try to consider different formats, which might help you find a simpler one, and also help you detect unintended logical omissions.

Ryan: We still have to write the code for that two_adjacent_D function. Can I try and write it down explicitly, though, without the call to that function? I think it will be short enough.

Coach B: Sure, go ahead.

Ryan steps up to the board and adds to the code as in listing 4.5.

Listing 4.5 A Visit To The Mooseum

```
1   char rooms[N][N];
2   int must_visit = 0;
3   int optional_visit = 0;
4   bool visited_food = false;
5   for (int row = 0; row < N; ++row) {
6       for (int col = 0; col < N; ++col) {
7           if (rooms[row][col] == 'D' ) {
8               // Dinosaur room
9               must_visit++;
10              continue;
11          }
12          // Adjacent room
13          int cnt = 0;
14          if (row > 0 && rooms[row - 1][col] == 'D') cnt++;
15          if (row < N - 1 && rooms[row + 1][col] == 'D' ) cnt++;
16          if (col > 0 && rooms[row][col - 1] == 'D' ) cnt++;
17          if (col < N - 1 && rooms[row][col + 1] == 'D' ) cnt++;
18
19          if (cnt >= 2) {
20              optional_visit++;
21              continue;
22          }
23
24          if (rooms[row][col] == 'F' && !visited_food ) {
25              // Food-concession room
```

```
26          visited_food = true;
27          optional_visit++;
28          continue; // We do not really need this continue
29        }
30      }
31  }
```

Coach B: Written nicely, Ryan. Well done. In general, the level of details we get into when writing algorithms may vary. Both approaches, leaving it as a function or writing the details, are perfectly valid. And the important thing is that you wrote it correctly.

Ryan: Thanks. For me, getting into these details really helps.

Coach B: Great job, everyone. I'll put the practice problems on the club's page. There will be more than usual, since this is a popular category in USACO, and is usually not too hard. However, pay careful attention to details. And remember: "Hard work beats talent ..."

The group joins in: "... any time talent doesn't work hard." They all sigh.

EPILOGUE

We solved a static modeling problem by implementing the rules in a given situation. After understanding the rules, the implementation is mostly a matter of technique. It is important to pay attention to the order of applying the rules, if specified, and consider special cases where the rules might seem to conflict. The problems in these competitions go through a thorough vetting, so you should assume that the rules are indeed consistent and cover all possible cases and scenarios.

Also, remember that "simple" does not mean "easy." Careful attention must be given to the details and to possible special cases.

 VOCABULARY Corner: **ADJACENT** is a formal term meaning "nearby, or closely related to," stemming from a Latin word meaning "bordering, or lying near." We often talk about adjacent rooms, as we did in this problem—or adjacent properties, buildings, even towns. Fun fact: an "adjective" is, more or less, a word that borders or lies near whatever word it's describing!

PRACTICE PROBLEMS

Hints and full solutions to the problems can be found on the club's page: http://www.usacoclub.com

1. USACO 2020 January Bronze Problem 1: Word Processor

   http://usaco.org/index.php?page=viewproblem2&cpid=987

   a. You will need to read strings from the input.

   b. Space characters are tricky: You don't see them when they appear at the end of a line. So be careful **not** to print any extra spaces at the end of a line.

2. USACO 2022 January Bronze 1: Herdle

   http://usaco.org/index.php?page=viewproblem2&cpid=1179

   a. You are given rules for when a guess should be marked green and when it should be marked yellow.

   b. Hint: Replace "used" characters in the guess and in the answer (namely characters that were already accounted for in green or yellow) with special characters, say * and +, respectively.

3. USACO 2014 December Bronze 2: Crosswords

   http://usaco.org/index.php?page=viewproblem2&cpid=488

   a. You are given rules for when a square should be numbered for a clue.

ON THE CLUB'S PAGE:

Note from Coach B: Problems involving modeling

The next few problems involve more than just modeling a process. Often it means you need to assume a value, and then model the resulting process. These are usually harder problems. These can frequently also fall under the search category, which we will cover in chapter 5.

4. USACO 2017 January Bronze 2: Hoof, Paper, Scissors

   http://usaco.org/index.php?page=viewproblem2&cpid=688

   a. You need to assume what values Hoof, Paper, and Scissors correspond to, and then model a series of games.

   b. There are 6 ways in which Hoof, Paper, and Scissors can be mapped into the numbers 1, 2 and 3. You can try all of these, model the game for each case, and find the answer.

   c. Hint: Do you really need to check all 6 cases? Consider the following two mappings: the mapping where Hoof is 1, Paper is 2, and Scissors are 3; and the mapping where Paper is 1, Scissors are 2, and Hoof is 3. Would these two different mappings give different results when modeled through the program?

5. USACO 2022 February Bronze 3: Blocks

   http://usaco.org/index.php?page=viewproblem2&cpid=1205

   a. This is not an easy problem.

   b. Loop over all possible orderings of the cubes, and for each ordering, model the game and determine if you can produce the word.

6. USACO 2022 January Bronze 2: Non-Transitive Dice

   http://usaco.org/index.php?page=viewproblem2&cpid=1180

   a. This is a hard problem.

   b. You can create all possible four-sided cubes and see if one of these will create a non-transitive set.

   c. The code will be clearer if you create a function: `int firstWins(int A[], int B[]);` This function takes as input two dice, and returns 1 if the first die wins, 0 if it's a draw, and -1 if the second die wins.

4.3. Modeling a Periodic Process

A process is said to have a periodic behavior if the process state repeats every certain number of steps. Maybe the most intuitive examples are processes in which we step through time. If every T time-units the state repeats itself, the process is said to have a period of T. We can often use this kind of periodicity to accelerate modeling. For example, if a process has a period of 10 minutes, and we need to find the state after 94 minutes, we can simply find the state at time 4. Since the system has a period of 10, the same state as at time 4 will repeat at time 14, time 24, time 34, and so on until time 94.

However, even with no explicit time component in the problem, a process can be periodic. For example, consider the shuffling problem we solved in section 4.1.2, "Where is The King?" In that problem, you might be given a shuffling arrangement that has a period, which means the cups go back to their original locations after a certain number of shuffles. This would lead to a similar savings pattern: If the pattern repeats every 10 shuffles, we do not need to model more than 10 cases.

On the board, Coach B draws a big circle.

Coach B: Welcome and happy Tuesday! Today we will solve a modeling problem that has a circle in it. If we move around a circle, we eventually return to the starting point. This will be our introduction to solving modeling problems that contain periodicity. Periodicity can also be used to accelerate modeling, but we'll save that for problems on the club's page once we're done here.

Problem 4.4: The Ferris Wheel

Bessie loves amusement parks, and her favorite ride is the Ferris wheel. Luckily, Coney Island's boardwalk and its giant Ferris wheel are a Brooklyn icon, and Bessie is determined to go and visit the park.

The Ferris wheel has N tubs, $N \geq 1$, each able to carry up to 4 cows. Cows can enter or exit only at the lowest point. Cows stay in their tub as long as no other cow is waiting to board. If there is a cow waiting to enter when a tub arrives at the bottom point, all the cows in that tub need to exit.

The wheel starts empty of cows. On each round, the wheel stops turning, and there is a tub at the bottom. At each such moment, the operator logs in his notebook the number of new cows arriving to enter, p_i where $0 \leq p_i \leq 100$. After K rounds of this process, $K \geq 0$, the manager comes by and wants to know how many cows are on the Ferris wheel at this moment. Please help the operator.

Determine how many cows are on the Ferris wheel after K rounds.

Input Format

Two lines.

The first line contains two integers: N, K.

The second line contains K integers: $p_1, p_2, \ldots, p_K$.

Output Format

One number, the number of cows on the Ferris wheel after K rounds.

Sample Input

3 8

2 7 0 5 5 2 5 1

Sample Output

10

The Ferris wheel started with three empty tubs.

- First, 2 new cows arrived, and these 2 cows entered the first tub, call it tub A.
- Then, 7 new cows arrived, and 4 cows entered the next tub, tub B, while 3 were still waiting.
- Then, 0 new cows arrived, and the 3 cows in waiting entered tub C.
- Now we're back at tub A. 5 new cows arrived, which prompted the 2 cows to exit from tub A , and 4 climbed in, with 1 more still waiting.
- Then 5 cows arrived, causing 4 cows to exit from tub B. 4 cows entered, and 2 are still waiting.

The process continues as such for a total of 8 rounds, and the final answer is 10.

DISCUSSION

This problem has a periodic component. The tubs of the Ferris wheel come back down every N rounds. However, the number of cows arriving, the number of cows waiting, and so forth, are not necessarily periodic.

Visualize it: Rachid goes first to the white board, and in a few seconds, everyone joins. Rachid starts by drawing a circle with 3 tubs as seen in figure 4.13. He then writes 0 in each of the tubs, and proceeds to draw the wheel after the two cows have entered.

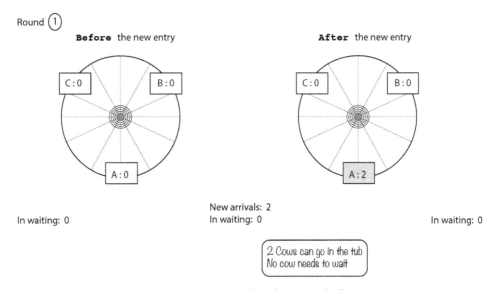

New arrivals: 2

In waiting: 0

2 Cows can go in the tub
No cow needs to wait

Figure 4.13 First round on the Ferris wheel.

TIP: The tubs are identified as A, B, and C, rather than as one, two and three. This is exactly as we did for the cup's name and location in the hidden King problem. It is much less confusing to say "tub A has 2 cows" than to say "tub 1 has 2 cows." Every little thing that avoids confusion in periodic problems is helpful.

Annie suggests that a table would be helpful to keep track of things. She draws one underneath.

Table 4.1 Using a table to describe the process.

	Before				After				
Round	A	B	C	Waiting	Arriving	A	B	C	Waiting
1	0	0	0	0	2	2	0	0	0

Coach B: It's nice how both of you, Rachid and Annie, emphasized the newly populated tub. It helps identify which is the most recently loaded tub, which is the one at the bottom. These little things help a lot in periodic problems.

Rachid continues, and draws the second round in figure 4.14, when 7 new cows arrive. Four of the cows will enter tub B, and 3 will have to wait. Annie adds one more row to the table.

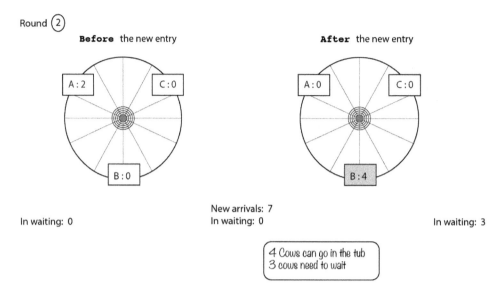

Figure 4.14 Second round on the Ferris wheel, and the appropriate table form in table 4.2.

Table 4.2 Table form for 2 first rounds.

	Before				After				
Round	A	B	C	Waiting	Arriving	A	B	C	Waiting
1	0	0	0	0	2	2	0	0	0
2	2	0	0	0	7	2	4	0	3

Rachid sees that writing the table is much easier, so he joins in. Together, everyone completes the table as in table 4.3.

Table 4.3 Table form for all 8 rounds.

	Before				After				
Round	A	B	C	Waiting	Arriving	A	B	C	Waiting
1	0	0	0	0	2	2	0	0	0
2	2	0	0	0	7	2	4	0	3
3	2	4	0	3	0	2	4	3	0
4	2	4	3	0	5	4	4	3	1
5	4	4	3	1	5	4	4	3	2
6	4	4	3	2	2	4	4	4	0
7	4	4	4	0	5	4	4	4	1
8	4	4	4	1	1	4	2	4	0

Mei: And the number of cows after the eighth round is $4 + 2 + 4 = 10$, which is indeed the answer for the sample input.

Coach B: Very nice. It was really impressive to see how, once you got the hang of filling in the table, it went very fast.

The team looks at the table and smiles in satisfaction.

Coach B: Are there any special cases to consider?

Ryan: What if there is only 1 tub? Then it's the same tub all the time. Only... I'm not sure it actually would make any difference.

Coach B: Good point. Indeed, Ryan, you are right on both counts: having only one tub is a special case, and it wouldn't make any difference for our algorithm. So, if there are no objections, do we have a volunteer to write the algorithm?

ALGORITHM

Mei goes to the board and describes her code.

Mei: This is a modeling problem, and I am going step by step and implementing the process. Each step is one round of the Ferris wheel. I loop on all K rounds. For each round I see how many cows want to climb in. This is equal to the sum of those waiting and the new arrivals. If there is at least one cow waiting to enter, we put up to 4 cows in the tub, and update the number of cows waiting. And then we are off to the next round. After all the rounds are done, we sum up all the cows in the tubs.

Listing 4.6.a The Ferris Wheel (a work-in-progress code)

```
1   int tub[N];
2   int waiting = 0;
3   for (int k = 0; k < K; ++k) {
4       int tub_at_bottom = k;   // <-- This line will be modified!!
5       int total = waiting + new_arrivals[k];
6       if (total > 0) {
7           // Not more than 4 cows can go in a tub.
8           tub[tub_at_bottom] = min(total, 4);
9           waiting = max(total - 4, 0);
10      }
11  }
12
13  int ans = 0;
14  for (int i = 0; i < N; ++i) {
15      ans += tub[i];
16  }
```

Ryan: I really like the way you used the min() and max() functions for managing how many entered, and how many are left waiting. I myself used two if statements to achieve the same. Your code is much cleaner that way.

Mei: Thanks. I gotta admit that while I'm coding, to make sure it works, I substitute in a few values. For example, it works right for total = $0, 3$, or 5, so I figured it's good.

> *TIP*: When writing a concise code which you are not too confident about, it is a good idea to substitute in some simple values and check that it works as expected.

Ryan: I think there's a problem with the line int tub_at_bottom = k; I don't see how it accounts for the tubs repeating. Well, you know, if K is 10 and N is 3, we will end up with tub_at_bottom getting values above 3. We need to cycle back to the first tub after N rounds.

This is exactly where the periodicity of the problem comes to light. Ryan goes to the board, erases the part tub_at_bottom = k, and ponders. He can use "if" statements, but there must be a better way to do it.

Coach B: Can you use a modulus operator there?

Ryan looks again, and corrects the code as follows:

Listing 4.6 The Ferris Wheel

```
1   int tub[N];
2   int waiting = 0;
3   for (int k = 0; k < K; ++k) {
4       int tub_at_bottom = k % N;   // <-- New modified line
5       int total = waiting + new_arrivals[k];
6       if (total > 0) {
7           tub[tub_at_bottom] = min(total, 4);
8           waiting = max(total - 4, 0);
9       }
10  }
11
12  int ans = 0;
13  for (int i = 0; i < N; ++i) {
14      ans += tub[i];
15  }
```

Mei: Okay, let me see if it works using your method. It looks right, but I want to check. Let's say $N = 3$ as in our sample input. When $k = 0, 1, 2$ the modulus operator will result in $0, 1, 2$, which works fine. It simply uses tubs 0, 1, and 2. When $k = 3$, we get to the first interesting case, and then it sets the tub to 0 again, which is the right thing to do! It cycles back to the first tub. And $k = 4$ will cycle to tub 1. Yes, I can believe that!

 TIP: To avoid making an "off-by-one" error, it is a good practice to check modulus expressions at interesting points: check x % N for values like x = 0, 1, and x = (N - 1), N, and (N + 1). If x might be negative, be careful of how the modulus operator works in your programming language. One way to mitigate the issue of negative numbers is to add N, or multiples of N, to x, and *then* use modulus. That way, x will be positive, and modulus will yield a predictable result.

Coach B: Great job, everyone! Seems like we figured this one out. And it seems like there are no questions. So now you just need to code it and submit. I'll stick around for a little more if you have any questions. I will post new problems on our club's page. Feel free to share comments and thoughts on the club's page. Next week, we'll finish the unit on modeling problems. That's when we'll look at methods to accelerate solutions. Alright, see you then!

EPILOGUE

In this section, we had a problem that involved periodic behavior: The tubs on the Ferris wheel rotated, and after N tubs, we were back to the same one. This required careful programming and the use of a modulus operator.

In the practice problems, you may find many similar cases—and also cases where the periodicity happens in the state of the process itself, which can be used to shorten the modeling process altogether.

 VOCABULARY Corner: **PERIOD AND FREQUENCY** A phenomenon that repeats in a regular manner is called a cyclic, or periodic, phenomenon. For example, when a satellite orbits the earth every four hours, that's a periodic phenomenon. All periodic phenomena have two qualities of interest: a period and a frequency. The period is defined as the time between two exact repetitions; in the case of our satellite, the period is 4 hours. And the frequency is defined as the portion of a cycle which is completed in one time unit. In our case, in one hour the satellite completes $\frac{1}{4}$ of its cycle, so its frequency is $\frac{1}{4}$ per hour. Once you understand that the period is the inverse of the frequency, and vice versa, you can more easily solve problems involving cyclic processes.

PRACTICE PROBLEMS

Hints and full solutions to the problems can be found on the club's page: http://www.usacoclub.com

1. USACO 2018 December Bronze Problem 1: Mixing Milk

   http://usaco.org/index.php?page=viewproblem2&cpid=855

   a. Cycle through the buckets to mix.

   b. Hint: The code should have something similar to the snippet below:

```
1    for (int i = 0; i < 100; ++i) {
2        int from = i % 3;
3        int to = (i + 1) % 3;
4        // Your code here, pouring the right amount
5    }
```

2. USACO 2016 February Bronze Problem 1: Milk Pails

   http://usaco.org/index.php?page=viewproblem2&cpid=615

   a. Not a periodic process per-se, but does include a good use of modulus operator.

4.4. Simulation Acceleration

In this last section of the unit on modeling problems, we will discuss one common way to accelerate the modeling process. We already learned in section 4.3 that in periodic modeling problems, if the state is periodic, we may reduce the number of steps we need. In non-periodic cases, we can accelerate the modeling time by focusing only on interesting events. Although this technique is more commonly used in the advanced levels of USACO, it is also beneficial at the Bronze level.

Coach B: Welcome to our last session on modeling problems! We are about to finish this unit. Who can list some types of modeling problems we've covered so far?

Mei: We did dynamic processes; these were the ones that change as we move along. We did the problem with walking around the lake, which has time steps, and then the one with the cup shuffling.

Ryan: And then we did the static modeling problems. These are the ones where we just need to apply rules. We did the one with the dinosaur rooms, where we should have noticed not to double-count. And for practice my favorite was the crossword question.

Annie: We also had the one with Coney Island, the Ferris wheel. This was the part on periodic processes where things repeat.

Coach B: Very good! You remembered all of them! As you said, when we model dynamic processes, we step through the modeling. If there are many steps to take, this process can be slow. Now, although at the Bronze level there is less emphasis on the time complexity of the solution, in some of the modeling problems you may need to use acceleration methods to get the algorithm to work within the time limit for all cases—and to get full credit. Acceleration is usually done by combining, or skipping, steps in the modeling while still preserving the accuracy of the simulation. Our next example demonstrates this.

Problem 4.5: Walking To The Opera House

Bessie and her friends love opera, and they want to visit the famous Mootropolitan Opera House in Manhattan.

The streets in Manhattan can be modeled as a two-dimensional grid. Bessie is starting her walk from the point $(a, 0)$, and she is heading straight up parallel to the y-axis to the opera house located at the point (a, b). Bessie is moving at a fixed speed of 1 city block per minute. Her N friends, $1 \leq N \leq 10^5$, are walking from various points across town denoted as (x_i, y_i). All cows walk at the same speed as Bessie, and all walk parallel to the x-axis directly toward Bessie's route, trying to join her along the way. If a cow reaches the route no later than Bessie, then they will walk together the rest of the way. (In this case, the cow will wait as needed for Bessie so they can walk together.) If a cow reaches the opera house before Bessie, she stops and waits there.

Determine how many cows are walking with Bessie when she reaches the Mootropolitan.

Input Format

$N + 1$ lines.

The first line contains three integers N, a, b.

Each of the next N lines contains two integers, the coordinates of one of the friends, x_i, y_i.

All input integers satisfy $0 \leq a, b, x_i, y_i \leq 10^9$.

Output Format

One number, the number of cows walking with Bessie at the end of her route.

Sample Input

```
3 8 15
1 4
14 6
4 8
```

Sample Output

```
2
```

Bessie walks straight up from $(8, 0)$ to $(8, 15)$. After 6 minutes, she will meet the cow that left from $(14, 6)$, and after 8 minutes, she will be also joined by the cow originating from $(4, 8)$. Bessie and the two other cows will then walk together, reaching the opera house at the same time.

DISCUSSION

The problem describes Bessie and her friends moving at a constant speed, albeit starting from different locations. Moving at the same speed means that during each time unit they all progress the same distance. Thus, this problem is very similar to the problem "Walk Around The Lake" from section 4.1, where the solution entailed stepping through the process with fixed time steps.

Coach B: Well, here we have another modeling problem with time steps! Any volunteers to draw the problem?

Visualize it: Annie walks up to the board and draws figure 4.15, indicating the starting positions of all cows, and the goal location (the Mootropolitan).

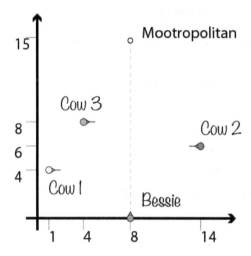

Figure 4.15 The starting positions of all cows.

Rachid: How did you know where Bessie is? The problem just gives all the other cows' coordinates, and the opera house coordinates. I don't see anywhere that Bessie's coordinates are given.

Annie: The problem states that the opera house is at location (a, b), and that Bessie starts from $(a, 0)$. They emphasize that Bessie needs to walk "straight up" to the opera house. So, Bessie has the same x-coordinate as the opera house, which is a.

Rachid: Oh, right! I get it now, thanks. So here, let me try and draw the first few steps in the sample input.

Rachid goes to the board, thinks for a second, and draws figure 4.16.

Rachid: I think there's no real need to draw anything before 4 minutes. They all just move along their lines. Four minutes is the first interesting time, since this is when things start happening. At time 4 minutes, we see that Cow-1 will never catch up to Bessie, and that Cow-3 already reached the route and will need to wait for Bessie.

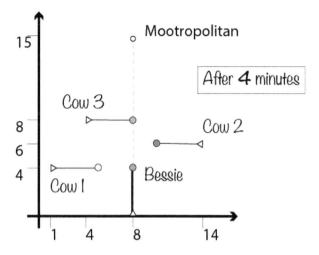

Figure 4.16 Cows' locations after 4 minutes of walking. Cow 3 already reached the route, and it is clear that Cow 1 will reach it after Bessie has already passed.

Ryan: Mei, can we draw the next important steps together?

Mei and Ryan head to the board and draw figures 4.17, 4.18 , and 4.19.

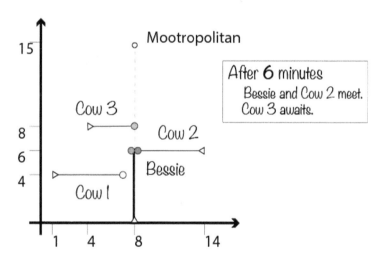

Figure 4.17 Cows' locations after 6 minutes. Bessie and Cow 2 meet. Cow 3 still awaits.

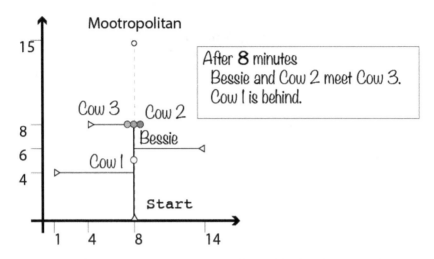

Figure 4.18 After 8 minutes, Bessie is reunited with two of her friends: Cow 2 and Cow 3.

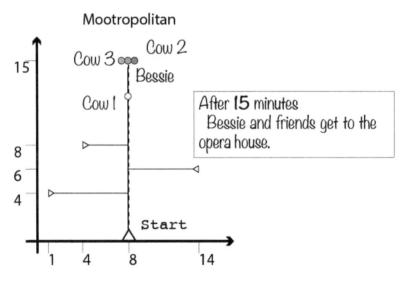

Figure 4.19 Bessie and two of her friends reach the end.

Ryan: Wait, so there are 3 cows getting together by the end. Why is the answer 2?

Mei: The question asks for the number of cows walking *with* Bessie. So that doesn't include Bessie herself.

Coach B: Very nice. Seems like you got the problem right away. Any thoughts about how to solve it?

Rachid: This looks very similar to the "Walk Around The Lake" problem we did a few meetings ago. I guess we can use time steps here as well. We can start from $t = 0$, and calculate for every subsequent minute where each cow is. If it gets to the route before or at the same time as Bessie, then this cow will join Bessie. If the cow reaches the route after Bessie, then she missed her and will never catch up.

TIP: Making connections and finding similarities to previous problems is a very helpful habit.

Coach B: Any objections?

Everyone nods in approval.

Coach B: I concur. This seems like it would work. But we do have two things to briefly check: special cases and complexity. Special cases first: Any thoughts?

Rachid: What if one cow comes from above? I mean if it starts above the end point.

Annie: We can just ignore any cow that has a y coordinate above, or equal to, the end point. These cows will reach the opera house and meet with Bessie there. They will never walk any segment together.

Rachid: Wait, and what about a cow that starts below Bessie? Can it ever catch up to Bessie?

Annie: Interesting. No, I don't think it ever can. But wait, there's no cow that can be below Bessie. Bessie starts from $y = 0$, and the problem clearly states that all cows' coordinates are positive.

Rachid: Yes, you're right. Okay, no need to worry about these issues.

With no other special cases suggested by the team, Coach B moves to the next item.

Coach B: Okay. Now, how about complexity: How many time steps do we need to perform?

Ryan: We need to keep going until Bessie reaches the end. She walks from the x-axis point $(a, 0)$ to the point (a, b), which means we need to do b steps. That's all.

Coach B: And, how large is b? And what do we need to do in each step?

Ryan: The problem says b can be up to 10^9. In each step we need to move Bessie and N cows, and N can be up to 10^5. Wow, that's a lot of friends! So the time complexity is of order $10^9 \times 10^5 = 10^{14}$. That's getting to be a large number!

TIP: It's a red flag if you find yourself needing to simulate over 10^8 steps. You can sometimes go beyond 10^8 if only very simple operations are required in each step. But, as is the case here, getting to 10^{14} is far away from this number, so this is a sign to try and look for a simpler solution.

Coach B: A large number, indeed. Any thoughts on how we can take some shortcuts?

The group is quiet for a moment. Then Mei points to the second figure on the whiteboard, drawn by Rachid (figure 4.16).

Mei: When Rachid drew this one, he didn't need to consider every minute, right? He just went straight forward to a time when a cow reaches the route, or when Bessie reaches a cow location. That's why we have only 4 pictures on the board and not 15.

Ryan: And after the last cow reached the route, we actually didn't need to step all the way to the end. Nothing changes after Bessie reaches the 3rd cow. We could have stopped there.

Coach B: Very good! This means that rather than step through every minute, we can just consider specific times of interest, or interesting events. This is exactly the point of this exercise. The interesting events here are only when any of Bessie's friends reaches the route. And there are at most 10^5 cows! So we have only 10^5 possible interesting events. That sounds much better than the 10^{14} we had considered before.

TIP: Choosing only interesting events usually requires us to have a formula for finding the state at the appropriate time. In our case, we could readily calculate the location of any cow at a given time. Thus, if we know what the times of interest are, we can calculate the state of all cows at that time.

Coach B: Well, I think we covered it all. Any volunteers to put the algorithm on the board? This will require finding times of interest, and then calculating locations there.

ALGORITHM

Ryan heads to the whiteboard and writes the code as in listing 4.7.

Ryan: I'll loop over all the cows. For each cow, I'll calculate when it reaches the route, and when Bessie is going to reach the same point on the route. If the cow gets there before or with Bessie, then they'll walk together.

Listing 4.7 **Walking To The Opera House**

```
1   int ans = 0;
2   for ( int cow = 0; cow < N; ++cow ) {
3       // Don't consider cows above the end goal.
4       if ( y[cow] > y_end) continue;
5       // Time for a cow to get to route.
6       int t_cow = abs( x[cow] - x_end );
7       // Time for Bessie to get to the point of cow on route.
8       int t_bessie = y[cow];
9       if ( t_cow <= t_bessie ) ans++;
10  }
```

Rachid: Let's see if I can follow your code. Every cow walks horizontally toward the route, so she walks from x[cow] to x_end, which is where the route is. Why did you put an absolute value function there? Why not simply the difference?

Ryan: We need to find the distance between x_end and x[cow]. We don't actually care which one of these is larger, and we certainly don't want to get a negative number. Absolute value gives the distance between two points. Distance is always positive.

Coach B: Very nice. Safe coding can save a lot of headaches later on. We will talk much more about it in the Geometry unit. But this is great thinking on your behalf, Ryan.

Rachid: Okay. So the cow reaches the route at the point (x_end, y[cow]). For Bessie to get so high, it would take y[cow] minutes, since Bessie is going up from y = 0. So then you compare them, and if the cow arrived first, she'll be walking with Bessie. Nice and simple!

Impressed, Annie and Mei give Ryan a round of applause, who dramatically takes a bow.

Ryan: Thank you, thank you.

Coach B: Nice work, Ryan! Okay, that was a great workout. You immediately recognized it as a modeling problem, and were able to follow the sample input given. We then recognized that the complexity of our solution might be an issue, and we found a way to make the modeling much faster. I will leave a few practice problems on the clubs' page. Beware that there are no easy problems this time. But, you can always ask a question on the club's page, and use the hints there. See you next week!

EPILOGUE

Modeling problems are often straightforward to code. You just need to understand the model, then follow it. Sometimes, though, this kind of direct implementation of a model might not meet the time constraints for the problem. In these cases, we need to find a way to accelerate the modeling. In the example we solved, we pulled this off by looking only at important events. As you will see in the practice problems, this is a commonly used method.

TIP: For modeling problems, it is worth implementing a slow solution even if it fails in some of the cases. You will get partial credit for the cases solved, and moreover, you'll see if your understanding of the problem is correct. Then, you can look for faster solutions.

VOCABULARY Corner: **Parallel Processing** is one way of accelerating computations. It means that multiple processors are working on the same task at the same time. If a task would take one processor 10 seconds to complete, then maybe if we have 10 computers working on it in parallel, we can complete the task in only 1 second. With this in mind, you can easily see how the word "parallel" comes from a Greek phrase meaning "beside one another;" picture all those processors working together, side by side. Parallel processing is deployed widely today in many systems, from the graphics card in your computer to huge computer-farms in the cloud. Parallel processing does have its limitations, as some algorithms cannot be converted into this mode of operation. But there's a very popular and active field of research that utilizes parallel processing to perform and accelerate algorithms.

PRACTICE PROBLEMS

Hints and full solutions to the problems can be found on the club's page: http://www.usacoclub.com

Coach's note: There are no easy practice problems here. By nature, problems that require accelerations demand not only that you solve the problem correctly, but that you do it efficiently as well. It bears repeating: If you don't see an easy acceleration, go ahead and solve it without an acceleration, which will help you move toward a full solution.

1. USACO 2015 January Bronze Problem 3: It's All About The Base

   http://usaco.org/index.php?page=viewproblem2&cpid=509

   a. The problem itself hints that acceleration will be required: "Note that due to the potential size of X and Y, a program that searches exhaustively over every possible value of X and Y will not run within the time limit, so it would not receive full credit."

   b. As we noted before, even if you do not see a way to accelerate, go ahead and solve it by searching over all possible options. You will get partial credit, and verify you understand the problem.

   c. Hint: There are different ways to avoid having a nested loop that tries all the possible combinations of bases. Here are two possible ways:

   - Observe that any three-digit number, like 832, will be larger, as the base it is in is larger. Thus, 832 base 1001 would be larger than 832 base 1000. This can lead us to starting with both bases assumed as 10 (the minimum value), then evaluating the number, and incrementing the base of the smaller between the two. Keep on doing this until the evaluated numbers are equal.
   - Following the given example in the problem, 419 base 10 is smaller than 792 base 10, so increment it to evaluate 419 base 11. And so on.
   - Assume a base Y, evaluate the number accordingly, and find (numerically) the possible base X. Remember that X has to be a positive integer in the specified range.
   - Following the given example: 419 base $Y = 10$ is equal to 419. 792 base X is equal to $7X^2 + 9x + 2$. Solve the equation $7X^2 + 9x + 2 = 419$ for X, and if this is an integer satisfying the requirements, this is your solution. If not, increment Y.

2. USACO 2020 January Bronze Problem 3: Race

   http://usaco.org/index.php?page=viewproblem2&cpid=989

   a. The problem itself hints that acceleration will be required:

   - Test cases 2-4 satisfy $N = X = 1$.
   - Test cases 5-10 satisfy no additional constraints.

   b. The above should give you a hint that, for the smaller cases, you can step through time. For larger cases, you will need to find an accelerated method.

c. As I said so many times before, even if you do not see a way to accelerate, go ahead and solve it by searching over all possible options. You will get partial credit, and verify you understand the problem.

d. To see how to accelerate, try and draw a graph of the problem with the vertical axis as speed, and the horizontal axis as distance. Can you use this graph to accelerate the modeling? Figures 4.20, 4.21 and 4.22 show the graphs for three cases given in the problem sample input.

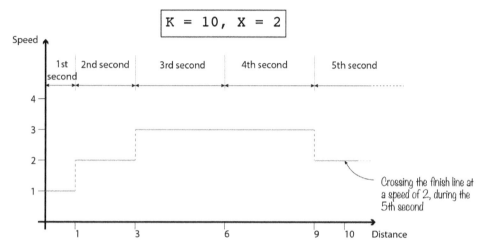

Figure 4.20 Speed versus distance for a sample case of Race. Bessie must slow down to meet the speed requirement at the end.

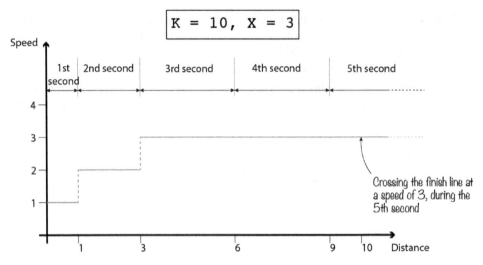

Figure 4.21 Speed versus distance for a sample case of Race. Bessie cannot keep accelerating after three seconds, as she will pass the finish line with too high of a speed.

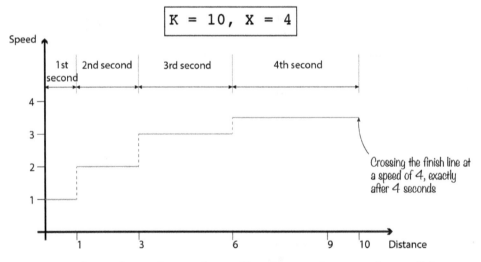

Figure 4.22 Speed versus distance for a sample case of Race. Bessie can keep on accelerating all the way to the finish line.

3. USACO 2020 December Bronze Problem 3: Stuck In A Rut

   http://usaco.org/index.php?page=viewproblem2&cpid=1061

   a. The problem is very similar to the "Walking To The Opera House" problem we did earlier. It can be modeled by stepping through time.

   b. The problem itself hints that acceleration might be required:

- In test cases 2-5, all coordinates are at most 100.
- In test cases 6-10, there are no additional constraints.

c. The above should give you a hint that, for the smaller cases, you can step through time. For larger cases, you will need to find an accelerated method.

d. Hint: Here is a way to solve that follows a similar methodology to what we did earlier, albeit things are more complicated now that we've associated a specific direction with each point.

- Calculate the collision time between any two ruts.
- While there is still a possible collision time that was not processed: Find the minimum collision time that was not yet processed; Process the two ruts at this collision time: which of them proceeds, and which of them stops; Mark this collision time as processed.

e. This is a hard problem. Remember: it's okay to look at a solution after devoting a reasonable amount of time to the problem. Look at the solution, try to understand it, and then implement it in your own code.

Thus, the main goal of the problem is to assess one's ability to understand the process, to pay attention to the fine details of implementation, and to code it correctly.

4.5. Summary

- **Modeling problems** are focused on careful attention to detail and technical mastery of the programming language.
- **Dynamic process** problems require stepping through the process, either as time steps or process steps. The solution is often either the final state of the process, or a parameter of the process.
- To solve a dynamic process problem, you:

  - Identify the state of the problem, and specifically the collection of variables that define the state.
  - Determine how the state changes in every step of the process.
  - Step through the process to the final state. A "step" can be either a time step or a process step.
  - If the required solution is the final state, you found it.
  - If the required solution is a parameter that leads to a specific final state: determine if the final state is the one required. If not, change the parameter, and repeat the modeling.

- **Static process** problems define rules and a scenario, and the answer requires applying the rules to possible scenarios.
- To solve a static process problem, you:

- Identify the rules and the scenario they are applied to.
- Verify the precedence and consider possible overlap of the rules.
- Consider special cases and understand how the rules work to resolve these.
- Code the rules in a clear and simple manner.
- If you find your algorithm does not work for a specific case, examine where you went wrong in applying the rules. Try to avoid the natural tendency to add a specific conditional statement to deal with a specific case. This is not the right approach. The rules should work with no additional special-case conditions.

- **Periodic process** problems are characterized by either cyclic process steps, or some other periodicity in the application of the rules. You can simplify and shorten the solution by taking advantage of the periodicity.
- When solving a periodic process problem, you:

    - Identify the periodic part of the problem.
    - Consider using a modulus operator to handle periodicity. Check your code to operate correctly around the cycle. That is, if you use a modulus operator, be sure to plug in values.
    - Examine if you can use the periodicity to accelerate the process by dropping full cycles.

- **Accelerating** a modeling process might be required at the Bronze level. Usually, the problem statement gives a direct hint to that, letting you know that the first few test cases can be solved without acceleration, but in order to get full credit, you would need to accelerate.
- When solving a modeling problem that might require acceleration, you:

    - Remember that a partial solution, namely without acceleration, does award you partial credit. It can also help you understand the problem better.
    - Identify opportunities to skip parts of the modeling steps and advance directly to important events.

Chapter 5. Searching and Optimization

This chapter covers

- Recognizing search problems in the context of USACO.
- Solving search problems using an exhaustive search algorithm.
- Choosing a domain for performing the search.
- Enumerating the chosen domain.
- Accelerating an exhaustive search algorithm.
- Solving search problems using a greedy algorithm.

In search problems, as the name implies, we are searching for something. Search problems are a wide and intensive field of research and algorithms development in computer science. You are probably familiar with many of the applications of search algorithms: searching for a word in a document you are typing; searching for phrases on the web; searching for the shortest path to get from point A to point B. But searching problems have even broader applications, many of which involve searching in covert ways. For example, your autocorrect identifies the word closest to the one you tried to spell. Behind the scenes, it searches over all the possible words in its dictionary, refers to its knowledge of which words are used more frequently, and suggests a new word.

Often, search problems are called optimization problems. Optimization problems strive to achieve the best result possible for a certain condition. For example, consider the problem of designing a traffic intersection to allow for the maximum flow of cars. We can try giving certain green light time periods to the different directions (not at the same time!), then model how many cars will flow in each direction. Then, we can change those assigned green light times, and model the newly resulting flow of cars. In this problem, we are searching: trying to find the best allocation of green light times, the one that would yield the maximum flow of cars. In optimization problems like this, we often find the solution by using search algorithms.

Search problems are very common in all levels of USACO. However, worry not: this chapter covers only the search algorithms needed at the Bronze level. You will learn more as you advance through the USACO levels.

The chapter map is described in figure 5.1. The most common searching algorithm at the Bronze level is the exhaustive search, also known as a complete search or brute-force search, described in section 5.1. This type of algorithm entails searching over all possible options. For example, the spellchecker might search over all possible words in the dictionary and decide which is the closest to your misspelled word. Doing an exhaustive search involves two main decisions. First, what "space" are we searching over? For example, are we searching over all the words in a particular British-spelling or American-spelling dictionary? This "space" to be searched is called the domain of the search and is discussed in section 5.2. Second, how do we know we searched all options? Or in other words, how do we order the elements in the domain? In the case of the autocorrect function, we can go over all the words in alphabetical order. In the case of the shortest path between two points on the map, where we need to consider many roads, the answer is not that clear. We need some kind of process for setting an order to search over all the elements. This kind of process is called enumeration and is discussed in section 5.3.

Section 5.4 describes ways to accelerate the search algorithm. This concern is worth exploring for the Bronze level, although it plays a more central role in the advanced levels of USACO. We close in section 5.5 with a discussion of a different search algorithm, the greedy algorithm. Unlike an exhaustive search, a greedy algorithm may reach a solution without examining all options. This may result in a significant reduction in execution time of the algorithm—but might fail to find the best solution. We will examine cases where a greedy algorithm works, as well as describe cases where it fails.

Throughout the chapter, we will encounter many search and optimization problems. One of the main goals of this chapter is to teach you to recognize a problem as a search problem, a skill that makes it much easier to devise an algorithm for a solution. Pay special attention as we highlight the key terms and concepts that indicate we're dealing with a search problem.

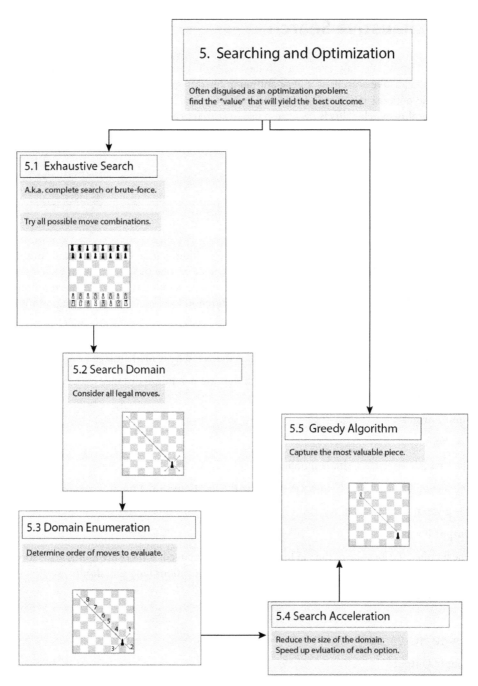

Figure 5.1 Searching and Optimization chapter map. We cover two types of search algorithms: Exhaustive search and Greedy algorithms.

5.1. Exhaustive Search

Coach B: Happy Tuesday, everyone. Today we will learn about exhaustive search algorithms. "Exhaustive search" is a very apt name for this method: it means we search over all possible options; it also alludes to the fact we, or at least the computer, is exhausted after doing this search. This is because it has to search over many, many options. Our first problem finds Bessie and her friends in Hawaii! Go ahead and read the problem, and we'll discuss it.

Problem 5.1: Tiki Torches

Bessie loves Waikiki Beach at night, with tiki torches illuminating the golden sand. But it's expensive to keep these torches lit, and the folks at the Office of Conservation have asked Bessie to help. Her job is to suggest one torch that can be removed that will cause minimum disruption. This torch cannot be the first or last torch in the line, as those are important to orient the guests.

Bessie noted in her notebook that there are N tiki torches, $2 < N < 10^5$, located along the beach in a straight line. A tiki torch location is indicated by a single integer, x_i.

Determine which torch can be removed such that the maximum distance between any two adjacent remaining torches is minimal.

Input Format

Two lines.

The first line contains a single number, N.

The second line contains N integers denoting the locations of the torches, $x_1, x_2, \ldots, x_N$.

It is given that $x_1 < x_2 < x_3 < \ldots < x_N$.

Output Format

One number, the location of the tiki torch that can be removed. If there are multiple locations that would yield the same result, output any of these locations (any will do).

Sample Input

6

1 8 10 16 20 23

Sample Output

20

If we remove the torch at location 20, the maximum distance between two adjacent torches is 7, which is the smallest possible.

DISCUSSION

The team reads the problem, then looks around at each other in puzzlement.

Coach B: I see there are a few confused looks around. So let's start from the very beginning. The problem asks us which tiki torch we should remove, right? And there are only so many tiki torches. This tells us this might be a search problem: we will need to search among all tiki torches and find the best one to remove.

Ryan: Thanks, Coach B. I got this part, but I'm still confused about what they actually are asking for. They ask for a maximum distance, but then they want it minimal. Am I reading it wrong?

Coach B: You read it right, Ryan. This is a very common phrasing in optimization problems. In optimization problems, we're searching for the best configuration. In our case, we are looking for the best tiki torch to remove. So let's try and see if we can figure this out by sketching out the problem. Since the problem doesn't totally make sense to us, we start with the parts that do make sense. I know it's hard, but let's try and get comfortable with the uncomfortable! Ryan, or anyone else, can you please draw the sample input for us? That will get us started.

TIP: Don't get stuck on the parts of the problem you don't understand. Start with the things you do understand, and see if you can figure out the rest.

Visualize it: Ryan walks to the board as the rest of the team joins. While Ryan draws the locations, Annie adds the tiki torches, as in figure 5.2.

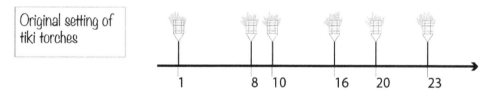

Figure 5.2 The initial placement of the tiki torches.

Coach B: Great. Love the tiki torches. Now, the problem talks about removing one torch. Let's pick one, remove it, and see how it looks.

Rachid: We can't remove the first or the last, so let's remove the one at location 8.

Rachid redraws the setting, as in figure 5.3, without the torch at location 8.

TIP: If possible, try not to erase, or write over, previous drawings. This will allow you to see the progress of your work, and how things evolve. Of course, some problems are too intricate to redraw every time. Find the right path for you, but keep in mind that having clear drawings helps with clear coding.

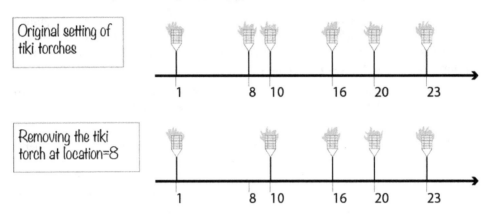

Figure 5.3 Removing tiki torch at location 8.

Coach B: Looks perfect. We are making progress. Now, what is the maximum distance between any two neighboring tiki torches?

Rachid writes the distance between all neighboring torches, as in figure 5.4.

Rachid: The maximum distance is 9, between the torches in location 1 and 10. I'm looking at 1 and 10 together because we removed a torch that was initially between them, the one at location 8.

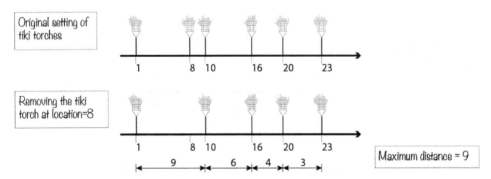

Figure 5.4 After removing one tiki torch, we examine the sketch to find the largest distance between two torches in this setting.

Annie: Oh, I think I get it. Now we need to try and remove other torches, and see what the maximum distance will be then. In the end, we take the minimum among those. Is this correct?

Coach B: Sounds right to me! Go ahead, the board is yours.

Annie and the team start drawing the different cases as in figure 5.5.

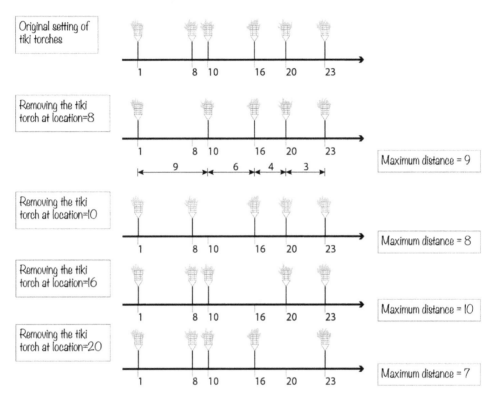

Figure 5.5 Examining all possible tiki torches to remove, and for each case indicating the resulting maximum distance between neighboring torches.

Mei: If we want to take the minimum among these, it's 7. That was when we removed the torch at location 20.

Coach B: And lo and behold, this is the answer they have in the problem for the sample input. Well done! Ryan, does it make sense now? Can you phrase it in your own words?

Ryan: I can try... So here is how I would phrase it: "Bessie wants to help the team and remove one torch. The problem is that any torch she removes makes a stretch of the beach a little less lighted. So her task is to remove one torch such that the resulting length of the beach without a tiki torch is the shortest. Help Bessie determine which tiki torch she should remove."

Mei: Wow, can we nominate Ryan to write USACO questions?

Coach B: I think the prerequisite is passing Bronze. But I agree, this was nicely phrased, Ryan! And I think this also helps us appreciate the use of the Minimum/Maximum phrasing in the original problem: It is much more succinct. The problem said, "Determine which torch can be removed such that the maximum distance between any two adjacent remaining torches is minimal." And we needed to parse that as, "Look at all the possible resulting largest distances, and pick the smallest one of those." The Minimum/Maximum phrasing here will fit in many optimization problems, as you will see in the practice problems, whereas the tiki torches phrasing will fit only this specific case. But it was fun rephrasing it, so thanks again, Ryan!

TIP: When you see a phrase like this: "such that the maximum distance between any two adjacent remaining torches is minimal," it tells you this is probably an optimization problem. Specifically, this type of problem is called a minimax problem. Yes, all in one word, "minimax." A combination of "minimum" and "maximum".

ALGORITHM

Coach B: Now, any concerns about special cases, or are we ready to move to the algorithm?

Mei: Sharks are born ready. I am ready to give it a try.

Coach B: That's the attitude! Go Mei!

Mei takes the marker and writes listing 5.1.

Mei: First I loop over all the relevant tiki torches. Keep in mind we need to skip the first and last. For each one of these, I have a loop over all the remaining tiki torches, and calculate the distance between neighboring ones. I just calculate distance to the neighbor to the left, and keep the largest value among these.

Listing 5.1 Tiki Torches

```
1   int min_max_distance = INT_MAX;
2   int min_max_location;
3
4   for (int tiki_removed = 1; tiki_removed < N - 1; ++tiki_removed) {
5       int max_dist = 0;
6       int dist = 0;
7
8       for (int i = 1; i < N; ++i) {
9           if (i == tiki_removed) continue;
10          // Are we to the right of the removed torch?
11          if (i == tiki_removed + 1) {
12              // Yes: Our left neighbor is the previous one.
13              dist = tiki_location[i] - tiki_location[i - 2];
14          }
15          else {
16              // No: Distance from the left neighbor.
```

```
17          dist = tiki_location[i] - tiki_location[i - 1];
18       }
19       max_dist = max(max_dist, dist);
20    }
21
22    if (max_dist < min_max_distance) {
23       min_max_distance = max_dist;
24       min_max_location = tiki_removed;
25    }
26 }
```

Rachid: I can see why you did the first loop from 1 to $N - 1$. This is because you wanted to avoid the first and last torches. But why do you skip torch number 0 in the inner loop? You go just from $i = 1$ up to N.

Mei: When I calculate distance, I calculate it from the current torch to its neighbor to the left. The very first torch does not have a neighbor to the left, so I am skipping it. Does this make sense?

Rachid: Oh, I see. Thanks.

Coach B: Very nice. Any comments?

The team seems to be happy with the code.

Coach B: Very well then. Actually, I have one more question before we move on from this problem. Any thoughts about what the time complexity of this algorithm might be?

Silence in the room. Complexity is, well, complex.

Ryan: I can try. If the number of tiki torches is N, then this is our base for talking about the order of the problem. Now, we are doing a nested loop over all the tiki torches, so that means we are going over N^2 cases. So that means our time complexity is $O(N^2)$. Is that... right?

Ryan trails off, uncertain.

Coach B: Very good, Ryan! The only thing missing is some more confidence in your answer! Can you say it with more confidence?

Ryan speaks louder.

Ryan: Our time complexity is $O(N^2)$!

The team shares a laugh.

Coach B: Right you are! Very nice. We will not try it now, but I would like to mention that there is a solution to this problem with a time complexity of only $O(N)$. I invite you to revisit this problem after we talk about accelerating search algorithms.

Mei: Wow, that sounds impossible. Can you please give us a hint at least?

Coach B: I really don't want to confuse you now, so here is what we'll do: I will leave the code, with comments and explanations, on the club's page. But this is a good point to emphasize: In Bronze, you do not necessarily have to find the most efficient algorithm in order to pass a problem. We will see that in some cases you are expected to accelerate your algorithm, but this is not always the case. If you have a solution, and it passes all the test cases, you should move on to the next problem! So, in our case, you passed all the test cases, we can move on!

The team cheers.

Coach B: Okay. I believe this completes our first search problem! Very nice. In the process, we learned a common phrase used for Minimum/Maximum in optimization problems. We then did an exhaustive search: We tried to remove each and every one of the relevant tiki torches, and found the best one to remove. And to top it all off, Ryan helped us analyze the time complexity of this algorithm, with confidence. Well done!

The team starts packing, ready to bid farewell.

Coach B: I will put a few search problems on the club's page. I will also sprinkle in some hints, as usual. Oh, and I will also put the $O(N)$ solution if you want to see how it is done. See you next week!

 TIP: If you are stuck for too long on a problem, you can always take a peek at the solution, and then write it on your own. It is better to get a big hint than to get discouraged. It's a learning process.

EPILOGUE

In exhaustive searches, we examine all possible options. This might be too time-consuming, but at the Bronze level it is often a valid approach. Still, even in exhaustive searches, there are opportunities to save on computation time. We will see ways to save computation time later in this chapter when we discuss acceleration.

 VOCABULARY Corner: **OPTIMIZATION** is the process of bringing something to its best, or optimal, position. As a fun note, the words "optimize" and "optimization" grew out of the word "optimist." And Mei here is an optimist: a person with a hopeful and positive attitude, focused on the best of all possible options. Optimists always look on the bright side and expect the best things to happen. Like saving fuel costs while keeping Waikiki Beach well-lit and safe.

PRACTICE PROBLEMS

Hints and full solutions to the problems can be found on the club's page: http://www.usacoclub.com

1. USACO 2014 January Bronze Problem 1: Ski Course Design

    http://usaco.org/index.php?page=viewproblem2&cpid=376

a. Can you pose the problem as a search question? What are you searching for?

b. Hint: We are searching for the range of hill-heights that would not need any change.

c. Hint: If you happen to know the lowest hill-height in the admissible range, can you find the cost of the ski course?

d. Big hint: You will search over the height of the lowest admissible hill. Given that, you can calculate the cost of the ski course. The lowest hill you should consider is the lowest hill height in the provided input, and the largest value to consider is the highest hill (possibly minus 17).

2. USACO 2016 Open Bronze Problem 1: Diamond Collector

   http://usaco.org/index.php?page=viewproblem2&cpid=639

   a. Can you see the similarity to the "Ski Course Design" problem? (2014 January Bronze Problem 1)

   b. Hint: If you happen to know the size of the smallest diamond you can display, can you determine how many diamonds will be presented?

3. USACO 2019 December Bronze Problem 1: Cow Gymnastics

   http://usaco.org/index.php?page=viewproblem2&cpid=963

   a. Arranging the input data in a two-dimensional array would make things easier.

   b. Then, it is exhaustive search over all possible pairs.

4. USACO 2019 December Bronze Problem 2: Where am I?

   http://usaco.org/index.php?page=viewproblem2&cpid=964

   a. Searching over strings.

   b. Exhaustive search over all substrings would work within time.

5.2. Search Domain

The two main components of solving a search problem at the Bronze level are identifying the domain you need to search over, and being able to go over all the elements in this domain. We will cover the first in this section, and the latter in the next.

Coach B: Welcome back, team! Let's get straight into it today. Choosing the domain is not always simple, nor is it always unique. The problem today is not easy, so take your time reading it carefully.

Problem 5.2: Bessie Searches Seashells by the Seashore

Bessie enjoys photographing seashells and wants to arrange a collection from Hawaii. She is heading to Tunnels Beach, rumored to be the birthplace of the puka necklace.

Bessie collects N shells, $0 < N < 10^4$. She then puts the shells in one long line, and assigns a photogenic value to each shell, denoted as a_i, $0 < a_i < 10^4$.

Bessie walks down the line taking photos, with each photo containing one or more consecutive shells. In addition, no shell can be moved from its position along the line, , and every shell must be photographed exactly once.

Bessie would like all her photos to have the same overall photo value, which is the sum of the photogenic values of each shell in the picture.

Determine the smallest possible overall photo value of each picture.

Input Format

Two lines.

The first line contains a single number, N.

The second line contains N integers denoting the photogenic value of each shell, $a_1, a_2, \ldots, a_N$.

Output Format

One number, the overall photo value of all the pictures Bessie takes.

Sample Input

7

1 2 3 5 1 4 2

Sample Output

6

If we group the shells as $(1, 2, 3)$, $(5, 1)$, and $(4, 2)$, each group will have the same photogenic value of 6.

DISCUSSION

Coach B: Any volunteers to draw the problem?

The team is still thinking about the problem. Eventually, Annie walks up to the board.

Annie: I don't know how to find the solution, but I can explain the situation, at least.

Coach B: That's a great place to start! Here's the marker.

Visualize it: Annie takes the marker and draws figure 5.6.

Ryan: Nice seashells!

Coach B: I concur. Very nice indeed.

Annie: Thanks. As I said, I can explain what their solution is, but I don't really know how they got it. They grouped the first three shells into one photo, and the overall photo value is then $1 + 2 + 3 = 6$. Then, the next group of two shells is of value $5 + 1 = 6$. And the last group is again two shells with overall photo value of $4 + 2 = 6$. So all photos share the same overall photo value of 6.

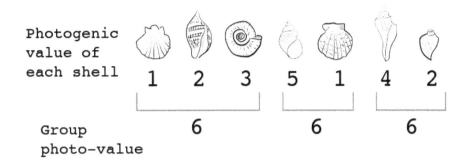

Figure 5.6 Visualizing the sample input. Three photos will be taken, each with an overall photo value of 6.

Coach B: Any ideas on how to go about finding a general solution?

The team is silent, looking puzzled.

Coach B: Okay, so one way to deal with a situation like this is to make your own example. Let's do it as a team: Annie, can you come up with a different example? And please don't tell us the solution.

TIP: When you understand a solution that is given to you, but can't find a general algorithm, try and build up a new example. This will help you understand the problem, and get better insights.

Annie thinks and writes on the board as in figure 5.7.

Figure 5.7 Annie's new example for shell photogenic values. Can you find the grouping in this case?

Rachid immediately steps up, and with another marker draws the solution in figure 5.8.

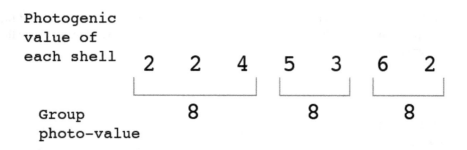

Figure 5.8 Rachid's solution. He's grouped the shells into photos with overall photo values of 8.

Coach B: That was fast. Both on coming up with a sample, and solving it. Rachid, how did you solve it?

Rachid: I started from left to right. If the first group has one shell, just the 2 by itself, then the photo value is 2. Then I can take the second shell by itself, but when I get to the third shell of value 4 it doesn't work, because the photo value will be too big. So if I take the first two shells together, then the photo value is 4, and I can take the third shell on its own, but it fails with the fourth shell of value 5. Then I took the first three shells as a group, which yields a photo value of 8, and everything worked!

Ryan: I think the photo value we are looking for should be at least as large as the value of the best shell. I mean, this shell will appear in one photo group, right? If this is the only shell in this group, then the value of the photo will be equal to the value of this shell. If there are additional shells in this group, the photo value will be larger.

Coach B: Very nice solution and explanation, Rachid. And great observation, Ryan. This kind of observation can make our algorithm faster and maybe even simpler to understand. However, for now, we will avoid adding these adornments. This is a common workflow when first solving a problem: First, we try to get the basic algorithm working; then, we incorporate optimizations if needed. Makes sense?

Ryan nods in agreement.

Coach B: I wonder: Annie, how did you build up your example? Maybe we can learn something from that.

Annie: I decided on a number for the photo value, 8, and then started writing numbers for the shell values and made sure, as I go left to right writing the numbers, that I get to this value with any new group.

TIP: You can sometimes imagine a good fairy gave you a number which might be a solution, and all you have to do is check it. If it's not the solution, the fairy will give you another number to try. If the fairy is lucky enough, or very rigorous, this will lead you to a solution. You can act like this fairy when trying to understand a problem, and in some cases you might be able to write a program that mimics such a fairy. This good fairy is called an Oracle.

Coach B: Interesting. I think we have two different approaches, and both may lead us to a good algorithm. Let me draw a table, and you can help me fill it up.

Coach B draws table 5.1 on the board and fills it with the team's help.

Mei: Rachid's method is searching for the length of the first group. This means he will check all options for the length from 1 to N, the total number of shells.

Ryan: For Annie's method, she will consider all the possible photo values. The photo value should be, at a minimum, equal to the highest value shell, so this is the starting point. The maximum photo value is the case when we have all the shells in one photo. So we can loop over all the values between these minimum and maximum values.

Coach B completes the table by writing the algorithm row.

Table 5.1 A table for analyzing the two different methods. The methods use different domains to perform an exhaustive search.

	Rachid's method	Annie's method
Domain	Length of the first group	Photo value
Enumeration of the domain	Length of group goes from 1 to N, the total number of shells.	From the highest value of a shell, up to the sum of values of all shells.
Algorithm	Calculate the photo value of the first group, and check if it works. - If the value works, done. - If the value does not work, increase the length of the first group, and repeat.	Assume a photo value. Check if this value works. If not, increase the photo value.

Rachid: These two methods look very similar to me. See? Because they both need to check if a photo value works for the problem. Is there really even a difference between these two methods?

Coach B: Let's consider the following case: There are 100 shells of value 1, and at the end there's one more shell with a value of 100. How will the two algorithms work on this?

Mei: Wait, the solution is one group of 100 shells, each has a value of 1, followed by the second group with one shell of value 100. With Rachid's algorithm, we would start with a group of 1, then 2, and so forth, until we reach a group of 100, and then we have a viable solution. With Annie's method, we'll start with a photo value of 100 (as this is the value of the best shell), and this is immediately the final result. Wow, that's a big difference!

The team takes time to digest the surprising result: such a big difference in the execution time, for two algorithms that seem very similar.

Coach B: Can anyone think of an example where the situation is reversed? I mean, a situation when Rachid's algorithm will do much better than Annie's?

This question throws the group off: Is there really a case where the other algorithm could be much better? Does Coach B have one in mind, or is he just being thorough? After some silence, Ryan tries.

Ryan: I think I've got one. Let's say there are four shells with values 100, 101, 100, 101. The solution will be a photo value of 201, where the first 2 shells form one group, and the next two a second group. In Annie's method, we will need to step through all the values from 101 to 201. That's 100 values to try. In Rachid's method, we will have only 2 steps. Trying a group length of 1, and then 2.

Rachid: This is wild. Two methods, which seem really similar, and yet they produce such different efficiency. How can we decide which one to use?

Coach B: Let's take a step back. Both methods are doing an exhaustive search, right? Both look over all possible values in their respective domain, right? In most cases at Bronze level, the selection of a search domain would not matter. But, if you find your solution runs into time issues, certainly consider whether moving to a different search domain can help. I'll have more to say about acceleration methods later in this unit.

The team looks again and ponders the table on the board.

Rachid: I wonder. The problem specifically states that we should look for the smallest possible photo value. Are we indeed finding the smallest one? Is there another possible value?

Coach B: Very good point, Rachid. I think we can all agree we do find the smallest possible value, right? We are going from the smallest group, or the lowest possible value, and moving up from there. Agreed?

The team nods in agreement.

Coach B: But, they do mention it specifically in the problem. Any idea as to why they do that? Is there another possible solution?

Mei: Well, we can always take the whole group of shells in one picture, right? This will be the largest group size, as well as the largest possible photo value for the photo.

Coach B: Right on! If the problem didn't specify the need for the smallest possible photo value, we could always have this trivial solution: One picture, with all shells in it. That would be too easy, wouldn't it?

The team sighs in agreement.

Coach B: But again, thanks Rachid for pointing this out. Watching for these little signs can give us good insight into the problem. Now, Let's move to coding.

ALGORITHM

Coach B: Okay, let's bring the cows home. Almost literally. Anyone up for writing the algorithm? Just one of them will do. Ryan and Mei, why don't you two go ahead and write it. Pick whichever method you prefer.

Ryan and Mei walk up to the board and write the code as in listing 5.2.

Listing 5.2 Bessie Searches Seashells by the Seashore (a work-in-progress code)

```
1   // Not final code!
2   // Rachid's algorithm
3   int photo_value;
4   int answer;
5   for (int group_len = 1; group_len <= N; ++group_len) {
6       photo_value = 0;  // need to reset for every new group size
7
8
9       // Calculating the photo-value for this group size. Code will be
10      // modified.
11      for ( int i = 0; i < group_len; ++i ) {
12          photo_value += shell_value[i];
13      }
14
15      int index = 0;
16      int sum = 0;
17      while (index < N) {
18          sum += shell_value[index];
19          if (sum == photo_value) sum = 0;
20          if (sum > photo_value) break;
21          index++;
22      }
23      if (index == N) {  // Code will be modified.
24          answer = photo_value;
25          break;
26      }
27  }
```

Coach B: Thanks, Ryan and Mei. This is not a simple code, is it? Looks very readable, though. Let's zoom in on a couple of important parts, starting with this:

```
1  photo_value = 0;  // need to reset for every new group size
2  for (int i = 0; i < group_len; ++i) {
3      photo_value += shell_value[i];
4  }
```

Coach B: This part calculates the `photo_value` of the group, right? But we know that in every step we increase the first group size by just one, namely adding one more shell. So maybe we can just add this shell's value to the `photo_value` so far?

Mei: Oh, I see. Here, let me change this.

Mei replaces these four lines of code with:

```
1  photo_value += shell_value[group_len - 1];
```

Mei: Since the array indexing starts from 0, the last shell to include for a group of length `group_len` would be `group_len - 1`. Let me check. So, for a group of length 1, we just need to add `shell_value[0]`. That's good. And when the group is of length N, including all shells, the last shell to add is `shell_value[N - 1]`.Yes, that looks right as well. We are good to go.

 TIP: When faced with zero-indexed arrays and lengths, substitute values to make sure you did not make an "off by 1" error.

Coach B: Great. Looks good. The next item is a little tricky. Take a look at the code where you check that the `photo_value` actually works.

```
1  int index = 0;
2  int sum = 0;
3  while (index < N) {
4      sum += shell_value[index];
5      if (sum == photo_value) sum = 0;
6      if (sum > photo_value) break;
7      index++;
8  }
9  if (index == N) {
10     answer = photo_value;
11     break;
12 }
```

Coach B: You are going over the shells, `index = 0` to N. For each one, you are adding the value, and there are three options:

1. If the value is less than the photo_value, we need to add another shell.
2. If the value is equal to photo_value, it means we have another group, and we should start a new group.
3. If the value is greater than photo_value, that means the photo_value is not a viable option, and we need to look for another value.

Is that correct?

Ryan: Yes, that's our intention. Anything wrong here?

Coach B: Oh, no, this looks perfectly correct. Now, why do you have the condition after that section, I mean the if (index == N)?

Ryan: This is our indication that we actually reached the end of the shells' array, and it means that all is okay, and the value worked.

Coach B: Does it? It does tell you that you reached the end of the array, and that all the groups so far worked fine. But, does it tell you if the last group reached the correct sum? What if the very last group did not reach the photo_value?

Ryan: Oh, I see. We can then add a condition if this is the last group, and ...

Ryan trails off, thinking.

Coach B: Try to keep it simple. Any idea for a small modification to make it work?

 TIP: Keep your code simple. Adding special conditions for special cases can produce a big entanglement. If your code is mostly right, maybe all you need is just a little adjustment.

Annie walks to the board and adds if (index == N && sum == 0).

Annie: This will make sure that the last group really did have the right photo_value, and sum was reset to zero in the loop.

```
1   int index = 0;
2   int sum = 0;
3   while (index < N) {
4       sum += shell_value[index];
5       if ( sum == photo_value ) sum = 0;
6       if ( sum > photo_value ) break;
7       index++;
8   }
9   if (index == N && sum == 0) {  // Added by Annie
10      answer = photo_value;
11      break;
12  }
```

The team looks at the resulting new code in listing 5.3, then laughs.

Annie: This was a real difficult problem!

Listing 5.3 Bessie Searches Seashells by the Seashore

```
1   // Rachid's algorithm
2   int photo_value = 0;
3   int answer;
4   for (int group_len = 1; group_len <= N; ++group_len) {
5       photo_value += shell_value[group_len - 1];
6
7       int index = 0;
8       int sum = 0;
9       while (index < N) {
10          sum += shell_value[index];
11          if (sum == photo_value) sum = 0;
12          if (sum > photo_value) break;
13          index++;
14      }
15      if (index == N && sum == 0) {
16          answer = photo_value;
17          break;
18      }
19  }
```

Coach B: Yes, this was not an easy problem. But we learned a lot! Great job on finishing this. So right now I suggest you just rest a bit and enjoy the solution. For me, the biggest part was getting to an algorithm. Recall how we had to create our own test case and solve it—thanks Annie and Rachid—and then we had a pathway to an algorithm.

Rachid: Yes, Annie's made-up example paved the way. Well done, Annie!

The team cheers for Annie.

Coach B: Indeed. It's a team effort, and we did it. Okay, I will post the practice on our club's page, and will see you next week. Thanks, everyone!

EPILOGUE

Search problems involve searching over a domain. As we learned and explored in the seashells problem, there might be more than one domain that can be used to search for the solution. As you choose which domain to work in, you can consider many aspects: the size of the domain; the ease of going over all the elements in the domain; the simplicity and readability of the resulting code; and the complexity in terms of execution time. At the Bronze level, in most cases the choice of the domain is not significant. However, if your program runs into an issue with the execution time, changing the search domain might be the solution.

 VOCABULARY Corner: **ENUMERATION** is the action of assigning a number to items. This often helps us when we want to be able to identify each item, and make sure we go over all items. For example, in real life, putting numbers on houses on the street allows us to give an address that identifies each home. Here's a different example from coding: say you try to solve a maze with an algorithm, and you are positioned in a spot with a few possible directions to pursue. You can assign a number to each direction, and then go over them one by one. Enumeration plays an important role in search algorithms. Naturally, you recognize almost the entire word "numeral" within the word "enumeration." You might also recognize the prefix, "e-," which here means "out." Think of enumeration as a process of passing *out* numbers: one for every single item.

PRACTICE PROBLEMS

Hints and full solutions to the problems can be found on the club's page: http://www.usacoclub.com

1. USACO 2022 February Bronze Problem 1: Sleeping in Class

   http://usaco.org/index.php?page=viewproblem2&cpid=1203

   a. This one is very similar to the seashell problem.

   b. For the domain you can use the number of classes to combine, or alternatively use the sum of sleeping hours.

2. USACO 2020 January Bronze Problem 2: Photoshoot

   http://usaco.org/index.php?page=viewproblem2&cpid=988

   a. Is this a search problem? Yes, in disguise.

   b. What is the domain you are searching over?

   c. Method 1:

   - If an oracle tells you the value of a_0, could you find all subsequent values a_i? Can you determine if the resulting sequence of a_i is a viable solution?
   - Use an exhaustive search over all possible values of a_0.

   d. Method 2:

   - If an oracle tells you which element is equal to 1, could you find all values a_i? Can you determine if the resulting sequence of a_i is a viable solution?
   - Use an exhaustive search over all possible options i for $a_i = 1$.

   e. Method 3:

- Can you find how all the terms are dependent on the first element? In other words, if we increase a_0 by 1, how will the rest of the values change?
- Hint: fix the first element to 1, then calculate all the rest. Find the minimum of the even and odd numbers.

f. The computation time for Methods 1 and 2 is $O(N^2)$. For Method 3, it's $O(N)$.

5.3. Domain Enumeration

As we've seen, exhaustive searches entail searching over all the possible options of our domain. This next process, enumeration, deals with ordering the elements in the domain so that we are sure to check all the options, and not miss any.

Coach B: Happy Tuesday! Today, we continue in our study of search problems, and specifically with the exhaustive search algorithm. Who can remind us: in the problems we've covered so far, how did we make sure we went over every single option?

Mei: The first problem we had was the tiki torches. We needed to see which tiki torch would be the best to remove. We just went over all of them one by one. The second one was the seashells, and like with the torches, we went over all possible group sizes of the first shell group. Neither of these was complicated nor hard. I don't even think we stopped to check that we'd covered every option. It was just baked into how we approached the problems. Not exactly hard!

Coach B: Very good, Mei, and you are absolutely correct. So far, it was relatively easy, or at least intuitive, to make sure we go over all options. The problem today is a little different. Go ahead, read this, and we'll discuss it. We'll see that counting all the options might be a little tricky sometimes.

Problem 5.3: Crossing Volcanoes

Bessie is heading to Hawaii Volcanoes National Park, excited to see the various lava forms and learn more about the earth she calls home. At the end of the tour, she steps into the souvenir shop, where she finds an adventure game called "Crossing Volcanoes" that immediately captures her imagination.

The game is played on a two-dimensional grid. Your starting point is at the bottom left, coordinate $(0,0)$. Your goal is to get to the top right, coordinate (N, N), $N \le 10$. There are K volcanoes spread on the grid, $K \le 90$. A safe path must dodge all the volcanoes. Your first move is to the right, and following that, you can only move up or to the right. You are allowed no more than three changes of direction after the first step.

Determine how many safe paths exist from $(0,0)$ to (N, N).

Input Format

$K + 1$ lines.

The first line contains two integers: N, K.

The next K lines each contain a pair of coordinates (x, y) describing the location of a volcano.

Output Format

One number, the number of possible safe paths.

Sample Input

4 1

3 2

Sample Output

8

DISCUSSION

Rachid: Is this a search problem? I would call it a counting problem: we need to count how many safe paths there are.

The team nods in approval.

Coach B: Yes, I can definitely see why you would say that. Honestly, this is one of the big challenges in search problems: just being able to identify the problem as a search problem. The only way to get better at this is seeing more examples, and this is one of these examples. So, if I may, I ask you to hold judgment on whether this is a search problem or not until we solve it. I think the algorithm will help us see behind the curtain. Anyone willing to draw the problem?

Visualize it: Ryan steps up and sketches figure 5.9.

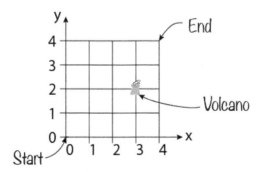

Figure 5.9 The game's two-dimensional grid, with one volcano located at (3,2).

Coach B: Thanks, Ryan. So, let's start counting. But we need to be organized, to make sure we count everything, and not double-count anything. We were told we cannot have more than 3 turns as we move along the grid. So let's start with one turn along our path. Can you count all the safe paths with only one turn?

The group tries different variations, draws and erases, and finally Annie presents figure 5.10. She speaks slowly.

Annie: Um, is it only one path?

Coach B: Let's have a little more confidence in our findings! Confidence is contagious. Can you walk us through with confidence?

Annie straightens, raising her voice.

Annie: Okay! There is only one path with one turn!

The team smiles as Annie continues.

Annie: We know the first move is to the right. And, we have only one turn. So we tried different points to turn. If we turn at point $(1, 0)$, we will go up and reach the edge of the board at the point $(1, 4)$, which is not the end point. The same goes if we turn at $(2, 0)$. At $(3, 0)$ we would actually hit a volcano. If we turn at the point $(4, 0)$, we reach the end point! So the only viable path is the one that turns at $(4, 0)$.

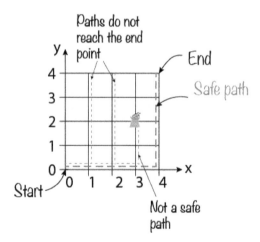

Figure 5.10 Drawing all paths with only one turn. There is only one safe path that has exactly one turn.

Coach B: Thanks, Annie. I really like the way you described it, and it jibes well with the way I saw the group searching for the safe path. Oops, here, I gave it away: "searching" for the safe path. Do you agree with this term?

Rachid: I didn't think about it this way, but that's exactly what we did. Interesting.

TIP: Identifying the type of the problem can help with using the right terminology and tools for the problem. And sometimes, like in this case, it takes a little fiddling with the problem to identify its type. Have an open mind to adapting as you learn more about the problem at hand.

Coach B: Okay. Now that we can call it a search, let's search for the number of safe paths with two turns.

The team huddles around the board, erases the paths that didn't work, and draws figure 5.11.

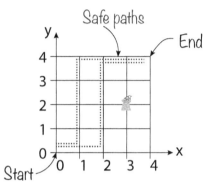

Figure 5.11 Drawing all paths with exactly two turns. There are two safe paths with two turns.

Coach B: That seemed to go much faster. You realized you need to have one turn up at the bottom, then proceed all the way to the top edge, and have a second turn to the right. Okay, the big one: three turns! Go ahead, don't let me stop you.

The team turns energetically to the drawing, but this time it takes much longer. Eventually, they come up with the drawing in figure 5.12.

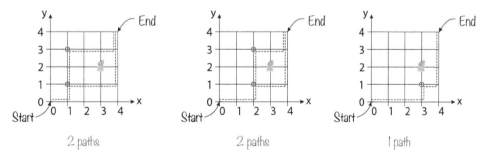

Figure 5.12 Drawing all paths with 3 turns. There are five such paths. Circled are the turning points in the middle of the grid for the different paths.

Coach B: Impressive! Still, this round took much longer. Any reason?

Mei: First, it took us time to realize that for three turns, we need to have one turning point in the interior of the grid. Then, there were too many paths to consider, so we got organized, and went over all the interior points one by one. We started with the column at $x = 1$, and there were two points, $(1, 1)$ and $(1, 3)$, that resulted in safe paths. We marked the interior turning points with circles. Then, we proceeded to the next column, $x = 2$, and so on. I mean, what I'm saying is, it took longer because it was a lot of work!

Coach B: And that's why they call it an exhaustive search!

The team laughs.

Coach B: But look at what you have done here. You searched over all the paths with three turns. This was your domain. Then, you had a hard time figuring out how to go over all these in an orderly manner, until you found a way to enumerate them: Each three-turn path is uniquely identified by its middle turning point! Which, as you rightly pointed out, has to be in the interior of the grid. Once you got this out of the way, you were able to go over all possible three-turn paths, and find the viable ones.

Can you describe your search for the two-turn paths in a similar manner? Spell it out for us: what's the domain, and what did you enumerate?

Mei: I'll try... For the two-turn paths, our domain was... all possible two-turn paths. We realized that every two-turn path can be uniquely identified by the turning point at the bottom, because once we turn up, we have to go all the way to the top, and make a turn to the right. That was how we enumerated the domain.

Coach B: Perfect use of enumeration! Great. And what about the one-turn path?

Rachid: I don't think we had a need for any special process in this case. We realized that there's only one possible path using one turn only: We need to go all the way to the end of the row, and then head up to the end. We just needed to check that this path is safe. But otherwise, there's only one such path possible. So, nothing to enumerate.

Coach B: Sounds right to me. Keeping it simple always helps. We do not have to force the terminology on every single case. Only when it is helpful.

ALGORITHM

Coach B: Now for the algorithm. In truth, I think that you already did the heavy lifting in this problem. Now it is only technique, but, technique is important! Let's do it in three steps. First, the case for a one-turn path.

Ryan leaps up to claim this shortest section. He writes listing 5.4a.

Listing 5.4a Crossing Volcanoes (One-turn path)

```
1   int path_count = 0;
2
3   int grid[N + 1][N + 1];  // Note: The array goes from 0 to N, inclusive
4   // grid[r][c] == 0 when there's no volcano
5   // grid[r][c] == 1 when there is a volcano
6
7   // x coordinates are in columns
8   // y coordinates are in the rows
9
10  // Moving to the right is them moving along the columns
11
12  bool safe = true;
13
14  // Going from the starting point to the right on the 0th row, until the
15  // end of the row.
16  for ( int c = 0; c <= N; ++c) {
17      if (grid[0][c] == 1) safe = false;
18  }
19
20  // Going up on the Nth column to the end point.
21  for (int r = 0; r <= N; ++r) {
22      if (grid[r][N] == 1) safe = false;
23  }
24  if (safe) path_count++;
```

Ryan: Since there is only one path, we just follow it, and check that there's no volcano along the way. One thing I was careful about is the fact the array should include both the $(0,0)$ coordinate and the (N, N) coordinate, which means its size should be $N + 1$.

Coach B: Thanks, Ryan. That's a very important point indeed. Well done! I appreciate the way you commented on the relation between the x and y coordinates and the columns and rows of the matrix. This is something that might be confusing, and you clearly wrote it down. It's a clean and concise code, and what's more important, it is written in a way that sets us up very nicely for the other cases. Great job!

Sheepish at the praise, Ryan turns a bit pink.

Ryan: Well, of course I planned it as such.

The team laughs. Mei and Rachid head to the board, writing the case for two-turn paths, as in listing 5.4b.

Listing 5.4b Crossing Volcanoes (Two-turn paths)

```
1   // continuing the code from before, listing 5.4a
2
3   // Enumeration loop
4   for (int c_turn = 1; c_turn < N; ++c_turn) {
5       bool safe = true;
6
7       // Going from the starting point to the right on the 0th row, until
8       // the (c_turn)th column.
9       for (int c = 0; c <= c_turn; ++c) {
10          if (grid[0][c] == 1) safe = false;
11      }
12
13
14      // Going up along the (c_turn)th column.
15      for (int r = 0; r <= N; ++r) {
16          if (grid[r][c_turn] == 1) safe = false;
17      }
18
19
20      // Going to the right along the Nth row to the end point.
21      for (int c = c_turn; c <= N; ++c) {
22          if (grid[N][c] == 1) safe = false;
23      }
24      if (safe) path_count++;
25  }
```

Mei: Our outer loop is going over the enumeration of the paths. And inside it we are going first right, then up, and then right again.

Ryan: Now I see what you meant by setting up the code for others. The loops of going over the path are very similar. The only difference is that now, for example, they needed to go only to c_turn on the 0th row. But yeah, it's very similar to my portion of the code.

Coach B: Indeed. So Annie, hopefully now you have the patterns established, so the three-turn paths shouldn't be that hard to write.

Annie: Yes, I think I can see the pattern. Loop over the enumeration, and for each, walk along the path and check it for volcanoes.

Annie walks to the board and writes the code in listing 5.4c.

Listing 5.4c Crossing Volcanoes (Three-turn paths)

```
1   // continuing the code from before, listing 5.4b
2
3   // Enumeration loop
4   for (int c_turn = 1; c_turn < N; ++c_turn) {
5       for (int r_turn = 1; r_turn < N; ++r_turn) {
6
7       bool safe = true;
8
9       for (int c = 0; c <= c_turn; ++c) {
10          if (grid[0][c] == 1) safe = false;
11      }
12      for (int r = 0; r <= r_turn; ++r) {
13          if (grid[r][c_turn] == 1) safe = false;
14      }
15      for (int c = c_turn; c <= N; ++c) {
16          if (grid[r_turn][c] == 1) safe = false;
17      }
18      for (int r = r_turn; r <= N; ++r) {
19          if (grid[r][N] == 1) safe = false;
20      }
21      if (safe) path_count++;
22      }
23  }
```

The team watches as Annie finishes writing, and all clap in unison. Annie takes a curtsy.

Coach B: Well deserved, Annie, and all of you! Very nice work. I would like us all to appreciate how the three parts follow the same pattern, or in computer science lingo, follow the same paradigma. They use the enumeration to loop over all the options and go over the paths in similar manner. It's nice to appreciate the aesthetic beauty of a well-organized code. It has a pattern of its own. Okay, okay, I admit it might be a matter of personal taste. But that's how I see it.

TIP: Well-written code has an intrinsic beauty to it. Keep your indentation and style consistent, and look for opportunities to unify patterns. Aesthetics, and beauty, are often in the eyes of the beholder, and it's totally okay to develop your own style in these. But, if you pay attention to these, in whatever form you like, you will become a better programmer, and produce a better code.

Ryan: Can't we actually combine all three cases into one loop? I think we can use the last case, for three turns, and calculate all the other paths with the same code.

Coach B: Great point Ryan. I think you are right, and it will make an even more concise and clear code. It is often very beneficial to look back after finishing writing the code, and explore ways to improve it. Having said that, let's leave this as homework this time around, since we are running low on time, and I would like to let you all go home soon.

The team smiles in approval.

Coach B: Let's wrap up: I hope you can all see why this can be considered a search problem, and how we benefited from identifying it as such. Agreed?

All nod in agreement.

Coach B: And the other aspect that I wanted to bring up is that enumeration was not a trivial matter in this problem, was it? Especially for the three-turn case, it took time and effort to realize the interior point is the way to enumerate the domain. But, once you knew it was a search problem, you were actually looking for a way to enumerate it, and found the pattern.

The team nods pensively in agreement.

Coach B: Okay, I will put a few problems on the club's page. Keep in mind things are getting harder. But, you do have the advantage of knowing that all these are search problems. When competing, you won't know the types of the problems! So, when you are solving one of these problems, try to see how you could have noted that it is a search problem without this clear direction, and also pay attention to how you are using this fact to help you find the algorithm. See you next week!

EPILOGUE

In this section we focused on enumeration of the domain. We needed to enumerate the different possible paths. The solution was to find a unique characterization for each path. For paths with only two turns, we saw that by specifying the first turning point, the path is uniquely identified. For paths with three turns, the unique identifier was the middle inflection point: the point inside the grid where the path turns. Once we had this correspondence between a path and a point on the grid, going over all the paths meant going over all the grid points.

Knowing that you need to find a way to enumerate your domain should guide you in looking for, and finding, the right domain and enumeration method for a given problem.

VOCABULARY Corner: **PARADIGMA** A paradigma (or, if you prefer to use the less fancy, less specialized term: a paradigm) is a typical pattern of something. These are used often in computer science to represent common schools of thought on how to do things. For example, Java is part of the object-oriented paradigma. Haskell is part of the functional-programming paradigma. In our example, we explored the "exhaustive search" paradigma: identifying the domain, establishing an enumeration of the elements, and looping over each element. No matter the example, whether in programming or beyond, a paradigm is a pattern, highly established and often followed. In the business world, when one wants to suggest breaking out from an old pattern of thought, one may say "This is a paradigm shift: We no longer consider a brick-and-mortar presence necessary for a business."

PRACTICE PROBLEMS

Hints and full solutions to the problems can be found on the club's page: http://www.usacoclub.com

1. USACO 2021 December Bronze Problem 3: Walking Home

    http://usaco.org/index.php?page=viewproblem2&cpid=1157

    a. This is a hard problem. It's similar to Crossing Volcanoes.

    b. There's a notable difference here from Crossing Volcanoes: You do not have to go along a row first. You could go along a column as your first step. As a result, for example, with one turn, there are two paths to consider.

    c. Enumeration is very similar to what we did in Crossing Volcanoes.
2. You already did this problem earlier in this chapter! The exercise here: Can you solve the same problem here with a different domain and different enumeration?

    USACO 2022 February Bronze Problem 1: Sleeping in Class

    http://usaco.org/index.php?page=viewproblem2&cpid=1203

    a. For the domain you can use the number of classes to combine, or alternatively use the sum of sleeping hours. Choose a different option than what you used before.

5.4. Search Acceleration

As the team walks into the room, they follow the sugary scent of donuts to an open box on the table.

Coach B: Please help yourselves to a donut: Happy Friday! I am happy we were able to find another day to meet this week. That's the best way to prepare for USACO, to spend time learning and practicing. So, thanks again for making it twice this week.

Each student chooses a favorite donut from the box.

Coach B: As you enjoy your donut, please listen closely, all. We've got some information to absorb before we jump into the practice. Today we're focusing again on the exhaustive search.

Exhaustive search is inherently slow as it searches over all possible options. In other words, for every possible option the algorithm must check whether it is the solution we are looking for. There are two main methods to accelerate such an algorithm:

1. *Reduce the number of possible options by a judicious selection of the domain space–* This can usually be done if we've made some sort of insight into the problem. For example, consider the problem of finding all the prime numbers between 1 and 100. Choosing as our domain all the integers between 1 and 100 will mean that an exhaustive search algorithm will need to check one hundred numbers. However, we know that all even numbers are divisible by 2 and therefore cannot be prime numbers (other than 2 itself, which *is* a prime number). Choosing only odd numbers as our domain reduces the size of the domain by half. We accomplished that by using our understanding of prime numbers. Using our insights is the first way to accelerate that algorithm.

2. *Reduce the complexity of checking each possible option–* For every potential option, the algorithm needs to check whether it is the solution we are looking for. Reducing this evaluation time will accelerate the total solution time.

 TIP: At Bronze level, only a few search problems will need acceleration. Moreover, even in problems that do need acceleration, the first few test cases are designed to pass even without any acceleration. Remember: you will get partial credit for every test case that passes. You will also gain insights into the problem by submitting a working solution, even if it doesn't meet all the time limit constraints.

Coach B: So far in this unit, we talked about the exhaustive search algorithm, and the choice of domain and enumeration. Today we are concluding our tour of exhaustive search algorithms with a discussion on how we can accelerate the execution time of the search algorithm. Please read the following problem, and we'll discuss it afterwards. Just a heads-up: We will need to be a little extra creative for this problem. Maybe the extra sugar from the donuts will help with that.

Problem 5.4: Luaus and Leis

Bessie and her friends are near the end of their visit to magical Hawaii, and their host invites them to a luau. Bessie and her friends are excited, busily stringing flowers into leis that they will wear to the event.

When they are done, they have N leis, $1 < N < 10^6$. Each has x_i flowers strung on it, $1 < x_i < 10^4$. However, some of the leis have more flowers than others! Bessie wants to make the leis a little more uniform, so no cow has a significantly shorter or longer lei than the others.

Given two positive integers K and M,, Bessie will leave untouched all leis that have between $(M - K)$ and $(M + K)$ flowers. If a lei has over $(M + K)$ flowers, she will take out flowers to bring it down to $(M + K)$, and add those flowers to any lei that has fewer than $(M - K)$ flowers, to bring it up to $(M - K)$. At the end of the process, Bessie might end up with a few extra flowers from the too-long leis, or she might be missing some flowers that she needs for the shorter leis.

Given K, determine the value of M that will leave Bessie with the minimal number of extra or missing flowers.

Input Format

Two lines.

The first line contains two integers: N, K.

The second line contains N integers denoting the length of each lei, $x_1, x_2, \ldots, x_{N-1}, x_N$, where $x_1 \leq x_2 \leq x_3 \leq \ldots \leq x_N$.

Output Format

One number, the value of M that will yield the minimal number of extra or missing flowers. The value of M should be in the range $x_1 \leq M \leq x_N$.

If there are multiple values of M that would yield the same minimal number of flowers, give the smallest value among those M values.

Sample Input

7 3

4 7 8 10 12 14 19

Sample Output

11

For $M = 11$, the leis with lengths between 8 and 14 are admissible. Bessie will need a total of 5 flowers to fill in for the leis of length 4 and 7. She has exactly 5 extra flowers from the lei of length 19. Thus, the total extra or missing flowers she will have in this case is 0.

DISCUSSION

Rachid: This was a long problem!

Everyone nods in agreement.

Rachid: But, I think I get it, and I think I even know how to go about solving it.

Coach B: That's great! Go ahead, the board is yours. First, can you please draw just the sample case? This will make sure we are all on the same page.

Visualize it: Rachid goes to the board and draws figure 5.13.

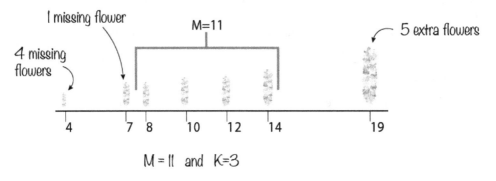

Figure 5.13 Seven leis with different sizes as given in the sample input, with 4,7,8,10,12,14, and 19 flowers. If we choose M=11, all the leis from size 8 to 14 are admissible.

Rachid: I drew the number of flowers as the x-axis. It's easier for me to see it this way. I needed a variable to represent the flowers in the "middle" lei, so I used M. And we allow leis with $(M - K)$ up to $(M + K)$ flowers.

> *TIP*: Like Rachid did here, it's a good idea to assign your own names to abstract variables, so that you can understand and solve the problem. However, keep in mind that if you misunderstood anything, then the terminology that you picked might mislead you. So, definitely use your own terminology, but be willing to adapt it. For example, in this specific case, did you notice that there might not be any actual lei with M flowers? It's still okay to call it the "middle lei," as long as you understand this limitation of your terminology.

Rachid: The question tells us the solution is when $M = 11$, so I drew that as well. If M is 11, and $K = 3$, this means we accept as-is all the leis from $(11 - 3)$ to $(11 + 3)$. For the ones that are out of this range, Bessie needs one flower for the lei of length 7, in order to bring it up to 8 flowers, and 4 flowers for the one of length 4. Luckily, on the other side, she has 5 extra flowers from the lei of length 19, since she will bring it down to 14 flowers. So, for $M = 11$, we don't have any extra flowers left.

Annie: That makes sense. Thanks. We still need to show that for, say, $M = 10$, we don't get zero left over as well. Because they want the smallest M that achieves the best solution, right?

Rachid: Oh, you're right. Let me check that.

He draws figure 5.14.

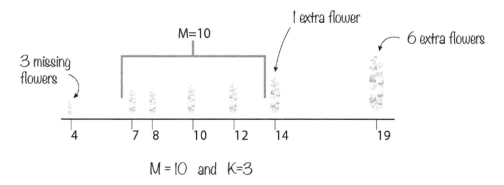

M=10

l extra flower

6 extra flowers

3 missing flowers

4   7 8   10   12   14   19

M = 10 and K=3

All leis between (10-3) and (10+3) are admissible

Figure 5.14 Choosing M = 10 leads to 7 extra flowers, and 3 missing flowers, which brings the total number of extra left flowers to 4.

Rachid: Well, for $M = 10$ we are missing 3 flowers for the lei of 4, and we have 7 extra from the other side. In total, we have 4 flowers left. So $M = 11$ is still better.

Ryan: Yeah, but what about $M = 9$? Or $M = 8$? We need to check if any of these is better than $M = 11$, because we need to find the smallest M according to the question.

Rachid: Hmm... I see what you're saying. And you're right. But, this will be resolved automatically with my idea about how to solve the problem. Let me show you. My idea was to go over all values of possible M, from the shortest lei to the longest one, and calculate the value of extra flowers for each. I think this will check all the M values possible, so we'll be okay.

Coach B: Very nice. I see you are using an exhaustive search, going over all the values of M. Will this address your concerns, Ryan?

Ryan: Yes, and one more thing... I just realized that if we start from the smallest M, we can stop the search whenever we reach the number of extra flowers to be zero, because we can't have less than zero extra. So, in these cases, we don't even need to search over all the values of M!

Coach B: Great observation! Indeed, we can stop searching when we find zero, because we can't do any better than that.

TIP: If we find the answer before searching over all possible values in exhaustive search, we can stop searching. Going over all possible values is just a tool at our disposal, and not a requirement. The right answer is the right answer. No need to keep searching any longer.

Coach B: Before we go to the algorithm, any special cases we need to consider?

Mei: Let's see. If all the leis are of equal length, I don't see this causing any problem. We'll just do the exhaustive search on one option. I wonder if K can be zero? No, I see in the problem it says that both K and M are "two positive integers," so that means they're both greater than zero. So I don't see any other interesting cases.

Coach B: Good. All clear on that front, so we can write the algorithm now.

ALGORITHM

Annie writes listing 5.5a.

Coach B: Let's try the following. Annie just wrote the code, but let's have someone else describe it. It can help us notice how clear the code really is. Anyone?

Rachid: I'll try. I think this is following the exhaustive search algorithm pattern we've seen before. First, she loops over all the possible values of m. This means going over all the options in the domain. Then, for each of these values of m, she has another loop, the inside loop, that checks for every lei if there are any flowers missing, or any extra flowers that need to be removed. She combines all these missing and extra flowers together and determines if this is the smallest we've seen so far. Is that how it goes, Annie?

Annie: Yes. High five!

Listing 5.5a Luau and Leis (a work-in-progress code)

```
1    int min_m;
2    int min_extra = INT_MAX;
3
4    for (int m = leis[0]; m <= leis[N-1]; ++m) {
5        int extra = 0;
6        for (int i = 0; i < N; ++i) {
7            if (leis[i] < (m - K)) {
8                extra += leis[i] - (m - K);
9            }
10           if (leis[i] > (m + K)) {
11               extra += leis[i] - (m + K);
12           }
13       }
14       if (abs(extra) < min_extra) {
15           min_extra = abs(extra);
16           min_m = m;
17       }
18   }
```

Ryan: I noticed just now, we can add a break if we find a min_extra of zero. That'll make sure we stop searching if we already found the best option.

Annie: Oh, right. My bad. Thanks for reminding us. Here, I'll add it.

And Annie updates the bottom of the code as follows:

```
if (abs(extra) < min_extra) {
    min_extra = abs(extra);
    min_m = m;
    if ( min_extra == 0 ) break; // new addition
}
```

Ryan: Do I get a high-five as well?

Annie: Yeah, assuming you're not covered in too much powdered sugar!

Annie, Rachid, and Ryan lean into a triple high-five.

Coach B: Well done. I think this will work, and the code is clear and simple. Question: What is the time complexity of this algorithm?

The team ponders.

Mei: We have a loop over all the possible values of m, which is of the order of the largest lei, given in the problem as 10^4. Then, for each of these values of m, we have a loop over all the leis to check their contributions to the extra flowers, so that means going over all N leis, which is not larger than 10^6. So I would say it is $O(10^4 \times 10^6)$. That's weird: Usually we express it in terms of N or something like that.

Coach B: You are correct on all fronts! As for the numbers, we can denote the largest lei size as L, and as you said it is given in the problem that $L < 10^4$. Then, the complexity would be $O(L \times N)$, which is still a little weird because it has two variable names rather than one. As Mei mentioned, for every value of m, we need to go over all the leis and determine the extras. That might eat up a lot of time. If we're able to reduce this check to something that doesn't need to go over all the leis, we may be able to reduce the complexity from $O(L \times N)$ to $O(L)$. Any thoughts on how we can do this?

Ryan: Are you sure we can do it? I mean, we do have to check all the leis for extra flowers, right?

Coach B: Well, you are right that we need to determine the number of extra flowers for each value of m. The question is, can we do it based on, for example, the previous value of extra flowers? Here, let me give you an example.

Visualize it: Coach B draws figure 5.15.

TIP: "Going back to the drawing board" means, metaphorically, rethinking or adjusting our entire approach. But, we can use it literally: When modifying your algorithm, don't hesitate to go back to pencil and paper, and visualize the modifications.

Coach B: I drew only part of the problem, and only two values of m. Can you find a way to compute the extra flowers for m = 10, without needing a loop?

Ryan: I think I get it. If we know that the two leis contributed 9 extra flowers when m = 9, then when we move to m = 10, each one will contribute one flower less, which means they'll contribute together only 7 extra flowers.

Mei: And in general, if we had X leis that are too large, then every time we increase m by 1, the number of extra flowers will be reduced by X. In your drawing, we just had X as two leis, so we subtracted 2 each time.

Rachid: That's very cool. And I bet something like that works for the other situation, for too-short leis. Probably we'll need to increase the number of the missing flowers every time we change m.

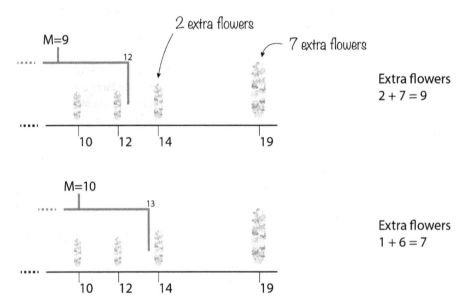

Figure 5.15 Determining extra flowers without the need to loop over all leis every time.

Coach B: Wow, what did they put in those donuts? That's amazing. I don't have anything to add. Well, no, I do. Just one more thing: Let me draw the next two steps as well.

Coach B draws figure 5.16.

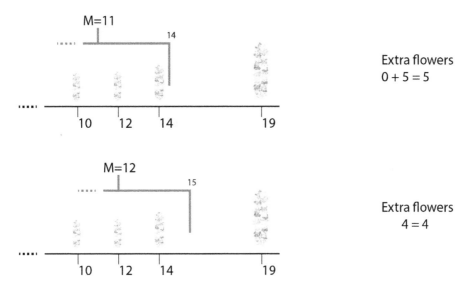

Figure 5.16 Two more cases for changing m and calculating the extra flowers.

Mei: Oh, I see. Something changes when a lei is getting into the allowed range. We don't need to subtract 2 anymore, because there's only one lei contributing to the extra flowers. So from m = 11 to m = 12, we need to subtract only 1.

Coach B: Correct. So, let's take a step back for a second, and recall why we started all these shenanigans. The instigating issue was the need to reduce complexity. In our original algorithm, we had to loop every time over all leis to determine extra flowers. With this new method, once we establish a baseline for a specific value of m, we just need to keep track of things, and then we can calculate the extra flowers for every consecutive value of m with no loop! That's a huge acceleration, agreed?

The team nods in agreement.

Coach B: So, to recap: it is still an exhaustive search process. We're still searching over all possible values of m. However, the evaluation at each value of m is now much, much simpler. This right there is one of the ways to achieve acceleration in exhaustive search algorithms.

Coach B looks at his watch.

Coach B: Okay, I see we are running out of time, but I still want you to see the code. Let me put it up really quickly.

Coach B writes the code as in listing 5.5.

Coach B: You can run the code later at home, and go over the different steps. It's pretty tricky, so make sure you take time to explore it. As you can see, we improved on our "brute-force" method of looping over all the leis to calculate the extra flowers. We now use more elaborate bookkeeping to keep track of how many leis are above and below the range. This bookkeeping requires careful coding and attention to details. The critical line in the code for this is

```
1   extra = extra - num_below - num_above;
```

and it works because:

- All of the leis below are now newly too low or one flower worse off than for the prior range, so each one takes away one of our extras.
- All of the leis above now have one fewer flower to give than for the prior range, so each one takes away one of the extras that they gave us before.

The team seems a little confused.

Coach B: Again, I know it is not simple. I recommend you run the code at home, either with a debugger or with printouts, and see how it moves over the values of m.

Listing 5.5 Luau and Leis

```
1   int num_above = 0;
2   int index_above = N;
3   int num_below = 0;
4   int index_below = 0;
5   int extra = 0;
6
7   int m0 = leis[0];
8   // At the beginning, we can only have lei's above,
9   // since we are starting with lowest possible lei size.
10  for (int i = 0; i < N; ++i) {
11      if ( leis[i] > m0 + K) {
12          num_above++;
13          index_above = min(index_above, i);
14          extra += leis[i] - (m0 +K );
15      }
16  }
17
18  int min_m;
19  int min_extra = INT_MAX;
20
21  for (int m = leis[0] + 1; m <= leis[N - 1]; ++m) {
22      while (leis[index_below] < m - K && index_below < N) {
23          index_below++;
```

```
24          num_below++;
25      }
26
27      while (leis[index_above] < m + K && index_above < N) {
28          index_above++;
29          num_above--;
30      }
31      // Update the number of extra flowers.
32      extra = extra - num_below - num_above;
33      if (abs(extra) < min_extra) {
34          min_extra = abs(extra);
35          min_m = m;
36      }
37  }
```

Coach B: Any questions before I send you off to the weekend?

Ryan: Can we have another donut please? There are a few left in the box.

Coach B: Oh, take another, but give it to a friend. Make their day. I don't want you to give yourself a sugar crash. Okay, I'll put a few practice problems on the club's page. Remember, you've got to work through those problems if you want to get good at accelerations. Have a great weekend!

EPILOGUE

Accelerating an exhaustive search algorithm can be done in two ways: reducing the size of the domain so we do not have to search so many options, and reducing the evaluation time of each option so we reduce the overall computation time. In this example, we focused on the latter, reducing the evaluation time. There are no hard and fast rules on how to find these acceleration methods. Each problem requires its own examination and understanding, but the more problems you do, the more familiar you become with possible methods.

VOCABULARY Corner: **ORACLE** In myths, an oracle was a person who offered a prophecy, usually coming from a divine source. Even today, we sometimes refer to people who predict the future (correctly or incorrectly!) as oracles. In algorithm development, it sometimes helps to postulate, "If we had an oracle that told us some key fact that's missing, could we then solve the problem?" If your answer is yes, you can try to create such an oracle in an algorithm. For example, in our last problem, we started exploring the solution, saying, "If we know the value of m, can we find how many flowers are moved around?" In essence, we're asking, "If an oracle tells us m, can we solve the problem?"

PRACTICE PROBLEMS

Hints and full solutions to the problems can be found on the club's page: http://www. usacoclub.com

1. USACO 2016 Open Bronze Problem 3: Field Reduction

   http://usaco.org/index.php?page=viewproblem2&cpid=641

   This problem will be revisited in the chapter on Geometry.

   a. You get a clear hint in the problem statement itself that acceleration is needed: "Finally, note that since N can be quite large, you may need to be careful in how you solve this problem to make sure your program runs quickly enough!"

   b. You do need an exhaustive search here, namely removing one cow at a time.

   c. If you do not find any way to accelerate it, go ahead and implement the brute-force method. You will get partial credit.

   d. The saving will happen if you efficiently evaluate the new resulting area after a cow is removed.

   e. Hint: Keep track of the two largest and smallest values in each dimension. If a cow that is removed caused the maximum (or minimum) value in this dimension to change, you just need to use the second-largest (or second-smallest) cow, which you already have saved.

2. USACO 2014 December Bronze Problem 1: Marathon

   http://usaco.org/index.php?page=viewproblem2&cpid=487

   a. This problem is very similar to the tiki torch problem.

   b. Solving this problem directly will require looping on each relevant checkpoint, and calculating the course distance with this checkpoint removed.

   c. Without acceleration, your program will fail for some test cases.

   d. Hint: To accelerate the computation, for each checkpoint, you can calculate the distance *saved* by its removal.

   e. Figure 5.17 is the drawing for the sample input. Remember: we are using Manhattan distance, and Bessie has to visit the checkpoints in order.

   f. Figures 5.18 and 5.19 demonstrate the accelerated way of calculating distance saved, which searches for the checkpoint to omit.

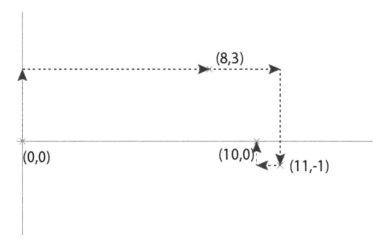

Figure 5.17 Drawing the whole course depicted in the sample input for Marathon.

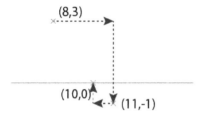

```
distance_ran =
{ from (8,3) to (11,-1) } + { from (11,-1) to (10,0) } =
{   | 8-11| + |3-(-1)|  } + {    |11-10| + |(-1)-0|   } = 9
```

Figure 5.18 Distance to run when the checkpoint (-11,1) is included.

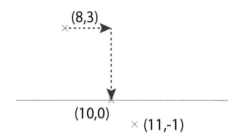

$$\texttt{distance\_ran = \{ from (8,3) to (10,0) \} =}$$
$$\texttt{\{ |8-10| + |3-0| \} = 5}$$

Figure 5.19 Distance to run when the checkpoint at (-11,1) is omitted.

3. USACO 2014 Open Bronze Problem 1: Odometer

   http://usaco.org/index.php?page=viewproblem2&cpid=430

   a. This problem is hard for many reasons:

   - You need to work with large numbers, long long in C++.
   - An exhaustive search, i.e., simply going over all numbers from X to Y and checking each one of them, would fail on time constraints.
   - Depending on your implementation, you might need to work with Strings and convert these to long long numbers.

   b. An alternative to exhaustive search: You can generate all the relevant interesting numbers, and check if they are in the specified range.

5.5. Greedy Algorithms

So far, we have used the exhaustive search algorithm to solve searching problems. Exhaustive search's main advantage is that it is guaranteed to find the right answer, but its big disadvantage is a long execution time. The greedy algorithm, on the other hand, is often very fast, and will find an answer, but it might not be the right one. For example, recall the tiki torch problem we did earlier, in section 5.1. Removing the torches at locations 8, 10, 16, and 20 yielded maximum distances of 9, 8, 10, and 7, respectively. The correct answer, using an exhaustive search, was to remove the torch at location 20, to achieve a maximum distance of 7. The greedy algorithm might have searched from left to right, stopping just before the maximum distance increases. This would lead us to stop at a maximum distance of 8, since the next distance is 10 which is larger. Though the greedy solution of 8 is definitely better than some other options, it is not the best solution if we were to keep on searching.

For the Bronze level, the greedy search algorithm is the only additional search algorithm you need to know. As you advance through the levels of USACO, you will learn many other search algorithms.

Coach B: Welcome back! It's our last session in the unit on search problems. Today we will explore a different search algorithm, or maybe we can call it a different search concept, called the greedy algorithm. It is called greedy because it chooses the best option for right now, and not considering what will happen down the road. In other words, the algorithm does not consider all possible options, but rather looks at only some of the options, and decides accordingly.

Rachid: So maybe we should call it a hasty, or impatient, algorithm?

Coach B: Yes, that would also be an appropriate name. Or maybe a nickname? Now, a greedy algorithm, as its new nickname implies, is much faster than an exhaustive one, but it may miss the optimal answer sometimes. I think an example can clarify. Without further ado, here's the problem! Go ahead and read it, and then let's hear your thoughts.

Problem 5.5: Kayaking

The beaches in Hawaii are great, and an exciting way to explore them is in a kayak. Bessie and her friends are heading to the kayak rental shop for a group tour. The group has N cows, $1 < N < 10^5$. Each cow weighs x_i, a positive integer less than 10^3. The sign on the rental shop says that each kayak can accommodate up to two cows, with a total weight not to exceed W.

Determine the minimum number of kayaks the group needs to rent.

Input Format

Two lines.

The first line contains two integers: N, W.

The second line contains N integers denoting the weight of each cow, $x_1, x_2, \ldots, x_N$, where $x_1 \leq x_2 \leq x_3 \leq \ldots \leq x_N$.

Output Format

One number, the minimum number of kayaks the group needs to rent.

Sample Input

```
5 10
2 4 5 7 9
```

Sample Output

```
3
```

One kayak will hold the cow of weight 9, the second will hold two cows weighing 7 and 2, and the third will hold the cows weighing 5 and 4.

DISCUSSION

Ryan: I can see why this is a search problem. We're looking for the best distribution of cows in the kayaks, so that we need to rent the minimal number of kayaks.

Rachid: So, for an exhaustive search we can go over all possible assignments of cows to kayaks, and for each one of these we check if it keeps the weight limit. From those that do follow the weight limit, we just take the best one. And that'll be the one requiring the minimum kayaks to rent.

Coach B: That sounds great. Two things to verify first. First, how do you go through all possible assignments? And second, how many arrangements are there?

The team puts their heads together. They try to figure these questions out by starting with only 3 or 4 cows. But then, things get messy. They can't see a pattern emerging.

Coach B: Okay, let me be the bearer of bad, and good, news. The bad news: There is no easy way to answer either of the questions I posed. First, to go over all possible arrangements of cows into kayaks requires intricate programming, using permutations and set concepts, which are beyond the scope of Bronze. Second, the number of arrangements grows very large very fast. And again, estimating it is beyond the scope of Bronze.

Rachid: No wonder we couldn't find any path through. Give us the good news!

Coach B: Right you are, Rachid. The good news is that a greedy algorithm can help us to solve this! Let's see how a greedy algorithm works in this case.

Visualize it: Coach B goes to the board and draws figure 5.20.

Weights   2   4   5   7   9

Figure 5.20 The cows' weights.

Coach B: I just wrote down the cows, and remember they are given in order of weight. Let's start from the heavy side. For the cow that weighs 9: Is there any other cow that can share a kayak with her?

Annie: No. The lightest cow is 2, and even adding her would bring the total over our weight limit of 10.

Coach B: Okay, so we can put the cow weighing 9 in her own kayak.

He draws figure 5.21.

Figure 5.21 The cow with weight 9 gets a kayak of her own.

Coach B: Now for the next cow, with weight 7. Is there any cow that can share the kayak with her?

Mei: Yes, the cow that weighs 2 can share with her. The total will be 9.

Coach B draws figure 5.22.

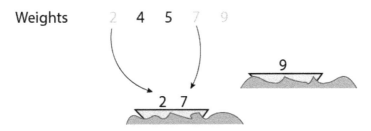

Figure 5.22 The next two cows can share a kayak.

Coach B: And now the last two can certainly fit together, 5 and 4, right?

He completes the set by drawing figure 5.23.

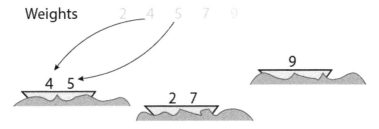

Figure 5.23 The next two cows can share a kayak.

Coach B: And here it is, this is our solution: 3 kayaks are needed. Now that we've seen an example, can anyone describe what they think a greedy algorithm is?

Mei: I'll try to generalize from the example we saw. The greedy algorithm doesn't look over every single option. It chooses, or builds, one option that works, and this is the answer. It doesn't bother comparing this to other options.

Coach B: That's pretty close to the official definition, so it's a classic example of a greedy algorithm. Very nice. But I want us to notice that, just on a smaller local scale, we are, in fact, making a decision and considering different options. What I mean is that in every step, we actively chose which cow to put on a kayak, the heaviest we had left—and we checked if we could add a second cow to the same kayak. In some sense, at every junction, we made a decision based on what we knew right then and continued. We never went back to modify this decision. This decision process that we made, of taking the heaviest cow, is called a heuristic. If you have a good heuristic, your greedy algorithm may perform well.

 TIP: The greedy algorithm depends on a heuristic, or decision, that you make at each point. Not all heuristics guarantee that you'll find the best solution, but better heuristics have a better chance of finding a solution closer to the optimal one.

ALGORITHM

Coach B: So, what would the code for this greedy algorithm look like? Any volunteers?

Annie goes to the board and writes the code as in listing 5.6.

Annie: The index `top_cow` always points to the heaviest cow we didn't assign yet. Similarly, `bot_cow` points to the lightest. On every turn, we make sure to assign the heaviest cow to a kayak, so we need to increase our answer by one, as well as move `top_cow` down by one, since we have just assigned the heaviest cow. Then, we try and fit the `bot_cow` into the same kayak. If it works, we move the `bot_cow` to the next cow in line. If not, then we don't assign the `bot_cow`, and we move to the next heaviest one that we didn't assign yet.

Listing 5.6 Kayaking

```
1   int answer = 0;
2
3   int top_cow = N - 1;
4   int bot_cow = 0;
5
6   while (top_cow >= bot_cow) {
7       answer++;
8       int cow1 = weight[top_cow];
9       top_cow--;
10      if (cow1 + weight[bot_cow] <= W) {
11          bot_cow++;
12      }
13  }
```

Coach B: Very nice solution, Annie. You remembered the two pointers method from Section 3.2! You are making use of two indices pointing into the same array, one moving from the top downward, and one moving from the bottom upward. That's an advanced technique that we will be using in other cases, and you demonstrated it here very nicely. Well done! Any questions, anyone?

Ryan: Whenever we have room to put an additional cow, we choose the lightest cow possible to add. Wouldn't it be better to check if we can add any heavier cow?

Coach B: Interesting point. I see your logic: We want to put as much weight as we can on each kayak. But you need to keep in mind that we do have to put all the cows on kayaks. Here is how I would explain it. We do have to put this light cow on a kayak, right? So let's say we were able, instead of putting this cow, to put a heavier cow on the kayak. Would it gain us anything? Not really. Because either of these two cows could have gone on this kayak, and they could have interchangeably gone on any future kayak. And both should be on a kayak at the end. Does this make more sense now?

Ryan: Sort of. I think the point is, as you said, that if we can put a heavier cow on this kayak, then we will need to put the lighter on a future kayak, so it won't really buy us anything. Yes, I think I get it.

 TIP: Using two indices to point into the same array, or the same list, is a common coding pattern. We will use it in more advanced algorithms at the Silver level and beyond, for example, in the binary search algorithm. However, even in Bronze, knowing this technique and using it when appropriate can simplify your code.

Annie: I am not sure this will fit into your lesson plan, but do you have any simple examples where a greedy algorithm doesn't work?

Coach B: That's an excellent question, Annie! Thanks for bringing this up. Let's look at one of those examples, because it'll help you understand greedy algorithms better. Here's a classic one where a greedy algorithm isn't going to work.

Sample Problem: Knapsack Problem (we will use a piece of luggage instead)

You are packing for your flight. You can check one piece of luggage, and the rest you need to take as carry-ons. The weight of your checked luggage cannot exceed 20 kg. You have four items to take with you:

A boom box–17 kg

A stack of books–8 kg

A laptop–6 kg

Hiking boots–5 kg

Which items should you pack in the luggage, so your carry-on weight is minimal?

Coach B: I think the problem is simple and clear. Is it?

Ryan: Yes, you want to pack as much weight as possible in the luggage, so whatever is left out, and you have to carry it yourself, is minimal.

Coach B: Correct. Now, what would a greedy algorithm do?

Mei: It would take the heaviest one, the 17 kg boom box, and put it in. Then, it will look at the biggest item it can still fit in. Since there's only room for another 3 kg item, and all our items are heavier than that, we can't fit anything more.

Coach B: Right. So the total weight in the luggage is 17 kg, and the total weight we need to carry ourselves is $8 + 6 + 5 = 19$ kg. Agreed?

Everyone nods.

Coach B: But is this the optimal solution? Can we do better than carrying 19 kg?

He pretends to hold heavy items on each shoulder, staggering under their weight.

Rachid: Yes, we can do better! Don't injure yourself! We can put the stack of books in our checked luggage, which is 8 kg so far, then add the laptop and the hiking boots, which brings the total to 19 kg packed in the luggage. Then, all we need to carry is only the 17 kg boom box.

Coach B: Exactly. So you see? We were greedy, we put the heaviest thing in first, and since our greedy algorithm didn't try any other options, we didn't find the optimal solution.

Annie: So how do you solve this problem with the luggage? It seems like the only other option is an exhaustive search.

Coach B: I see what you mean! And yes, an exhaustive search will always find the optimal solution, but it is often not practical. This problem only involved a handful of items, but that's not very realistic, is it? For example, when you're packing products in containers for shipping overseas, there are hundreds or thousands of items to pack in each container. And let's say we want to pack the containers to be as heavy as possible, to make the best use of the ship. There are way too many options. An exhaustive search just wouldn't be feasible. The common way to solve this problem is with dynamic-programming methods, which are beyond the scope of Bronze.

Annie: Alright, let's do it that way!

Coach B: Soon! You'll get to learn these for the Silver level. I'm happy it piqued your interest. Yes, there are interesting things to come.

The team is excited.

Coach B: Okay, then we'll wrap up for today. Great job, everyone. Now you know the greedy algorithm. And its limitations! I'll post the practice problems. Next week we start a new unit!

EPILOGUE

This section introduced greedy searching algorithms. Because these don't check all the options, they might miss the optimal solution. However, they work very fast, and in some problems they do give the right solution.

At Bronze level, consider first an exhaustive search approach, possibly with some of the acceleration methods we studied. If the number of options is too large, or the time required to check each option is too long, then that's the time when you should resort to a greedy algorithm.

When designing one, you always need to consider: "What's the one decision that I should make at each step?" After you implement it, if your algorithm fails, you can always try to design a different greedy algorithm using a different decision process, for the same problem.

 VOCABULARY Corner: **HEURISTIC** A heuristic is an argument or a decision that relies on intuition or an analogy to other cases, rather than on a rigorous argument. This term derives from the Greek *heuriskein*, which means "to seek, to discover, or to invent," and indeed a heuristic is a way to discover a solution, by making a choice. For example, a grandmaster chess player—the human kind—might make choices by prioritizing the safety of the king, or the centrality of a pawn. And so the first computer chess programs relied on heuristics based on those same intuitive principles. The programs were given the rules to follow, and they obeyed. But, like a novice chess player, these heuristic programs ran the risk of oversimplifying things: of making errors by always obeying the rules when a grandmaster would have bent the rules instead. That's why today's computer chess programs rely on rigorous searches among many possible options, and very few heuristics.

PRACTICE PROBLEMS

Hints and full solutions to the problems can be found on the club's page: http://www.usacoclub.com

Coach's note: We start with two problems from CSES and Codeforces, as these are simpler. Greedy algorithms are often considered an advanced topic in USACO Bronze, so those problems are not simple. We do give three of those.

1. CSES, Sorting and Searching : Ferris Wheel

   https://cses.fi/problemset/task/1090

   a. Very similar to the kayaking problem.
2. Codeforces, Round #587 (Div. 3) Problem B: Shooting

   https://codeforces.com/contest/1216/problem/B

   a. Initially taking cans with large durability will reduce the total count.

   b. The number of cans is small, so you do not have to use sort. You can look every iteration for the remaining can with largest durability.
3. USACO 2021 Open Bronze Problem 2: Acowdemia II

   http://usaco.org/index.php?page=viewproblem2&cpid=1132

   a. Solve this with a greedy algorithm.

   b. In this context, greedy algorithm means not to look over all possible options. Rather, "whenever you find an evidence of seniority", log it in and use it.

4. USACO 2022 December Bronze Problem 3: Reverse Engineering

http://usaco.org/index.php?page=viewproblem2&cpid=1253

a. Use a greedy algorithm.

b. If you can figure out a way to reverse-engineer one bit, go ahead and do it.

c. Remember to mark "done" on the rows that can be explained by this bit, so you do not have to consider these again.

5. USACO 2016 February Bronze Problem 1: Milk Pails

http://usaco.org/index.php?page=viewproblem2&cpid=615

a. Would a greedy algorithm work here? Try a few examples of your own.

b. Try this example: 4 9 24.

c. If the greedy method doesn't work, you can always resort to an exhaustive search.

5.6. Summary

- **Search problems** can be hard to identify. They come in many shapes and forms, and often are presented as optimization problems. In optimization problems, we search for a parameter of a process to achieve the best outcome.
- To identify a search problem, try asking yourself the following questions.

  - Could you try different values, and see which one works best? If it seems possible, then maybe you can search over all these values.
  - Would an oracle allow you to solve the problem? That is, if someone appeared, poof, to magically reveal to you the value of the parameter, would you be able to evaluate how good this value is? If yes, then you can build an exhaustive search going over all possible values from the oracle.
  - What's the first decision you'd need to make to solve the problem? For example, taking the heaviest cow. If you kept making this same type of decision again and again, would that lead you to the solution? If yes, maybe a greedy algorithm is possible.

- At the Bronze level, we solve search problems with two main types of algorithms: exhaustive searches and greedy algorithms.
- **Exhaustive searches** evaluate all possible options and choose the best one.

  - Determine the domain of the problem. These are the values you will search over.
  - Enumerate the domain. How are you going to go over the domain one element at a time?

- **Accelerating exhaustive searches**. We do this in two ways:

  - Choose a smaller domain. This way, you get to examine fewer options.
  - Accelerate the evaluation of each option.

- **Greedy algorithms** are based on making simple and quick decisions at each step.

    - They are usually very fast.
    - They don't necessarily guarantee an optimal solution (they work only for some problems!).
    - You may get a better result with a greedy algorithm if you design a new one using a different greedy decision.

Chapter 6. Geometry Concepts

This chapter covers

- Recognizing what geometry problems are in the context of USACO.
- Breaking down geometry concepts that appear in USACO problems about searching and modeling.
- Solving geometry problems in one and two dimensions that involve points, lines, line segments, rectangles, and coordinate grids.
- Using and calculating Manhattan distance.
- Analyzing problems that include a circle as a geometric concept, and applying the appropriate concepts and tools.
- Recognizing geometric concepts for more involved shapes and settings, such as the perimeter of an enclosed area.

Geometry problems rely on coordinates to describe a configuration in space. At the Bronze level, these problems are typically limited to dealing with basic geometric shapes such as lines, line segments, rectangles, and two-dimensional grids. As such, the quantities of interest are often distance and area. There are, of course, exceptions to this generalization. For example, some problems require you to find the perimeter of a two-dimensional shape, or the direction of travel on a grid, or even the number of possible paths. The key to all these problems is a strong grasp of the one- and two-dimensional concepts that they're built on.

In fact, when you understand these basic geometric structures, you're better able to solve many problems that, at first glance, do not even appear to have any geometrical component. For example, consider a problem that asks you to determine the amount of time during which there are two or more lifeguards on duty, given the start and end times of all shifts. Even though there is no direct mentioning of a line or geometry, this problem is equivalent to a geometrical question about the overlap of line segments. In this case, each time interval, a lifeguard shift, is a line segment. That concept of overlapping line segments is one we will dive deep into in section 6.1.2. Thus, understanding the underlying geometrical structure will be beneficial in many USACO problems. And this holds true for the more advanced levels as well, though the geometric constructs get more involved, e.g., graphs and meshes.

Our chapter structure follows this progression and is shown in figure 6.1. It starts with one-dimensional problems in section 6.1, covering three basic geometric quantities: location, length, and distance. We first discuss these three quantities, then we consider interactions between multiple line segments.

In section 6.2, we consider two-dimensional settings, meaning we deal with rectangles and areas. You'll need extra finesse to deal with interactions between two rectangles, since in two dimensions, compared to one, there are many more possible configurations of two objects.

The chapter continues with a discussion of less common shapes and other quantities of interest. Section 6.3 starts with problems involving circles. Although a circle is inherently a one-dimensional line closing on itself, it has interesting implications for even the most basic geometric quantities. For example, if you are moving on a circle, there are two ways to get from one point to the other. And one of these ways might be shorter than the other. This is very different than moving along a straight line, where there is only one way to get from one point to another. After exploring circles, we then move to polygonal shapes in two dimensions. These shapes might be defined using a descriptive construction process or through a drawing, and the problems related to these shapes can vary quite a bit. For example, you may need to determine a shape's perimeter, or its orientation.

After reading this chapter, you will be well equipped to solve geometric problems in USACO Bronze, and even beyond that, you will have the tools to recognize geometric concepts in other types of USACO problems, such as search problems and modeling problems.

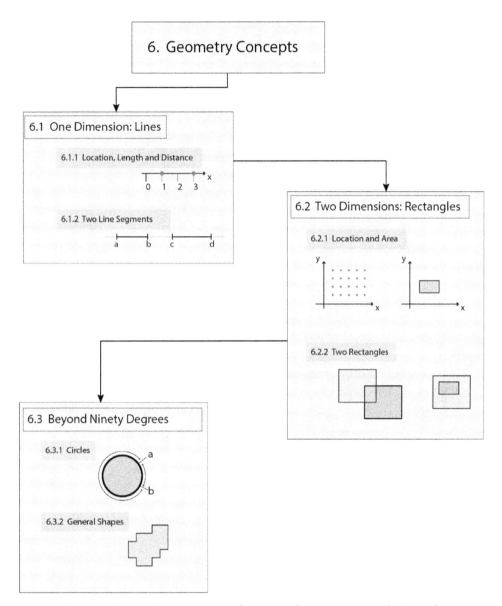

Figure 6.1 Geometry Concepts chapter map. From lines in one dimension, to rectangles in two dimensions, and to general shapes in two-dimensional space.

6.1. One Dimension: Lines

We start our geometry chapter with problems involving the simplest geometry construct we will deal with: a straight line in a one-dimensional space. This is a very common setting for USACO problems, so once you understand it, you can handle many USACO problems.

These problems deal with quantities we are very familiar with, like location and distance. However, familiar does not mean simple, and throughout this section we will elaborate on different aspects of these quantities.

6.1.1. Location, Length and Distance

It's Tuesday, and the team meets for the weekly practice session.

Coach B: Welcome everyone! Today we are starting a new unit on geometry problems. And, we'll start from the very beginning: lines and points.

Annie: Geometry?!?! Ahhhhh, no, no, no, no, no... Are we going to do proofs?

Rachid: ... and memorize theorems?

Coach B smiles.

Coach B: No, no, no worries about that. No proofs, and you don't need to memorize theorems or definitions. Remember, this is USACO, so we are focusing on problem solving, algorithms, and coding proficiency. But, you will need to draw a lot. Well, we do it all the time, but even more so in these problems.

The team relaxes: USACO problems are familiar turf. Now, let's see how geometry fits into the mix.

Coach B: Let's look at the first problem that takes place on a line, and you'll see what I mean. A point on a line is described by a single coordinate or location x. If we have two points, denoted x_1 and x_2, we can also define an order between them: a point can be larger than, equal to, or smaller than another point. In addition, one can calculate the distance between two points, which is the length of the segment connecting them. The first problem revolves around the calculation of distance.

Coach B projects problem 6.1 on the board.

Coach B: Oh, it seems Bessie and the crew reached San Francisco, so I guess the problem takes place on a line located within San Francisco. Please go ahead and read the problem, and we'll discuss it.

Problem 6.1: Walk or Bus?

Bessie visits San Francisco and enjoys Market Street. Market Street can be modeled as a straight number line stretching from coordinate 0 to coordinate 100. Bessie is at point a on the street. She wants to visit another location on the street, point b. She can either walk directly from point a to point b, or take advantage of the bus. The bus has stops at points c and d, and it goes back and forth between these two points.

Determine the shortest distance Bessie needs to walk to get from point a to point b.

Input Format

One line with 4 integers: a, b, c, d.

All integer values are in the range 0...100.

Output Format

One number, the minimum distance Bessie needs to walk.

Sample Input

20 70 10 85

Sample Output

25

The shortest route is walking from coordinate 20 to the bus station at 10, riding the bus to the station at 85, and then walking from 85 to 70, for a total distance of $10 + 15 = 25$ units.

DISCUSSION

Coach B: Clearly a geometry problem, right? As the problem describes, we have a straight line with four points on it: The start and end points, a and b, and the bus stops, c and d. And the quantity of interest is distance. Who's up for drawing our first geometry problem?

Visualize it: Mei walks to the board and draws figure 6.2, including the bus glyph.

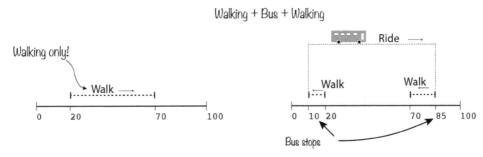

Figure 6.2 Walk or Bus? Two options are presented. Walking directly is 50 units from start to end. Taking the bus requires only 25 units of walking.

Mei: I first drew the walking-only option. Starting from point a and walking to point b. This entails a walking distance of 50. Then, I drew the option where Bessie uses the bus. This involves walking to the station, from 20 to 10, and then walking from the station at 85 to the end at 70. The total walking in this case is $10 + 15 = 25$. So, the shortest option is definitely 25 units.

Coach B: Nice and simple. Any special cases we need to be aware of?

Ryan: If the start and end are the same point, then the walking distance is 0. But I think that's not a big issue. It will come out anyway when we calculate the distance between a and b.

Coach B: Correct, Ryan. Indeed, the problem doesn't say that they are different, so a walking distance of zero is a valid answer. Nice. Any other special cases?

Ryan, Mei, and Rachid all shrug to signal the problem seems pretty simple, and that no additional special cases come to mind.

Annie: Now that I think about it, what if b is less than a? I mean, the question doesn't specify that either, right? Let me explain. At least the way I thought of finding the distance for walking directly from a to b was to calculate the difference $b - a$. However, if b is less than a we will get a negative number.

Coach B: Very good point, Annie. Distance cannot be negative. And how can we solve it?

Rachid: We can check if b is less than a, in which case we'll calculate the difference $a - b$, to make sure distance is positive.

Annie: Or, we can take the absolute value of the difference, to make sure it is always positive.

Coach B: You are both correct. The important thing is to make sure distance is positive. I think taking the absolute value would keep the code cleaner, but it is up to you.

 TIP: Distance should always be positive. You can ensure a positive result by taking the absolute value whenever you calculate distance. Alternatively, you can check which point is larger before subtracting.

Ryan: Wait. If we don't know that a is less than b, what can we say about how the bus stops are arranged or located? For example, how do we know which bus stop is closer to the start? And maybe both stops are closer to the start than to the end? I totally confused myself now. I thought this was a simple problem!

Coach B: Very good, Ryan. That's a very good point, pun intended! The problem is simple to describe and understand, but it is not easy to solve. We need to be careful. Does everyone understand Ryan's point?

Everyone nods, understanding the issue but confused about how to fix it.

Coach B: Great. Understanding the issue is the first step. The next step is to solve it. Any thoughts?

Rachid: We can check which bus stop is closest to the start and walk there. This is just adding an "if" statement.

Coach B: Yes, we can do that. Beware, though, that too many conditional "if" statements tend to make for a convoluted code. I think you can get away with using one more "if" statement in this simple problem. But, how about a little challenge? Let's see if we can find a way to solve this without even a single "if" statement. Can we do that?

Rachid: Well, we can always calculate the two options and take the shorter one. I mean, one option is that we go from point a to the bus stop at c, and the other is that we walk from point a to the bus stop at d.

Rachid goes to the board and draws figure 6.3.

```
Route I  :  a ──▶ Walk to ──▶ c ┈┈┈▶Bus ride ┈┈┈▶  d ──▶ Walk to ──▶ b

Route II :  a ──▶ Walk to ──▶ d ┈┈┈▶Bus ride ┈┈┈▶  c ──▶ Walk to ──▶ b
```

Figure 6.3 Consider the two different bus options. In the first route, Bessie is going from the start to bus stop c. In the second route, she goes from the start to bus stop d.

Coach B: Thanks, Rachid. Yes, I think I like this option better than using an "if" statement. It is not too much computation to calculate both options, and it keeps the code clearer and simpler. And simpler is good: less prone to bugs!

The group nods in agreement.

Coach B: Okay, I think we are ready to write the algorithm. Ryan and Annie, why don't the two of you write it together? Make sure there are not too many "if" statements please.

 TIP: Simple code is less prone to bugs than code with many conditional statements. The more code you write, the more chances there are to misspell a condition or make a typo. These types of bugs can be very hard to fix, especially under the pressure of time during the competition. Simple and concise code is your friend.

ALGORITHM

Annie and Ryan walk to the board and write the code in listing 6.1.

Listing 6.1 Walk or Bus?

```
int dist1 = abs(a - b);  // Walk a->b
int dist2 = abs(c - a) + abs(d - b);  // Walk a->c -> Ride -> Walk d->b
int dist3 = abs(d - a) + abs(c - b);  // Walk a->d -> Ride -> Walk c->b
// Taking minimum of the three options
int ans = min(min(dist1, dist2), dist3);
```

Annie: Voila! No if's or buts.

The group smiles.

Mei: Seems a really clean and concise code. Simple and straightforward. You're calculating the three different options: one is walking directly from start to end, and the other two involve the bus. And you're using absolute value to calculate distance, and therefore you don't need any "if" statements to determine which point is larger. Lastly... you are using the minimum function, in a composed way, to get the minimum out of the three options. I might have done it in two lines of code.

Coach B: Very nice analysis, Mei, and of course thanks to Annie and Ryan for writing such great code. Any other comments or thoughts before we wrap up?

Rachid: I might be missing something, but it really looks simple and very short. How come it's so easy?

Coach B: Well, there are two things to say about it. The first, as you probably personally witnessed many times, is that USACO problems, at least at the Bronze level, often look really simple and easy after you've already found the solution. The reason is that, at the Bronze level, all you need are creative thinking, logic, and proficiency in coding. Specifically, you are not expected to know or use any advanced algorithm in order to solve a problem. Thus, you truly have all the tools to solve the problem, and once shown a solution, it seems very easy. But getting to the solution on your own might be a different story.

Rachid: Yeah, I know the feeling all too well. Too often I can't solve a problem, and then after seeing the solution, I wonder how come it is so easy.

The team nods in agreement.

Rachid: But, you did say "two things" about it seemingly so easy. What was the other thing you wanted to say?

Coach B: Yes, here's the second thing. Consider all the little issues we had to resolve in order to write such a short code block. We had to deal with how to calculate distance if the points are reversed, and to consider different configurations of the location of the bus stops. If we missed any of these, it is safe to assume some of the test cases wouldn't work. All this is to say that you learned a lot from this example: now you know that you've got to use absolute value for distance, and you've got to consider the order of the points. These are important special cases that appear time and again in USACO problems. Don't underestimate how much you learn in the process.

The team sits back, smiling.

Coach B: Okay, I hope you all enjoyed a bit of geometry. And, I hope you appreciate the subtleties of the special cases. Geometry is such a rich subject, and I really hope you'll grow to love it. It doesn't have to be about theorems and proofs. It's about elegance and solutions. I will put a few problems on the club's page to help you fall in love with the subject.

EPILOGUE

Our first geometric problem dealt with location and distance along a line. This is the most common problem to appear in the geometry category. Often, the actual USACO problem has an additional layer on top of the basic line geometry, requiring search or modeling algorithms. In all these cases, it is important to remember the fundamentals of line geometry: that distance is always positive, and that a point can exist on either side of another point, or even at the exact same location.

VOCABULARY Corner: **GEOMETRY** is a mathematical field that boasts numerous practical applications. It plays a crucial role in designing efficient road networks by determining the shortest routes between hills, calculating the optimal flight paths for airplanes while considering the Earth's curvature, and even in planning interstellar trajectories for NASA's space expeditions. No wonder the word "geometry" itself rests on two concepts: measuring (from the Greek *metria*, as in "meter") and the earth (from the Greek *gaia*, as in "geography"). Geometry enabled the ancient Greeks to measure the earth, literally. And these days, it takes us to the sky and beyond!

PRACTICE PROBLEMS

Hints and full solutions to the problems can be found on the club's page: http://www.usacoclub.com

1. USACO 2018 February Bronze Problem 1: Teleportation

   http://usaco.org/index.php?page=viewproblem2&cpid=807

   a. This problem is very similar to problem 6.1, "Walk or Bus?"

   b. Be sure to check the different possible cases for the location of the points.

2. USACO 2016 January Bronze Problem 2: Angry Cows

   http://usaco.org/index.php?page=viewproblem2&cpid=592

   a. This problem involves calculating distance on a line.

   b. This is also a search problem: You need to search among all hay bales and find the best one to start with.

   c. Hint: You can make your code much less prone to errors if you separate the progression of the explosions of hay bales into two cases: left and right.

   d. Hint: Your domain is all the hay bales, and for each one you need to model how far you can go.

3. USACO 2020 Open Bronze Problem 2: Social Distancing II

   http://usaco.org/index.php?page=viewproblem2&cpid=1036

   a. This problem involves calculating distance on a line.

   b. Determine R first, and then the number of groups.

   c. Hint: You will probably need two passes on the data:

   - A first pass to determine the largest R.
   - A second pass, using the previously determined R, to find out how many groups there are.

6.1.2. Two Line Segments

Still within the realm of one-dimensional problems and lines, we are now moving to a case involving two line segments, and how these might interact. Specifically, these two segments could overlap, touch at one point, or be completely disjointed with zero points of contact.

Coach B: Happy Tuesday, everyone! Here, I brought some rulers and papers, and there are some writing instruments in the box over there. We are continuing with geometry problems, and it's really important to practice drawing things out. We always do this in USACO problems, but it is especially important in geometry problems. You don't really have to use the rulers, freehand is totally fine, but I know some feel more comfortable with these, so I brought a few. Oh, and I hope everyone fueled up on plenty of protein... today's problem is a doozy, even though it might not seem like it.

Ryan reaches for his backpack and takes out an energy bar. Just in case, to have in the ready.

Coach B: Okay, without further ado, here is the problem for today. This time, we are dealing not with mere points, but with line segments. Go ahead, read it, and we'll talk afterwards.

Problem 6.2: Golden Gate Bridge Patrol

Bessie is heading to walk the Golden Gate Bridge, one of San Francisco's most famous icons. The bridge can be modeled as a straight line stretching from coordinate 0 to N, where $N < 10^9$. While walking the span of the bridge and enjoying the beautiful views, Bessie notices there are two patrol officers, on bikes, going back and forth along the bridge. The first patrol officer is assigned the section between points a and b, and the other is assigned the section between points c and d.

Determine the length of the bridge covered by at least one officer.

Input Format

One line with 5 integers: N, a, b, c, d.

All integer values are in the range $0 \ldots N$, and it's given that $a \le b$ and $c \le d$.

Output Format

One number, the length of the bridge covered by at least one officer.

Sample Input

```
100 10 50 40 80
```

Sample Output

```
70
```

The two officers cover the bridge from point 10 to 80.

DISCUSSION

Coach B: Clearly a geometry problem again, right? As the problem describes, we have a straight line, and then two sections, one for each patrol officer. The quantity of interest is length. Is anyone up to drawing our first geometry test case?

Visualize it: Ryan walks to the board and draws figure 6.4.

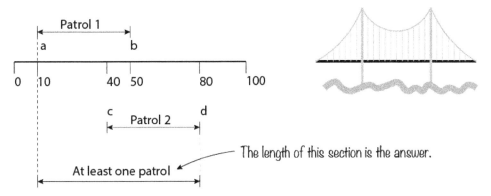

Figure 6.4 Two patrol officers on the Golden Gate Bridge. The segment covered by at least one patrol officer is from 10 to 80, for a total length of 70.

Annie: Nice drawing of the Golden Gate Bridge, Ryan.

Ryan: Thanks.

Coach B: Looks good to me. Thanks, Ryan. Any objections?

The team is happy. Looks pretty simple.

Coach B: I wonder, what do you think is the tricky part in this problem? Or maybe it's just a straightforward implementation?

Ryan: I think it is pretty much straightforward. If there's no overlap between the two segments, we just need to add the length of the two individual segments. If there is an overlap, we need to account for that, and take the two edges of the segments. But I think we can do it...

As Ryan trails off, thinking, Rachid has an idea.

Rachid: Wait, I think I have a way to do this that doesn't need any geometry at all!

Everyone turns to Rachid with puzzled looks.

Rachid: No, really. Let me show you.

Coach B: That would be great, Rachid. My hunch is that we will see three different solutions for this problem. I planned on two geometric ones, and you have yet another. Each of these with its own merits and deficiencies. Studying all three will help us appreciate the differences and consider the best scenarios in which to use each one of them. So, show us what you've got, Rachid. The board is all yours!

TIP: When practicing, a great way to gain better understanding is by solving a problem in multiple ways. This allows you to understand tradeoffs in the solutions. In competition time, practice is over, and it's crunch time: when you solve a problem, you should go to the next one. Don't try to beautify your code or examine alternatives. If it works and you got full credit for the problem, just move on. Time is of the essence.

ALGORITHM 1: BRUTE-FORCE IMPLEMENTATION

Rachid goes to the board, writes listing 6.2, and explains.

Rachid: My idea is to do a brute-force search. I'll go over each section of the bridge, which means in the middle of every unit of the bridge from 0 to N, and check if there's a patrol officer responsible for this small section. So, for example, I check at 0.5: If this falls within one of the patrol officer's sections, that means that the unit from 0 to 1 is covered. Then I check at 1.5, and so on.

Listing 6.2 Golden Gate Bridge Patrol: Brute Force

```
1   int units_covered = 0;
2   for (float x = 0.5; x < N; ++x) {
3       if ((x >= a && x <= b) ||
4           (x >= c && x <= d)) {
5           units_covered++;
6       }
7   }
```

Coach B: Very nice. I think we can all agree it is a very short code, clear, and correct! Any questions?

Everyone shakes their heads.

Annie: Really, it looks very, very simple. And effective. Do we really need to look any closer?

Coach B: Let's revisit this question after we see the other methods. Just so we don't forget, I'll start a table with the pros and cons of each of the algorithms we explore.

Coach B draws on the board table 6.1.

Table 6.1 Advantages of the brute-force algorithm for the solution of the two line segments problem. Perhaps some disadvantages, too, can be discovered.

Algorithm	Pros	Cons
Brute-force	Simple	
(a.k.a., an	Short	

Algorithm	Pros	Cons
exhaustive search)		

Coach B: The pros are clear: Simple and short. Any ideas about the cons?

Annie: Yup, it's actually evident in the table already. By definition, a brute-force algorithm means we're doing an exhaustive search over all options. This means it's a slow algorithm.

Coach B: Correct. Can you quantify it for this case?

Annie: Well, we need to go over all the units on the line, from 0 to N. For each of these we just do a simple comparison, so I would think it is $O(N)$.

Coach B: Very nice. If you recall, we did mention back then, when we talked about computational complexity, that doing more than 10^7 steps might get us into time constraints. So, in this case, with $O(N)$ complexity, and $N <= 10^9$, time constraints might be an issue. As we will see, we can do much better than $O(N)$ for this problem, so I will add it on the side of the drawbacks for this algorithm. Any other drawbacks?

The group thinks and shakes their heads.

Coach B: Okay, so let's leave it as is for now. Maybe we'll come back to this later on when we see other algorithms.

Coach B writes the time complexity into the table; see table 6.2.

Table 6.2 Adding time complexity as a drawback of the brute-force method.

Algorithm	Pros	Cons
Brute-force	Simple	Time complexity–O(N)
(a.k.a., an	Short	
exhaustive search)		

Coach B: And there we have it! Now let's pivot back to Ryan's original idea. He wants to look at the different patrol sections, and determine when there's an overlap between them. That's an example of casework.

ALGORITHM 2: GEOMETRIC CASEWORK

"Casework" is a term used to describe a method where we divide the problem into separate cases, and then we proceed to solve each case by itself. In the Golden Gate Bridge Patrol problem, for example, it means we divide the problem into a case where there *is* an overlap between the segments, and a case where there is no overlap, and solve each one separately. Finding the cases might need some work though, so let's see how the team handles it.

Coach B: Okay Ryan, and everyone. We are back to your idea of adding the length of the sections, unless they are overlapping. Was that the idea you wanted to pursue?

Ryan: Yes, but now I'm confused about how to figure out if there's an overlap... and what to do in that case.

Coach B: This is totally natural. Drawing is going to clear that confusion right up. Remember what I said? In geometry problems, drawing is your friend. Let me help you get started.

Coach B draws on the board figure 6.5.

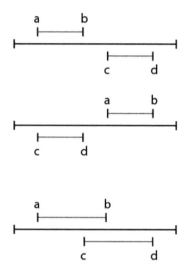

Figure 6.5 Three different cases for the relations between the two segments. Two cases where there's no overlap, and one case with overlap.

Coach B: I drew three different cases of how the two segments of the patrol officers can be positioned in relation to each other. There are three more. Can you add those?

The group goes to the board, and after some trial and error, and discussion, completes figure 6.6.

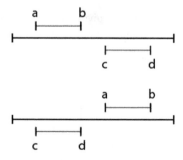

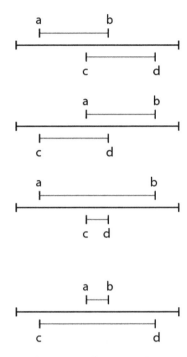

Figure 6.6 All six cases for the possible relations between the two segments.

Coach B: Very nice. These are indeed all the possible six cases. Now, let's look at the first case in detail.

Coach B points to the case in figure 6.7.

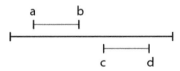

Figure 6.7 A deep dive into the first case. How can we characterize it? And what will be the final answer in this case?

Coach B: How can we characterize it? I mean, can you find any "i f" statement that will be true only for this case?

The team looks puzzled.

Mei: This is the only case where the segment from a to b is completely to the left of the segment from c to d , right?

Coach B: Yes! And how about if we use the condition $if(b <= c)$? Would that be true for this case, and only for this case?

Ryan: Oh, I see now. This is the only case where b really is less than c. I didn't notice it before.

Coach B: Right. And the last piece of the puzzle: What is the answer in this case? Remember, we are looking to figure out where at least one patrol officer is covering the section.

Annie: For this case the answer would be $(b - a) + (d - c)$.

Coach B: Perfect! So here, let me put it in a table.

Coach B draws table 6.3.

Table 6.3 Organizing the casework, starting with case #1. For each case, we will write the characterizing condition, and the answer, which is the length of the bridge that is covered by at least one patrol officer.

Case #	Drawing	Condition	Answer
1	a b / c d	`if (b <= c)`	`(b - a) + (d - c)`

Coach B: And this is how casework is done. We identified six different cases. For each we find a corresponding characterization, and then we solve for this specific case. Can you fill in the rest of the cases?

The team gathers around. Filling in the fourth column, the expected answer, is easy and they do it fast. Filling in the second column, with the condition, proves to be quite tricky. After discussion and comparison, they settle on table 6.4.

TIP: When doing casework, being organized pays extra dividends. Take the time to make a chart, and you'll ensure that you've identified the cases correctly without ignoring any of them. Casework always takes time, and taking that time is always worth it.

Table 6.4 Casework for overlapping segments. In this problem, there are six different cases.

Case #	Drawing	Condition	Answer
1	a b / c d	`if (b <= c)`	`(b - a) + (d - c)`
2	a b / c d	`if (d <= a)`	`(d - c) + (b - a)`

Case #	Drawing	Condition	Answer
3		`if (a <= c && c` `<= b && b <= d)`	`(d - a)`
4		`if (c <= a && a` `<= d && d <= b)`	`(b - c)`
5		`if (a <= c &&` `d <= b)`	`(b - a)`
6		`if (c <= a &&` `b <=d )`	`(d - c)`

Coach B: Wow, that wasn't that easy, was it?

The team sighs.

Annie: Um, no, not even! But we made it! I think now we can just program this, and we have a solution.

Coach B: Indeed! Annie, can you please just walk us through one of these? Say case #3 in the table? Just to make sure we are all on the same page.

Case #	Drawing	Condition	Answer
3		`if (a <= c && c <=` `b && b <= d)`	`(d - a)`

Annie: Sure. This is the case where we have an overlap. To characterize it, we see that the edge at point a needs to be to the left of the other segment, so we put the condition $a \leq c$. Then, we need the edge at b to be inside the other segment, so we required $c \leq b$ and $b \leq d$. putting all these together we got the condition in row 3. Then, from just looking at the drawing, we see that the answer is $(d - a)$. Right?

The team nods in approval.

Coach B: Looks right! Just looking at the table, it gives you kind of reassurance with its nice thorough structure. That's part of what we call the aesthetic of algorithms and code. Remind me at the end of the lesson, and I will tell you the story of Erdős and the book of proofs.

Mei: What's that? Tell us now!

Coach B: All in good time! Take another look at the table. Should we be concerned about any special cases?

They look for a moment, then shake their heads.

Coach B: Right, I don't think we do. I mean, you drew out all possible cases and have solutions for them, so things should go smoothly, right?

The team nods.

 TIP: Often, there are multiple equivalent ways to write the conditions that characterize a case. For example, both of the following expressions would characterize the same case: "if (a <= c && d <= b)" and "if (d <= b && !(a > c))", where exclamation mark is the "not" logic operator in C++. In competition time, don't waste time trying to simplify logical expressions unless there's a good reason to do so. If the condition truly characterizes the case, you're good to go with it!

Coach B: Since we are all happy with the casework, let's go and write the code for it!

Mei goes to the board and starts writing the code as in listing 6.3. The team comes to her help by reading her the rows from the table.

Listing 6.3 Golden Gate Bridge Patrol: Geometric Casework

```
1   int units_covered = 0;
2
3   // Only *one* of the below cases will be true.
4   if (b <= c) units_covered = (b - a) + (d - c);  // case 1
5   if (d <= a) units_covered = (d - c) + (b - a);  // case 2
6   if (a <= c && c <= b && b <= d) units_covered = (d - a);  // case 3
7   if (c <= a && a <= d && d <= b) units_covered = (b - c);  // case 4
8   if (a <= c && d <= b) units_covered = (b - a);  // case 5
9   if (c <= a && b <= d) units_covered = (d - c);// case 6
```

Mei: Thanks everyone for reading the table to me. This was pretty easy; I was literally just copying the table.

Coach B: You worked hard on the table, so yes, it was straightforward. Great. Any thoughts on how this algorithm compares to the previous one? Here's that comparison table we started. Maybe you could fill in the next row.

The team goes and adds another row to the table, as in table 6.5.

Table 6.5 Adding the geometric casework algorithm.

Algorithm	Pros	Cons
Brute-force	Simple	Time complexity–O(N)
(a.k.a., an exhaustive search)	Short	
Geometric casework		Long, tedious work to prepare all cases

Mei: Well, the only thing we can say is that it was much harder! We had to work on all these cases.

The team shares a smile.

Coach B: Oh, you can say more than that for sure. What about the time complexity?

Mei: We just had to consider 6 cases. Independent of N . So that would make it $O(1)$, right?

Coach B: Yes, and that is a huge improvement in time. Even if N is very large, say 10^9, it will still require us only 6 cases to solve the problem. Isn't that amazing?

The team reluctantly agrees.

Rachid: Yeah, only 6, it was just so much work to get there.

Coach B: Okay, can you see another big advantage of this method? Or maybe better said, can you now see a drawback to the previous method?

The team looks puzzled.

Coach B: Here's a hint. What if the edges of the segments, $a, b, c,$ and d, were not integers? Would the casework method still work? Would the previous one, brute-force, still work?

The team takes several moments to consider this.

Ryan: Well, the brute-force method would definitely not work. In the code, I checked only in the middle of each unit. So, for example, if the segment were to start at a non-integer point like 0.6, and I checked at 0.5, I wouldn't know that the section from 0.6 to 1 is actually covered. The brute-force method works only if the segments' edges are integers.

Rachid: Oh, and now I see. The casework method would work regardless! It doesn't assume anything about the edges being integers.

Coach B: So what's the con for the brute-force method? What should go in the table?

Annie: The segment edges had to be integers.

The team nods in agreement, and Coach B updates the table as in table 6.6.

Table 6.6 Adding the drawback for the brute-force method that it can handle only integers.

Algorithm	Pros	Cons
Brute-force	Simple	Time complexity–O(N)

Algorithm	Pros	Cons
(a.k.a., an exhaustive search)	Short	Segment edges have to be integers
Geometric casework	Time complexity–O(1)	Long, tedious work to prepare all cases

Coach B: I know you are ready to be done with this problem, but there's still one more thing we need to do.

Annie: Why, though? The geometric casework is a fast method and works for non-integers. What else can we ask for?

Coach B: Less work for us! Remember how time-consuming it was to deal with 6 cases? And the code had six if statements. When we move to a two-dimensional setting in a couple of weeks, the number of cases to consider is much larger. Can you imagine having to deal with 18 cases?

Rachid: Oh, please no. Not eighteen!

Coach B: I totally agree, and that's why we will try and use some geometric reasoning to solve this problem in a simpler way. So, let's do some geometry! But before that, let's take a 5-minute break and go outside for some fresh air. Doing all this casework was pretty intense.

The team gladly springs out of their seats.

ALGORITHM 3: GEOMETRIC ANALYSIS

After 10 minutes, the team is finally ready to start again.

Coach B: Okay, I hope you are all re-energized for the last part. It is not going to be too long nor hard, but it does require focus. Ready?

Annie: Awake and ready!

Coach B: Great. We're about to leave the one-dimensional world for a few minutes, and look at a two-dimensional scenario.

Coach B draws figure 6.8 on the board.

Coach B: Say we want to calculate the total area of the circle and the ellipse. Since there's no overlap, it is simply the sum of the two individual areas. Agreed?

The team nods in agreement.

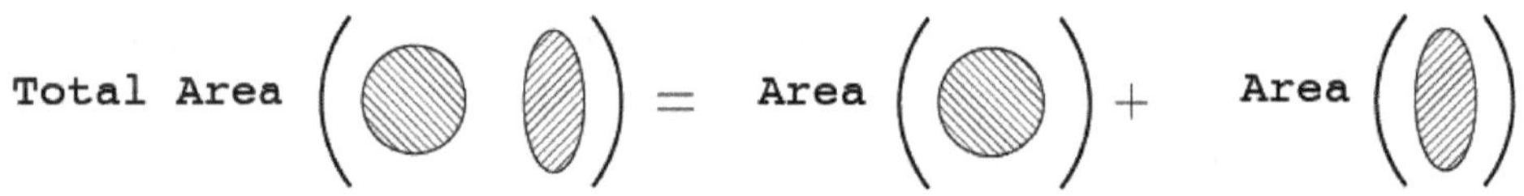

Figure 6.8 Calculating the total area of two shapes with no overlap.

Coach B: Now, say we want to calculate the total area when these two shapes have an overlap, as in figure 6.9. How do you suggest we go about this?

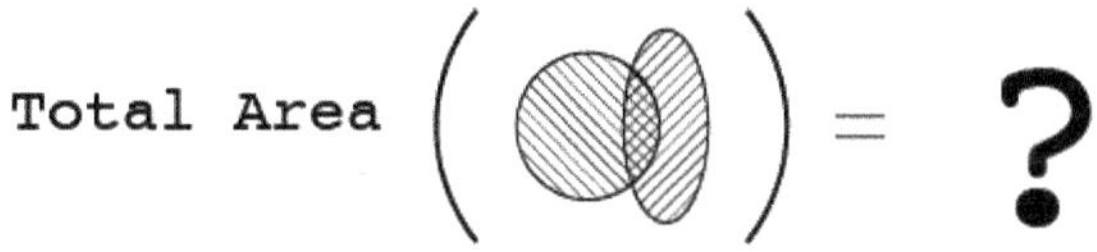

Figure 6.9 Calculating the total area of two shapes with an overlap.

Annie: Well, you need to add the two basic shapes, the circle and ellipse, and then subtract the shared part.

Coach B: Why subtract?

Annie: Because you added this part twice! You counted it in the area of the circle, and also in the area of the ellipse, so you have to subtract it. Can I draw what I mean?

Coach B hands Annie the marker, and she draws figure 6.10.

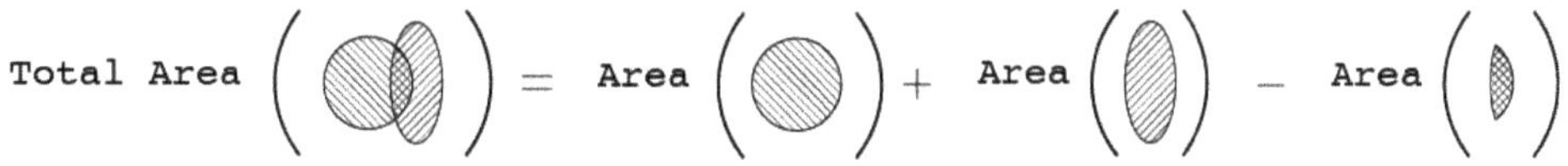

Figure 6.10 Calculating the total area of two shapes with an overlap.

Coach B: I see. This makes it much clearer. Everyone agrees?

Ryan: Yes, I think we learned something like this in grade school. Aren't these Venn diagrams?

Coach B: Good memory, Ryan. Yes, these definitely look like Venn diagrams. It's a different usage here, but the same look. Now, let's go back to our one-dimensional case of line segments. I want us to notice two things. First, we can write the total length as the sum of the individual lengths minus the overlap. Second, we can do this even if the length of the overlap is zero! Here, let me write it on the board.

Coach B draws figure 6.11, and adds three sample cases.

Coach B: We can draw all six different cases to see that it works for all of them, but I just drew three. Do you agree with this general formulation?

The team examines the drawing, and then Mei speaks up.

Gerneral formulation:

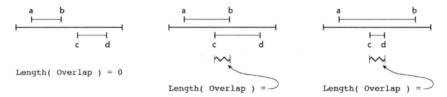

Three sample cases:

Figure 6.11 A general formulation for calculating the length of two segments, and three specific examples.

Mei: It looks perfectly fine, and makes sense. But, why would you want to subtract a zero when there's no overlap? We can just ignore the last term for this case. Can't we?

Coach B: You are absolutely correct, but there's a reason I wrote it this way. What we will now see is how we can write each of these terms without resorting to any special cases! So, rather than checking if this is the no-overlap case, I rather we *always* subtract the overlap, and in the case when there's no overlap, we simply subtract zero. Makes sense? I see you're not fully convinced. Let's do it. Let's just calculate each of the terms.

The team is still unconvinced, but is willing to play along and see where it will lead.

Coach B: What is the length of the segment a, b?

Mei: It's just $b - a$.

Coach B: Correct. And what is the length of the segment c, d?

Mei: It's just $d - c$.

Coach B: There you go, we already have two of the terms. Let me write these in figure 6.12, and then we'll calculate the overlap.

General formulation:

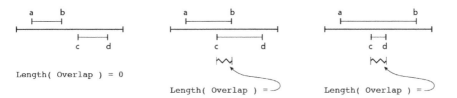

Three sample cases:

Figure 6.12 Adding the two lengths of the segments, but we still need to resolve the length of the overlap.

Coach B: Let's consider the left edge of the overlap segment. Question: Can the left edge of the overlap be to the left of edge a?

Rachid: No, because then it would be out of the first segment. It also can't be to the left of edge c.

Coach B: Good. So it cannot be to the left of either a or c. And if there is an overlap, where would the left edge be? Take a look at the drawings in figure 6.12, and the previous ones in figure 6.6. These might help.

Annie: It looks like it's always going to be the rightmost between edges a and c.

Coach B: Yes! This means we can say something like

```
left_edge_of_overlap = max(a, c);
```

Would you agree with that?

The team looks at the formula and the drawings, and checks that it works.

Rachid: Yes. When we say "to the right" we mean the larger value, so this means taking the maximum. But it doesn't make sense when there's no overlap, does it?

Coach B: Hold on to that thought, please. We'll get there. So let's look at the right edge of the overlap. Similar to before, think whether it can be to the right of either edges b or d. Then, try and find a formula similar to the one we found for the left edge.

The team thinks, and Annie writes:

```
1  right_edge_of_overlap = min(b, d);
```

Annie: The right edge needs to be to the left of the other two, so it's the minimum operator.

Coach B: I think we have it now! Let me write it all together:

```
1   left_edge_of_overlap = max(a, c);
2   right_edge_of_overlap = min(b, d);
3   length_of_overlap = right_edge_of_overlap - left_edge_of_overlap;
```

Coach B: Look at this: Isn't it beautiful? We are able to find the length of the overlap segment without any "if" statement or special cases. This formula would hold for any case.

Rachid: But then we still have to address the no-overlap case, right?

Coach B: Let's see. Can you write the result of this operation for the non-overlap case?

Rachid adds the part for the non-overlapping case in figure 6.13.

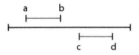

```
Length( Overlap ) = 0
```

```
left_edge_of_overlap = max( a, c );        ==>   c
right_edge_of_overlap = min( b, d );       ==>   b

length_of_overlap = right_edge_of_overlap  - left_edge_of_overlap;

==>   length_of_overlap =  b  -  c
```

Figure 6.13 Substituting values for the non-overlapping case.

Coach B: Do you notice anything special about the result?

Rachid looks, then shakes his head.

Annie comes to his rescue.

Annie: It's negative! The length is negative.

Rachid: Oh, you're right. And we said length can't be negative. So we just need to check that the overlap length is not negative.

Coach B: Can you do it without using an "i f" statement?

Rachid thinks, and adds to listing 6.4.

Rachid: Here, I can use a maximum function to make sure it's not negative. Oh, and now I see why we end up subtracting zero if there's no overlap. It's because the length of the overlap will come out to be zero in that case. Neat.

Listing 6.4: Length of Overlap Segment

```
1  left_edge_of_overlap = max(a, c);
2  right_edge_of_overlap = min(b, d);
3  length_of_overlap = right_edge_of_overlap - left_edge_of_overlap;
4  length_of_overlap = max(0, length_of_overlap);  // <== Added line
```

Coach B: We made it! Can anyone please "bring the cows home"? I mean, finish writing the code for this problem?

Ryan steps up to the task, and writes listing 6.5.

Listing 6.5 Golden Gate Bridge Patrol: Geometric Analysis

```
1  int units_covered = 0;
2  left_edge_of_overlap = max(a, c);
3  right_edge_of_overlap = min(b, d);
4  length_of_overlap = right_edge_of_overlap - left_edge_of_overlap;
5  length_of_overlap = max(0, length_of_overlap);
6  units_covered = (b - a) + (d - c) - length_of_overlap;
```

Coach B: What do you say about this? Let's fill in the comparison table and finish it up.

Ryan walks up and fills in table 6.7.

Ryan: Time complexity is again independent of N, so it's $O(1)$. Are there any disadvantages to this method?

Coach B: I don't see any. Well, we did have to spend some brain cycles to find it, and I expect you will need to always put some effort to adapt it to a specific scenario. But other than that, no real drawbacks. And in fact, we're going to see that this approach is even more valuable when we move to two dimensions. Any thoughts or questions? I can see it's getting late.

The team seems exhausted, slouching in their seats.

Table 6.7 Adding the geometric analysis method to the table.

Algorithm	Pros	Cons
Brute-force	Simple	Time complexity–O(N)
(a.k.a., an exhaustive search)	Short	Segment edges have to be integers
Geometric casework	Time complexity–O(1)	Long, tedious work to prepare all cases
Geometric analysis	Time complexity–O(1)	

Coach B: Well done, everyone! This was a real workout. We covered three different ways to get to a solution, and I think we learned a thing or two in the process. And, as you'll see in the practice problems and as we move on, this subject appears very frequently in various forms in USACO, so this was time well spent, I assure you. Okay, let me send you off.

Mei: Wait, what about Erdős? And his book thing? Weren't you going to tell us a story?

Coach B: Oh, right! Let's get to that next time. My stomach is grumbling. Thank you, and I will put the practice problems on the club's page. See you next week!

The team shuffles out of the room, with high fives and sighs of exhaustion.

EPILOGUE

We used three different methods to solve a problem involving two line segments. The first method uses a brute-force search and is very easy to code, but does not support non-integer boundaries and will fail on execution time for large N. The second method uses casework and is much more efficient in terms of execution time, but requires more coding, as each case must be handled individually. The third method, geometric analysis, showed the power of abstraction. We wrote a general formula for calculating the result, one that could accommodate all the cases. This ability to abstract and simplify will prove very useful when we deal with two-dimensional spaces later on.

VOCABULARY Corner: **PAUL ERDŐS AND "THE BOOK" OF PROOFS** Paul Erdős was a Hungarian mathematician (1913–1996), one of the most prolific mathematicians of the 20th century. He published about 1500 papers during his lifetime, with many collaborators, on a wide spectrum of mathematical subjects, including proofs and conjectures. Erdős often referred to a hypothetical book in which God would keep the most elegant proof of each mathematical theorem. This concept of a beautiful proof, or code, is something worth aspiring to. When you see a beautifully written code, one that seems glorious or even divine in its grace and ingenuity, you can imagine it coming from "The Book."

PRACTICE PROBLEMS

Hints and full solutions to the problems can be found on the club's page: http://www.usacoclub.com

1. USACO 2015 December Bronze Problem 1: Fence Painting

    http://usaco.org/index.php?page=viewproblem2&cpid=567

    a. This problem is very similar to problem 6.2, Golden Gate Bridge Patrol.

2. USACO 2018 January Bronze Problem 2: Lifeguards

    http://usaco.org/index.php?page=viewproblem2&cpid=784

    a. This is a search problem. The search domain is all cows.

    b. How do you check if no other lifeguard covers the same time slot?

    c. Hint: Create one array of length 1001, that holds all the time intervals 0 to 1000. Initially it is full of zeros, and for every cow you add one to each time interval she is covering. Then, for every time interval, you know how many cows cover it.

3. USACO 2015 December Bronze Problem 2: Speeding Ticket

http://usaco.org/index.php?page=viewproblem2&cpid=568

a. This problem discusses line segments, but you do not have to use the methods discussed here verbatim. Rather, you can use the understanding of the geometric setup.

b. This problem can be solved in a direct method, namely with no need to resort to calculating segments.

c. Hint: Create two arrays, each of length 100: in the first array fill in the speed limit in each mile, and in the second array fill in Bessie's speed in each mile.

d. The answer is the maximum difference between the corresponding elements of these arrays.

6.2. Two Dimensions: Rectangles

We are now moving from one-dimensional problems to two-dimensional problems. Each point is now described by a pair of coordinates, (x, y). The shape we most commonly encounter now, at the Bronze level, is the rectangle. Adding one more dimension adds complexity in several aspects, and we will explore these in this section. For example, in the first problem, we will encounter a new way to define distance in two dimensions.

6.2.1. Location and Area

Things are different in two dimensions. Even distance.

Coach B: Welcome back to another episode of "USACO and Geometry," and today we go on a picnic! Well, Bessie goes on one!

Annie: Wait, can we join her? Can we do this practice outside? There's a big whiteboard over near the offices on the grass. Please...

Mei: Yes! Can we?

Rachid: Picnic! Picnic!

Coach B: Sure, let's do it.

Instantly, the team grabs their laptops and bolts outside, not hearing the rest of Coach B's answer.

Coach B: I'm sure no one is going to be distracted by anything out there on this beautiful sunny day.

Under the afternoon sun, everyone settles into the soft grass, positioning their laptops away from the glare.

Coach B: Okay, here we are. I'm posting this problem on the club's page. Take a look, and once you're done, come to the whiteboard to draw it. I'll leave the marker and eraser up here.

Problem 6.3: Going Around the Fence

Bessie is looking forward to dining in the best place in San Francisco: Crissy Field! It's a huge expanse of green grass right by the beach, with views of the Bay, the Golden Gate Bridge, Alcatraz Island, and the city skyline.

Crissy Field can be imagined as a square of grass with a side measure of 100 units, aligned with an (x, y) coordinate system. Bessie arrives at location (a, y_0), and she wishes to walk closer to the beach, to the point $(a, 100)$. Bessie cannot leave the grassy field, and she moves parallel to the axes only. Due to maintenance work, there is a fence on the grass, stretching from (b, y_1) to (c, y_1). Bessie cannot climb the fence and thus might have to walk around it. The fence is of negligible thickness.

Determine the shortest distance Bessie will have to walk to get from (a, y_0) to $(a, 100)$.

Input Format

One line with 5 integers: a, y_0, b, c, y_1 .

$0 \leq a \leq 100$, and $1 \leq b, c, y_1 \leq 99$ (this ensures the fence does not abut the edge of the field)

Output Format

One number, the minimum distance Bessie needs to walk.

Sample Input

70 20 65 90 50

Sample Output

90

Recall that Bessie must walk parallel to the axes; she can't cut across the field diagonally. Her shortest route, then, is walking 30 units from $(70, 20)$ to the fence at $(70, 50)$, then passing the fence by first walking 5 units left to $(65, 50)$, and (now on the other side of the fence) back 5 units to $(70, 50)$, and finally walking 50 units straight to the destination at $(70, 100)$, for a total of $30 + 5 + 5 + 50 = 90$ units.

DISCUSSION

Coach B: How appropriate it is that we are sitting on a square patch of grass! We may be looking at the administration buildings rather than the golden beaches, but, we've still got our green square. Well, no doubt this is a geometry problem again, and it takes place in two dimensions. Any volunteers to draw this for us?

Visualize it: Mei walks to the board and draws figure 6.14.

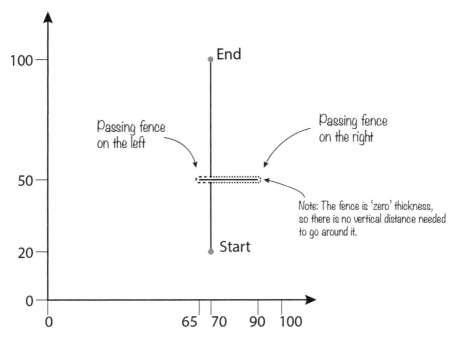

Figure 6.14 Bessie wants to go from "Start" to "End," going around the fence.

Mei: Bessie starts at $(70, 20)$, and she wants to reach the point $(70, 100)$. She goes up until she reaches the fence, and then has two options: pass it on the right or on the left. Passing on the left adds only 5 units out and 5 units back, whereas passing on the right would add two times 20 units. Obviously, going around on the left is shorter.

Coach B: Thanks, Mei. Simple and nice. Any questions or comments?

Ryan: Well, I've got a question, but... it's more of a complaint! Hear me out, though, because I'm curious. In real life, if Bessie wants to go the shortest distance, she would go diagonally. She'd go from the start to the edge of the fence, and then from the edge of the fence straight to the end. Why does the question have to impose this weird constraint that she walks parallel to the axes? It doesn't make sense to me.

Coach B: Very good question. At Bronze level, all the problems to date have used this kind of constraint. I'll open it up to the team. Why do you think this is?

Rachid: Maybe because it's easier to calculate distance this way?

Coach B: Tell us more. What do you mean by "easier to calculate"?

Rachid: Here, I'll draw it.

Rachid draws figure 6.15, and explains.

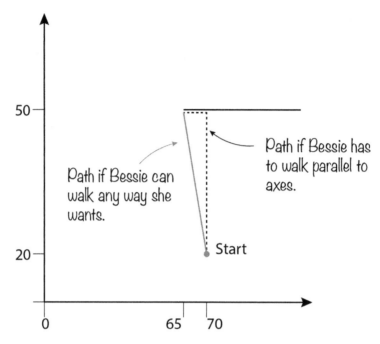

Figure 6.15 What if Bessie could walk diagonally? She can then make it a shorter distance.

Rachid: What I mean is that if she walks diagonally, we'd need to use Pythagoras to calculate the exact distance she walks. That involves squaring the two sides, and then taking the square root. That's way more involved than just subtracting integers.

Coach B: You're correct. Can you calculate both?

Rachid: The diagonal length is $\sqrt{5^2 + 30^2}$. Annie, you brought your calculator, right? Would you mind plugging that in?

Annie: It's 30.4138 and some more digits.

Rachid: Thanks. And using the two straight segments, I don't need the calculator; it's much simpler. Her walking distance would be $5 + 30 = 35$. So, what I'm saying is, Ryan was right that the diagonal path is shorter, but it's much harder to calculate.

Coach B: Very good, Rachid. And it's more than avoiding hard calculations: When we are walking parallel to the axes, we only deal with integers! That simplifies our programming and is almost always the rule in USACO Bronze. Really, I can't remember a single case that used non-integer numbers.

TIP: The vast majority of USACO Bronze problems use integer numbers. You might need to use a variable of type `long long`, rather than of type `int`, in order to accommodate large numbers. But, type `long long` are still integers.

Coach B: But moving parallel to the axes has an even deeper meaning. It is so common in mathematics and CS that it has a name. It's called Manhattan distance. Yes, that Manhattan, as in that borough of New York City. The streets there are laid out in a perfect grid. It's a very organized system! You've got avenues going north to south, and streets going east to west. Imagine using the sidewalks, or getting in a taxi to go from one place to another in Manhattan; you have to stick to avenues and streets, and you can't move diagonally. Unless you are Superman and can fly over the buildings.

Annie: You mean Supercow!

Coach B: Of course, SuperBovine! Just before we move on, I wanted to mention one of the many practical examples for using Manhattan distance. In a big warehouse, people and forklifts need to move around and collect items from the shelves. They have to move along shelves and on main aisles. They can't go diagonally, crashing through the boxes! If we want to calculate their distances within the warehouse, we will need to use Manhattan distance.

Rachid: Okay, thanks. This "parallel to the axes" thing makes much more sense now. I kinda like it because it means we get to stick with integers, anyway! But it's also just really interesting!

TIP: Manhattan distance, namely moving parallel to the axes, is the most common way of moving in two-dimensional grids in USACO Bronze.

Coach B: Agreed! It's definitely interesting how we can define different ways to move in two-dimensional space, and how these change the structure of the problem. Everyone gets the idea, right? Moving only up, down, left, and right, and never diagonally, when you're using Manhattan distance?

The team nods.

Coach B: Great! Then, try this out. I've got a question for you. When we're using Manhattan distance, that is, when we're walking parallel to the axes, how does that influence our view of the space?

The team is quiet as they look at each other.

Ryan: Our view of the space? What does that mean?

Coach B: Here, I'll draw a grid on the board. There's the origin, $(0,0)$. And over here I'll draw one point. Can you tell me, what's its distance, specifically its Manhattan distance, from the origin?

Coach B draws figure 6.16 (a).

Mei follows and draws one path from the origin to the point.

Mei: The distance is 6.

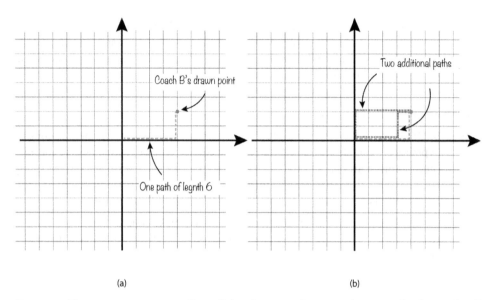

(a)   (b)

Figure 6:16 There are many ways to walk parallel to the axes and arrive at the point. The shortest for all these is length 6.

Coach B: Is there any other path, parallel to the axes, that could get me to the same point?

Rachid joins in, and draws two more paths, as in figure 6.16 (b).

Rachid: There are actually even more. I just drew two of them.

Coach B: Yes, very good. And it is interesting to note that as long as you go parallel to the axes, the distance you walk on all these paths is the same, 6 units.

The team looks and absorbs the information.

Coach B: Okay, now go ahead and take turns, and mark all the grid points that are 6 units away from the origin. I know, it sounds like busy work. But trust me. We'll see something interesting.

The team uses a few markers, and eventually produces figure 6.17 (a).

Coach B: Well done. Many points. Now watch what happens when we connect all these dots.

And Coach B draws figure 6.17 (b).

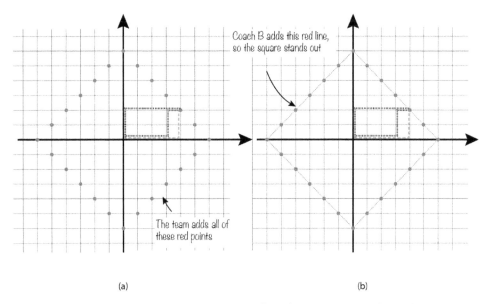

Figure 6.17 All the points that are exactly 6 units from the origin, using Manhattan distance.

Coach B: Now, what do we call a shape that has all its points the same distance from the center?

Annie: That's a circle!

Coach B: Correct! And if we use Manhattan distance to find all the points the same distance from the center, what shape do we end up with?

Annie: A rotated square?

Coach B: Yes! Isn't that strange: we know what a circle is in our normal two-dimensional space. Now, we defined a new kind of distance, and as a result, the circle looks different.

Ryan: We literally squared the circle! Ha ha, it's like we're living in Minecraft.

Coach B: Indeed. We won't dwell on it much more. But I just wanted to give you a taste and see how defining a distance gives a different shape to a space.

The team still stares at the board in amazement. A circle that looks like, and basically is, a square.

Coach B: Okay, I think now you have a better grasp of Manhattan distance and what interesting things it can add to our space. For now, let's try and finish our problem. Any special cases with Bessie or the fence?

The team ponders.

Annie: If we don't hit the fence at all, that's probably a special case. Here, I'll draw it.

Annie draws figure 6.18.

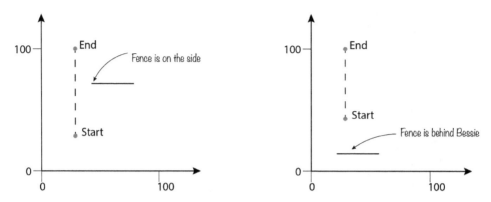

Figure 6.18 Special cases where Bessie misses the fence altogether.

Coach B: Thank you, Annie, for including both cases where Bessie misses the fence. Now, let's do this. Let's write the algorithm!

ALGORITHM

Coach B: So what would the algorithm look like?

Rachid: I would first check if I hit the fence. If I don't, I'd just calculate the distance from start to end. If I do hit the fence... then I need to calculate how much distance it would be to pass it on the left and on the right, and take the smaller between those two.

Rachid writes the code as in listing 6.6.

Listing 6.6 Going Around the Fence (a work-in-progress code)

```
 1  int dist;
 2
 3  // b and c are the left and right edges of the fence
 4  // a is the x-coordinate of Bessie's line
 5  // y_0 is Bessie's y-coordinate
 6  // y_1 is the fence's y-coordinate
 7
 8  if (a > b && a < c && y_0 < y_1) {  // Do we hit the fence?
 9      // Yes: Have to go around fence
10      dist = 100 - y_0;  // Distance from start to end without a fence.
11      int d_left = 2 * (a - b);
12      int d_right = 2 * (c - a);
13
14      dist += min(d_left, d_right);
15  } else {
16      // No: Go directly to destination
```

```
17      dist = 100 - y_0;
18  }
```

Coach B: That looks right. But look, you have the line `dist = 100 - y_0;` in two places in the code. Can you combine these?

Rachid: Oh, you're right. Sure.

He edits his code into listing 6.7.

Listing 6.7 Going Around the Fence

```
1  int dist = 100 - y_0;
2  if (a > b && a < c && y_0 < y_1) {
3      int d_left = 2 * (a - b);
4      int d_right = 2 * (c - a);
5
6      dist += min(d_left, d_right);
7  }
```

Coach B: Well done! I think we've solved it! Thanks to Annie for suggesting we move the meeting outside. I think it was fun, right?

Ryan: It was moooognificent!

The team groans and laughs.

Coach B: Yes, agreed. So to recap: We solved a two-dimensional problem, and we learned about Manhattan distance. We dealt with points and their locations (start and end), and lines and lengths (the fence and the walking distance). Next meeting, we'll deal with rectangles and areas in two dimensions. I'll leave some problems on the club's page, and please reach out if you have any questions.

EPILOGUE

As our first foray into two-dimensional space, we solved a problem that involved location and distance. Manhattan distance is an important topic in USACO Bronze, and we will encounter it many times. It's interesting to note that as we move from one to two dimensions, things tend to get more complicated. For example, in one dimension, one point (or one line segment) can exist to the left or right of another point or segment, or the two can overlap; those are the only three options. However, once we move into two dimensions, those options expand dramatically: relative to another object, an object can exist to the left, to the right, above, below, overlapping, or any combination thereof, such as "below and to the left." We will see more about this increased complexity in the next section.

VOCABULARY Corner: **DISTANCE** is a very familiar concept. The conventional distance we usually use is called Euclidean distance. In the last example, we complicated this simple, familiar quantity by introducing the Manhattan distance. There are even more ways to measure distance in mathematics. No matter what method we're using to conceptualize distance, when we imagine a space and associate it with distance, we refer to the space as a metric space. Now, should you bother with learning all this terminology—metric space, Manhattan distance, and more to come? Yes! These terms are important for communication in computer science, and especially important as you build your own internal understanding of concepts and problems. The next time you see a problem involving Manhattan distance, you will already have a name for it, and a context. From there, you're well on your way to a solution.

PRACTICE PROBLEMS

Hints and full solutions to the problems can be found on the club's page: http://www.usacoclub.com

1. USACO 2019 Open Bronze Problem 1: Bucket Brigade

   http://usaco.org/index.php?page=viewproblem2&cpid=939

   a. It's simpler than it looks.

   b. You are now familiar with Manhattan distance.

   c. Draw a few of your own cases on a two-dimensional grid.

   d. The only cases that pose a problem are when the Rock is in the way. Check for those cases.

6.2.2. Two Rectangles

Coach B: Happy Tuesday, and welcome back! Today we're diving deeper into geometry, and we'll be looking at rectangles in two-dimensional space. I believe that you'll see many similarities to a previous problem we did. Remember the overlapping segments problem?

Annie: The one with the patrols on the Golden Gate bridge? That took us forever.

Rachid: Yeah, that problem was so long! I couldn't forget about it if I tried!

The team rumbles in agreement.

Coach B: Yes, that one. And I'm glad you remember it took us so long. Now, who remembers why? Why did it take us so long to find the solution?

Annie: I think we all do.

Everyone nods.

Annie: We solved it in three different ways. First was the brute force, checking every point on the bridge. Then, we solved it using all those "if" statements. What was it called?

Rachid: Casework.

Annie: Oh, yes, thanks. Casework. And then we finally solved it with this tricky way where we just found the overlap length, and if there was no overlap, it was zero.

Mei: And now I remember you said that this last method, geometric analysis, would come in handy in two dimensions. Is this the glory moment this method has been waiting for?

Coach B: Indeed! Geometric analysis gets its moment, at last! Or at least one of its glorious moments. But hey, since you remembered the previous problem so well, I think this one will be a breeze. You'll see. So please, go ahead and read it, and when you're done just come and draw it on the board.

Problem 6.4: Two Blankets for the Picnic

Bessie is heading to Ocean Beach in time to enjoy the sunset over the Pacific Ocean. She has two rectangular blankets to lay on the sand. The beach can be considered as a two-dimensional surface. Bessie places the first blanket with one corner at (x_1, y_1) and the diagonally opposite corner at (x_2, y_2), where $x_1 \leq x_2$ and $y_1 \leq y_2$. Similarly, she places the second blanket from (x_3, y_3) to (x_4, y_4), where $x_3 \leq x_4$ and $y_3 \leq y_4$.

Determine the total area covered by the two blankets.

Input Format

Two lines.

The first line contains 4 integers, x_1, y_1, x_2, y_2.

The second line contains 4 integers, x_3, y_3, x_4, y_4.

All given integer values are in the range $0 \ldots 10^6$.

Output Format

One number, the total area covered.

Sample Input

```
20 10 50 50
40 40 70 70
```

Sample Output

```
2000
```

The first blanket has an area of $(50 - 20) \times (50 - 10) = 1200$, and the second blanket has an area of $(70 - 40) \times (70 - 40) = 900$. However, there is an overlap between the blankets of the portion from $(40, 40)$ to $(50, 50)$, which amounts to an area of 100. The total area covered by the two blankets is therefore $1200 + 900 - 100 = 2000$ square units.

DISCUSSION

Visualize it: Ryan heads to the board and draws figure 6.19.

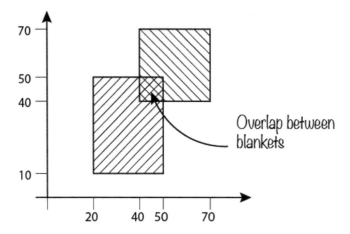

Figure 6.19 Two blankets on the beach, with an overlap.

Ryan: The first blanket has one corner at $(20, 10)$ and the diagonal corner at $(50, 50)$, so I drew these and connected them to create a rectangle. The same for the second blanket.

Coach B: Thanks, Ryan. I like how you clearly drew the overlap area. Any questions, anyone?

No questions. The problem looks pretty clear.

Coach B: Okay, now, rely on what you remembered so well from the problem with the two segments on the Golden Gate Bridge. How would you implement the brute-force method for this case, and what's going to be its complexity?

Rachid: That's when you check literally every point to find the answer. Since we know the whole beach stretches between 0 and 10^6 on two axes, we can just poke each unit area and see if it is covered by at least one blanket. Like we did back then, we'll poke the unit areas at the center, that means at $(0.5, 0.5), (1.5, 0.5), (0.5, 1.5), (1.5, 1.5), (0.5, 2.5)$ and so on. Makes sense?

Coach B: Makes sense to me. And the complexity? Back then it was $O(N)$. What is the complexity for this case?

Rachid: Hmm... We have an $N \times N$ grid, which means N^2 unit areas to poke, so it would be $O(N^2)$.

Coach B: Yes! And that's a big jump from $O(N)$ to $O(N^2)$. We said the complexity was a drawback of the brute-force method for a one-dimensional case. It is even more so for a two-dimensional case. Again, if this is the only method you can think of at competition time, and it is easy to implement, go ahead and try it. It would at least get you partial credit, and you would gain more insight into the problem. But it might not pass time constraints on some of the test cases.

TIP: It's very common for algorithms that worked in one dimension in $O(N)$ time complexity, to work in $O(N^2)$ in two dimensions, and to work in $O(N^3)$ in three dimensions. This increased time complexity requires us to get more creative in these higher dimensions.

Coach B: I suggest we won't code this, unless there are any special requests? No? Good, so let's move to the second method we used back then: casework. This means we need to decide how many cases there are, then characterize each one, and finally calculate the area for each case. Do you remember how many cases we had last time?

Mei: Six cases! I had to code these, and the team read me the cases from the table.

Coach B: There's nothing like muscle memory! Right. How about you all go to the board and draw two cases each, which will bring us to eight cases. That means, each needs to draw the two blankets in a different relation to each other. Make sure we have eight different cases at the end!

Ryan: Why eight? Did I miss something? Did we figure out there should be eight cases?

Coach B: You didn't miss anything! Good point. We haven't decided if there are eight cases, or more. For now, we just want to get a few on the board to get a sense of the cases.

The team nods, goes to the board, and comes up with figure 6.20.

Coach B: That was pretty fast. So these are eight different cases. Are there any more cases?

Annie: Oh, I think there are many more. For starters, even for the case at the top left, with one blanket above the other, with no overlap, there's actually also the case of the blankets reversed. So we'd have to check for both cases.

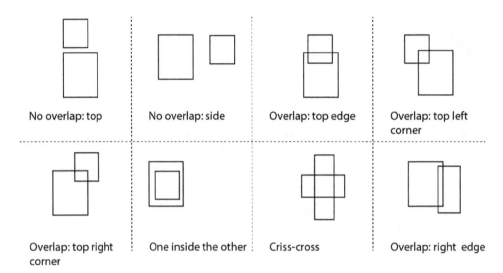

| No overlap: top | No overlap: side | Overlap: top edge | Overlap: top left corner |

| Overlap: top right corner | One inside the other | Criss-cross | Overlap: right edge |

Figure 6.20 Different possible relations between two blankets. If you are doing casework for this problem, there are more cases to consider.

Coach B: Yes, you're right. On the one hand, there are more cases. On the other hand, I want to point out that the area calculation for different cases would be the same. For example, for all the cases with no overlap, and as you correctly pointed out there are quite a few of those, the total area is going to be the same, the sum of the two individual blanket areas. I don't think we need to delve into this option too much. You are most welcome to try casework for this problem later on, and definitely keep it as a viable option for new problems. But I want us to move to the fastest method.

TIP: If you are trying the casework method, and your solution doesn't work for some of the test cases, it might be that you missed some of the cases in your casework. Go back to the drawing board and try to draw different configurations of the problem at hand. See if your solution can address these new cases.

Coach B: We saw that brute-force might be too slow for two-dimensional problems, and casework might be, well, too many cases to work out. Let's try the third method, geometric analysis.

TIP: It might be tempting to think that when you move from one dimension to two dimensions, the various quantities related to the problem will double: for example, that the number of cases will double, or that the complexity will double. However, in the context of search problems, it is often more accurate to think about the change as an exponential growth. Thus, quantities move from N^1 in the one-dimensional case, to N^2 for two dimensions, to N^3 for three dimensions. A line segment is the most basic shape in one dimension, with 2 edge points; a rectangle is the most basic shape in two dimensions, with 4 corners, which is 2^2; and a cube is the most basic shape in three dimensions, with 8 vertices, which is 2^3. Wonder about 4 dimensions? We will talk about four dimensions and n-cubes in our vocabulary corner.

Coach B: Anyone willing to take us through the geometric analysis for this problem?

Like deer caught in headlights, no one moves a muscle. Coach B smiles.

Coach B: No worries. Here, I'll give you a hint, and then I'm sure you can do it as a team. Actually, I'll make it two hints. The first is that, very similar to what we wrote back then, we want to add the basic areas, and subtract the overlap. So the solution would be of the form

```
total_area = Area(blanket_1) + Area(blanket_2) - Area(overlap);
```

And the second hint is that the overlap area will always be in the shape of a rectangle. Thus, to calculate the overlap area, you'll need to calculate the overlap in the x-direction, the overlap in the y-direction, and then multiply them! That's all. Does it look doable now?

The group sighs in relief.

Annie: Sure, we can do it. Can we still call you as our lifeline if needed?

Coach B: Of course. Go ahead. I'll be sitting over there, and when you're done, we'll go over it.

The team goes to the board. It takes some drawing, as in figure 6.21, and some code writing, as in listing 6.8; eventually Mei turns back and declares the team is ready to present their solution.

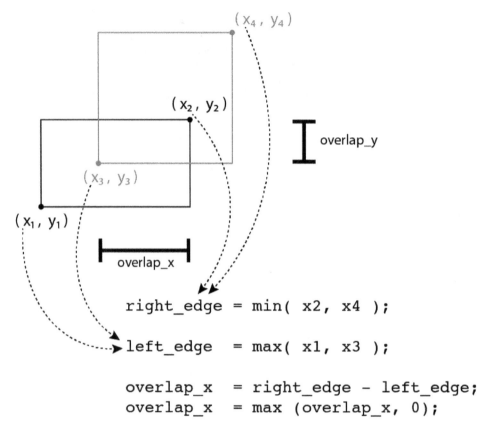

```
right_edge = min( x2, x4 );

left_edge  = max( x1, x3 );

overlap_x  = right_edge - left_edge;
overlap_x  = max (overlap_x, 0);
```

Figure 6.21 An overlap between the two rectangles. This is the notation used in the problem, in order to calculate the overlap in the x-direction.

Mei: We started writing the code and were in a big mess right away because of the notation, so we went back and drew figure 6.21. This was really helpful. From this, it was pretty clear how to calculate the overlap in the x-direction. Just like we said back then: the left edge of the overlap is determined by the left edges of the individual segments. And the same goes for the right edge of the overlap. And then we calculate the difference, and make sure it's not less than zero.

Rachid: Once we had that on the board, we went to write the code as in listing 6.8. It was pretty straightforward. The drawing saved us a lot of confusion.

Annie: And, as you like to say, Coach, it looks very aesthetically pleasing! There is a clear symmetry between the overlap_x and the overlap_y equations.

The team smiles. They did it.

Listing 6.8 Two Blankets for the Picnic (a work-in-progress code)

```
1   // Overlap in x
2   int left_edge = max(x_1, x_3);
3   int right_edge = min(x_2, x_4);
4   int overlap_x = right_edge - left_edge;
5
6   // Overlap in y
7   int bottom_edge = max(y_1, y_3);
8   int top_edge = min(y_2, y_4);
9   int overlap_y = top_edge - bottom_edge;
10
11  // Overlap area
12  int overlap_area = overlap_x * overlap_y;
13  overlap_area = max(overlap_area, 0);  // This line will be changed
14
15  int area_blanket_1 = (x_2 - x_1) * (y_2 - y_1);
16  int area_blanket_2 = (x_4 - x_3) * (y_4 - y_3);
17
18  int total_area = area_blanket_1 + area_blanket_2 - overlap_area;
```

Coach B: Very well done. This drawing is a great help to understand your code, and I'm sure it helped you to avoid confusion with all these different x's and y's. And indeed, it's nice to see the symmetry between the different parts of the code.

Mei: I know, right? It's awesome. We should probably leave early and get some ice cream.

Coach B: The only problem? It's not correct. I mean, it will work for some cases, but not for all of them.

The team groans and protests.

Ryan: Are you sure, Coach? We did exactly what we did last time, with the one-dimensional problem.

Coach B: Yes, something is off. And as a hint: Your drawing is correct; the listing has a bug.

The team gathers around the listing and starts chatting. After a few minutes, they turn back.

Annie: We don't get it. If the drawing and what we wrote over there is correct, then we think our code should be correct as well. What are we missing?

Coach B: What happens if there is no overlap?

Annie: The area would be negative, and we checked for it. This is the line

```
overlap_area = max(overlap_area, 0);
```

The team nods in agreement.

Coach B: Let's walk slowly through that. We know that if there's no overlap in the x direction, then `overlap_x` would be negative, right? And the same goes for `overlap_y`: if there is no overlap in the y direction, `overlap_y` would be negative. Do we all agree on that?

Everyone nods.

Ryan: Yeah, that's exactly the same process we followed.

Coach B: Now, what would happen if there's absolutely totally no overlap, neither in the x direction nor in the y direction? `overlap_x` would be negative, and `overlap_y` would be negative as well, but, and this is important, their product, which is the `overlap_area`, would be positive!

Surprised, the team starts talking all at once. Mei takes the lead.

Mei: Oy vey. Now I get it. We actually had it right initially, but then we wanted to make the code shorter and nicer. We thought we were being efficient by checking only the area and not each of the individual overlaps. But we missed this case. Oh well. Here, I'll bring it back.

And she writes down listing 6.9.

Listing 6.9 Two Blankets for the Picnic

```
1   // Overlap in x
2   int left_edge = max(x_1, x_3);
3   int right_edge = min(x_2, x_4);
4   int overlap_x = right_edge - left_edge;
5   overlap_x = max(overlap_x, 0);   // Added line!
6
7   // Overlap in y
8   int bottom_edge = max(y_1, y_3);
9   int top_edge = min(y_2, y_4);
10  int overlap_y = top_edge - bottom_edge;
11  overlap_y = max(overlap_y, 0);   // Added line!
12
13  // Overlap area
14  int overlap_area = overlap_x * overlap_y;
15  // overlap_area = max(overlap_area, 0);   // Removed line
16
17  int area_blanket_1 = (x_2 - x_1) * (y_2 - y_1);
18  int area_blanket_2 = (x_4 - x_3) * (y_4 - y_3);
19
20  int total_area = area_blanket_1 + area_blanket_2 - overlap_area;
```

Coach B: Well done! This is a very common mistake, so good thing we were able to see it together. I am sure you'll remember this now.

The team sighs.

Rachid: I bet you're about to say "No pain, no gain." It was painful enough for plenty of gain.

Coach B: And indeed, you gained a lot from this problem. You were able to extend what you learned in the one-dimensional problem into a two-dimensional problem. That's a big thing. And as you can see, the solution is elegant and short. Well done, you earned it! I think this is a great place to finish today. Break time! I'll put the practice problems on the club's page, and don't forget: we have an extra practice meet this Friday. We want to be ready for the December competition!

EPILOGUE

Continuing our journey in a two-dimensional space, this section dealt with rectangles (which can overlap) and calculating area. The problem was very similar to the one-dimensional Problem 6.2 involving overlapping segments. We were able to extend our learning and apply it here. The key here was to take a big problem that we don't know how to solve and separate it into two smaller problems that we do already know how to solve. We didn't know how to find an overlapping area, but we did know how to find overlapping segments. So we did that twice: once for the x-direction and once for the y-direction. When we can separate a task in two dimensions into two separate tasks in each of the directions, we call this a separable task. Later on in this chapter, we will encounter problems that are not separable. Whenever a problem is separable, namely whenever you can solve it in a one-dimensional setting, take advantage of it!

 VOCABULARY Corner: **N-CUBE** An n-cube, also called a hypercube or an n-dimensional cube, is a mathematical construct that generalizes the concept of a cube to different dimensions. In zero dimensions (yes, this is a thing), a 0-cube is a point. In one dimension, a 1-cube is a line segment. A 2-cube is a rectangle, and a 3-cube is, well, a cube. In four dimensions, a 4-cube is called a tesseract. And the n-cubes continue. You might think, "Who cares about more than three dimensions? It's not real anyway." Turns out that n-dimensional analysis is a very important tool in analyzing big data. Linear algebra is one of the branches of mathematics that explores large-dimensional problems.

PRACTICE PROBLEMS

Hints and full solutions to the problems can be found on the club's page: http://www.usacoclub.com

1. USACO 2016 December Bronze Problem 1: Square Pasture

   http://usaco.org/index.php?page=viewproblem2&cpid=663

   a. This problem is concerned with rectangles, but all you really need to watch for are the corners.

   b. Look for the maximum and minimum coordinates on both axes.

2. USACO 2017 December Bronze Problem 1: Blocked Billboard

   http://usaco.org/index.php?page=viewproblem2&cpid=759

   a. You are looking for one rectangle obscuring another, and you will need to do it twice.

   b. If a brute-force algorithm would work, it can be the simplest to code. Maybe it's worth trying.

3. USACO 2018 January Bronze Problem 1: Blocked Billboard II

   http://usaco.org/index.php?page=viewproblem2&cpid=783

   a. Things get trickier compared to the first Blocked Billboard problem from December 2017. In this problem the answer not only depends on the area covered, but also on the shape of this area.

   b. Draw the given sample case and make a few of your own.

   c. There are a few plausible ways to solve it. For example, a brute-force method would look for the maximum and minimum coordinates covered in each of the axes.

4. USACO 2016 Open Bronze Problem 3: Field Reduction

   http://usaco.org/index.php?page=viewproblem2&cpid=641

   This problem was already given as homework in the chapter on Search, so no need to solve it twice if you already solved it. On the other hand, if you had difficulties solving it then, you might benefit from the new insights on geometry problems as well as the additional hints given here.

   a. Only cows that are on the edges or corners can change the area needed.

   b. If a cow standing on the edge is removed, how would you determine the amount of area saved?

   c. If a cow is on the corner, it contributes to two edges. This is an important special case to consider. How would you determine the savings if a cow on the corner is removed?

   d. Hint: Think about a simple solution to the cow in the corner case.

   e. Hint: Find the two largest coordinates (and the two lowest coordinates) in each axis. This can be done in one loop. Then, do another loop on all cows, and for each one, determine what coordinates she will impact if removed.

   f. This is the code for the second loop, going over all the cows:

```
1    int area;
2    area = (max_x - min_x) * (max_y - min_y);
3    for (int i = 0; i < N; ++i) {  // loop over all the cows
4        int xbig = (X[i] == max_x) ? max_x_2: max_x;
5        int xsmall = (X[i] == min_x) ? min_x_2: min_x;
6        int ybig = (Y[i] == max_y) ? max_y_2: max_y;
7        int ysmall = (Y[i] == min_y) ? min_y_2: min_y;
8        area = min(area, (xbig - xsmall) * (ybig - ysmall));
9    }
```

5. Codeforces, Round #587 (Div. 3) Problem C: White Sheet

   https://codeforces.com/contest/1216/problem/C

   a. Brute-force method would work here.

   b. Hint: Consider using geometric analysis to solve it. This may require finding the overlap of 3 rectangles.

6.3. Beyond Ninety Degrees

So far, we have focused on basic shapes (points, lines, and rectangles) and straightforward quantities (distance, length, and area). In this section, however, we break new ground. We first solve a problem where the shape of interest is a circle; we then solve a problem where the quantity of interest is the direction of a path in a two-dimensional space. The practice problems will introduce additional shapes and quantities, like triangles and perimeters.

6.3.1. Circles

Circles are common not only in geometry problems but also in modeling and search problems, and understanding them will help with many problems that involve periodic behavior.

Coach B: Welcome, everyone! Glad to see you today, Friday, for this extra practice. We will try to make it short and sweet. We've already covered lines, line segments, and rectangles. We also covered points in one and two dimensions. So today we tackle this last shape: the circle.

Ryan: Circles, okay! Will we need to deal with pi and stuff? To calculate area and circumference?

Coach B: Well, not really. As we've found, most USACO Bronze problems deal only with integer numbers. Now, if your calculations need to involve pi, you are out of the realm of integers. So that's why we don't really see pi in USACO Bronze. We will mostly be concerned with the geometry imposed by the circle, and once we dive in, you'll see that we often treat a circle like a line segment that closes on itself.

Annie: So in that case, are these problems considered one-dimensional problems or two-dimensional problems?

Coach B: Very astute question, Annie! You can consider it either way, and it really depends on the specific problem at hand. However, the important thing is still that you are able to solve the problem. So, let's get to it. Here's a typical example. Read the problem, and we'll discuss it together.

Problem 6.5: Seats Around the Arena

Bessie is a great fan of basketball and loves to watch NBA games. And this is her lucky day: San Francisco is home of the famous Golden State Warriors, and they are playing tonight!

Bessie has purchased N first-row tickets for herself and friends, $1 \le N \le 100$. The tickets are for seat numbers $x_1, x_2, \ldots, x_N$. In the arena, the first row forms a big ellipse around the court, with seats numbered from 1 to 100. Seats 1 and 100 are adjacent.

When Bessie and her friends arrive at the stadium, they enter single-file, arriving at a seat number S on the first row, and then walk around to their designated seats. For example, suppose that all entered at seat $S = 23$,. If Bessie's designated seat is number 37, then she will have to walk 14 seats over. If her friend, Elsie, is at seat number 22, then Elsie will need to walk only 1 seat over to her place. The total distance Bessie and Elsie have to walk is therefore $14 + 1 = 15$.

Determine which seat number S would yield the smallest total walking distance.

Input Format

Two lines.

The first line contains one integer, N.

The second line contains N integers, $x_1, x_2, \ldots, x_N$.

Output Format

One number, the smallest seat number S that would yield the smallest total walking distance.

Sample Input

3

4 90 3

Sample Output

3

If the group enters at seat number 3, the cow in seat 4 needs to walk 1 seat over, the cow in seat 90 has to walk 13 seats over, and the cow in seat 3 does not need to walk at all. The total distance in this case would be $1 + 13 + 0 = 14$ seats.

DISCUSSION

Ryan: Hey! This is actually an ellipse, or an oval, and not a circle.

Coach B: Right you are, Ryan. For our purposes, it behaves just like a circle: the important thing is that it is a line that closes on itself, and that you can walk circles around it.

Mei: Pun intended, I guess!

The team smiles.

Ryan: Also, is this really a geometry problem? It looks to me more like a search problem, or an optimization problem. We're searching for the best seat to enter.

Annie: I agree. This is just like the ones we saw in the search unit, and we can probably use an exhaustive search here. We'll just search over all the seats from 1 to 100, and find the best one to enter.

Coach B: Wow, you two are really fast! Yes, you are absolutely correct, and I mean both of you. It is a search and optimization problem, and we can, and will, solve it with an exhaustive search. Well done! The reason we have it now, here in the unit on geometry, is because we do have a circle here. Well, an oval. And this shape imposes some geometric characteristics on the problem. So, yes, we will solve it using an exhaustive search. Let's keep on going and see where the circle affects the solution.

Mei: Ryan and I will take this one! We're the basketball players in the group. We'll draw it!

Visualize it: Mei and Ryan head to the board and draw figure 6.22.

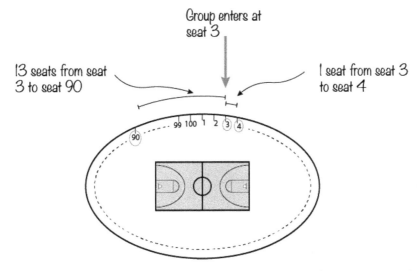

Figure 6.22 A row of one hundred seats around the arena, arranged in an oval. Seat number 1 is adjacent to seat number 100.

Mei: We drew the problem as described. The group enters at seat 3. Then one cow needs to go one seat over to seat 4, and one cow needs to go over 13 seats to seat 90. The cow at seat 3 can stay put. All together, they need to walk over $1 + 13 + 0 = 14$ seats.

Coach B: Can you show us what would happen if the group entered at, say, seat 4?

Ryan: Sure. In that case... the distance to seat 90 would be 14 seats over. The distance to seat 3 would be 1 seat over, and... the one at seat 4 wouldn't have to move. So, the total would be $14 + 1 + 0 = 15$. This is more than the 14 seats required if we enter at seat 3.

Coach B: Okay, and if we enter at seat 2?

Mei: Then it would be 12 seats to get to seat 90, 1 seat over to get to seat 3, and 2 seats over to get to seat 4. A total of $12 + 1 + 2 = 15$. Again, more than the original 14 seats required.

Coach B: Great. Makes sense to everyone?

The team nods.

Annie: Yup! It seems simple enough so far.

TIP: When you are solving an optimization problem and you follow the explanation for the optimal solution, it is worth exploring other, non-optimal values, as well. This will give you a better understanding of why the optimal value is indeed the best. It will also help you identify ways to look for the optimal value.

Coach B: Does anyone see what might be special about the circle—okay, oval—in this problem? Why does the shape matter?

Annie: I think it's because there are actually two ways to get from one seat to another. Not just one.

Coach B: Can you show us what you mean?

Annie draws figure 6.23.

Annie: Here, we chose to go from seat 3 to seat 90 by going left, or counterclockwise. It took us 13 seats that way. If we were to go to the right, or clockwise, it would take us 87 seats. So, I think we need to always consider the two options and choose the shortest one.

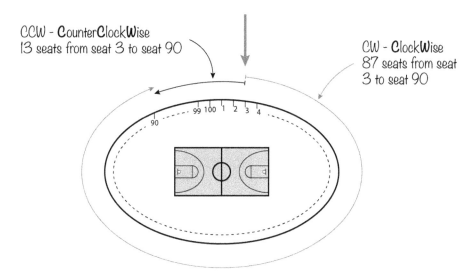

Figure 6.23 Two ways to get between two points: move clockwise or counterclockwise.

 TIP: Clockwise and counterclockwise are terms derived from the movement of the hands on a clock face, as shown in figure 6.24. Since these are very long words, we often use the abbreviations CW and CCW.

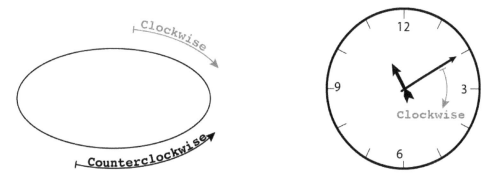

Figure 6.24 Clockwise and counterclockwise directions, and the classic clock face that inspired the terms.

Coach B: Sounds like a plan. Let's say you need to calculate the distance from seat a to b. How do you suggest calculating both options?

Rachid: Here, I would use an "if" statement. Is this correct?

```
1   if (b >= a) {
2       dist_CW = b - a;
3       dist_CCW = 100 - dist_CW;
4   } else {
5       dist_CCW = a - b;
6       dist_CW = 100 - dist_CCW;
7   }
```

Coach B: Well, you can try and check it for yourself. You can substitute the case we already have, $a = 3, b = 90$.

Rachid annotates his code:

```
1   if (b >= a) {                    // 90 >= 3 --> True
2       dist_CW = b - a;             // dist_CW = 90 - 3 = 87
3       dist_CCW = 100 - dist_CW;    // dist_CCW = 100 - 87 = 13
4   }
```

Rachid: Yes, that's exactly what we got for this case.

> *TIP*: Plugging in numbers is a great way to check your code. It's fast, and it's easy, but it doesn't always guarantee correctness. Nor is it always easy to find good numbers to plug in! But if you do have some good numbers, and if you have doubts about your code, go ahead and plug them in to check it.

Ryan: How did the calculation of dist_CCW come about? I mean, how did you get the formula:

```
dist_CCW = 100 - dist_CW;
```

Rachid: My thinking is that if you add both directions, of walking CW and CCW, you actually cover all the seats in the first row. So, dist_CW + dist_CCW should be equal to the total number of seats, 100.

Ryan: Oh, yes. I get it. Nice. I wonder, can we use a modulus operator here? We used it often in periodic problems before, and this looks similar.

Coach B: Good observation, Ryan. Although we could certainly do that, I wouldn't recommend it for this first try, because a modulus might not behave the way we expect it to for negative numbers, and even worse, the behavior might be different in different programming languages. We've talked before about a way to avoid using negative numbers altogether, by adding the modulus amount. So for the moment, let me just write it here on the side; later on, you can try putting this snippet in your code. The way you should put it in is like this:

```
1   dist_1 = (100 + b - a) % 100;
2   dist_2 = (100 + a - b) % 100;
```

Ryan: It's cool. It avoids the need for "if"/"else" blocks, but I do see what you mean about it being tricky. Okay, we might come back and use that later.

TIP: Be careful when using modulus operators, especially if there are negative numbers involved. The modulus operator is a great tool, able to make your code clearer, cleaner, and less prone to errors, when used correctly. However, if you are not sure about how well it will work in a specific setting, you can always deploy some alternatives.

Coach B: Okay, I think once we clear up this geometric issue of having two plausible ways to calculate a distance on a circle, then we're ready to do our exhaustive search. So, Mei and Ryan: you're still our basketball team! Ready to write the algorithm for us?

They head to the board, Mei passing the marker to Ryan behind her back, and Ryan pretending to slam-dunk it.

ALGORITHM

Mei and Ryan write the code in listing 6.10.

Listing 6.10 Seats Around the Arena

```
1   // We cannot do any worse than everyone stepping over 100 chairs.
2   int min_total_dist = N * 100;
3
4   int min_entry_seat = 0;
5   for (int entry_seat = 1; entry_seat <= 100; ++entry_seat) {
6       int total_dist = 0;
7       for (int cow = 0; cow < N; ++cow) {
8           int cow_seat = seats[cow];
9           int dist_CW, dist_CCW;
10          if (cow_seat >= entry_seat) {
11              dist_CW = cow_seat - entry_seat;
12              dist_CCW = 100 - dist_CW;
13          } else {
14              dist_CCW = entry_seat - cow_seat;
15              dist_CW = 100 - dist_CCW;
16          }
17          total_dist += min(dist_CW, dist_CCW);
18      }
```

```
19      if (total_dist < min_total_dist) {
20          min_total_dist = total_dist;
21          min_entry_seat = entry_seat;
22      }
23  }
```

Ryan fakes a layup and passes the marker to Coach B.

Coach B: Thanks, Mei and Ryan. It's a clean and clear code. You used the patterns we learned for exhaustive search problems: the outer loop is over all possible `entry_seat` values, and for each you calculate the `total_dist` traveled by the group. Then, you take the minimum of that. Well done. Any questions?

The team shakes their heads, looking restless.

Coach B: Okay, I see you are all ready to get out of here and go play. Good thing we didn't try this practice over on the basketball court! At any rate, let me wrap this up. We solved a search problem that had a circle geometry in it. This is a very common occurrence in USACO Bronze. The problem itself focused on searching or modeling, but there was an underlying geometric structure component to it. Bringing these two concepts together, you were able to easily solve the problem. I'll leave some similar problems on the club's page. You've done good work today. Now go and play! See you next week.

EPILOGUE

On a circle, there are two ways to travel from one point to another. This is true in general for any segment in which the two edges are joined to form a closed loop. Once we understood this underlying geometric structure, we could solve the problem.

In more advanced levels of USACO, a common problem is to have multiple segments joined together. These problems lead to more involved geometric structures and are often solved using graph algorithms. Later, in Chapter 8, we will mention a special kind of graph called trees.

VOCABULARY Corner: **CLOCKWISE AND COUNTERCLOCKWISE** When talking about moving on a circle, too often people use the ambiguous terms "right" and "left." You've probably heard the phrase "Righty tighty, lefty loosey," in reference to opening and closing containers, or tightening and loosening screws. However, "right" and "left" are ambiguous: if the top part of a circle moves to the right, the lower part moves to the left! See also figure 6.25. It is better to refer to directions as CW and CCW, even though the phrase would lose its poetic appeal: "CW tighty, CCW loosey"?!?

Top part moves to the **right**

Bottom part moves to the **left**

Figure 6.25 Clockwise direction cannot be directly associated with turning 'right' nor turning 'left'. 'Right' or 'left' depends on whether you consider the top part of the circle or the bottom part.

Alas, though, even the terms CW and CCW can be ambiguous. They depend on the side you are looking at the circle from. See figure 6.26. If you are facing a friend, and you wish to turn a bicycle wheel between you, the CW direction will be opposite for each. This ambiguity is resolved in physics and vector analysis by using the right-hand rule, which also involves the direction of viewing. Not to worry, though: that rule is beyond the scope of USACO Bronze.

Figure 6.26 CW and CCW depend on the direction you are looking from.

PRACTICE PROBLEMS

Hints and full solutions to the problems can be found on the club's page: http://www.usacoclub.com

1. USACO 2016 February Bronze Problem 2: Circular Barn

    http://usaco.org/index.php?page=viewproblem2&cpid=616

    a. Note that the cows are allowed to walk only in a clockwise direction.

    b. Therefore, you do not need to calculate two distances.

6.3.2. General Shapes

We close this chapter with problems involving general shapes and different qualities of these shapes. At the Bronze level, you are always able to visualize the shapes; by drawing them, you will understand them.

Coach B: Happy Tuesday! Tuesday is an auspicious day. Let's get rolling. This is our last meeting in the geometry unit. Yes, exciting! We learned a lot, and what's really important, the things we learned here will serve you well in many other USACO problems. For now, let's look at a problem that describes a general shape in two dimensions, and asks about its orientation. Don't be alarmed by the general description: we'll do plenty of drawing, and things will become clearer. I hope.

Problem 6.6: Path Around the Lake

Bessie loves history and nature, and a great way to explore both is a hike in the Presidio of San Francisco, a large urban national park. As part of her hike, she goes around Mountain Lake, a small pristine lake in the Presidio.

Bessie's walk around the lake can be described by a string of characters. Each character represents one meter of progression in a specific direction. For example, "WNNESS" represents a progression of 1 meter to the west, 2 meters to the north, 1 meter to the east, and 2 meters to the south.

We know that Bessie started and ended her hike at the same point, and that the path she took never crossed itself.

Determine if Bessie's path describes a clockwise or counterclockwise walk around the lake.

Input Format

One line, containing a string describing the path.

The length of the string is less than 100 characters.

Output format

One line containing either "CW" if the path is clockwise, or "CCW" if it is counterclockwise.

Sample Input

NENENEESSWSWWW

Sample Output

CW

This problem is similar to USACO 2021 February Bronze 3: Clockwise Fence. Credit there goes to Brian Dean.

DISCUSSION

Coach B: Okay, it seems like everyone is done reading, and it's still very quiet, so let me start. The problem describes a path and asks about its direction. Do we have a volunteer to draw the path?

Rachid: I don't really get it. Are we supposed to know what the path looks like?

Coach B: Not really. But, you should know how to create it! The problem gives you the recipe.

Annie: Here, Rachid, let's go try it together.

Visualize it: Annie and Rachid go to the board and describe as they draw figure 6.27.

Annie: The first letter in the string is "N", which means we go north one meter. Let's just put it like a map: north at the top, west on the left, and so on. Then, "N" means going one meter up.

Rachid: The second letter is "E", so we move to the right one meter.

They keep on going over the letters, until they get back to the starting point.

Rachid: Hey, that worked out perfectly! The last letter brought us right back to the start.

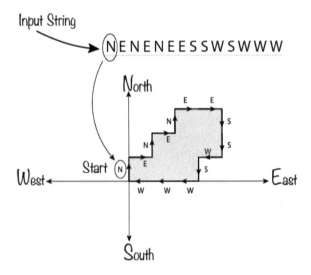

Figure 6.27 Drawing the shape letter-by-letter. The resulting path has a CW orientation.

Coach B: Nicely done. It would have been a mess if the path didn't finish at the same point.

Mei: The problem clearly states that "We know that Bessie started and ended her hike at the same point," so, exactly—it should be a closed loop.

Coach B: Good eye for details, Mei. Thanks. Let's see, the problem actually asks for the direction of the path. Any ideas?

Ryan: This is clockwise.

Coach B: Thank you for not saying "right" or "left"! Yes, it is clockwise, so we need to output "CW".

The team looks at the strange shape on the board, and tries to digest the problem. It still looks pretty hard.

Coach B: Let's see. Given an input string, do you feel comfortable drawing the shape?

The team nods.

Annie: Yup, that part we can definitely do.

Coach B: And, given a drawn shape, do you feel comfortable finding if it's CW or CCW?

The team nods.

Ryan: Yeah, that's easy.

Coach B: Any ideas on how to determine the direction of the path algorithmically?

The team is quiet.

Ryan: It's really strange. It was so obvious once we looked at the drawing that the path was clockwise. But I can't explain how we knew.

Coach B: Very true! These cases can be frustrating, but it can also help us understand "how" we understand what we know. What I'm saying is, once you translate your thinking process into an algorithm, you will understand much better what "CW" and "CCW" actually mean.

Mei: I totally agree with Ryan. I can easily see the last case was "CW", but I don't have a clue how I know it!

Coach B: Okay, one way to deal with this is a few more examples. Let's see. There are four of you. So why don't we have each of you draw two cases on the board, one that is "CW" and one that is "CCW", and maybe when we see all these together, we'll have a better idea. Can you do that?

The team approaches the board hesitantly but starts working. After erasing a lot, and redrawing, eventually they come up with figure 6.28.

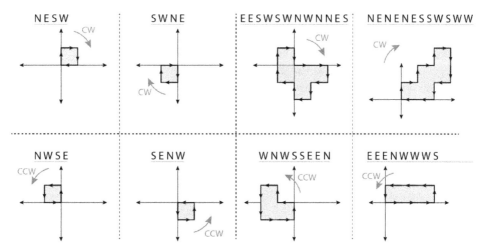

Figure 6.28 Eight examples of possible paths. Paths on the top row are all CW, and paths on the bottom row are all CCW.

Coach B: A very rich collection! Now we have plenty of examples. Take a look at these. First, I hope we all agree with the notation of CW and CCW on these drawings, right?

The team scans for mistakes. Finding none, they nod in agreement.

Coach B: Okay, now to the million-dollar question: can you suggest an algorithm that would distinguish between these two types?

The team thinks.

Mei: It might sound really weird, but here goes. I noticed that the rightmost segment in all the CWs is going south, and in all the CCWs it's going north. It doesn't really make sense that this is how we can find the direction, but it works on all these examples.

The team looks in amazement (at figure 6.28) and tries to validate this observation.

Rachid: Wait, yeah it's really weird, but now I see that all the top segments for the CW are pointing east, and the top segments for CCW point west.

Annie: Yes, both are true, and, there's also a consistent direction for the left and bottom segments. Can this be it?

Coach B: Try and create an example where it doesn't work. Can you make one?

The team tries, drawing shapes in the air with their fingers, to no avail.

Ryan: I think we found it!

The team talks excitedly.

Annie: That was amazing! We can just look at one segment of the path and know the answer!

Coach B: Well, but it has to be a special segment, right? Either the top one, or the right-most one, etc. But yes, I agree, it's amazing indeed. I think we are ready to write the algorithm.

 TIP: The team has identified a pattern that effectively resolves the problem at hand. They have tested the pattern on various examples and found it to work consistently. Although some members of the team may have insights into why the pattern is effective, there is currently no rigorous proof of its correctness. In the competition, remember that time is of the essence, and that it is not necessary to provide a formal proof of your algorithm's correctness. Rather, your algorithm must function accurately on all test cases. Therefore, if you recognize a pattern that appears to be sufficiently general and sound, it is advisable to convert it into an algorithm. It might be the actual solution.

ALGORITHM

Annie and Mei join forces at the board to write the algorithm as in listing 6.11.

Listing 6.11 Path Around the Lake

```
1   // considering only the top segment
2   int y = 0;  // y coordinate of the point on the path.
3   int top_y = -1;
4   char direction_top_y = ' ';
5
6   for (int i = 0; i < input_string.length(); ++i) {
7       if (input_string[i] == 'S') y -=1;
8       if (input_string[i] == 'N') y +=1;
9
10      if ( input_string[i] == 'W' || input_string[i] == 'E' ) {
11          if (y > top_y) {
12              top_y = y;
13              direction_top_y = input_string[i];
14          }
15      }
16  }
17
18  if (direction_top_y == 'W' ) answer = "CCW";
19  else answer = "CW";
```

Mei: And we could have done a similar thing for any of the other sides, like for the rightmost segment.

Coach B: Nice. Very clear code. You could have used a switch statement, but this is still very clear as is. Thank you. Any questions?

The team is happy with the code.

Coach B: I have a small question. I was both impressed and intrigued by your choice to initialize top_y = -1. Can you please explain that?

Annie: Yes, we were thinking about it. At first we thought of initializing it to a very large negative value, but then we realized that eventually, since we start and end at the same place, there must be a horizontal segment at least the height of the start point. I'm not sure I'm explaining it right, but we did think about it and convinced ourselves about it.

Coach B: Interesting. So, if you were looking for the left_x segment, how would you initialize it?

Annie: For left_x, where we're looking for the leftmost segment going north or south, we would have initialized it to 1. In that case, the leftmost vertical segment has to be either at $x = 0$ or to the left of it.

Coach B: Yes, I think this is all correct. Very nice that you were very conscious about it and made a judicious choice of value to initialize. For the rest of us: if you followed Annie's reasoning, that's great. If not, you can put in your implementation a very large number (negative or positive, as the case may be). It's really nice to implement all these subtleties. However, your main focus in the competition is getting the right answer, and fast. Okay, before we wrap up, any comments? What can we take away from this problem?

Ryan: The big thing for me in this problem was the contrast between how easy it was for us to just eyeball the direction, and how hard it was for us to translate the process into an algorithm.

The team nods in agreement.

Coach B: I agree. I just want to add that there are more ways to solve this problem. For example, we could sum up all the angles we are turning. This means that if we move east and turn north, we add 90 degrees. If we move east and turn south, we subtract 90 degrees. After we complete the full path, the sum will be either 360 degrees, which means the answer is "CCW", or the sum will be -360 degrees, in which case the answer is "CW". I mention this method not in order to confuse you, but for two reasons: one, to show you that the way we actually find it as humans might be different than the algorithm we choose; and two, because this kind of path orientation is very important in modeling real-world physics.

Rachid: "Physics modeling"? That sounds scary.

Coach B: hmm... "That sounds very" you say? Well, yes, it is! It's a very interesting area combining math, programming, and science!

Is coach B not hearing well or is he just pretending?

Coach B: Okay, we did a lot of drawing today. Appropriate for closing the unit on geometry! I will post a few more problems on the club's page for next week. And remember, drawing is your friend when solving geometry problems! Thank you, and I'll see you next week.

EPILOGUE

As hard as this problem was, we solved it by following a very prescribed series of steps. We started by visualizing the given example. Then, we created our own examples and looked for patterns. Eventually, when we nailed down the pattern (actually, multiple patterns), it was easy to translate it into an algorithm. The balance between the hard and easy parts of this process may change, but the process is pretty common to all the problems we've encountered so far.

 VOCABULARY Corner: **METACOGNITION** Cognition is thinking, and the prefix "meta-" often means "on a higher level." So, metacognition is thinking about thinking, or understanding our understanding! It's the way we're aware of our own thought processes. In the last problem, we had to rely on metacognition: we tried to understand *how* we understood the path's direction. Humans often think and process things very differently than computers. That is to say, some of the algorithms we use in our thinking process are constructed very differently than the algorithms we use when coding a solution to a problem.

PRACTICE PROBLEMS

Hints and full solutions to the problems can be found on the club's page: http://www.usacoclub.com

1. USACO 2021 February Bronze Problem 3: Clockwise Fence

   http://usaco.org/index.php?page=viewproblem2&cpid=1109

   a. This is essentially the same problem as problem 6.6: Path Around the Lake.

   b. You may want to try two different solution methods. For example: using the bottom segment to determine direction, or using the sum of turning angles.

2. USACO 2024 Open Bronze Problem 2: Walking Along A Fence

   http://usaco.org/index.php?page=viewproblem2&cpid=1420

   a. Manhattan distance is important here.

   b. Think about creating a 2D array of size 1001x1001 (just like the farm), and tracing over this array the distance (along the fence) from the starting post.

   c. One way to accomplish (b) is by reading the first post, assigning it a distance 0, and then marching from there (along straight lines) to the next post, updating the distance and recording it in the array at every step of the way. Then doing the same from the second post to the third, and so on.

   d. You will need to 'close the fence' by going from the last post to the first. This will also give you the total perimeter of the fence.

   e. Then, for each cow, you need to read the distance at it's starting point and end point, subtract these, and compare it to the total perimeter minus this size.

3. USACO 2020 February Bronze Problem 1: Triangles

   http://usaco.org/index.php?page=viewproblem2&cpid=1011

   a. This is a search problem with underlying geometric shapes: triangles this time.

   b. Figure 6.29 is a drawing of the sample case.

   c. Below is one suggested method of determining the domain and enumeration. There are others.

   - The domain is all combinations of three points that form a right triangle.
   - Enumeration: this is the hard part that requires geometric insight. In every right triangle, there is only one vertex with a 90-degree angle. This can be our cue for enumeration.

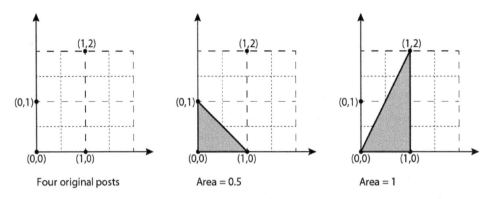

Figure 6.29 The four posts and two possible right triangles for the sample input of Triangles.

4. USACO 2017 Open Bronze Problem 3: Modern Art

   http://usaco.org/index.php?page=viewproblem2&cpid=737

   a. This is a hard problem.

   b. Draw a few examples of your own, even with just two rectangles on a blank canvas.

   c. Hint: You can determine the bounding box for each color. Then, if there is any other color within this area, it means that the other color could not have been first.

5. USACO 2013 February Bronze Problem 3: Perimeter

   http://usaco.org/index.php?page=viewproblem2&cpid=243

   a. We will solve this problem here as a geometry problem. This problem can also be solved using recursion.

   b. Given a starting hay bale, you can walk along the perimeter and count the sides.

   c. When walking around the hay bales, follow the same rule as walking through a maze: keep your right hand on the wall. This will ensure you are walking around the perimeter in a consistent manner.

6.4. Summary

- **Geometric concepts** appear in many USACO problems:

  - They appear in problems that are focused on shapes in one and two dimensions.
  - They also appear in searching and modeling problems where the underlying concept might have a geometric structure, like a circle or a timeline.

- We have three different methods for solving geometric problems:

  - **The brute-force** method checks all possible points in the problem. This method is often the simplest to code, but it is slow. It is useful when there is a small number of coordinates to check.

- The **casework analysis** method discerns the different spatial configurations, and treats each one of them appropriately. This method is most useful when there are only a handful of different cases to consider.
- The **geometric analysis** method is based on geometric insights into the problem. This often leads to the fastest execution time and the most succinct code, but it requires a careful understanding of the geometry involved.

- **Manhattan distance** is the distance calculated in a two-dimensional space when one is limited to moving parallel to the axes. This is the most commonly used type of distance in USACO Bronze.
- **A circle** can be considered in most settings as a one-dimensional line segment with the edges connected. There are two ways to move from one point to another on a circle: clockwise or counterclockwise.

Chapter 7. Strings

This chapter covers

- Representing strings as sequences of characters.
- Solving problems with collections of characters.
- Using and solving problems deploying strings as words or labels.
- Evaluating the costs and benefits of string functions.
- Using lexicographic order on strings.

Although humans communicate with words, computers use numbers. To allow computers to handle words, we represent words in code as strings. And just like words are composed of letters, strings are composed of characters. This chapter deals with strings and characters, and covers their use on the Bronze level.

You may be wondering why we use the terms "strings" and "characters" in computer programming, rather than "words" and "letters." The reason is that "strings" and "characters" are broader terms. In English, letters are all the symbols A through Z, both lowercase and uppercase. Characters, however, include all those letters plus many other symbols, such as question marks, exclamation points, and even blank spaces between words. Likewise, in English, words are combinations of letters, like "hello." Strings, however, are combinations of characters, many of which are definitely not words, such as "Lleho," "lehlo," "HhhhHHHello," or even "?!.,;:."

In programming, we're often interested in strings that aren't words. Take the human genome, for example, which we conceptualize as a chain of bases that we label A, T, C, and G. These bases form a string of approximately 3.2 billion letters, a highly complex string that computational biologists work to analyze.

Still, we don't always need to toss words out the window in favor of strings! There are many cases where a USACO problem focuses on words, or names, which are indeed pronounceable and are real words. Remember, strings are a superset of words: just like every dog is a mammal though not every mammal is a dog, every word is a string though not every string is a word.

The chapter map is described in figure 7.1. We start In section 7.1 with characters, the basic elements of strings. We explain how characters are represented in a computer, and then move to problems that consider the individual characters of strings. In section 7.2 we consider strings that are words: names, labels, and so on. In section 7.3 we discuss specific functions that can be applied to strings. Finally, in section 7.3.2, we close by paying special attention to the lexicographic order of words.

283

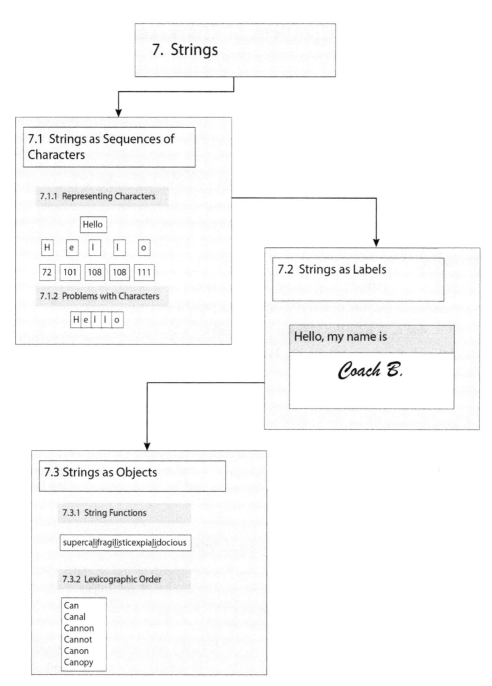

Figure 7.1 Strings chapter map. Looking at strings from three different perspectives.

7.1. Strings as Sequences of Characters

In this section, we will discuss problems where strings are used to store characters in an ordered way. These problems are not concerned with the meaning of the string as a whole, but rather with its individual building blocks, the characters.

7.1.1. Representing Characters

Coach B: Welcome to our new unit on strings! In USACO Bronze, strings are frequently used to conveniently represent the input data when you're working with problems about searching, modeling, and more. We will solve these types of problems in this unit. But before we dig into our first problem, sit back, close your laptops, and let's talk a little bit about words and letters.

The team settles in.

Coach B: Let's start from the beginning. What are words?

The team laughs, but they trust that Coach B has a point. They try to answer.

Ryan: A word is... a collection of letters that we can say and understand.

Rachid: Well, that seems too specific; I think words are collections of letters that have an agreed-upon meaning.

Annie: Yeah, it's a word if it's included in the dictionary.

Ryan: Except that doesn't include people's names, like "Rachid" or "Annie." These are words, but they're not in the dictionary.

Coach B: Okay, I'm glad you see the need for precision! But we don't really need to go into the dictionary to define the word "word" right now. I think we got the idea. Rachid pretty much nailed it: a word is a collection of letters that have an agreed-upon meaning for us. Does this sound right?

The team nods in agreement.

Coach B: Okay, a collection of letters. So what are letters?

Mei: In English, there are 26 letters, A to Z. But it really depends on the language. Oh! And some words have other things in them; my friend D'Angelo has an apostrophe in his name.

Coach B: Perfect. So does anyone have an idea why in computer science, and here in this unit, we use the term "character" rather than "letter"?

Mei: Well, I think all the letters are characters, but characters can also be other symbols. You know, everything else you can hit on the keyboard? Like the apostrophe, or the semicolon. There are way more characters than letters.

Coach B: Correct. So if we say that a string is a collection of characters, what do you think the differences are between words and strings?

Annie: For one, words are things you can always say, and they always mean something. Strings aren't like that, necessarily. Like for example, my passwords are strings, but not words.

Coach B: That's a good thing! Words alone make terribly weak passwords! And you've got it, exactly: words are a small subset of strings. Strings are much more general objects than words. There are many more strings in the world than words.

The team ponders this statement.

TIP: Don't use single words, or even combinations of words, as your passwords! Many password-cracking algorithms do a brute-force search over many combinations of words. Use strings rather than just words, and use characters rather than just letters. Mix in various symbols and numbers. This will make it much harder for a brute-force algorithm to crack your password.

Coach B: So, one more thing before we jump into a practice problem. Please bear with me for another five minutes, as I want to cover one more very important aspect of how computers deal with characters. We all know the computer "thinks" only in numbers, so how can it deal with characters?

Rachid: I think it represents the characters as numbers. Is that correct?

Coach B: Very good. Yes! In the early 1960s, ASCII coding was established. ASCII stands for "American Standard Code for Information Interchange," and as the name implies, it was focused on the American, or English, set of letters. It assigned each letter a unique code, a number. For example, the lowercase letter 'a' is represented by the value 97, lowercase 'b' by the number 98, and so on. Uppercase 'A' is represented by the number 65, uppercase 'B' by the number 66, and so on. But like we just said, there are many more characters than there are letters, and ASCII deals with these, too. For example, '!' is represented by 33, and ':' is represented by 58. Overall, there are 128 symbols defined in the ASCII code. Any idea why 128?

Mei: Because it fits into one byte? One byte is 8 bits, which has room for 256 codes actually.

Coach B: Correct on all fronts. They wanted the code to fit into one byte in the computer memory, and they also wanted to leave one bit spare for possible other usages. Do you all follow me so far?

Rachid: Sort of, but computers work with zeros and ones. So what do you mean lowercase 'a' is represented by 97?

Coach B: Yes, it is zeros and ones, but we can represent it as a base 2 number, right? Remember binary numbers? So, in this sense, the lowercase 'a', which has value 97, is actually written in memory as '01100001', which is 97 in base 2. Okay, now let's move on to why all this matters for Bronze.

The team members frown at each other, then start laughing.

Annie: Coach B, did you memorize all the binary representations? How did you know that so fast? Are you sure it's right?

Coach B: Ha! Well, let's see!

He writes on the board:

```
01100001 base 2 = 1*1 + 0*2 + 0*4 + 0*8 + 0*16 + 1*32 + 1*64 = 97
```

The team follows in agreement.

Ryan: Yeah, that checks out! Coach, you were about to say how all this relates to Bronze. I thought the idea was that programming in languages like C++ or Python means that we get to ignore the nitty-gritty details. So, yeah... how does this relate to the competition?

Coach B: Thanks for getting us back on track, Ryan. Once you know these details, your understanding goes deeper, so you're able to grapple better with Bronze problems. Here's an example. To the computer, is the string "12" the same as the number 12?

Ryan: Oh, I see what you mean. The number 12 is represented as zeros and ones in binary, but the string "12" is a combination of two characters, so it will be two bytes in our ASCII code, the first representing "1" and the second representing "2."

Coach B: Yes, very good. Okay, let's open your laptops and solve a problem!

The team cheers. They are ready!

TIP: In C, and C++, you can treat characters (variables of type `char`) as (unsigned) numbers. This is beyond the Bronze level, but now that you know how characters are represented, operations on characters may make more sense to you. For example, in C++ you can perform the subtraction of two characters, say the operation '9'-'5', and the result would be the number 4. How can it be? The character '9' is represented by ASCII code 57, and the character '5' is represented by ASCII code 53. When you do the subtraction, 57-53, the result is indeed 4. Again, you are unlikely to use this method in USACO Bronze.

7.1.2. Problems with Characters

Coach B: Okay then, let's dive right into the first string problem. Bessie and her friends are in beautiful Minnesota, also known as the Land of 10,000 Lakes. That's a lot! But before heading to the boundary water and the lakes, the group visits the capital, St. Paul, and its famous cathedral. Please read the problem, and we'll discuss it when you're done.

Problem 7.1: Double Doors

Bessie is visiting St. Paul, Minnesota, where the average low temperature in January is 6 degrees Fahrenheit. That's well below the freezing point. Brrr... In order to keep warm air within the structures, and keep the snow and sleet outside, all farms have a system of doors in their entryways.

A system of doors has N doors, $N < 10^6$. The system is composed of left doors, each marked as a left-parenthesis '(', and right doors, each marked as a right-parenthesis ')'. An example of a system of doors is the following string.

()((()))

A valid system of doors is one which is balanced. This means that for every left door, there's a corresponding right door that closes it. Each door can be matched with only one other door, and the left door should, of course, be on the left of the right door.

Determine if a given string describing a system of doors is balanced.

Input Format

Two lines.

The first line contains one integer N, the number of doors in the system.

The second line contains a string of length N, describing a system of doors.

Output Format

One word. 'Yes' if the system is balanced, and 'No' if it is not.

Sample Input

8

()((()))

Sample Output

Yes

The doors can be paired as shown by the corresponding symbols below.

() ((()))

aa b c dd c b

DISCUSSION

The team finishes reading the problem.

Ryan: I kind of got confused with what "balanced" means here, but I think they're trying to say it's a normal math-expression set of parentheses, right?

Coach B: What do you mean by "normal math-expression"?

Ryan: I mean one where you can put numbers and plus signs into it, and it'll be a mathematical expression. Because whenever you opened a set of parentheses, you remembered to close it.

Annie: Oh, that's a cool way to think about it. I see what you mean. Here, let me draw the problem's sample case like this.

Visualize it: Annie takes the marker, and draws figure 7.2.

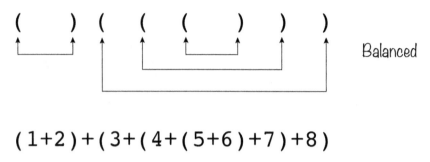

Figure 7.2 Drawing the sample case, and demonstrating its possible use as an arithmetic expression.

Annie: First, I re-drew their example, and connected the different right and left parentheses. Then, I drew a math expression that fits into these.

Coach B: Very nice. Can you draw an example that is *not* balanced?

Annie: Sure, I'll just flip the middle ones.

Annie adds one more case, as in figure 7.3.

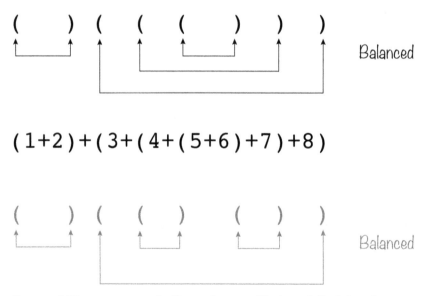

Figure 7.3 Adding one more case, by flipping the two middle doors. Still, a balanced system.

Annie: Oh, wait, it's still balanced. Hmm...

Mei: I think if we flip two more, it'll be unbalanced. Here, let me try.

And Mei draws the case as in figure 7.4.

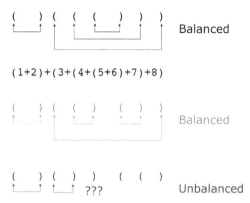

$$(1+2)+(3+(4+(5+6)+7)+8)$$

Figure 7.4 Finally, an unbalanced set of doors. We cannot find a pairing for the 5 door.

Coach B: Yes, this one seems unbalanced. Thanks, Mei. Now that we have an example of both cases, any thoughts about how to solve this problem?

 TIP: When you are asked to discern between two or more cases, it is helpful to draw examples for each case. This will help you see the differences, giving you insight as to how to differentiate between the cases.

ALGORITHM

Rachid: To start with, I think the first door can't be a right door. It has to start with a left door. So we can check for that. Then, we can go left to right, and whenever we see a right door, we pair it with the last unpaired left door that we already encountered.

Ryan: How will you keep track of the doors we already paired?

Rachid: I'll have another array for those. So if I see a right door, I'll go backward on this array until I find a left door that wasn't paired yet. And I need to watch out for cases when it's an unbalanced system, because then I need to make sure I end the search at index zero and not fall off the array.

Coach B: That sounds right, and probably even doable, but seems it's getting a little too complex. Is there a much easier way to do this?

 TIP: Although you won't always find a simpler way to solve the problem, it's worth looking for one. Once you have an algorithm, assuming it is correct, it means you understand the problem and are able to solve it. The next step is coding it, and fast. But before you do, you could look back and find an easier way. It may take some extra time (which admittedly is in short supply during a competition!), but it could save you a lot of time and effort in coding and debugging.

The team pauses to think. A long moment passes.

Coach B: Here's a hint. We don't really need to find the matching pairs of doors. We just need to say if it's balanced or not.

The team stays quiet, unsure how to use the hint.

Coach B: Okay, here's another hint. Let's assume from the get-go that the string is balanced. We then move along it from the left, following something similar to Rachid's algorithm. If we get all the way to the end of the string, and didn't find any reason for it to be unbalanced, then it *is* balanced, right? What this tells us is that we should only look for the case where it is *not* balanced. So, in other words, can you tell me how you would notice if it were unbalanced?

Mei: Maybe... I think, if there are more right doors than left doors?

Rachid: Yeah, that makes sense, I think. Because we're always trying to match doors to the ones we've already seen, and if at any stage there are more right doors, then we definitely won't be able to match it to anything we've seen already.

Annie: Oh, that's brilliant. I think I got it. We can just go left to right, and count how many left doors we have. For every right door we bump into, we subtract one from this count, because it'll be matched with one of the left doors. If this count ever goes negative, there's no way it was balanced.

Ryan: Wow, so we only need to have a counter?

Rachid: That's so much simpler. Here. Let me write this one.

Rachid writes down the code as in listing 7.1.

Listing 7.1 Balanced Doors

```
1   int cnt = 0;
2   for (int i = 0; i < N; ++i) {
3       if (str[i] == '(') cnt++;
4       else cnt--;
5       if (cnt < 0) break;
6   }
7
8   string ans;
9   if (cnt == 0) ans = "Yes";
10  else ans = "No";
```

Ryan: Wow, that's so much simpler than the original one we were thinking about!

The whole team looks with admiration and surprise over the simple code.

Coach B: I concur. Such a simple and clean solution. Kudos to Rachid for writing it so concisely! Any questions? Alright, then. It seems our first string problem went very smoothly. I'll tell you right now, that's a green-light code! Well done.

Now, look back at how this algorithm was set up. Even though the input was a string, our algorithm examined one character of the string at a time. Next week we will see the extreme reverse case: We'll be interested only in the string as a whole, and not with its individual characters. But until then, let me put a few homework problems on the site, and we'll see you next week.

EPILOGUE

We started by exploring the differences between words and strings and between letters and characters. In the problem dealing with doors, the characters were '(' and ')' rather than letters, and naturally, the string was not a word. In some sense, the string served as a container that preserved the order of the characters. We could have used an array of characters in C++, or a list of characters in Python. If we wanted to take it another step further, the program could have read and processed one character at a time. In this problem, we didn't need to store the characters, or the whole string, at all.

 VOCABULARY Corner: **UNICODE** The Unicode Standard is the accepted modern-day way to handle symbols used in writing systems. It transcends the ASCII system in the sense that it allows for many more symbols, as well as encompasses many more aspects of the text representation process. Text representation includes such things as writing in multiple languages, writing in multiple directions, and using multiple encoding schemes. UNICODE includes about 150,000 symbols that cover 161 modern and historic scripts, as well as symbols and thousands of emojis (even in color).

PRACTICE PROBLEMS

Hints and full solutions to the problems can be found on the club's page: http://www.usacoclub.com

1. USACO 2012 November Bronze Problem 1: Find the Cow!

   http://www.usaco.org/index.php?page=viewproblem2&cpid=187

   a. Read one character at a time going from left to right.

   b. Every pair of '((' can be a pair of left legs. Keep a count of these.

   c. Every pair of '))' can be matched to all the pairs of left legs seen so far.

2. USACO 2017 US Open Bronze Problem 2: Bovine Genomics

   http://www.usaco.org/index.php?page=viewproblem2&cpid=736

   a. Process one character at a time, but across a few strings.

   b. When looking at a specific location across strings, if there is any letter that appears in both spotted and non-spotted cows, than this location cannot be an indicator of spottiness.

7.2. Strings as Words

Coach B: Welcome back to another session of our USACO training! We are getting close to the first competition event, and we are close to wrapping up all the material you need to ace the Bronze!

Ryan: Yes!

The team echoes Ryan. They're excited to see the finish line ahead.

Coach B: Today we continue our exploration of strings. Whereas last time, strings were merely a collection of characters, this time around our strings are actual words, or names, and we treat them as such. Without further ado, let me present the problem for today. Go ahead, and we'll discuss it after you're done reading.

Coach B projects the problem on the board.

Problem 7.2: Arrange by Age

Bessie and her friends are excited to explore the beautiful Boundary Waters. This is a wilderness area in northeast Minnesota, accessible primarily by canoe. Full of lakes and greenery, it's a cow's heaven.

The canoe rental owner has a minimum age limit of 6 years old for cows who want to take the trip. Bessie is 8 years old, and was born in January.

Given the input declarations from the cows, determine if there is any cow who was born more than two years before Bessie.

Input Format

The first line contains one integer N, the number of cows in the group in addition to Bessie ($1 \leq N \leq 100$).

Each of the next N lines contains a 7-word phrase specifying the relationship between the birth month of two cows. It is of the form

"`Rosie was born in April after Bessie`", or

"`Rosie was born in April before Bessie`".

The first word is the name of a cow on the farm who is not "Bessie" and who has not yet been mentioned in the input. All cow names are a single sequence of letters.

The last word is also the name of a cow on the farm, which is either "Bessie" or a cow that has already been mentioned in a previous line of input.

Words 2 through 4 are always "was born in".

The 5th word is a name of a month: January, February, March, April, May, June, July, August, September, October, November, or December.

The 6th word is either "before" or "after".

The number of months separating two cows mentioned on the same line can be any number between one and twelve (for example, if both cows are born in April, then they are 12 months apart, not 0 months apart).

Output Format

One word. 'Yes' if there is any cow who was born more than 2 years before Bessie, and 'No' otherwise.

Sample Input

```
4
Rosie was born in April after Bessie
Daisy was born in April before Rosie
Elsie was born in March before Daisy
Betty was born in August after Rosie
```

Sample Output

```
No
```

If Bessie was born in January 2020, then all the cows were born as follows:

Bessie was born in January 2020

Rosie was born in April 2020

Daisy was born in April 2019

Elsie was born in March 2019

Betty was born in August 2020

No cow was born more than two years before Bessie.

DISCUSSION

The team finishes reading the problem.

Annie: Yeah, um, that's a lot of words, and sentences. Even the input is real sentences and not just numbers.

Ryan: Yes, but at the end of the day these are just names of the months and of cows. We could have called it month 1, month 2, and so on, and even for the cows we could call them cow 1, cow 2, and so forth. We don't really care about the names, per se.

Coach B: Interesting. I think we do care about the fact that Daisy is the name of the same cow appearing in the second and third input sentences.

Ryan: Oh, for sure. What I meant is that we don't care what the name is, as long as it's the same in both places.

Coach B: Agreed. So, do we have any volunteers to draw the sample case on the board?

Mei: I think it is very simple. We just follow each line of the input, and add one more cow at a time. I might be missing something, as it looks too simple.

Visualize it: Mei stands up, walks to the board, and draws table 7.1.

Coach B: Great. Let's see if anyone else can explain the table. Anyone?

Table 7.1 Analyzing the input, line by line.

Input	New cow name	New cow month	New cow age (in months, relative to Bessie)
(This we know)	Bessie	January	0
Rosie was born in April after Bessie	Rosie	April	0 + 3 = +3
Daisy was born in April before Rosie	Daisy	April	3 - 12 = -9
Elsie was born in March before Daisy	Elsie	March	-9 - 1 = -10
Betty was born in August after Rosie	Betty	August	3 + 4 = +7

Annie: I can try. So the first line, with Bessie, is just given in the question. Bessie was born in January, and we want all the ages relative to Bessie, so she is zero months away from herself. Then, Rosie was born in April after Bessie. Since Bessie was born in January, April is 3 months away. So Rosie is 3 months older than Bessie. Is this correct?

Coach B: Works for me. Anyone else for the next line?

Ryan: Daisy was born in April before Rosie. Since Rosie was also born in April, this means we have to go a full year back, 12 months. Normally, like for humans, I would think if two friends were born in April then it may have been in the same year, but the problem says "The number of months separating two cows mentioned on the same line can be any number between one and twelve." So her age is Rosie's age, which was 3 months after Bessie's, minus 12, which is -9. Well, she is not -9 months old, of course. She's 9 months older than Bessie.

Coach B: Very nice. Seems clear enough to me. Any questions? I think we also covered an edge-case, where the two cows have the same birth month.

The team seems content with the table.

Coach B: There is only one subtle point I want to highlight here. We already encountered it when we dealt with the seats around the arena. Remember that problem?

Mei: Yes, when we needed to find the best seat to enter into the arena. This was a search problem. But I can't see the connection to this problem...

Coach B: The seats in the arena were arranged in a circle, so the numbering went from 1, 2, 3... all the way to 100, and then back to 1, 2.... This is very similar here. We start with January, February, all the way to December, and then back to January, February... So the point is, how do we calculate the distance, in months, between two months?

The team seems not to follow this line of thought.

Coach B: Here, let's take a concrete example. Say we need to calculate the age difference between a cow that was born in October before a cow that was born in September. How would you do it?

Mei: Do we start counting months from 0, or from 1? I'll just choose 1 here because it's easier for me. Though I'm sure in the code we're going to start at 0. I just know it! Alright. September is 9, and October is 10. Just one month off. So this means the difference should be 11 months.

Coach B: Right. You did that in your head, but how would you get an algorithm to do it?

Rachid comes to the rescue.

Rachid: I think I get the connection to what we did in the arena, with the seats. What we need to do is first calculate September–October = 9-10 = -1. If the result is negative, we need to add 12. This way we get to 11. We add 12 just like we did back then: going around the arena the other way, we added 100, because we had 100 seats.

Coach B: Mei, does this ring a bell?

Mei: Oh, yes. Now I remember. It's like going around the circle clockwise or counterclockwise.

Coach B: Exactly. Now, if the difference between the two months is positive, do we need to add the 12? Say we need to calculate the difference going from April to June. Would we need to add 12 then?

Mei: Well, no. The difference is simply 2, which is the right answer.

Coach B: Yes! So, if it's negative we need to add 12, and if it's positive, we don't add anything, right?

The team nods.

Coach B: So indeed, the way we did it back then was with a conditional statement. Let me show you a different way to achieve the same result. This time we will do it with a modulus operator. Let me write the expression here:

```
diff_months = (month_to - month_from + 12) % 12;
```

Ryan: Um, actually, how did you get to that expression?

Coach B: Let's see. You for sure recognize the part with `month_to - month_from`, right?

Ryan: Yes, that's our original.

Coach B: Now, if this expression is negative, we need to add 12. We do just that in the expression I wrote. This will bring the part in parentheses into the range 0 to 11. Then, we take modulus 12 which doesn't matter at all if the quantity is between 0 and 11. So we are fine. Do we agree?

The team nods slowly in comprehension.

Ryan: So why do we need to take the modulus 12 if it doesn't do anything?

Coach B: Well, there's the second case. The second case is when the difference between the months is positive. In that case, we still add 12, but when we take modulus with 12, we come back to the original number. For example, if the difference between the months was 5, then we add 12 to get 17. How much is `17 % 12`? It's 5 again! So, the modulus 12 ensures that this expression, with adding 12, works well for all cases, and there's no need for a conditional statement.

The team ponders. It's working, but it still looks like magic.

TIP: It's a common pattern to use $(\text{variable}+N) \% N$. It helps deal in a consistent manner with negative numbers. Keep it as a tool in your toolbox.

Coach B: I know it looks strange the first time you see this pattern. Consider it one more tool you can reach for. Maybe you will grow to love this one, and maybe you'd prefer using the conditional statement. Your choice. Let's keep with it for now, and see if we can code everything in. Are you ready for coding all this? After all, Keep in mind, we do need to handle strings, both in the input and when processing the months and the cows' names.

Ryan: Oh, it's very easy to do it in Python! I would use dictionaries for this. Can I show you on the board?

Coach B: That would be lovely, but first let's try and do it without any dictionaries, in plain vanilla C++.

TIP: Indeed, dictionaries in Python are a very convenient data structure to assign values to labels. For example, we could use a Python dictionary to associate each cow-name (a label) with that cow's age (a value). Or we could assign to each month (a label) a month value (January=0, February=1, ...). C++ and Java have similar data structures, called maps. Those advanced data structures are not required for USACO Bronze, and although we could use them to solve this problem, here we will do it without them.

Coach B: Since the main issue here is writing the code, and it is going to be long and verbose if we do it in C++, let's go ahead and write it together. I'll project it on the board, and you can follow along on your laptops. I don't think you'll find it hard, but it's certainly longer than most programs we've written.

ALGORITHM

Coach B projects his screen on the board, and starts writing listing 7.2.

Listing 7.2 Arrange By Age (First part)

```
1   #include <iostream>
2   using namespace std;
3
4   int main() {
5
6       int N;
7       cin >> N;
8
9       string months[] = {"January", "February", "March", "April",
10      "May", "June", "July", "August", "September", "October",
11      "November", "December"};
12
13      string cow_name[N + 1];
14      int cow_age[N + 1];   // Age in months, relative to Bessie
15      int cow_month[N + 1]; // The month the cow was born
16
17      cow_name[0] = "Bessie";
18      cow_age[0] = 0;   // Bessie is our reference
19      cow_month[0] = 0; // January
```

Coach B: Pretty standard stuff so far, right? We created the various arrays, and initialized them with Bessie. She is our reference. Any questions?

Ryan: Why did you create the arrays with size of $N + 1$? We have only N string lines in the input.

Coach B: Yes, there are only N strings of input, and each one contains information about a new cow. But, we also have Bessie, our reference, so we need to store her somewhere.

Ryan: Oh, right.

Coach B: Okay, let's go over the next part, which takes care of the input and setting up.

Coach B continues the code, as in listing 7.3.

Listing 7.3 Arrange By Age (Second part)

```
1      for (int i = 1; i <= N; ++i) {
2
3          string cow_to, cow_from, tmp;
4          string before_after, mon;
5          cin >> cow_to >> tmp >> tmp >> tmp >> mon
6          cin >> before_after >> cow_from;
7
8          // Rosie was born in April after Bessie
9          cow_name[i] = cow_to;
10
11         // Translate month into a number
12         for (int j = 0; j < 12; ++j) {
13             if (mon == months[j]) {
14                 cow_month[i] = j;
15                 break;
16             }
17         }
18
19         // Find the index of the cow_from
20         int cow_from_ind;
21         for (int j = 0; j < i; ++j) {
22             if (cow_from == cow_name[j]) {
23                 cow_from_ind = j;
24                 break;
25             }
26         }
```

Annie: It sure is a lot of work translating from the names and months into numbers.

Coach B: Yes, that's the price we pay when dealing with strings, and when we are not using many of the available standard library functions dedicated to dealing with strings.

Ryan: If we're using Python and dictionaries, it's way faster!

Coach B: You'll get your time shortly when we are done, no worries, Ryan. Now, to the rest of us, any questions? It's just like Annie said: it's cumbersome dealing with strings. There are many ways to make it much simpler, like using maps in C++, enumerated types (for the case of the months), and so on. But I want to make sure you can see this: that we can solve it with basic C++. If there are no questions so far, let me now go to the logic part of the algorithm! I think we all agreed that we could do it after seeing Annie's table, so we didn't think too hard about it. But here it is, in C++.

Coach B continues the code, as in listing 7.4.

Listing 7.4 Arrange By Age (Third, and last, part)

```
1        int month_to = cow_month[i];
2        int month_from = cow_month[cow_from_ind];
3
4        if (before_after == "after") {
5            int diff_months = (month_to - month_from + 12) % 12;
6            cow_age[i] = cow_age[cow_from_ind] + diff_months;
7            if (cow_month[i] == cow_month[cow_from_ind])
8                cow_age[i] += 12;
9        } else {   // "before"
10           int diff_months = (month_from - month_to + 12) % 12;
11           cow_age[i] = cow_age[cow_from_ind] - diff_months;
12           if (cow_month[i] == cow_month[cow_from_ind])
13               cow_age[i] -= 12;
14       }
15   }
16
17   string ans = "No";
18   for (int j = 0; j < N + 1; ++j) {
19       if (cow_age[j] < -24) {
20           ans = "Yes";
21       }
22   }
23   cout << ans << endl;
24 }
```

Annie: Wow, I'm glad you've written it out for us. It's just so much code to write.

Coach B: Exactly.

Coach B peeks at his watch.

Coach B: Hmm... seems like writing all this code together took us quite some time. And Ryan, I know you wanted to show us how short and easy it can be to write it in Python with dictionaries. Here is what I suggest: I will put on the club's page the code we just did in C++, as well as whatever Python code you'll send me, Ryan. Would that be okay with you?

Ryan: Sure. I actually already wrote it, just now.

Coach B: Great. So just to recap: this problem had us dealing with strings that were real labels. We had names of cows and names of months. The input lines were full sentences.

We did have to be careful with calculating the difference between months, but most of the difficulty in this problem was handling the strings. As Ryan mentioned, there are advanced techniques to do it more swiftly. However, you are not expected to master those for Bronze. We were able to solve the problem with basic data structures and careful coding. For practice, I will put a few homework problems on the site, and we'll see you next week. Happy coding!

EPILOGUE

Strings can be easily represented in every modern programming language, including C++ and Python. However, the "Arrange by Age" problem presented two hurdles. The first dealt with converting between strings and numerical values; for example, from "April" to 3 ("January" is 0). The second hurdle dealt with matching the name of a cow to her location in the array: for example, matching "Bessie" to index 0. These issues created a more involved code. There are tools, like dictionaries in Python and maps in C++ and Java, that can handle these situations more conveniently; however, these are not required for the Bronze level.

 VOCABULARY Corner: **ASSOCIATIVE ARRAY** Python dictionaries, and C++ maps, are examples of associative arrays. These data structures hold key-value pairs. In other words, they associate, or link, a key with a value. They then allow you to retrieve a value by referencing its key. For example, a dictionary of months in Python can hold as key the names of the months, and as value their sequential number in the calendar. So the pairs in the dictionary would be `months_dict = {"January":0, "February":1, "March":2, ...}`. To retrieve the value for any month, we can simply access `months_dict["January"]`, and retrieve the value 0.

PRACTICE PROBLEMS

Hints and full solutions to the problems can be found on the club's page: http://www.usacoclub.com

1. USACO 2021 February Bronze Problem 1: Year of the Cow

   http://www.usaco.org/index.php?page=viewproblem2&cpid=1107

   a. Very similar to the problem "Arrange by Age" we solved.

   b. Read one line at a time from the input, and find the relevant age of the newly introduced cow.

2. USACO 2019 January Bronze Problem 3: Guess Animal

   http://www.usaco.org/index.php?page=viewproblem2&cpid=893

   a. Use strings as labels.

   b. Count the number of similar characteristics among any two animals.

3. USACO 2023 Open Bronze Problem 2: Moo Language

   http://www.usaco.org/index.php?page=viewproblem2&cpid=1324

   a. This is a search problem that uses string labels.

   b. It is a hard problem.

c. Partition the problem into two parts. The first part is searching for the optimal configuration and type of sentences. The second part is composing these sentences.

d. Using C++ vectors will simplify the coding a little. Alternatively, you can use fixed-length arrays, as you are given that N cannot be more than 1000.

7.3. Strings as Objects

We have already seen strings as a mere collection of characters, and we also saw strings as labels and names. In this section we are considering strings as objects, which have built-in functions that can work on them. After we solve an example problem, we'll briefly talk about how to arrange strings by order.

7.3.1. String Algorithms

String algorithms are a very broad and active area of research. At Bronze level, you are not expected to be familiar with these algorithms, but rather, at most, only use some predefined functions on strings. For example, one common function is to find the first occurrence of a short string within a larger string. For example, can you find a "rad" in "camaraderie"?

In this section, we will put that common function to use, and then we will consider alternatives as well.

Coach B: Welcome, everyone! Today we will close our discussion of strings. Strings is a very large subject, and an important component at the more advanced levels of USACO. For Bronze, however, we mostly covered all that is needed: strings as collections of characters and strings as labels. Today we will examine one more aspect, that of built-in functions on strings. These functions can be a good resource when handling strings, even on Bronze, and I hope the example will serve as a good segue about string algorithms in the future. It's exciting stuff, team! We're on the cutting edge here, the most advanced stuff that's still on Bronze. And here it is!

Coach B projects the problem on the screen.

_____

Problem 7.3: Bessst Bracelet

Bessie visits a history museum dedicated to the two largest tribes who called Minnesota home: the Dakota and the Ojibwe. She is fascinated to learn about how the tribes lived in such a harsh environment.

At the souvenir shop, on the way out, she sees a bowl full of friendship bracelets with her favorite letters: B, E, S, and I. Each bracelet has N letters ($6 \leq N \leq 10^6$). Bessie wants to pick the bracelet that has the most resemblance to her name. She gives each bracelet points as follows:

Every match in the bracelet to the first letter of her name, B, gets one point.

Every match in the bracelet to the first two letters of her name, BE, gets two points.

Every match in the bracelet to the first three letters of her name, BES, gets three points.

Every match in the bracelet to the first four letters of her name, BESS, gets four points.

Every match in the bracelet to the first five letters of her name, BESSI, gets five points.

Every match in the bracelet to the full name BESSIE gets ten points.

Given a bracelet, help Bessie determine its point score.

Input Format

Two lines.

The first line contains one integer N, the number of letters in the bracelet.

The next line contains one string of N letters.

Output Format

One number, the point score of the bracelet.

Sample Input

14

BESSIEBEBESSIE

Sample Output

53

DISCUSSION

The team finishes reading and everyone talks at once.

Ryan: Well, this looks like a problem with both character and string components to it.

Rachid: And I tried to start counting, and got all confused.

Mei: And they didn't give any explanation for the answer, they just gave the number. They usually also have some short explanation.

Coach B: You all sound overwhelmed. Just to address your point, Mei: Indeed, they did not give an explanation as to how to get to the sample result. That does happen sometimes. Maybe they think it will give away too much of the answer. Anyway, no need to worry about that. Let's see if you can reproduce the answer they give. Here, go to the board and try counting it together.

The team goes to the board, and after a few trials and errors produces the table as in table 7.2.

Table 7.2 Counting points in the bracelet.

String	Substring	# of occurrences	Points
BESSIEBEBESSIE	B	3	3
BESSIEBEBESSIE	BE	3	6
BESSIEBEBESSIE	BES	2	6
BESSIEBEBESSIE	BESS	2	8
BESSIEBEBESSIE	BESSI	2	10
BESSIEBEBESSIE	BESSIE	2	20
Total points:			53

Coach B: Okay, can someone explain what you did?

Annie: We got really confused, so we picked a really simple method to be safe. As you can see, we counted how many B's there are. Each of these got us 1 point. Then we counted how many BE's there are in the strings, and so on, until finally we counted how many BESSIE's there are in the string.

Coach B: Yes, I see. What made it take you so long to get there?

Ryan: At first we tried to do it faster by counting everything at once as we scanned from left to right. We got a different number every time, and it wasn't even the expected answer! That's why we went with the slow and safe method.

Coach B: That's funny but understandable. And as we often say, better safe than sorry. Later we can improve on speed if needed.

The team looks happy with their solution.

ALGORITHM

Coach B: So I guess your algorithm will use the string `find()` function to find the occurrences, and just tally these up, right? Is anyone ready to write it for us?

Annie steps forward, takes the marker, and writes the code as in listing 7.5.

Listing 7.5 Besssst Bracelet (Using string functions)

```
string name = "BESSIE";
int pts = 0;

for (int len = 1; len <= name.length(); ++len) {
    // We use substr to take a substring of length 'len' from the name
    string name_sub = name.substr(0, len);
    int pos = 0;
    // str is the input string
    while ((pos = str.find(name_sub, pos)) != string::npos) {
        pts += len;
        if (len == name.length())
```

```
12                    pts += 4;  // completing 6 points to 10 points for full name
13            pos += len;
14      }
15  }
```

Coach B: Very nice, Annie. And impressive mastery of C++ string functions. Can you explain the two functions you used?

Annie: Thanks. I used `name.substr(0, len)`. `substr(start_pos, length)` takes `length` characters, starting with `start_pos`. Since we want to take characters from the beginning of BESSIE, `start_pos` here is 0.

Ryan: In Python it would just be `name[0:length]`. Very similar, only without calling a special function.

Coach B: Indeed so. Different programming languages, but similar string functionality. And the second function you used, Annie?

Annie: The second one was `str.find(name_sub, pos)`. It tries to find the string `name_sub` within the string `str`, starting from position `pos`. The fact that it starts searching from `pos` is important because we want to make sure we don't find the same string time and again. So, every time we start from just after the last string we found. Oh, and if it doesn't find the substring, the function returns `string::npos` which is defined in C++, in the header file `<string>` I think.

Coach B: Yes, correct. We need to include `<string>` to get this benefit. This is part of the abstractions in C++, but this is all we need to know about this for now. Ryan, how does that work in Python?

Ryan: It's actually the same! You use `long_string.find(substring, position)`. The only difference is that the return value is -1 if the substring is not found.

Coach B: Okay. This whole problem went very fast. Any questions or comments?

The team doesn't have any questions.

Annie: Are we already done? This was a short practice!

Coach B: Sorry to disappoint you, but not quite! We saw the ease afforded by these built-in string functions. However, what do you think the time complexity of this algorithm is?

The team looks perplexed.

Mei: The length of the name "BESSIE" is 6, so we run the `len` loop 6 times. So I know that for sure. But I'm not sure how many times we actually call the `find()` function in the inner while loop. It depends on how many times we find the substring. And I don't know the complexity of the `find()` function.

Coach B: You hit the nail right on the head, Mei. Those are the two main questions! As for the first one: any ideas how many times we execute the loop that calls the `find()` function?

Ryan: We need to take the worst case. So maybe this is the length of the bracelet divided by six, the length of the name?

Annie: But we also look for the letter "B" at the very beginning. And if our bracelet is "BBBB...B" we would need to call the function N times. That would be even worse.

Coach B: You are both correct, and we need to keep in mind that we don't worry about multiplication factors when computing complexity. So both of your cases would mean we execute the loop about N times, worst-case. Agreed?

Annie and Ryan nod.

Coach B: So that leaves us with the second question: What is the time complexity of `find()`? Let me answer this for you: It depends. This is a library function, and the C++ standard doesn't specify the time complexity of this algorithm. There are different implementations, and they might differ in running time!

Ryan: So then, if our algorithm fails on time, how would we know whether or not it was because of these functions? It's not our fault!

Coach B: This is something to discuss in more depth when you further investigate string algorithms. But for now, in the Bronze level, if something like this happens, you may need to think "Can I get this done without using these special string functions?" Here, take the example we just did. Can we do it more elegantly and without the use of the special string functions?

Mei: What do you mean by "more elegantly"?

Coach B: I think I mean, "less wastefully." In my mind, it seems wasteful to go so many times over the input string to search for the occurrence of B, then BE, then BES, and so on. If we found there's a B somewhere, we might as well check if there is a BE as well, and then BES, and so forth. Oops, I think I just revealed the solution, didn't I?

The team smiles.

Rachid: Yeah, you did give it away. I think I've got it.

And Rachid puts down listing 7.6.

Rachid: I'm going over each character of the input string, left to right, and comparing it to the first character of the name string. If there's a match, I record that by adding the points, and move on to comparing the next character in the string to the second character of the name, and so on. So, this accomplishes what you said: we find all the matches to all the relevant substrings of the name, and all in one fell swoop.

Annie: Nice and clean code. Very clear. And yes, I think it looks more elegant than the one with the string functions. The other one is a little shorter, but this one is nice because it really uses only very simple operations. Just comparing character by character.

Listing 7.6 Bessst Bracelet (with no call to string functions)

```
1   string name = "BESSIE";
2   int pts = 0;
3   int name_index = 0;
4
5   for (int i = 0; i < N; ++i) {
6       // We are trying to match as much as we can from the name.
7       if (str[i] == name[name_index]) {
8           name_index++;
9           pts += name_index;
10          if (name_index == name.length()) {
11              pts += 4;   // completing 6 points to 10 points for full name
12              name_index = 0;
13          }
14      }
15      else {
16          name_index = 0;
17          // If the matching broke,
18          // we need to re-start from the start of the name.
19          if (str[i] == name[name_index]) {
20              name_index++;
21              pts += name_index;
22          }
23      }
24  }
```

The team looks at the code in agreement.

Mei: Yes, this is much simpler. There's no functions that kind of hide how they work. I prefer this one.

Ryan: I see what you mean, Mei, but I prefer the one using the functions. I would only use this one if my code with functions failed on time. But otherwise, I prefer using the black box of built-in functions.

Coach B: Interesting discussion. As we said, in competition time, the important thing is to solve the problem. And now you have more than one way to do that, and you can also practice it in your homework.

The team starts folding their laptops, ready to head out.

Coach B: Oh, one more thing before we go. I wanted to mention lexicographic order.

7.3.2. Lexicographic order

Lexicographic order is alphabetical order. It's the order used in dictionaries. This is the common way to specify ordering among strings. Since in the Bronze level you are not expected to deal with sorting algorithms, or with string algorithms, you will not likely need to use this ordering. Still, since it is so common a phrase when dealing with strings, it's important to be familiar with it. If you plan to advance beyond Bronze, this is the right time to learn about it.

Coach B: So let's have a very short detour to talk about lexicographic order. This is the same ordering used in dictionaries. Remember, those paper things we have in the library?

Mei: Ha! I think we haven't touched them since second grade.

Coach B: Yes, I know. But, you still remember how to order words, right? Here, let me write a few here, and you'll order them.

Coach B writes on the board the following words:

```
Align, Alignment, Alien, Word, Wording, Encyclopedia, Can, Can't,
Off-limits, ASAP, Hors d'oeuvres, Sk8
```

The team heads to the board, and starts writing them in order. It takes them just a minute or so. They've written:

```
Alien, Align, Alignment, ASAP, Can, Can't, Encyclopedia, Hors
d'oeuvres, Off-limits, Sk8, Word, Wording
```

Annie: We decided on this order, but we weren't sure how to deal with the dashes and apostrophes.

Mei: Yeah, we weren't sure about the apostrophe in "Can't." But since "Can" is shorter, we put it first.

Coach B: And that looks like the right choice. If you had also the word "Cannot," then it would be an issue, right? Because then you would need to decide if the apostrophe comes before or after the letter "n."

Mei: Yes, and the same goes for the space in "Hors d'oeuvres," the hyphen in "Off-limits," and the number in "sk8."

Coach B: Well, considering all these, you did a great job! And it's true, comparing letters and other characters is complicated. Like comparing apples and oranges. And the same goes for capital and lowercase letters: which should go first? There is no unique solution for that, and it depends on what we define. But, that's beyond our scope. All I wanted to make sure is that you're familiar with the term, and the skill of alphabetizing, even though your paper-dictionary days are way behind you.

Ryan: Mercifully!

The team chuckles.

Coach B: And on that happy note, we will end today. I will post a few problems as homework, and next week we will start our last unit before the USACO competition. See you then!

The team cheers as they grab their backpacks and head outside, excited.

EPILOGUE

Many programming languages have a rich and useful library of functions that can work on string objects. For USACO Bronze, you may need to use only the very basic ones, like extracting a substring from a longer string, or finding the location of one string within another. Use these functions freely; they are there to help you. However, if you run into time constraint issues with your problems, know that these functions might be the culprit. Check if you can work more efficiently with them, or if you could even avoid them altogether. And, as you progress through the levels in USACO, you will learn more about how to implement these functions efficiently.

VOCABULARY Corner: **LEXICON AND SYNTAX** Lexicon is the vocabulary of a language. It means the words we use in that language. Human languages consist of two parts: a lexicon, which is the words we use; and a grammar, which is the system of rules that tell us how to combine words into sentences. Programming languages are very similar. There is a set of reserved words, and a set of variable names you can make on your own; these are your lexicon. And then there is syntax, which is the set of rules for combining these reserved words and variables to write a program; these are our grammar.

PRACTICE PROBLEMS

Hints and full solutions to the problems can be found on the club's page: http://www.usacoclub.com

1. USACO 2023 January Bronze Problem 3: Moo Operations

   http://www.usaco.org/index.php?page=viewproblem2&cpid=1277

   a. Examine three characters from the input at a time.

   b. There are only a handful of substrings that can be transformed as required into "Moo": "MOO", "MOM", "OOO", and "OOM".

2. USACO 2021 January Bronze Problem 1: Uddered but not Herd

   http://www.usaco.org/index.php?page=viewproblem2&cpid=1083

   a. Examine one character from the input at a time.

   b. If the index of the new letter in the alphabet is lower (or equal) to the index of the previous letter in the alphabet, then she must have looped around.

3. USACO 2019 December Bronze Problem 2: Where am I?

   http://usaco.org/index.php?page=viewproblem2&cpid=964

   a. We have seen this problem already in Chapter 5.

   b. Searching over strings.

   c. Exhaustive search over all substrings would work within time.

4. USACO 2015 February Bronze Problem 1: Censoring?

   http://usaco.org/index.php?page=viewproblem2&cpid=526

   a. Using the library function `find()` will be too slow for some of the test cases.

   b. Hint: Think differently - Rather than removing substrings from the original string, construct the output string while avoiding any of the censored substrings.

   c. Big Hint: Add one character at a time to the output string, and check that the last sequence of characters is not a censored substring.

7.4. Summary

- **Strings and characters, words and letters**: A string is a sequence of characters, whereas a word is a sequence of letters. Characters are symbols, which include letters, but can also be any other symbol, like exclamation marks, commas, and so on.
- **Strings** can be processed one character at a time. In this regard, a string is an array of characters.
- **Labels and names** in USACO problems can be regarded as strings.
- **String library functions** are useful tools to handle strings. You should feel free to use them in USACO Bronze, but if your code fails due to time constraints, such functions might be the cause of these problems.
- **Lexicographic order** is the same alphabetical order used in dictionaries.

Chapter 8. Ad Hoc Problems and Advanced Techniques

This chapter covers

- Approaching problems that do not fall into any of the previous categories.
- Solving problems using the forward-backward technique.
- Focusing on significant events to reduce time and space complexities.
- Using and manipulating tree structures.
- Simplifying programs using dictionaries and dynamic arrays.

Ad hoc problems, also called logic problems or general problems, are problems that do not fall into any of the categories already discussed: modeling, searching, geometry, or strings. Although there's no single approach that will always work to solve these problems, there are a handful of techniques that can help you solve many of these problems, or at least simplify them.

The chapter map is described in figure 8.1.

We start in section 8.1 with the forward-backward technique. It's a simple approach that often yields a straightforward solution, yet many programmers fail to take advantage of this approach, winding up with solutions that are needlessly cumbersome and complex. For example, consider the problem of finding the second-to-last occurrence of the letter 'A' in the string "ABACAACABA". Using the conventional line of thinking, our algorithm will scan the string left to right, keeping a record of the previous and current instances of the letter 'A', and do some bookkeeping to get the final answer. However, if we look at this problem as going backward on the string, finding the second-to-last 'A' would be a breeze. We will consider this forward-backward idea in different problems and settings and see how to apply it.

Section 8.2 discusses the method of focusing only on significant events. Although we've briefly encountered this method before in some of the practice problems on modeling, here in this section we'll give the method our full attention to harness its power. For example, assume you are modeling the energy level of a runner in a marathon. Every mile, her energy level decreases by a known amount, and at every aid station, depending on what the aid station holds and what she takes from it, her energy level rebounds. Given the location of the aid stations, you need to determine her minimum energy level. Rather than simulate every mile on the road, you can focus only on the aid-stations locations, the significant events in this case. You know that her energy level would be minimal just before an aid station (or at the end of the race), so you can calculate it only at these points. In doing so, you've saved time and effort, and you've created tidier, simpler code.

The rest of the chapter is dedicated to two topics that play important roles in the more advanced levels of USACO. Although it's not strictly necessary for you to know these topics to succeed at the Bronze level, they will give you a significant advantage. They will help you solve some of the problems faster and more efficiently, and they'll lay a strong foundation for your future studies if you plan to continue beyond Bronze.

The first of these topics is in section 8.3, where we cover trees. Trees are a special type of graph, an important way of structuring data that should be carefully studied for the Silver level and beyond. For Bronze, we will just introduce the structure and describe a few problems that use a tree. Traversing and building trees are beyond the scope of Bronze, and will not be covered here.

Finally, section 8.4 briefly discusses two different kinds of data structures: dictionaries, also known as maps, and dynamic arrays. A dictionary or map is a data structure that holds pairs of keys and values. Again, we already encountered this data structure when working with strings, and here we will explore it more formally so we can apply them to other types of problems. The second data structure we'll explore is the dynamic array: a List in Python, or an ArrayList in Java. Again, we will talk briefly about the benefits of using this data structure, but we won't dive into the intricate details, since they are beyond the scope of Bronze.

All of these advanced techniques that we'll explore through the chapter are the cherry on top of your preparation for Bronze. You don't truly need them to pass, but by mastering them anyway, you'll pass Bronze with greater ease.

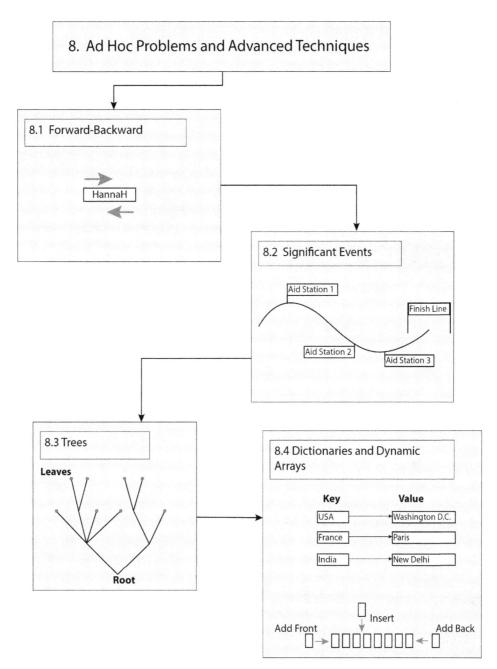

Figure 8.1 Ad hoc problems chapter map. We first discuss the forward-backward method, then the application of significant events. In the last two sections, we cover more advanced data structures that might prove useful to know at the Bronze level.

8.1. The Forward-Backward Technique

The forward-backward technique offers a new perspective on a problem. It will often allow you to solve problems in a more natural way, which translates to a simpler and faster algorithm and code.

Coach B: Happy Tuesday! We have reached our last unit of this practice season. Exciting. This unit is indeed the extra material!

The team cheers.

Ryan: Wait. Extra? You mean we don't actually need this stuff for Bronze?

Coach B: Well, yes and no. What I mean is that you do not *have to* know the topics we are going to cover. You can surely pass the Bronze without this unit. However, we are aiming to *Ace* the Bronze, right? *Acing* means solving it fast and simply, with confidence and a wide margin. For this, knowing this unit is a great help. Also, just as important is that this unit will set you up for learning more advanced topics and data structures that are part of the advanced USACO curriculum. In other words, we are finishing strong, and setting up for the next level.

Ryan: In that case, we're ready! Bring it on.

Coach B: I love the spirit! And it is a lot of fun. Here, let's start with the first problem, which might look a little familiar. We saw a version of this problem, albeit a little different, in section 7.1.

Problem 8.1: Double Doors Fixing

Bessie is visiting Wisconsin, the state known as "America's Dairyland." Wisconsin also appears on Bessie's favorite state quarter, which proudly features a Holstein cow and a wheel of cheese! Wisconsin sure knows how to appreciate cows.

Being in the northern part of the USA, where winters are harsh, Wisconsin also deploys systems of double doors, just like in Minnesota.

A system of doors has N doors, $N < 10^6$. The system is composed of left doors, each marked as a left-parenthesis '(', and right doors, each marked as a right-parenthesis ')'. An example of a system of doors is the following string.

'()((()))'

A valid system of doors is one which is balanced. This means that for every left door, there's a corresponding right door that closes it. Each door can be matched with only one other door, and the left door should, of course, be on the left of the right door.

An installer tries to install a balanced system of doors. However, it turns out she might have made a mistake, replacing one of the doors with the other type: she either put a left door in place of a right door, or vice versa.

Determine in how many places the installer might have made a mistake.

Input Format

Two lines.

The first line contains one integer N, the number of doors in the system.

The second line contains a string of length N, describing a system of doors.

Output Format

One number: the number of places a single door can be replaced to make the system balanced. If the system is already balanced, the output should be 0.

Sample Input

8

()(())))

Sample Output

4

The following four configurations would achieve a balanced system (The door to be changed appears in square brackets).

()((()))

()(()[))

()(())[)

([(())))

DISCUSSION

The team finishes reading the problem.

Mei: This is very similar to the double doors question. The one where Ryan called it a "normal math expression," remember?

Ryan: Yes, where you can put in numbers and plus signs and get it to work as a math expression.

Rachid: And we solved it in a cool way, with just using a counter and keeping it always non-negative.

Mei: Yes, we added one for each left parenthesis, and then subtracted one for each right parenthesis. Oh, so I know how we can solve this one. We'll just scan left to right, and whenever we get a negative number, we'll count how many before that we can flip.

Annie: Yeah, let's write it!

Coach B: Wow, you all seem very excited. And you think you know the solution. That's great, BUT... remember our mantra? "Things look perfect in your mind?" We've said it a lot. It's great if you think you have the solution, but you've got to stick with the procedure. If you think you have it and see it clearly in your head, and immediately start coding, it might be a big waste of time. So instead, go ahead and write things out, and give yourself a chance to verify your algorithm and find bugs. It will set you up for a quick solution of the problem. So please, let's follow our procedure.

The team sighs.

Mei: Okay, we'll do it, but seriously, it'll work fine!

> *TIP*: It's always important to write out your idea before you code it. But it's especially important in two cases: when you don't have a clue and need to find a place to start (which lets you move step by step), and when you're sure you have the perfect solution clear in your mind (which lets you verify whether you're right about that). In the latter case, slowing down to check over your idea is wise, like counting to ten before allowing yourself to shout out an angry comment. Following the procedure slows you a little, but it pays off, preventing you from making costly mistakes.

Coach B: The first step is visualizing, or following the sample case. Any volunteers?

Visualize it: Mei walks to the board and starts drawing the problem, following the sample input, as seen in figure 8.2.

Mei: I drew the sample case, and marked the pairing of the doors.

( ) (( ))))   Original: Not Balanced

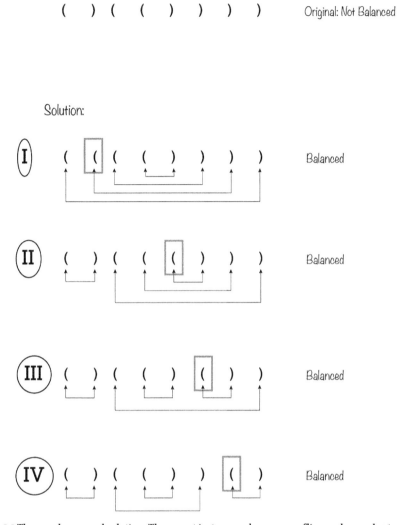

Figure 8.2 The sample case and solution. There are 4 instances where we can flip one door and get a balanced set.

Coach B: Thanks, Mei. Looks perfect. Annie and Rachid, would you like to explain your algorithm using these examples? Or feel free to draw a new one.

Rachid and Annie go to the board.

Annie: I think we can use the same example. Here, let me just draw it with the counters next to it.

Annie and Rachid draw figure 8.3, and then turn to the group.

Rachid: Voila! Annie drew these two counters here. The left door counter, that's counter 1, counts the left parentheses, which aren't paired yet. This part is the same as that other problem we did back then; we add one for every left door we find, and subtract one for every right door. If this counter goes below zero at any time, then we know we're in trouble! The system isn't balanced, and we have to repair it.

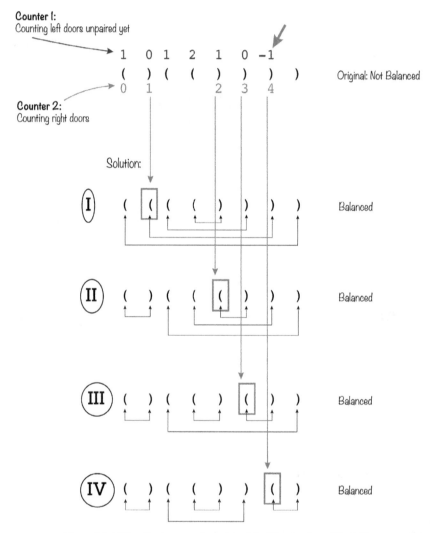

Figure 8.3 Adding the two counters as explained by Annie and Rachid.

Annie: And, to repair it, we need to flip one of the doors we already passed from a right door to a left door. And this is why we have the other counter: this one, counter 2, counts how many right doors we passed. As you can see, when the first counter goes negative, the second counter reaches 4. So this is our answer. We had come across four right doors already, and each one of those can be flipped to make a balanced set.

Ryan: Yeah, that completely works. See, Coach? It worked perfectly in our mind, and perfectly on the board also. We can turn to coding now!

Mei: Cool, yes! Let's move on to coding it!

Coach B: Okay, very nice indeed. You've made sure your idea works on paper. Well, on the board! Nice. But there's another part of our procedure, and that's to try it on some other cases if relevant, and edge cases. So here, let's try another case.

Coach B draws on the board the test case ((((( )))), as in figure 8.4.

Original: Not Balanced

Figure 8.4 New test case suggested by Coach B. How many doors can we flip to make this a balanced set?

Coach B: So this is an unbalanced set of doors. Can you first solve it by hand and see what we should expect as an answer?

The team clusters around the board, squinting at the parentheses.

Ryan: Okay, we got these four doors that can be changed.

He draws the doors as in Figure 8.5.

(((((   )   )   )   Original: Not Balanced

Solution:

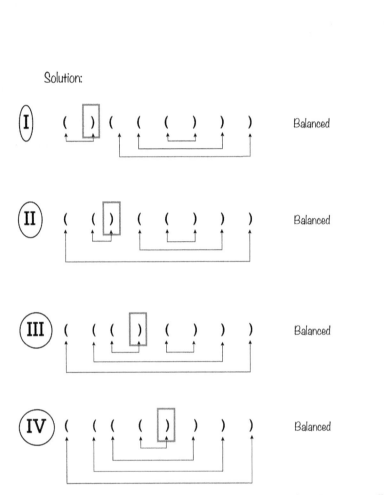

Figure 8.5 Solving the new test case by hand, we get that there are four doors we can flip.

Coach B: Looks good. So there are four doors we can flip. Now, can you try your algorithm?

Ryan annotates the board with the counters as in the algorithm, as seen in figure 8.6.

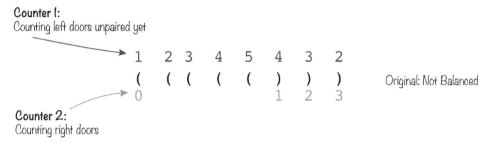

Figure 8.6 Applying the suggested algorithm to the new test case.

Rachid: Uh... okay, Houston, we have a problem. With our method, The counter of the unmatched left doors never turns negative, so there doesn't seem to be any issue with unbalanced doors. Moreover, if we were to take the counter of the right doors at the end, we would get the answer as 3, but we know the answer should be 4. We just showed the four options.

The team looks puzzled.

Ryan: Yeah, that's annoying. I thought we had it. The sample case worked just fine, so... what happened here?

They pause to think.

Annie: I see we ended up with the counter positive. If it's zero, it means we're balanced. If it's negative, it means we're missing a left door. So if it's positive, it means we have extra left doors. Meaning, we're missing some right doors.

Ryan: Yeah, I see it now. So we can check the counter at the end, and then...

He trails off, unsure.

Coach B: Well, you're almost there. You're stepping on the tail of the dragon, or in our case on the threshold of a new door. Now, listen carefully: what happens if you apply your algorithm backward? What happens if, instead of going left to right, you go right to left? Look closely and think about it. Instead of watching when the left door counter goes below zero, you watch for when the right door counter goes below zero, and so on. Would things work then?

Mei: Let's try it!

The team regroups at the board, then slowly updates the drawing to produce figure 8.7.

Rachid: Yay, look: it gives us the right answer.

Ryan: That's really cool. The same algorithm, only backwards. Wow.

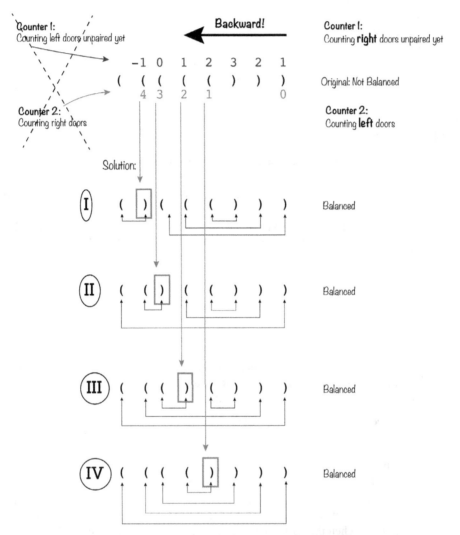

Figure 8.7 Applying the algorithm in a backward manner to the problem. It works!

Coach B: Yes, I agree. It's really interesting how we can modify the problem to come at it the same way from the opposite direction. Coding should be similarly simple. Once you solve one direction, you can copy-and-paste and make it work in the other direction. Let's do it!

TIP: In general coding, it's frowned upon to copy and paste your code. It's considered bad practice, prone to errors and hard to maintain. However, we are not in a general coding setting. We need to solve a problem under time pressure. If you can copy and paste your code, perform some minor modifications, and reach a quick and efficient solution, then, do it! It's not just allowed, it's recommended.

ALGORITHM

The team is getting ready to write the code when Coach B interrupts them.

Coach B: Here, we're short on time right now, so how about this: I will write the forward version of the code, and then you just need to copy it and change it to work backward. Are you folks okay with this?

Annie: For sure. It is only appropriate for a backward day that you will write the initial code, and then we will complete it.

Coach B writes the code on the board, as in listing 8.1.

Listing 8.1 Double Doors Fixing (Forward part)

```
1   // Left to right: have to flip ')' <-- left to '(' <-- right?
2   int ans = 0;
3   int cnt = 0;   // Counting '(' doors
4   int cnt2 = 0;   // Counting ')' doors
5   for (int i = 0; i < str.size(); ++i) {
6       if (str[i] == '(') {
7           cnt++;
8       } else {
9           cnt--;
10          cnt2++;
11      }
12      if (cnt < 0) {   // Stop if we ever get negative number of '(' doors
13          ans = cnt2;
14          break;
15      }
16  }
```

Coach B: I think this is a direct implementation of what you did on the board with the counters, right? Now it's your turn: ready to flip the code backward?

The team leaps into action, and after a few minutes presents the code as in listing 8.2.

Listing 8.2 Double Doors Fixing (Backward part)

```
 1   // Right to left: have to flip '(' <-- right to ')' <-- left?
 2   cnt = 0;
 3   cnt2 = 0;
 4
 5   // Going backward on the string
 6   for (int i = str.size() - 1; i >=0; --i) {
 7       if (str[i] == ')') {
 8           cnt++;
 9       } else {
10           cnt--;
11           cnt2++;
12       }
13       if (cnt < 0) {
14           ans = cnt2;
15           break;
16       }
17   }
```

Coach B: That was quick! Looks very nice. So in the final code, we'll have both parts, forward and backward, one after the other, and the problem is solved! Just one question: Why did you use ans = cnt2; in your code? Shouldn't you add whatever you find here to whatever you've found before? Shouldn't it be something like ans += cnt2;?

Rachid: Hmm, did we make a mistake?

Annie: No, no. We meant to do that. At the end of the day, for every string, only one of two cases can actually happen: either we have too many left doors, or we have too many right doors. It'll never be too many of both! So because of that, only one of the two statements ans = cnt2; will be executed. Either the one in the forward or in the backward direction. So the way we wrote it is fine, and, we could have written it the other way with the +=. It wouldn't matter.

Coach B: Good catch, Annie. You are absolutely correct. Any questions?

Ryan: Nah, we're good. It was kind of fun to flip the code around and write it backward.

Coach B: Great. Then we'll wrap it up there for today! The idea of using the forward-backward technique is simple enough, and coding it is usually very fast. Just watch out for the little details when you're inverting the code. Okay, I'll post some problems as practice, and... see you next week!

EPILOGUE

This problem invited us to apply the forward-backward technique in the most straightforward way. It is worth keeping an eye out for other variants of this idea. For example, in some problems, you can create a much simpler algorithm just by going over the input in the reverse order, without the forward component. In other problems, you can use a very similar piece of code to solve for two different cases. These options help to both simplify the algorithm and speed up the coding process.

 VOCABULARY Corner: **DIVIDE AND CONQUER** The divide and conquer algorithm is a common concept in algorithm design, in which we divide a problem into sub-problems, and solve each of these separately. Often, this process is repeated multiple times, with already subdivided problems divided again, until the resulting sub-problem is very simple to solve. As you continue your study of computer science beyond Bronze, you will learn many sorting and search algorithms that apply this concept.

PRACTICE PROBLEMS

Hints and full solutions to the problems can be found on the club's page: http://www.usacoclub.com

1. USACO 2012 November Bronze Problem 2: Typo

   http://www.usaco.org/index.php?page=viewproblem2&cpid=188

   a. This problem is very similar to the "Double Doors Fixing" problem that we just solved.

   b. Note that the input in the USACO problem is just the string, and it does not include one line with the string length.

2. USACO 2019 February Bronze Problem 3: Measuring Traffic

   http://www.usaco.org/index.php?page=viewproblem2&cpid=917

   a. Go left to right, and you will be able to determine the minimum and maximum values at the right end.

   b. You start by assuming that the minimum is 0 and the maximum is the largest possible. In each section of the road, you can update these according to the given information.

   c. Go right to left, and you can find the values on the left end.

8.2. Focusing on Significant Events

In some problems, although we're dealing with a very large domain, we might have only a few interesting objects or events within that space. For example, think about having only a handful of cows spread over a very long line. Or a handful of locations specified in a very large two-dimensional field. In all these cases, we might not have the time or space for a brute-force implementation. So, we're motivated to consider only special events, or special locations. This approach makes our algorithm manageable, but it may even give us a better insight into the essence of the problem, helping us find a simple and efficient solution.

Coach B enters the room with a spring in his step.

Coach B: Happy Tuesday, everyone! Hope you are ready for a fun practice today.

Ryan narrows his eyes.

Ryan: What kind of fun?

Coach B: Oh, it's probably going to be one of the hardest problems we've tried together, the most involved, but I think you can do it.

Ryan: Uh-huh, and where does "fun" come in?

Coach B: Well, if I know the team well enough by now, you will enjoy the challenge and have a lot of satisfaction from seeing the complete solution. You will get a chance to deploy a lot of the stuff we practiced this year, and bring it to good use.

The team groans good-naturedly.

Annie: Really, though, we ARE ready! Let's do it.

Coach B: Yes, let's go. Without further ado, here is the problem. It's similar to another you may have worked through, titled "Stuck in a Rut," and that one was written by Prof. Brian Dean for the USACO 2020 December competition. Okay, take a look!

Coach B projects the problem. It's quiet as the team reads.

Problem 8.2: Sharks and Moonnows

Bessie and her friends love to play "Sharks and Moonnows," a variant on the game "Sharks and Minnows." They are invited to a friendly match against Farmer Nhoj's team.

The game is played by two teams on a square field with a side measure of N units. The field is aligned with an (x, y) coordinate system, where x points to the east and y points north, and the field stretches from $(0, 0)$ all the way to (N, N). The Moonnows' goal is to reach the top of the field at coordinate $y = N$, also called the goal line, and the Sharks' goal is to prevent them from doing so.

The rules of the game are:

1. Moonnows can only run in a straight line to the north (that is, upward), and the Sharks can only run in a straight line to the east (that is, to the right). All cows run at the same pace.
2. Both the Moonnows and the Sharks create a line on the field as they run along, and no cow is allowed to cross such a line. If a cow reaches a line in the field, she has to stop.
3. If both a Moonnow and a Shark reach the same point at the same time, they can both proceed.

You are given the location of the Moonnows and the Sharks at the start of the game.

Determine how many Moonnows were able to reach the goal line at $y = N$.

Input Format

The first line contains three integers: the side length of the field, N; the number of Moonnows, M; and the number of Sharks, S.

The next M lines contain two numbers each, x and y, the coordinates of a Moonnow.

The last S lines contain two numbers each, x and y, the coordinates of a Shark.

All numbers are integers, and $N \leq 10^9$, $M + S < 50$.

Output Format

One number. The number of Moonnows who made it to the goal line.

Sample Input

```
10 3 3
3 1
6 4
7 1
1 2
4 3
1 8
```

Sample Output

```
2
```

The Moonnows that started from $(6, 4)$ and $(7, 1)$ made it to the goal line.

DISCUSSION

The team finishes reading the problem.

Ryan: Wow, yeah, that's hard. And it's really long.

Coach B: Yes, this is definitely among the hardest problems you'll encounter on Bronze. But I trust you folks by now. We can solve it!

Mei: Well, at least we can try... Here, I can do the first step.

Visualize it: Mei walks to the board and draws figure 8.8.

Mei: I just drew the field. It's a 10×10 square, and the goal of the Moonnows is to reach the line at the far end, at $y = 10$. Then, I placed the different cows.

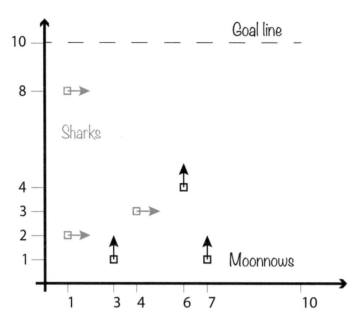

Figure 8.8 Drawing the playing field, with the location of all the cows, and their respective roles and directions.

Coach B: And you even drew little arrows with their direction. That's really useful. So this is the sample input. Now, what is the next step? Can you get us to the sample solution?

Mei laughs.

Mei: Uh, nope! Annie, how about you?

Annie: This is like a modeling problem, right? We can just move step by step. Here, I'll draw it after one time step—no, actually, make it two time steps. I just moved each cow along her defined direction. Is this correct?

Annie points to figure 8.9.

Coach B: Looks correct to me. It's really good you clearly marked every time step. That'll keep us on track. And it seems you just arrived at the stage where one cow blocks another. So that's perfect to get us rolling.

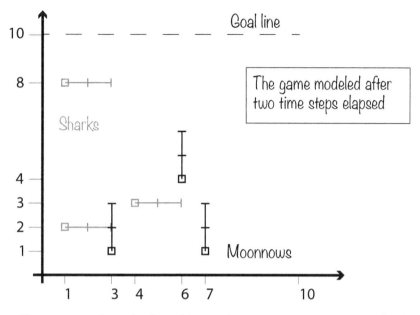

Figure 8.9 Moving two steps forward in the modeling. Each cow moves two steps in its prescribed direction.

Rachid: And now that you've drawn it, it reminds me of the problem we did back then with the walk to the opera house. I think it was in the modeling problems.

Ryan: Yeah, the one where Bessie walks to the opera house, and her friends join in.

Coach B: Exactly! And since you remember it was in the modeling chapter, how did we do it back then?

Rachid: We modeled it with time steps, just like Annie did.

Coach B: Sure. So you can model this one on the board. Go ahead, do it as a team. Keep going like Annie's done it so far, so we can see each time step as you move along.

The team gets up, and continues the drawing, to create figure 8.10.

Ryan: There we go, we did get to the right answer: two Moonnows made it to the goal line. It was kind of tedious to keep track of everything step by step, but we had to do it so we could see who's blocking who.

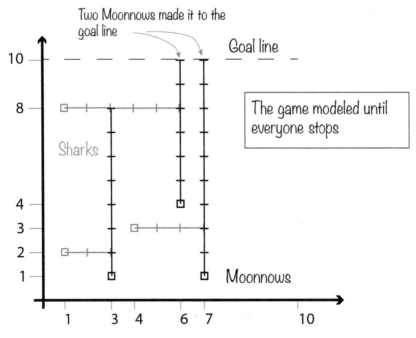

Figure 8.10 The game is modeled all the way through until everyone stops. Cows stop either because they got to the goal line, or because they were stopped by the trail of another cow who crossed their path first.

Rachid: But back then, in the opera problem, we used an acceleration method, where we looked only when the cows reached Bessie's path.

He turns to his teammates.

Rachid: Can we do it in this case as well?

Mei: Yup, I remember that now, too. Maybe we can do it here if we calculate all the intersection times between the paths. Because then we could see which cow reaches the intersection point first, and stops the other cow.

Coach B: Great idea, Mei! And that brings us exactly to the subject of today's practice: We need to consider only the significant events. In this case, these are the intersection times. This will save us the need to model all the steps, and just focus on a few.

Ryan: So we can just repeat what we did for the opera problem, right? Because this problem is the exact same?

TIP: Expect USACO problems to look similar, but not the same. It is very useful to recognize types of problems, like search and modeling, as it may give you a framework on how to analyze the problem. It is even better to actually identify a similar problem that you have already encountered, as it might give you ideas on the algorithm and patterns to use. But be aware that seldom do you get to encounter the same problem twice! Once you identify similarities, pay special attention to what might be different in this new problem. These differences might mean a slight change in the algorithm, or they might highlight a big change needed in the current scenario. Whatever the case may be, these insights will help you get to a solution faster.

Coach B: It's similar, yes, but it's not exactly the same. We are moving in the right direction, but we likely won't be able to repeat any exact method we've used before on any other problem. Remember, USACO problems are unique, and not easy, so you should watch for the distinct details.

Coach B marks the relevant cows and points as in figure 8.11.

Coach B: Consider the interaction between the Moonnow starting from $(7, 1)$ and the Shark starting from $(1, 8)$. If we just consider these two, who will get to their meeting point first, at $(7, 8)$?

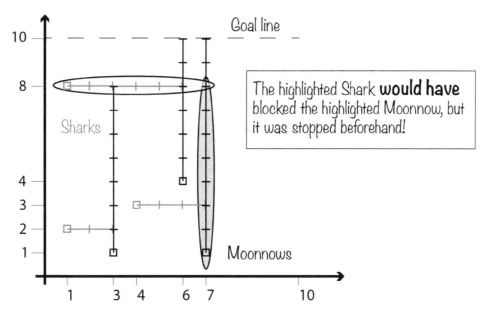

Figure 8.11 Coach B circles an example case. The Shark would have blocked the Moonnow, but the Shark itself was blocked beforehand.

Mei gestures to figure 8.11.

Mei: For the Shark, it'll take 6 steps to get from $(1, 8)$ to $(7, 8)$. Then for the Moonnow, it'll take 7 steps from $(7, 1)$ to $(7, 8)$. So, the Shark will get there first.

Coach B: That's right. But, it seems like this Shark is being stopped beforehand by the other Moonnow. So this supposed meeting at $(7, 8)$ will never happen!

Ryan: Wow, that really complicates things. I mean, we could calculate all the intersection points and see what's happening there, but some of these crossings might not be relevant at all. How do we untangle this?

Annie: We probably need to consider the time when these meetings are going to happen, and not just the location. This way we can see if the cow was stopped beforehand.

The team groans in agreement.

Coach B: Okay, I did say it is a hard problem, but I think we got a handle on it. And remember, we want to keep things simple. Here, let me try and draw some of the ideas you came up with as a flow chart.

ALGORITHM

Coach B draws figure 8.12 on the board.

Coach B: I tried to break it down into the big things we need to do. Then, we can do each of the parts separately. So first, as Annie suggested, we can calculate all the events of interest. These are the places *and* the times: the location of the intersections, and also when they occur.

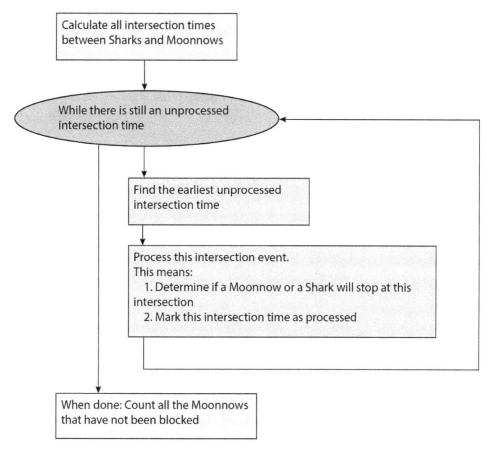

Figure 8.12 A flowchart of what needs to be done in the algorithm. Details will be added as we code.

Mei: These are the intersections between all the Sharks and all the Moonnows, right? So the total for the events would be $M \times S$.

Coach B: Yes, but keep in mind not all of them will meet. For example, the Moonnow starting from $(3, 1)$ going up will never meet the Shark that starts from $(4, 3)$ going right.

The team traces the two cows on the board.

Ryan: Yup, they'll never meet.

Coach B: So, we calculate and keep all the events that might happen. Then, we have a loop that goes over all these events, starting with the earliest one. We need to go over these events in the order that they occur, and keep in mind some of them might not actually happen.

Rachid: See, that really throws me off. That we need to go over all events, even if some of them don't happen. How do we deal with that?

Coach B: I hear you. Hold on, and I'm sure you can write a piece of code that does just that. You'll see, we'll break it into manageable parts. It's throwing you off now, but we'll make it simpler.

TIP: When you're overwhelmed by a large problem, it can help to break your algorithm into smaller pieces. One small step at a time can take you all the way to a full solution.

Coach B: So consider this. We need to process each event: See if any cow is stopped, and do any recordkeeping we might need to do, such as marking this event as completed.

The team nods slowly in approval.

Rachid: Yeah, that makes sense. But how do we code it?

Coach B: I'll show you how to get it started. Just to get us all on the same page, and using the same variable names, let me write this for our base, and then we can all use it.

Coach B writes the code as in listing 8.3.

Coach B: As I said, here we're just reading the input and setting variables. We have arrays for the Moonnows, denoted with _m, and arrays for the Sharks, denoted with _s. Also, I created a `time_active` array for each Moonnow and Shark. This will let us know when they've stopped. Does everyone follow?

The team nods.

Ryan: So at the end, we would just need to count the number of Moonnows that are active, right?

Coach B: Exactly. These are the ones who will make it all the way to the goal line.

Listing 8.3 Sharks and Moonnows: Setting up the code

```
1   int main() {
2
3       int N, M, S;
4       cin >> N >> M >> S;
5
6       const int MAX_TIME = N + 1;   // Useful to have this. Everything will
7                                     // surely be done by this time.
8
9       // Arrays for Moonnows are marked with _m
10      // These are the x, y, and time active
11      int x_m[M], y_m[M];
12      int time_active_m[M];
13      for (int i = 0; i < M; ++i) {
14          cin >> x_m[i] >> y_m[i];
15          time_active_m[i] = MAX_TIME;
16      }
17
```

```
18    // Arrays for Sharks are marked with _s
19    int x_s[S], y_s[S];
20    int time_active_s[S];
21    for (int i = 0; i < S; ++i) {
22        cin >> x_s[i] >> y_s[i];
23        time_active_s[i] = MAX_TIME;
24    }
```

Coach B: Any volunteers to do the first part, of calculating all the events? Mei, Annie? You two seemed interested in this part. Mei, do you want to give it a try?

Mei nods, steps to the board, and writes the code as in listing 8.4.

Mei: Phew, this wasn't easy. Lots of tricky spots. But I think this is correct.

Coach B: It looks spot-on! Can you walk us through it, please?

Mei: Sure, so I start with a nested loop on all the Moonnows and the Sharks. This will check all possible encounters. Now, actually, for a Moonnow and a Shark to cross paths, it has to be the case that the Shark is to the left of the Moonnow, and the Moonnow is below the Shark. Otherwise, they won't cross paths at all.

Ryan: Oh, I see it. If the Shark is to the right of the Moonnow, and the Shark is moving only to the right, it will never get to the path the Moonnow walks. Cool.

Listing 8.4 Sharks and Moonnows: **Finding all intersections**

```
1  // For each event we will save three things:
2  // 1. The time it happened
3  // 2. The Moonnow involved
4  // 3. The Shark involved
5
6  int t[M * S], moonnow[M * S], shark[M * S];
7  int times_counter = 0;
8  for (int m = 0; m < M; ++m) {
9      for (int s = 0; s < S; ++s) {
10         // Determine if the interaction will happen at all
11         if (x_s[s] <= x_m[m] && y_m[m] <= y_s[s]) {
12             // Distance for each cow to the intersection point
13             int dt = min(x_m[m] - x_s[s], y_s[s] - y_m[m]);
14             t[times_counter] = dt;
15             moonnow[times_counter] = m;
16             shark[times_counter] = s;
17             times_counter++;
```

```
18              }
19          }
20      }
```

Mei: Then, if they do cross paths, I need to see who gets there first. Here, let me draw it.

She draws figure 8.13.

Annie: Let's see. The Moonnow from $(3, 1)$ isn't going to meet the Shark on her right. We already established that. And now I see how you found the time of the crossing: You calculated how much time it will take the Shark to move to the right, and how much it would take for the Moonnow to go up, and then you took the smallest of those two. We want to know who got there first, because they'll block the other arrival. Great.

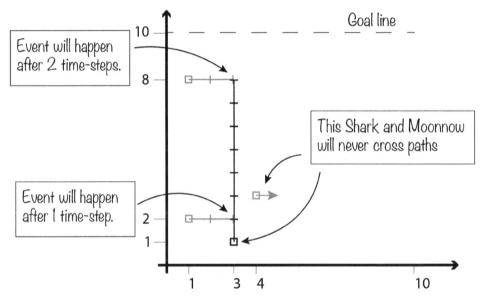

Figure 8.13 Events details for the Moonnow starting from (3,1).

Coach B: Great, Annie. And Mei, you see how someone else could easily explain your drawing? It means you've done it right!

Annie and Mei share a high-five.

Coach B: Any questions on determining the events and their timing? It wasn't that simple, but Mei did a great job. Nope, no questions? All right, moving on, then! Who's up for writing the loop over all the unprocessed event times, and finding the minimum?

Rachid: I think finding the minimum is a pretty standard pattern. Ryan, let's give it a shot.

Ryan and Rachid go to the board, and complete listing 8.5.

Ryan: Yup, it's like Rachid said, it's pretty straightforward. We just needed to find the minimum value in the array 't[]', and this is one loop. Now, all that's left to do is to determine what happens in this event. I mean, we have to see who stops, and who continues.

Listing 8.5 Sharks and Moonnows: Determine next intersection to happen

```
int total_times = times_counter;


while (times_counter > 0) {
    // Find the next closest time instance.
    int tt_min = MAX_TIME;  // it cannot take longer than this
    int tt_ind;
    for (int tt = 0; tt < total_times; ++tt) {
        if (t[tt] < tt_min) {
            tt_min = t[tt];
            tt_ind = tt;
        }
    }


    // These are the relevant participants
    int mm = moonnow[tt_ind];
    int ss = shark[tt_ind];


    // We will not use this time intersection again
    t[tt_ind] = MAX_TIME;
    times_counter--;


    // TODO: Determine what happens in this event


}  // Processing all events
```

Coach B: We're getting there! But there are two other things to do as well. One is at the very end, to count how many Moonnows are still active. But that's after everything. There is something we actually need to do right now, before determining what happens in this event. Remember? We aren't sure this event will happen at all! Why might it not happen?

Annie: Because one of them, a Shark or Moonnow, was stopped already!

Coach B: Perfect! So what would you add to the code?

Annie goes to the board and augments the code with one line, as shown in the snippet listing 8.6.

Annie: Here, I'm just checking that they are both still active at this time. And "this time" means the time of the current event, which is tt_min.

Listing 8.6 Sharks and Moonnows: Check if the intersection is valid

```
1   // We will not use this time intersection again
2   t[tt_ind] = MAX_TIME;
3   times_counter--;
4
5   if (time_active_m[mm] < tt_min || time_active_s[ss] < tt_min)
6       continue;
7
8   // TODO: Determine what happens in this event
9
10  }  // Processing all events
```

Coach B: Very nice. As you can see, we are just moving piece by piece through the required code, and we almost got it all done. And now we're ready for the grand finale of figuring out what happens in this event. Annie, since you are already up there on the board, can you finish it up?

Annie turns to the board again, and adds listing 8.7.

Annie: I think the only finicky point here is figuring out what to do with the active time for the one who's late to the crossing. I took the minimum, just in case there was another event that already blocked this cow.

Listing 8.7 Sharks and Moonnows: Processing the event

```
1       if (time_active_m[mm] < tt_min || time_active_s[ss] < tt_min)
2           continue;
3
4       int dx = x_m[mm] - x_s[ss];
5       int dy = y_s[ss] - y_m[mm];
6       // if (dx == dy);  // Both arrived together. Nothing to do
7       if (dx < dy)  // Shark arrived first
8           time_active_m[mm] = min(dy, time_active_m[mm]);
9       if (dy < dx)  // Moonnow arrived first
10          time_active_s[ss] = min(dx, time_active_s[ss]);
11  }  // Processing all events
```

Coach B: Very nicely done. It's a really complicated problem, but with building all the blocks separately, we were able to make it through. Here, let me just finish it all off.

He adds listing 8.8.

Listing 8.8 Sharks and Moonnows: Counting how many moonnows made it

```
1   int ans = 0;
2   for (int i = 0; i < M; ++i) {
3       if (time_active_m[i] == MAX_TIME) {
4           ans++;
5       }
6   }
7   cout << ans;
```

Rachid: Coach, how come you always get to do the easiest parts?

Coach B: Rachid, when you are a coach, you can do the same.

The group laughs.

Coach B: Okay, this has been a long and challenging one. It truly is one of the hardest problems in USACO Bronze. But you made it through. Breaking it into blocks, and doing one block at a time, was a good way to deal with a bigger problem of this sort. I hope you can appreciate how each of the blocks was not too complicated by itself, in terms of coding.

The team nods in agreement and stretches their limbs, eager to be done.

Coach B: You proved your mettle today. I will put this code in full on the web site, and a few relevant problems. Not as hard, and just one or two. See you next week!

EPILOGUE

This is a hard problem. I highly recommend that you try and solve it again on your own, or perhaps try the "Stuck in a Rut" problem from the practice set. There are many subtleties here that are revealed only when you code it on your own, and that's true whenever you deal with problems requiring you to focus only on important events. Unlike in brute-force modeling problems, in these cases, there is careful bookkeeping work that needs to be done. For example, here, we had to keep track of the time of the events, and process them in the right order. As we programmers like to say, when focusing only on relevant events, you save on time and space, but you pay with mental labor. It's a serious workout for your brain to write the correct algorithm.

 VOCABULARY Corner: **ABSTRACTION** The word "abstract" refers to thoughts or ideas with no physical or concrete manifestation. In software and coding, we apply the word "abstraction" to any function that, like a black box, has a known function even though we don't know concretely how that function is implemented. Abstraction is a crucial concept in large systems. We used it in our small program to simplify our thinking about a complex problem. We created a flow chart where we included various black boxes, just ideas about what functionality we want those blocks to have. This was simple enough to deal with. Later on, we implemented each of these black boxes, turning them from abstractions into concrete physical code. Again, dealing with each abstraction one at a time made it simple enough. We were able to focus on the big picture, and implement the details later on.

PRACTICE PROBLEMS

Hints and full solutions to the problems can be found on the club's page: http://www.usacoclub.com

1. USACO 2020 December Bronze Problem 3: Stuck In a Rut

   http://usaco.org/index.php?page=viewproblem2&cpid=1061

   a. We've encountered this problem already. Hopefully, by now you are familiar with many of the relevant subtleties.

   b. This is a hard problem. But, by implementing the significant events method, you should be able to achieve a simple code.

   c. Hint: Be sure to check the included solution. The code has simplicity to it that takes time to arrive at, but actually makes the code easier to think about and debug! Below is part of that code:

```
1    // Go left to right
2    // Find minimum and maximum values at the end
3    int min_e = 0, max_e = 999999;
4
5    for (int i = 0; i < N; ++i) {
6        if (s[i] == "none") {
7            min_e = max(min_e, a[i]);
8            max_e = min(max_e, b[i]);
9        }
10       if (s[i] == "on") {
11           min_e += a[i];
12           max_e += b[i];
13       }
14       if (s[i] == "off") {
15           min_e = max(min_e - b[i], 0);
16           max_e -= a[i];
17       }
18   }
```

2. USACO 2024 January Bronze Problem 3: Balancing Bacteria

   http://usaco.org/index.php?page=viewproblem2&cpid=1373

   a. If we assume (as given) that FJ is standing on patch N, the rightmost one, then the hardest patch to take care of is the furthest from him: This is the patch at location 1.

   b. Start by making sure this last patch is okay. Then, move one patch to the right.

   c. The notion of starting from the end, the furthest one, will get you on the right track.

d. If you are able to get cases 1 through 10 correctly, but your code fails for cases 11 and beyond, that means your algorithm is $O(n^2)$ instead of $O(n)$. It is a correct algorithm, but too slow. See the solutions if you need help.

8.3. Trees

Trees, as a data structure and as a base for various algorithms, hold an important place in USACO Silver and beyond. Although you don't necessarily need to know about trees to pass USACO Bronze, you'll have an easier time solving some of the problems if you do. In the context of programming, a tree is a special type of graph. By "graph," we mean a collection of vertices connected by edges. For example, think of cities as the vertices, and roads as the edges connecting them. Or think of people as vertices, with an edge between every two people who know each other. A tree is a graph that provides only one way to get from one vertex to another, and does not contain any loops. You are probably familiar with family trees, and with decision trees. We will have examples of both in this unit and in the practice problems.

Coach B enters the room with a box of donuts. The team cheers and heads for the box.

Coach B: Happy Tuesday, everyone! Yes, help yourselves, one per customer—it's a day for celebrating. This is our last USACO club practice before the competition! We have one more meeting next week to set you up for the test day, and then next weekend is the first USACO competition.

The team tries to settle in their seats, jazzed up by the upcoming competition and the sugar.

Coach B: Today we are going to put the icing on the cake. On the Bronze cake, that is. We will briefly cover a few subjects that will be useful to know, but they are not strictly required for Bronze. These subjects relate to data structures and the relevant algorithms. Data structures get a lot of attention in the more advanced USACO levels, but not so much in Bronze. Here, without further ado, I present to you the first problem.

Coach B projects the problem and waits for the team to read through it.

Problem 8.3: The Restaurant at the End of the Farm

Bessie loves to read sci-fi books, and in honor of Douglas Adams, she is celebrating in a restaurant named "The Restaurant at the End of the Farm." True to the restaurant in Adams's novel, this restaurant is a very special one.

The process of ordering is automated, and is done in front of a machine with three buttons labeled 1, 2, and Stop (S). In each step you are given a prompt, and you need to respond by pressing one of the buttons. Your order finishes when you press the Stop button. For example, the first prompt might be "1. Tofu. 2. Salad. 3. Stop." If you choose 2, the next prompt might be "1. Caesar. 2. Green. 3. Stop." The 3rd prompt might be "1. Side of Bread. 2. Side of Hay. 3. Stop," and so on.

As the kitchen prepares dishes by adding these options, every dish that builds upon a previous one is considered more involved. Thus, a dish with "Salad, Caesar, Side of Bread" is more involved than a dish of "Salad, Caeser," which in turn is more involved than a dish of "Salad." Final dishes are considered those that no other dish builds upon.

For example, if the first cow orders 12S, and the second orders 1211S, then the second cow's order builds on the first, and in this case of only two dishes ordered, the second order is a final dish.

Given N orders, where $N < 50$, determine how many different final dishes the kitchen has to make.

Input Format

The first line contains one number N, the number of orders made.

The next N lines each contain a string of digits 1 and 2, and terminates with the letter S.

Output Format

One number. The number of different final dishes the kitchen has to make.

Sample Input

5

121S

1211S

1212S

1S

2121S

Sample Output

3

The dishes 1211S, 1212S, and 2121S are all final dishes.

DISCUSSION

The team finishes reading the problem.

Rachid: This question makes me hungry. Not for tofu, though. Good thing we had the donuts. Thanks, Coach!

Coach B: You are very welcome, Rachid. Now, before anyone tries to visualize this, I want to mention the subject of our practice today, and of this problem specifically: Trees. Not the kind that grows in the woods, but rather decision trees, or maybe the more familiar family trees. A tree is a data structure that has vertices connected by edges.

Mei: Right. Actually I learned about trees in statistics, where each time you make a decision, you go a different route.

Coach B: Exactly! This is the tree we have here. Can you draw this problem as a tree for us?

Mei: I can try.

Visualize it: Mei walks to the board, and after some deliberation draws figure 8.14.

Mei: Okay, here's what I've got so far. In each step, you need to make a decision between three options, so there are three branches. Is this correct?

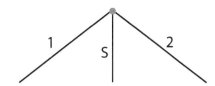

Figure 8.14 Start of a tree. There are three choices at each step.

Coach B: That's perfect! This is what a tree, well, a Computer Science tree, looks like. Okay, we can have the rest join you and draw all the orders.

The team joins Mei. It takes them a few minutes to draw all of the orders; there were a lot! Finally, they step back to examine their completed trees, as in figure 8.15.

Annie: Phew, that was a lot of work. Good thing they didn't have any longer orders.

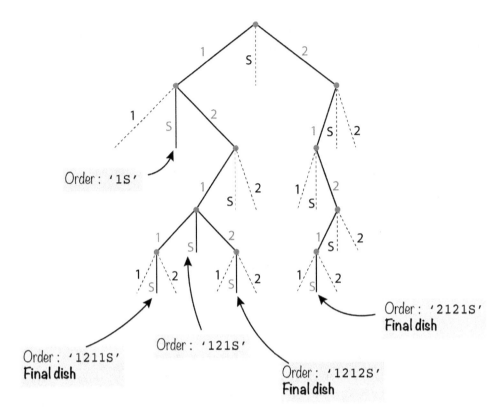

Figure 8.15 Drawing the full tree for all the orders. There were 5 orders, and three of those are final dishes.

Coach B: But it looks really impressive, and you did very detailed and careful work! That's great. For example, I see you noted all the choices *not* taken by anyone as dashed lines; you noted the order strings; and you noted all the final dishes. I have no doubt you now understand the problem!

The team nods in agreement. They essentially planted a tree, an upside-down tree, on the board.

Coach B: Okay, so any ideas about an algorithm?

Ryan: For each order, we can check whether it's the start of another order. If it is, then it's not a final dish. But that might be very slow time-wise, because we need to compare each order against all the rest. That would be $O(N^2)$.

Coach B: You are correct on all accounts, but look at N: it is really small, less than 50. So even a complexity of N^2 wouldn't be too bad.

Ryan: So is this it? Is this the way to do it?

Coach B: Yes, as far as I can tell. So you see, other than the fact that it looks like a tree, it's drawn like a tree, and it is, indeed, a tree, you didn't need any tree algorithm to solve it. And trust me, there are many tree algorithms we will learn for Silver and Gold, but we don't need these here. For example, in Silver and Gold you may have a problem like this with much larger N, and that would require an advanced algorithm. But for this problem, we are done. Even an $O(N^2)$ solution will do the work.

The team looks pleasantly surprised.

Coach B: There you go, you learned what a tree is, and now you can code it. Any volunteers to write our last code of the season?

Rachid: Let's do it as a team. Our last coding practice. It could get messy, though. Everyone up for it? Like, everybody write one line at a time?

The team agrees, laughing.

ALGORITHM

All four team members cluster around the board, and the writing begins. There's a buzz of talk and laughter, and a healthy amount of erasing, as the code takes shape one line at a time. Eventually, the team presents listing 8.9.

Rachid: Here it is. It was a little chaotic, but look, we made it! By the way, I think that this question might also fit into the strings practice. It was mainly using string functions.

Listing 8.9 The Restaurant at the End of the Farm

```
1   int ans = 0;
2
3   for (int i = 0; i < N; ++i) {
4       string s0 = s[i].substr(0, s[i].length()-1);
5       bool found = false;
6       for (int j = 0; j < N; ++j) {
7           if (i == j) continue;
8           // If s1 has fewer than s0.length() characters,
9           // substr will return as many characters as are available.
10          string s1 = s[j].substr(0, s0.length());
11          if (s0 == s1) {
12              found = true;
13              break;
14          }
15      }
16      if (!found) ans++;
17  }
```

Coach B: Nice. I see that you're determining for each s0 whether it is a final dish. Just one question.

He points at the code.

Coach B: Why did you trim the length of the string by 1? I see you took s[i].length()-1.

Annie: We needed to skip the last 'S' in our comparisons. In the short string, there would be an 'S' in the end, which wouldn't fit in the longer string. Basically, the whole problem would have been easier without any 'S's at the end.

Coach B: Oh, I see. Well, we don't get to write the problems, we just get to solve them.

Ryan: Not yet, anyways! The day may come!

The team chuckles.

Coach B: Okay, we are done with our last in-class practice problem! You made it. Let's take a five-minute bio-break—everybody, hydrate after those donuts—and then we'll have a short lecture on two more data structures, and call it a day.

EPILOGUE

Trees are a data structure that are very intuitive. We encounter them whenever we have multiple options to choose from. It's similar to a family tree, where every child is connected to two biological parents. In the problem we analyzed, at each junction, we had to choose one of three options. In the Bronze level, as you will also see in the practice problems, drawing the tree is all you will need to do with this data structure. It helps visualize the problem and see its underlying structure, but no special tree algorithm is required.

 VOCABULARY Corner: **GRAPHS AND TREES** As we saw earlier, trees are a specific kind of graph. A tree is a graph that has all its vertices connected, and there is no cycle (or loop) present. This means there is exactly one path between any two vertices. Trees, and graphs in general, are data structures, and their study involves two key aspects: how to store these structures in memory, and how to manipulate these structures. On more advanced USACO levels, you will learn how to build and manipulate these structures in a way that is efficient for different purposes. For example, you'll learn how to keep it balanced, trimmed and pruned (seriously!), or how to make it easier to search within it for prefixes of strings.

PRACTICE PROBLEMS

Hints and full solutions to the problems can be found on the club's page: http://www.usacoclub.com

1. USACO 2018 open Bronze Problem 3: Family Tree

   http://www.usaco.org/index.php?page=viewproblem2&cpid=833

   a. The relation to a tree, or a family tree, is strong.

   b. The basic information we need to keep track of is only the relation between mother and daughter. Then, we need to perform multiple searches on this relation.

   c. It's doable with simple arrays. No need for special structures.

   d. It's a lot of code to write:

   - Create all the ancestors of Bessie.

- Create all the ancestors of Elsie.
- Look for a common ancestor (a nested loop).
- Then, if you find a common ancestor, determine what to print.

2. USACO US Open 2019 Bronze Problem 3: Cow Evolution

http://usaco.org/index.php?page=viewproblem2&cpid=941 (Warning: This problem is difficult for Bronze.)

a. The tree is proudly shown and described in the problem itself!

b. Try looking at the problem in a reverse way: For each feature, record which populations it is manifested in.

c. In order for it to be a feasible tree, one feature must be a subset of another or the features must be disjoint. If they have partial intersection among the populations, then there's no feasible tree.

d. In Python, you can use dictionaries to save the features and populations, and sets to identify intersections.

8.4. Dictionaries and Dynamic Arrays

Coach B welcomes the team back, as they settle for a short lecture.

Coach B: The big day is almost here! You can close your laptops, relax, and settle back. This will be short, as we will cover two subjects that are not strict requirements for acing the Bronze. They can help make your algorithms simpler to write and implement, but they might also be the culprit if you run into execution time limits.

The team members frown at each other.

Coach B: Don't worry, these subjects are well worth our time. You'll see. Let's get you thinking about two kinds of data structures. The first one is known as dictionaries in Python, and maps in C++ and Java. It's the same concept. We briefly mentioned it when we talked about strings a few weeks ago. Ryan gave us a very elegant solution using dictionaries in Python, to deal with string labels. Remember?

Ryan: Yes, this was the one with the months the cows were born on. We needed to connect the name of the month and its number. For example (starting with January as 0), `October` is 9, and `November` is 10.

Coach B: Exactly. In dictionaries, and maps, we hold key-value pairs. So in this case, the key can be the name of the month, as a string, and the value is the respective number. In C++ and Java there are special ways to define these and interact with them. In Python, it is a much more natural part of the language. So this is the first data structure I wanted to mention. Who remembers from just a moment ago: what kind of problem might these cause?

Annie: You said they might cause trouble in execution time, right?

Coach B: Right. It's true that these data structures, in all languages, are well-optimized in terms of their performance. But they are inherently costly in terms of management. Here, let me give you a simple example, and hopefully it will convince you. We are not going to get too deep into this.

Coach B heads to the board and draws figure 8.16.

Coach B: In a regular array, if you know where one element is in memory, and you want to access the next, where would it be?

Annie: In the next memory location. The elements of the array are placed one after the other.

Coach B: Right, all the elements are stored in memory one after the other. Sequentially. This is what I labeled as "organized linearly in memory" in the figure. So it is very simple to go from one element of the array to the next, or even to any element in the array. As you said, they are just one after the other. With more complicated data structures, like dictionaries, this is not necessarily the case. Let's say we have a dictionary that holds the items in our pantry, together with how much we have of each. In this dictionary, the keys are the items, and the values are their respective amount. For example, say we have three tuna cans, two bags of sugar, and one bottle of ketchup. Here, I drew the dictionary as well.

Coach B points to the left side of the figure, and the team examines the figure again.

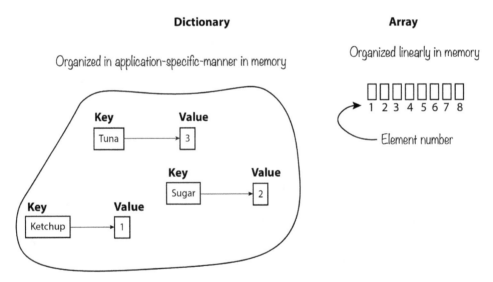

Figure 8.16 Dictionary and array data structures. A dictionary has a well-defined functionality, but it is not guaranteed to be stored in any specific way in physical memory.

Coach B: Now, how are these arranged in memory? Is the tuna next to the sugar, or next to the ketchup? If we want to go over the items, what is going to be their order? Every time you want to retrieve any of the items, the computer has to search where it is in memory. There are of course ways to make this search easier, but still, it's not like the elements are just waiting in a neat line, arranged one after the other. Does this make sense?

Annie: Yes, I think so. The drawing really helped me to see it.

Coach B: Great. So, dictionaries, unlike arrays, don't have a rigid indexing and placement in memory mechanism. There are other drawbacks to the rigidity of the structure of regular arrays. For example, say we have an array of numbers with values as in figure 8.17. Now, we want to insert a new element in location 5. In a rigid array, this means we need to move all the elements after that by one memory location to the right. That's a lot of work.

The team examines the figure, taking a moment to let it sink in.

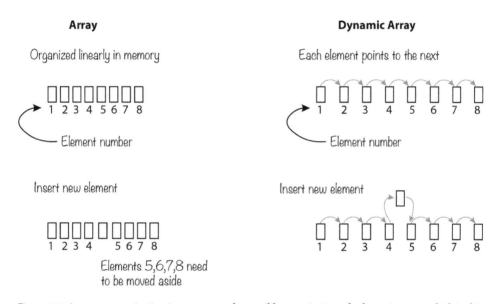

Figure 8.17 An array organization in memory, and a possible organization of a dynamic array, which in this case is implemented as a linked list. Inserting a new element is much simpler in a dynamic array, compared to a regular array.

Rachid: But you will always have to move all the elements to the right of the one inserted, right? I mean, there is no other way to insert a new element.

Coach B: Turns out, there is! For example, imagine every element in the array is not only holding its own value, but also holds the location of the next element! This is called a linked list, and it is one example of how to implement a dynamic array, where you can change the size of the array, and add and remove elements easily. In this case, as I've drawn in the picture, you just need to break one connection, and insert the new element in between.

Rachid: Wow, that's much easier!

Coach B: Indeed, and you will learn all about it if you continue to study data structures. Other examples of dynamic arrays are vectors in C++, ArrayLists in Java, or Lists in Python. There are different ways to implement dynamic arrays, but often there is either a time or space cost associated with any implementation. For example, a linked list is one way to implement a dynamic array. In a linked list, instead of just holding the element, we also need to hold the location of the next element. This is more memory, and more processing time. So, as they say, there's no free lunch!

Ryan: Yeah, that's... kind of disorienting.

Annie: I know what you mean. Most of the time we're just up here writing the code, but at the same time the computer chip is way down there trying to handle where locations are stored. And it's getting slowed down by all that work.

Coach B: Yes. So you see what I mean: with dictionaries and dynamic arrays, they might slow you down, but as Rachid pointed out, they can make your coding a lot easier. And that's it! If you have time, and if you're curious, go ahead and learn how to use these data structures, and feel free to use them at USACO. However, look first for a simpler solution that does not use these. If you do need to use them, and you get a time-limit or space-limit error, you know who your first suspect should be.

The team relaxes.

Rachid: Right. They're good to know, but it's good to know we don't HAVE to use them.

The team nods in agreement.

Coach B: Exactly. Now, next week we will not have a meeting on Tuesday, but rather on Thursday, just before the competition weekend. We'll just talk briefly about what to expect the day of the competition. Until then, I will post a few problems on the club's page, and also point to possible places to practice more if you wish. Have a great weekend!

Mei: Thank you, Coach B! I learned so much these last few weeks in the club!

The team joins in the chorus of thank-you's as they leave off until next week.

EPILOGUE

Dictionaries and dynamic arrays can help make your algorithm, and code, simpler. They do come with a certain amount of overhead or work required behind the scenes. At the Bronze level, you are welcome to use them, but they are not required. For now, it's enough to be familiar with these structures; you can appreciate their possible use, and lay the groundwork for their use as you advance to Silver.

VOCABULARY Corner: **ABSTRACT DATA TYPE** We just learned about dictionaries, which happen to be a type of abstract data type, or ADT. An ADT is a way to package the structure of data and the operations performed on it. In other words, an ADT defines the data it can hold and the operations a user can perform on it. These functions are separated from any specific implementation of this data structure. Dictionaries, as we just saw, can hold key-value pairs, where the keys are unique. You can add pairs to the dictionary, remove pairs, update pairs, and look for a pair given a key. Whether the dictionary is implemented by the language as a tree structure, or as a hash table, or as any other method, is not specified in the ADT definition. The definition is abstract, not including any specific, physical manifestation. Indeed, some languages have different implementations you can choose from. In general, as we saw earlier, this kind of abstraction allows us to put aside specific details and consider the big picture. The best programmers are able to use abstraction to see the big picture without losing sight of the details, to ensure the best implementation.

PRACTICE PROBLEMS

Hints and full solutions to the problems can be found on the club's page: http://www.usacoclub.com

1. USACO 2019 January Bronze Problem 3: Guess The Animal

   http://www.usaco.org/index.php?page=viewproblem2&cpid=893

   a. Each animal has a different number of characteristics.

   b. You can store characteristics in arrays of different lengths, or use vectors (dynamic arrays in C++).

   c. This is an example of a problem that can be solved without using dynamic arrays, but for which using them simplifies the program.

8.5. Summary

- **Ad hoc problems** are also called logic problems. These require an original and creative approach to solving them. The best way to prepare for these problems is to practice, which will help you recognize these problems in the first place.
- **The forward-backward method** divides the problem into two smaller problems, each using the same algorithm, but where that algorithm is applied in different directions.
- **The significant events method** focuses only on specific events, and helps us calculate what happens between these directly. This method is key to reducing the required time and space.
- **Data structures** allow you to store and manipulate data in convenient ways. They can make your algorithm and code much simpler. Knowledge of these is not strictly required in the Bronze level.

    - The tree structure can help you visualize problems that include multiple options and choices.
    - Dictionaries and maps help when you're dealing with string labels.
    - Dynamic arrays are most helpful when you wish to keep the linear structure of an array, but add the flexibility of removing and adding elements.

Part III. Competition Day and Beyond

Chapter 9. Competition Day

This chapter covers

- How to practice in the days just before the competition.
- What to prepare for the day of the competition.
- How to take part in the competition.
- What happens after you've finished the competition.

It seems like just yesterday you started practicing for Bronze, and now look how far you've come! Congratulations. Back then, the Bronze problems were intimidating, difficult, and even tricky. Now, you know all about search problems, modeling problems, following a problem-solving process, and so much more. And the problems don't look so tricky anymore, do they?

In this chapter, we will consider the last few days leading up to the competition. The chapter map is shown in figure 9.1. Section 9.1 starts with the week leading to the event. Even if it's not a full calendar week, it's the span of time after you've finished your regular practicing and before the event itself. We'll explore some good ways to review what you have learned and get some more practice in. We will also talk about what you need to prepare for the day itself. (It's pretty simple: uninterrupted time, pencil, and paper.)

The next section, section 9.2, details what to expect during the competition itself, and some advice for best practices. No surprises here: we're just summarizing what you've learned throughout the book.

Closing with section 9.3, you'll learn what to expect once you are done with the competition. What happens if you answered all the problems perfectly? And what if you didn't make it to a perfect solution? We'll cover all the possibilities.

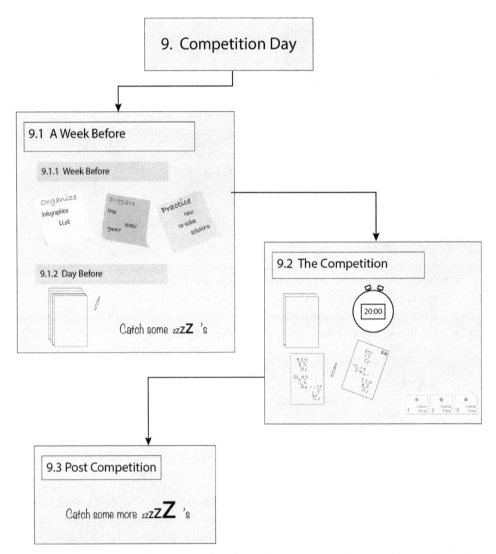

Figure 9.1 Chapter map. We'll cover the week leading to the competition, the competition itself, and what happens once you've completed the event.

9.1. A Week Before

It's Friday right after school, and the team gathers for one last meeting before the competition day.

Coach B: Glad you could all make it! I know it's a Friday, so we'll keep it short. We're just a week out from the competition, so we're just meeting for a final tune-up. So here, let's move the tables, as we won't need our computers today, and sit in a circle.

There's a moment of scuffing and scraping as the team circles up.

Coach B: Okay, I know you are all experienced test-takers. You have enough years of schooling to know how to prepare for a test. Still, I promise to give you one great new resource at the end of today's session. Something unique to USACO, that will help a lot. But first, let's go around, and listen to how each of you plan to do your final prep work for the competition.

Annie: What! No way. Tell us about this great new trick first.

Ryan: Yeah, what is it?

Mei and Rachid: Tell us!

Coach B: Nope, you'll have to wait! I will say, though, that, it really is great, it really is useful, and it works every year! I promise to tell you at the end of our meeting. But who knows, maybe one of you will suggest it first?

This possibility piques the group's interest, and they settle in.

Coach B: Before we start, let's just put things in perspective. You already know all the material you need for the competition. That's what we did in the club the last few months. This week is just to set the right tone, and get you comfortable for the competition. And, if anything goes awry, there's another competition in a month. So, without further ado, let's go around, and see how you plan to prepare during these last few days.

Coach B gestures to Mei, on his left.

Mei: Me first? Okay, so, I'm a flash cards person. Flash cards help me organize things and remember them, and I just love making them. I even hang onto them afterward, so for every subject I studied, I have a pack of them.

Coach B: That sounds very organized. So, what are your cards for USACO going to look like?

Mei: I already started making some... Each card has one problem on it. Either from the ones we did in class or from my own practicing. On the front side I put the question name, and some details, or drawings, to remind me what it is. Then, on the back side, I put what the tricky part was, or what the unique thing was about this question. For example, I might write that it's a search problem, and that we had to use a special acceleration. Or that it was a modeling problem where we used a modulus to deal with a periodic case. Oh! And I also use a color coding system for the cards: Modeling problems are green, searching ones are pink, geometry ones are bluish, and ad-hoc ones are white. Of course, not every single problem fits the color coding scheme perfectly. But it helps.

Ryan: Wow, uh, you're definitely doing a lot more than I have! What about after you make the cards? Do you memorize them?

Mei: Oh, definitely not. First, just making them really helps me organize things in my mind. But what I do with them is, when I want to review, I just go over some, pick out a card, and try to see if I can remember the problem.

TIP: Organizing the material in your head is probably the most important review process you can do. It helps you remember the material, make connections between different aspects, and understand the material at a deeper level. And a good way to organize the material mentally is to do it physically: with notes, flash cards, or whatever works for you!

Coach B: Indeed, Mei, this is commendable! I haven't heard that approach before in all my years of USACO coaching. I don't think we can top it. But, it's important to remember that different things work for different people. You've got to do what works for you. Okay, Annie, you're next. How do you prepare?

Annie: I like to draw, so I am actually making my own infographics. These are graphic organizers. I don't think they would exactly make sense to any other person looking at them, but they're helpful for me. I write down some of the big concepts, and then connect things with arrows.

She gestures, indicating bubbles and arrows with her hands.

Annie: So, for example, I might have the big subjects as modeling and searching in big letters, and then write down problems that have arrows to these subjects. I try to group things that I put down, so there's some structure to everything and it's not just a mess.

Coach B: I'd love to see some of these. Maybe we can turn your infographics into posters for next year!

Annie: Sure, but like Mei said about her flash cards, I think the most helpful thing was just the process of making them.

TIP: As Mei and Annie have both said, the most effective way to prepare, and to fully master the material, is to do the hard work of making your own study aids. For example, using someone else's flash cards is not as effective as making your own. Nor is using someone else's summary notes. Making these yourself is what makes the difference, as the process forces you to think deeply and find personally meaningful connections among the concepts.

Coach B: Rachid, how are you planning to prepare?

Rachid: Hmm.. I feel like I'm doing something wrong. I'm just going to solve more problems. Mostly USACO ones, but probably some from the resources you shared. I really liked the Codeforces site. Oh, and I'll look some more at the USACO Guide site. They have plenty of stuff there.

Coach B: Sounds good. But are you going to do some review of the stuff we did?

Rachid: Not really. I remember all the problems we did in club, and all the problems I did on my own. That's how I also prepare for math tests, for example: I just take the practice tests, and solve the practice questions, and that's it. Then I know I'm good to go if I can solve everything.

Coach B: Yes, some students really remember well what they learned, and just need to apply it. If this worked for you in the past, maybe that's you.

Rachid: Well, it didn't work on my history test last week, but that's different. I think with math and computer science, it is really just a matter of practice for me.

Ryan: Yeah, I'm pretty much the same. I do make a short summary of the highlights of the material, and I try to fit it all on one page, but otherwise, I just practice more questions. Oh, and I think for USACO, I'll also try and solve some of the problems I already did. I mean, I got the code right the first time by looking at the answers. I need to know that I can solve these on my own.

Coach B: That's a very good point, Ryan. Sometimes solving the same problem again can really help gain insights and improve your coding.

Mei: Um, yeah, there were so many times I took a look at the solution and, in a sense, copied some of it. I'm sure doing it now from scratch will really help!

Coach B: Which brings to mind another point, which you all do in some way, but not quantitatively. It is really important to see how many problems you solved. It's okay if you got hints and help, but we are talking about real USACO problems that you can confidently solve right now. A while ago, on the club's page, I posted a list of all the USACO Bronze problems available. Go back to that, and check off all the ones you did. From my experience, you need to solve around 30 of them to do well in the actual competition. If you solved 50 or more, you are seriously ready to ace it! Tally those up and see where you stand. It's a very good reality check. We often feel like we did many more than we actually did.

Ryan: Because some of them are so hard!

The group laughs in agreement.

 TIP: For Bronze, one of the best ways to practice is to solve Bronze-level problems. Make sure you solved enough of them by yourself. To comfortably ace the Bronze, you should complete about 50 practice problems. If you've done only 10 or 15, and these were hard for you, you definitely should do many more.

Coach B: Okay, any specific preparations for the day of the competition itself? Besides making sure you have scratch paper, a pencil, and an eraser?

Ryan: For me, the most important thing would be to make sure I have 4 hours with no disturbance. I have to make sure someone keeps the dog and my little brother away.

The team laughs.

Ryan: No, seriously! If this is on a weekend, my brother can start making noises and playing loud games. I can't exactly focus if he's blasting his music and, like, narrating his game at the top of his lungs.

Coach B: I totally agree. I think this is the number one thing to ensure: having an appropriate setting to do the competition. Hopefully, you can close the door to your room and not be interrupted. Talk with your parents. Make sure they know you have the competition. And remember, there's a window of three days to do it, and it includes the weekend. So choose a time you are sure will work for you, and will also work for everyone in your family.

Annie: Maybe we should do it here? I mean, come to school and have a room for us to take it?

Coach B: That would be nice, only, of course, it is over the weekend, and we will need a teacher to proctor, and there's some administration to do. But it's an idea. And the other thing is that it is nice to take it in a comfortable place for you to have a snack, take bathroom breaks, etc. I'm sure you can ask for four hours of silence at home. If not, the library is probably a great place!

The team smiles, confident that they'll find a place.

Coach B: Okay, we're almost ready to reveal my super-secret piece of advice. The one that'll make a huge difference. First, let's get all your ideas on the board, all those strategies you already mentioned. And then, in the center, I will put the new thing.

Coach B draws figure 9.2, pausing before adding in the centerpiece. He glances at the team, who, in anticipation, start up a drum roll.

Coach B: Yes, thank you! Now I've just organized all your ideas into three groups, and now let me explain the central part.

He adds to the center: "Watch a real-time video of a USACO Bronze competitor."

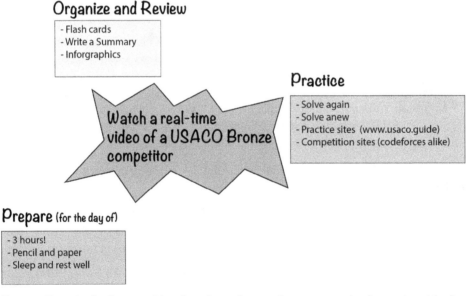

Figure 9.2 Preparing for the competition. Organize, review, practice, prepare, and make sure to watch a live competition solving.

Mei: What? Watch a YouTube video? Really?

Coach B: Yes, and at normal speed, please! What I am asking you to do here is to watch someone doing the competition and recording the process. Usually, I do it with the club in one of the meetings, but we ran out of time for that this year.

Ryan: Seriously? We just watch someone solving the Bronze questions?

Coach B: Yes, but I have suggestions for how to do it. First off, choose a video where it is someone who is actually a Gold or Platinum USACO competitor. I left a few links to these videos on the resources page. Any of these is fine. These are really strong programmers, with a lot of experience. And, they solve it in real-time, while being recorded. They are not there to teach and explain the problem, but rather to show you how they actually go about it. They see the problem for the first time with you, and then try to solve it.

Rachid: And do they always succeed?

Annie: I bet they do. Otherwise, they wouldn't post the recording.

Coach B: Yes, I guess you're right, but in truth, I believe they are really solving it for the first time, so it's possible they could fail. Now, there are two things you need to take away from watching this video, whichever one you pick. And by the way, although I strongly recommend watching all of it, you don't have to do it in one sitting. But please watch it at the original speed. If you speed up or jump ahead, you'll miss the most important part. So the first thing I want you to notice is how they approach what to solve first and then how they solve it. They first look at all the problems. All three of them. Then, they choose the easiest one to start with. Easiest one for them. And then they play with it a little bit to see they get it right, and only then do they start coding an algorithm.

Annie: Yeah, we know! You drilled that into us: "It always looks perfect in your mind."

The group nods in agreement.

Coach B: True, true. I'm glad it stuck. And the second thing I want you to notice is how they struggle, or should I say work, on some of the problems. Keep in mind: these are strong, very strong, competitors. They know very advanced techniques, and they have a lot of experience, yet, they need to think about the problems, try things out, and sometimes need a few iterations to solve these.

The team listens carefully.

TIP: When watching the videos, pay attention to how the advanced competitor approaches a new problem. They will probably understand the problem faster than you, and code it cleaner and nicer than you. But, they will also solve it much faster than the allotted four hours. You do not have to be that fast or that proficient; you are just starting your journey through these competitions. You have four hours to solve the questions.

Coach B: I can tell you from my own experience this is how it works, but you probably won't believe me. Watch these videos, and you'll see it for yourself. I know from previous years that students have found it so affirming and so validating of their experiences. You will probably see problems where you have absolutely no clue how to solve them at first.

That's normal. These are not easy problems. But you need to have the confidence of trying things, making some progress going from the sample case and onward, and know that you can eventually do it.

Mei: Wow, that should be interesting, actually. I do worry sometimes that even after all this prep, I won't be able to answer any of the questions.

Coach B: Exactly: the video should ease your mind! Hopefully, out of the three problems, you will at least recognize one where you have an idea and can relate to at least one problem we already did. This will get you started. But there's also likely to be at least one problem that will baffle you. This is where you'll need some confidence. And you'll get that confidence if you rely on our problem-solving process. And watch these videos.

 TIP: Perhaps the most important thing to take from these videos is the ability of the competitors to play with the problem, explore it from different angles, and enjoy while doing it. It is an integral part of the process to meander through, trying simple cases, before arriving at a plausible algorithm.

9.2. The Competition

Coach B: Okay, now, let's imagine: the big day is here. You had a good night's sleep, and you cleared a 4-hour block of time. You have some paper and a pencil, and an eraser. You are all set.

Ryan: Yes. And a silent room. We're ready!

Coach B: Yes, that's the spirit. You log into the USACO page, and follow the path to start the competition. You're given some general guidelines, you press a confirmation button, and your timer begins. You'll see the timer throughout, but it's a good idea to write this on the top of your paper: Competition Start-time. Here, let me write all these little items on the board.

Coach B draws figure 9.3.

Coach B: First thing, read all three problems. One of them will look easier than the others: this is the one you want to start with. Write the problem number and starting time for this problem. You don't want to be stuck on one problem for too long. When you start a problem, spend at least 15 minutes on it, but no more than 40 minutes. Those first 15 minutes are to ensure you're giving it a fair try, trying some examples, and playing a little with the problem. The 40-minute limit is to ensure you don't get stuck on one problem for too long. You can always come back to it.

Rachid: But if we really almost got it, we can stay a little longer, right?

Coach B: Of course, yes. But be careful that 40 minutes doesn't turn into 50, and then an hour, and so on. The idea is to move on to other problems. Maybe inspiration will strike when you come back to this problem, or maybe you have enough partial credit on this problem as-is. You do need to try the other problems as well.

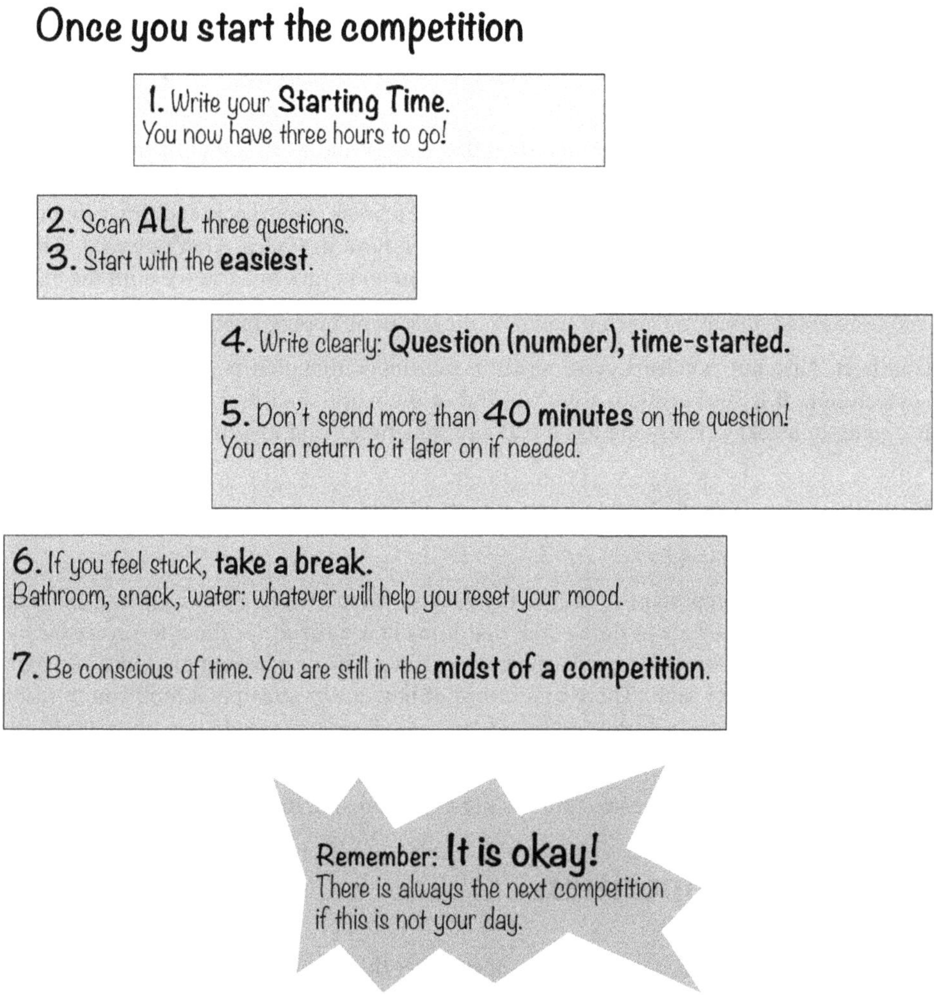

Once you start the competition

1. Write your **Starting Time**.
You now have three hours to go!

2. Scan **ALL** three questions.
3. Start with the **easiest**.

4. Write clearly: **Question (number), time-started.**

5. Don't spend more than **40 minutes** on the question!
You can return to it later on if needed.

6. If you feel stuck, **take a break.**
Bathroom, snack, water: whatever will help you reset your mood.

7. Be conscious of time. You are still in the **midst of a competition**.

Remember: **It is okay!**
There is always the next competition
if this is not your day.

Figure 9.3 The competition day. With all this practice, you can do it. Summon your confidence, and enjoy the challenge.

Coach B: Feel free to take a break, whether to reward yourself after solving a problem or if you are just stuck. Four hours is a long time. Taking a short break can help your mood and focus. Just make sure it is short and not a distracting break.

Annie: You mean no scrolling through social media, I guess.

The team laughs.

Coach B: Yes, exactly. Take a break to walk to get a snack, breathe in, take a bathroom break if needed, and then come back. Stay focused and avoid distractions.

TIP: It is highly recommended to close all other windows on your computer, and to silence your cell phone and any other devices. This is a competition, a test of sorts. You cleared four hours just for this, so make sure these are indeed clear for you to work.

Coach B: And that's it. It is really important that you try and work at it until you've finished all three problems, or until time is up. Please, pretty please, don't give up after two hours saying "Oh, I just can't do problem number 3." Take a break, come back, and think about the problem differently. Try another example, and look for a new idea. Don't give up. That's an important characteristic of a real competitor: you don't give up! You try until the end.

The team listens intently. Coach B points to the last item, hoping to break the tension.

Coach B: Last but not least, you need to remember that this is just one event, one competition. If it goes badly, it's not the end of the world, and there's always next time. It's going to be okay. Everyone has a bad day sometimes, and maybe this is not your day today.

Ryan: I feel like we're all about to take the football field.

The team bursts into laughter.

Coach B: Well, it's important to keep everything in perspective. I have seen students, and parents, get so stressed about doing well that it made it difficult for them to succeed. One more thing: there are no lasting consequences for not passing a competition. Once you pass, you achieve the Silver rank. There's no record of how many attempts it took you to reach that level. So again, it's important to keep everything in balance, and know there is always another day.

Annie: Yup, it's like our counselor always says, "Just breathe in."

9.3. Post Competition

Coach B: And now the last part: what happens after the competition.

Ryan: After that, we party!

The team cheers.

Coach B: Well, sort of. We will have a small party at the club meeting after the competition, but I mean immediately after the four hours. There are two things that could have happened during the competition. The first one is you solved all the problems, and got a full green light on all three.

Rachid: I want that one!

Coach B: Yes, we all do. In this case, you get an automatic message saying something like "Congratulations. You passed the Bronze competition." Right after that, you will have a prompt asking you if you want to do the Silver competition.

Annie: Seriously? They expect you to take the other one right away?

The team share surprised looks.

Coach B: Not necessarily, but they do allow it. Now that you passed, you are a Silver level. You are done with Bronze. From now on, in any USACO competition, you can take the Silver level. They just give you the opportunity to do it right away. Unless you specifically practiced for it, I would suggest skipping the opportunity this time. Just rest on your laurels for a little bit. Enjoy your success. Next time there's a USACO competition, go for it.

Annie: Wait, so I can get promoted from Bronze to Silver, and Silver to Gold, in one competition period?

Coach B: And while you are at it, go on to Platinum as well...

The team chuckles.

Coach B: So yes, you can. And some people do. These people practiced for the more advanced levels, and they just go ahead and do multiple levels at one USACO competition period. Again, if you haven't practiced for it—and we haven't—I would suggest avoiding this.

The team sits back, thinking how neat it would be to advance more than one level in the same day.

Coach B: Back to reality: hopefully, you will get the green lights on all problems and pass straight to Silver. But, otherwise, the second possibility is that you got only partial credit, at least on some of the problems. In this case, when the 4 hours end, your competition is done. You can try and determine your exact score by figuring out how many test cases you passed, but it is not really crucial. Whether you passed or not depends on a threshold, which is determined only after the competition period is done. This threshold depends also on the results of other competitors, so it fluctuates with each event. I would suggest in this case waiting for the final announcement from USACO, usually a few days after the end of the competition, to find out the threshold and your results.

Ryan: So you don't know your score and whether you passed until a few days after?

Coach B: Correct. This is how it works in conventional tests, right? You need to wait a few days for the teacher to grade it, and then, if the test was hard for many students, sometimes there's a curve for the final grade. So this is exactly the situation here.

Ryan: How do they determine the threshold? Is there a certain percentage that passes?

Coach B: In all honesty, I do not know exactly, and I wouldn't worry about it too much. Most of the people who pass, and this should be our goal, pass with full credit. That's what we are aiming for. If we don't get that, the option of being promoted through the threshold is a bonus for us.

Ryan: We can hope.

Coach B: Yes. Now, it seems like that's all I have for you today! I didn't even plan on any specific practice problems. But you do have the video to watch, right? Any questions? You can always reach me in school or on the club's page if you have any questions.

Annie: Let's do it. We got this, Coach!

The team cheers. They leave the room in high spirits.

EPILOGUE

You made it. You are ready for the competition. Still, a good review can make a big difference, reminding you of things long forgotten, and putting you in the right mindset for the competition. Be sure to watch the video, and be sure to get a few more problems under your belt.

 VOCABULARY Corner: **ALPHA, BETA, AND RELEASE** A software release life cycle is the process by which large software applications make their way into a product. The most common methodology relies on a few milestones on the way to a full release. The alpha version is the first version of the product, usually tested internally within the organization. Next up is the beta version, which is then tested externally as well, but only with a selected group of users. Finally, the release is the version that is released to the public as a product. Of course, in between there are many additional checkpoints. Software development processes are the subject of software engineering, a field within Computer Science. It's worth considering this process, now, as a metaphor as you prepare for your competition day. You've tested your skills again and again, honing them every time. First, in your alpha version, you worked your way through some problems, using hints and even looking at the answers to teach yourself how the problems work. Next, in your beta version, you worked through problems entirely on your own, with no help from friends or the answer key, and your skills grew. Finally, you're ready to "release" your skills onto the real competition, working entirely solo and under the pressure of the time limit. But you're ready for it, because you've done the work. You've passed through the milestones. You've got this.

PRACTICE PROBLEMS

Hints and full solutions to the problems can be found on the club's page: http://www.usacoclub.com

We mentioned a few ways to review and prepare. Please make sure to watch a video of a live solution, and choose any of the activities that work for you to prepare.

9.4. Summary

- In the **final week**(s) leading up to the competition, you can prepare in different ways:

  - **Review** by creating flashcards, a summary, or your own infographics.
  - **Practice** by re-solving old problems, solving new ones, and using competition sites like https://codeforces.com/.
  - **Study** using practice sites like https://usaco.guide/.

- In the **few days** leading up to the event, be sure to prepare:

- **A four-hour** block of time.
- **Pencil and paper.**
- A good night of sleep.

- **During** the competition:

  - Write down your **starting time** for every problem, so you can keep track of how long you are working on it.
  - Scan **ALL** three problems first, and start with the one that seems easiest.
  - **Take a break** when you need one.

- **After** the competition:

  - If you aced it, enjoy your success and then decide what you'd like to do next.
  - If you got partial credit, wait a few days for the final results.

- **It's okay if this wasn't your day!**

Chapter 10. Beyond USACO Bronze

This chapter covers

- How Silver is different from Bronze.
- How to start practicing for Silver.
- How to solve an example Silver problem.
- Moving beyond Bronze.

If you've passed the Bronze, you reached the Silver level! You made it. Congratulations. I hope you enjoyed the journey, learning all along the way, and that you're now energized and ready to scale the next level. (And, if you haven't passed Bronze: the next Bronze competition is not far away!)

This short chapter sees the USACO Bronze club transitioning into the Silver club. The chapter map is described in figure 10.1. We start in section 10.1 by describing, in general terms, the material needed for the Silver level, and how it differs from Bronze. This will also guide you in how to start studying for the Silver level. In section 10.2 we actually solve a Silver problem, which expands on the material we covered in Bronze. This taste of a Silver-level problem, and the subtleties involved, will hopefully inspire you to continue your learning journey to Silver and beyond.

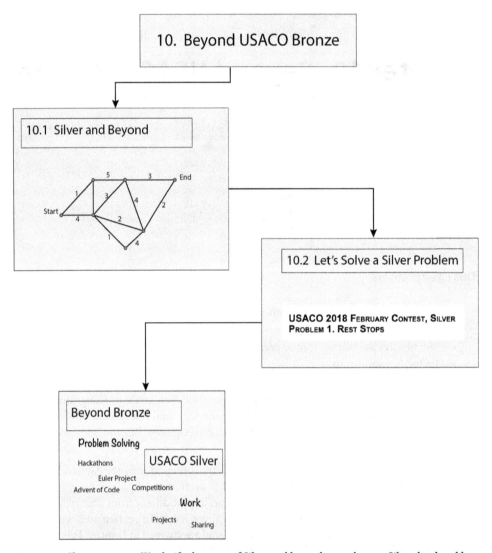

Figure 10.1 Chapter 10 map. We clarify the scope of Silver and beyond, we solve one Silver-level problem, and finally we explore how to apply your new skills beyond the world of competitive programming.

10.1. Silver and Beyond

The team is already assembled in the room, excitedly sharing their experiences from the competition the previous week. They don't even notice as Coach B enters. He smiles and clears his throat.

Coach B: Well, how was it?

Ryan: Uh, here's the bad news first, Coach. I didn't pass it. But everyone else did!

Annie: Yeah, but question 2 was really hard and confusing. I was lucky to solve it.

Mei: Me too!

Ryan: Yeah, I bombed that one.

Coach B: Okay, and did you get the other two? Walk us through it. There's a lot we can learn from your experience, if you don't mind sharing it?

Ryan: Sure, I don't mind. I did get green lights on the other two problems. Like you said, I started by looking at all three questions. The first question looked like a simple search problem, and the third one seemed like the crossword problem we did for the modeling. The one where you need to figure out the clue numbers. So, I started with the first question. This took me about 40 minutes. It was relatively easy. Then I went to question 3, which surprisingly I also found easy, because you just needed to follow the rules of the model. This was also about 45 minutes. So after 90 minutes, I was fully done with two questions, I was so pumped up, but then...

He grimaces.

Ryan: But then I went to the second question. The thing that threw me off there were all those names of the different parts.

Rachid: Yes, that was really confusing; it was hard for me to understand what they wanted. I eventually realized those were just labels, and that the specific names didn't really matter.

Ryan: Yes, I actually did realize that, but I was still confused about how to store things.

Coach B: Did you get to any algorithm? I mean, did you code anything on this problem?

Ryan: I ended up writing something, but it wasn't even producing the right answer for the sample case. That's as far as I got. It was really frustrating.

The other team members nod, understanding.

Coach B: I can understand. And did you figure it out afterward?

Ryan: After they published the solution, yes. I still think this was a hard problem.

Annie: Yeah, for sure. Very hard, with strings.

Coach B: Okay, thanks for sharing your experience, Ryan! And I'm glad to see you back here, because you know, there is another competition in just a month, and you can do it again! We will keep on solving problems, albeit Silver ones, and these will also help you. Any practice helps.

Ryan: For sure. And I'm gonna go back and re-solve all the String questions. I don't want to get stuck on the same kind of problem again.

Coach B: That's the right way to do it. To be resolved, and try again. You'll get it next time, Ryan!

The team echoes Coach B, slapping Ryan's back supportively, and Ryan smiles sheepishly.

Coach B: Now, Annie, Mei, and Rachid: I am so glad for you that you passed it. And on your first try! Impressive.

Ryan claps good-naturedly for his teammates.

Coach B: So today, this is just a short meeting. Kind of a party for after the competition. Next time, we can start practicing for the Silver competition. We'll go into detail about the Silver level next time, but in general, the big difference is that the Silver level does require you to know a few algorithms, like binary search for example. And, a little bit more about data structures, like how to represent a graph, or how to use stacks and queues. Oh, and you also need to know some common programming patterns, like how to traverse a tree, or how to sort according to specific criteria. Oh, and...

Ryan: Okay, that's a lot!

Coach B: Oh, sorry, I didn't mean to scare you off. So yes, it's very different in the sense that you do need to learn new things. But I think that's fun, and you'll all enjoy it. Learning how to represent a graph, and then how to work with it, for example, traversing and searching in a graph, are new and exciting things. So, for Silver, we will need also some lecture and practice time for new concepts.

Ryan looks at his teammates in doubt; they, too, are frowning.

Coach B: Trust me, learning about these new things, and bringing them right away to good use in some problems, is truly fun. You'll learn a lot about computer science. But, the core skill about Silver, as it was for Bronze, is the ability to solve problems. It is just that now you will have a larger number of techniques in your arsenal to deploy! And, we'll keep doing what we've always done: playing with problems, visualizing them, and trying things out.

The team is still frowning. Mei's eyebrows are raised at Coach B.

Coach B: Alright, you know what? I'll prove it. Why don't we solve a Silver level problem?

Ryan: What? Like right now? But you just told us how many new things we need to learn! I thought today was going to be easy.

Coach B: No time like the present! Besides, you already have the most important skill: a problem-solving attitude. So let's try it!

Mei: Alright. Lay it on us, Coach!

The team cheers in agreement.

10.2. Solving your first USACO Silver Problem

The team fires up their laptops, ready for the unexpected challenge.

Ryan whispers to Rachid.

Ryan: Coach said today was a party. I think he lied.

The team giggles.

Coach B: Let's go for our first Silver problem. It's going to be the one from the February 2018 contest, Silver level, Problem 1: Rest Stops.

He writes the URL on the board:

http://www.usaco.org/index.php?page=viewproblem2&cpid=810

He also projects the problem on the screen as in figure 10.2.

USACO 2018 FEBRUARY CONTEST, SILVER
PROBLEM 1. REST STOPS

Return to Problem List

Contest has ended.

Analysis mode

English (en) ▾

Farmer John and his personal trainer Bessie are hiking up Mount Vancowver. For their purposes (and yours), the mountain can be represented as a long straight trail of length L meters ($1 \leq L \leq 10^6$). Farmer John will hike the trail at a constant travel rate of r_F seconds per meter ($1 \leq r_F \leq 10^6$). Since he is working on his stamina, he will not take any rest stops along the way.

Bessie, however, is allowed to take rest stops, where she might find some tasty grass. Of course, she cannot stop just anywhere! There are N rest stops along the trail ($1 \leq N \leq 10^5$); the i-th stop is x_i meters from the start of the trail ($0 < x_i < L$) and has a tastiness value c_i ($1 \leq c_i \leq 10^6$). If Bessie rests at stop i for t seconds, she receives $c_i \cdot t$ tastiness units.

When not at a rest stop, Bessie will be hiking at a fixed travel rate of r_B seconds per meter ($1 \leq r_B \leq 10^6$). Since Bessie is young and fit, r_B is strictly less than r_F.

Bessie would like to maximize her consumption of tasty grass. But she is worried about Farmer John; she thinks that if at any point along the hike she is behind Farmer John on the trail, he might lose all motivation to continue!

Help Bessie find the maximum total tastiness units she can obtain while making sure that Farmer John completes the hike.

INPUT FORMAT (file reststops.in):

The first line of input contains four integers: L, N, r_F, and r_B. The next N lines describe the rest stops. For each i between 1 and N, the $i + 1$-st line contains two integers x_i and c_i, describing the position of the i-th rest stop and the tastiness of the grass there.

It is guaranteed that $r_F > r_B$, and $0 < x_1 < \cdots < x_N < L$. **Note that r_F and r_B are given in seconds per meter!**

OUTPUT FORMAT (file reststops.out):

A single integer: the maximum total tastiness units Bessie can obtain.

SAMPLE INPUT:

```
10 2 4 3
7 2
8 1
```

SAMPLE OUTPUT:

```
15
```

In this example, it is optimal for Bessie to stop for 7 seconds at the $x = 7$ rest stop (acquiring 14 tastiness units) and then stop for an additional 1 second at the $x = 8$ rest stop (acquiring 1 more tastiness unit, for a total of 15 tastiness units).

Problem credits: Dhruv Rohatgi

Figure 10.2 A USACO Silver problem, from 2018, February, Problem 1: Rest Stops.

The team finishes reading.

Ryan: Silver or not, I can definitely understand the question.

Mei: Yes, it's in plain English. Let's draw this!

The team gets up and goes to the board, excited to solve a Silver problem.

Mei: Okay, let's bust out our old reliable technique. Draw it out. And go from there.

They draw figure 10.3. Annie turns to Coach B.

Annie: We drew the sample case. Since it takes Bessie 3 seconds to cover 1 meter, it will take her 21 seconds to cover 7 meters to reach the first rest stop. It will take Farmer John 28 seconds to cover the same distance. So, Bessie has 7 seconds to stay there and eat the grass with tastiness 2.

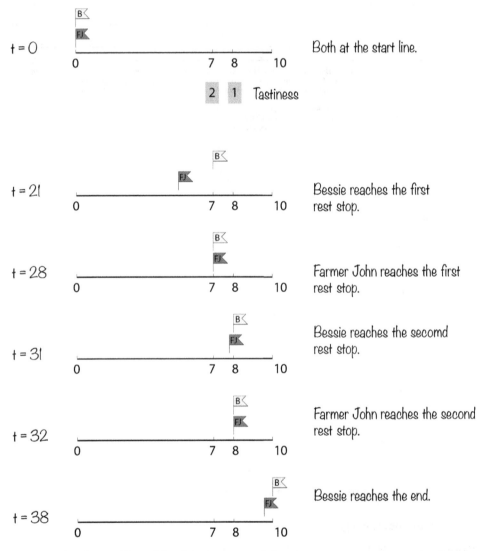

Figure 10.3 Sample case. The trail length is 10 meters, and there are two rest stops: one 7 meters from the start and one 8 meters from the start. Bessie is moving at a rate of 3 seconds per meter and Farmer John is moving at a rate of 4 seconds per meter.

Rachid: And then, when Farmer John catches up to the rest stop after 28 seconds, Bessie starts walking again, and reaches the second rest stop after another 3 seconds, which brings it to 31 seconds overall. She's there only for 1 second, since Farmer John catches up quickly. So, Bessie has 1 second to stay there and eat the grass with tastiness 1.

Ryan: And then they just head to the end of the trail, but she doesn't get to eat anything more. So here the total is 7*2 tastiness units from the first rest stop, plus 1*1 tastiness units from the second rest stop, for a total of 15 tastiness units. And this is what the sample output is.

Coach B: Great! I think you got it. What kind of problem do you think it is?

Ryan: Is it modeling? We just need to do time-steps and calculate how much she eats.

Coach B: But how do you know where she'll eat? In which rest stop?

Ryan: Isn't she going to eat in all of them? That's what we had in this problem.

Coach B: Let's add another rest stop at 3, with a tastiness of 1. Would your answer change in any way?

Coach B draws figure 10.4.

 TIP: Don't forget to try other sample cases to clarify your understanding of the algorithm. Especially in more complex problems, like on the Silver level, one simple example may not cover all the intricacies of the problem. Coming up with more test cases allows you to shed light on new aspects.

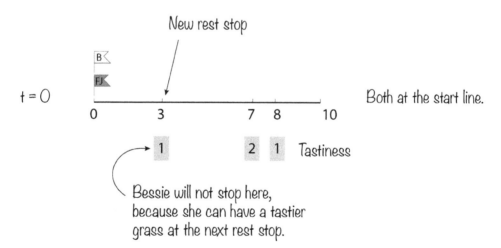

Figure 10.4 We have added a new rest stop. Will this change the solution?

The team considers, jots a few numbers, and then Mei reports back.

Mei: No, it's the same answer. It isn't worth Bessie's time to stop at this new rest stop, because she can spend the time at the tastier one. So, she'll go straight to the second rest stop, eat there, and the result is exactly the same.

Coach B: Good! So now we've realized something. Every time, you need to choose which rest stop she should go to, right? So maybe this is a search problem?

Rachid: But it's not really a search problem, because every time we just want to go to the rest stop that's the tastiest. We don't really have to search for which one is the best: the tastiest is always best!

Coach B: Hmm... I think we had a name for a search algorithm that always picks up the best next option, and it doesn't have to compare or search too much. Does anyone remember?

Annie: The greedy algorithm! I remember that.

There's a chorus of "Oh!" and "Right!" as the team nods..

Ryan: Yeah, so the algorithm is gonna pick the best option right now, and we don't have to pick any more complicated options.

ALGORITHM

Coach B: So, are you ready for the algorithm? Any volunteers?

Annie: I got this!

She starts writing the code in listing 10.1, while the team is helping with suggestions.

Annie: So first, let's assume we have a function that returns the next best rest stop for Bessie. We called this function `find_best_next_rest_stop()`. This is the greedy function; it's going to return the best next rest stop. Then, we need to calculate how much time she's going to stay there.

Mei: And to calculate the time Bessie spends at the rest stop, we need to know the difference between her arrival time and Farmer John's arrival time. The time it takes Bessie to get there is the distance multiplied by the pace, which is (`next_x - last_x`)*`rb`, and the time it takes Farmer John is (`next_x - last_x`)*`rf`. We calculate the difference, and then just multiply it by the tastiness of the rest stop.

Listing 10.1 Rest Stops (Main loop)

```
 1   int last_x = 0;   // Last place Bessie stopped
 2   int val = 0;
 3
 4   // Assume we have such a function that finds the best next rest stop
 5   int best_next_rest_stop = find_best_next_rest_stop();
 6
 7   while (best_next_rest_stop != -1) {
 8       int next_x = x[best_next_rest_stop];
 9       int t_bessie = (next_x - last_x) * rb;
10       int t_farmer = (next_x - last_x) * rf;
11       int dt = t_farmer - t_bessie;
12
13       val += dt * taste[best_next_rest_stop];
```

```
14    last_x = next_x;
15    best_rest_stop = find_best_next_rest_stop();
16  }
```

Coach B: I am impressed! What a clean and concise code. Who was your coach again?

The team laughs.

Coach B: Question: How do you know they are both leaving from the same place, `last_x`?

Rachid: Well, Bessie is going to stay and eat all the grass she can until Farmer John comes to the rest stop she is currently at. That's our greedy algorithm. So only when Farmer John gets to the rest stop, does Bessie start moving on. So they will always start together.

 TIP: When writing the algorithm, it is okay to delay the task of coding some detailed, complex part by labeling it as a function call. It is usually just a placeholder, and will be replaced later on with some direct code, or a real call to a function. When you do this, be sure to give the function a clear name, like `find_best_next_rest_stop()`, which will allow you to write a clear and concise algorithm idea, without clouding the more essential parts with too many details.

The group is still clustered by the board, nodding at the code, when they hear a knock at the door. Ms. Kramer, the art teacher, pokes her head into the room.

Ms. Kramer: Are you all coming soon?

Coach B: Yes, we got caught up. Be there in five minutes!

Ms. Kramer: Okay. It'll melt, you know.

Ms. Kramer leaves, and the team turns to Coach B to pepper him with questions.

Ryan: What was that? Coming where? Melting what?

Coach B: This was supposed to be more of a surprise, but it's okay. I told you we'd have a party after the competition, so this is it! I asked Ms. Kramer if we could use the art room, so there are some goodies and ice cream waiting for us.

The team cheers and scrambles to pack up their laptops.

Coach B: But just a second. I see we're not going to finish this problem, but let me summarize a few things.

Ryan: Wait, before you do, it wasn't too hard at all! I think I could have solved it in the competition if this one showed up as question 2 on the Bronze.

Coach B: Well, truth be told, there are a few subtleties here. So on the bright side, as you saw, it is written in plain English. You can understand and follow the problem, and find an algorithm. Of course, there are other Silver problems that have topics you are not familiar with, but you will learn these. The essential piece of problem-solving is something you are comfortable with, and this is a crucial part of the Silver level as well.

Annie: And the subtleties?

Coach B: A few things. For example, some of the variables in this problem might get too large for a variable of type integer, so you have to define these as `long`. This is just a matter of technique, and paying attention. Another more important issue is the function you left unwritten, `find_best_next_rest_stop()`. If you do this function as a naive implementation, it'll be too slow to pass all test cases. Remember how we talked about the forward-backward technique? Turns out there is a very simple way to implement this function if we scan the rest stops from the end, backward. So again, this is something you know, but you've got to bring it to good use here. And this is just part of the whole solution, which requires a very solid mastery of all the subjects you already know. Now let's say you ignored all these details, and you wrote a brute-force solution. What would happen?

Annie: You'd probably get partial credit.

The team nods.

Ryan: Okay, I see. This problem was within our reach, basically, but there's more to learn to do it well and get full credit.

Coach B: Exactly. And with that: it's time to party! I will put an annotated solution on the club's page. We will solve this one again, in full, at our first Silver practice. Now, let's go and have some ice cream!

The team barely hears the end of the sentence. They hustle to the art room.

EPILOGUE

You've finished studying for Bronze. Maybe you will need some more practice and another try, but you know all the material needed. As we mentioned in Chapter 1, there are numerous platforms, aside from USACO, where you can discover problems that will challenge your coding skills, as well as your algorithmic and problem-solving abilities. I strongly encourage you to explore various avenues simultaneously. While it's perfectly fine to prioritize USACO, solving Euler problems or participating in events like Advent of Code will undoubtedly enhance your overall problem-solving capabilities and expose you to a wider range of problem types.

Silver is a different story compared to Bronze. You still need solid coding and problem-solving skills, just as you did for Bronze. But on top of that, you need to study new algorithms, data structures, and coding techniques.

If you're interested in pursuing Silver and beyond, we encourage you to read and practice with the book *Algorithmic Thinking, 2nd Edition: Unlock Your Programming Potential* by Daniel Zingaro (2024). You'll learn all about trees, graphs, binary search, dynamic programming, and many other powerful data structures and algorithms that you'll encounter at the more advanced levels. And just like in our Bronze journey, you'll be solving competitive programming problems from day one. It continues right where we're leaving off here.

One of the great side effects of competitive programming is that you are honing your programming skills as you practice. Why not consider applying your new programming skills to personal or community projects as well? For example, you could learn how to make a game, or a homepage for a club.

Good luck!

 VOCABULARY Corner: **Natural Language Processing (NLP)** NLP is a field within Computer Science that deals with processing and analyzing natural language. It goes from understanding the different components of sentences, such as subjects, verbs, and so on, to understanding the structures of compound sentences, and even to inferring the meaning of paragraphs. Just like for the concepts in each vocabulary corner, it starts with a basic understanding of the meaning of a word, then moves to understanding it in a specific context, and from there, to reveal the idea and meaning associated with the use of this word in a specific sentence. I hope you enjoyed the vocabulary corners, and if you are intrigued by the words and phrases abounding in computer science, there is a lot for you to do in helping computers understand human language.

PRACTICE PROBLEMS

You can find the full annotated solution to the Rest Stop problem on the club's page: http://www.usacoclub.com

10.3. Summary

- **USACO Silver** requires the study of additional material:

    - **Algorithms**, such as binary search and traversing graphs.
    - **Data structures**, such as stacks and queues, graphs, and trees.
    - **Techniques**, such as dynamic programming and customized sorting.

- **Silver still revolves around problem-solving**: the art of investigating a problem, exploring it through different test cases, and devising an algorithm.
- **It also raises the bar on coding**, which you'll need to do fluently, confidently, and correctly. If you are thinking of moving to a new programming language for the Silver level, make sure you take plenty of time to develop proficiency in it.
- **Good luck!** If you enjoyed the problems so far, you will definitely enjoy Silver even more.
- If you're interested in trying **different types of competitions** or expanding your problem-solving experience, there are numerous places you can explore.

Part IV. Appendix

Appendix A. List of All USACO Bronze Problems

This appendix includes a comprehensive list of all the USACO Bronze problems published since 2012. You can utilize it to track and tally the problems you have solved or to locate a specific problem within the book. Additionally, the appendix also features a compilation of problems from https://codeforces.com/ and https://www.cses.fi/ that are referenced in the book.

USACO problems

2012-2013 Season

2012 Nov Bronze 1 Find the Cow![1]
2012 Nov Bronze 2 Typo[2]
2012 Nov Bronze 3 Horseshoes[3]

2012 Dec Bronze 1 Meet and Greet[4]
2012 Dec Bronze 2 Scrambled Letters[5]
2012 Dec Bronze 3 Crazy Fences[6]

2013 Jan Bronze 1 Mirrors[7]
2013 Jan Bronze 2 Painting the Fence[8]
2013 Jan Bronze 3 Liars and Truth Tellers[9]

2013 Feb Bronze 1 Message Relay[10]
2013 Feb Bronze 2 Cow Crossings[11]
2013 Feb Bronze 3 Perimeter[12]

2013 Mar Bronze 1 Cow Race[13]

---

[1]http://www.usaco.org/index.php?page=viewproblem2&cpid=187
[2]http://www.usaco.org/index.php?page=viewproblem2&cpid=188
[3]http://www.usaco.org/index.php?page=viewproblem2&cpid=189
[4]http://usaco.org/index.php?page=viewproblem2&cpid=205
[5]http://usaco.org/index.php?page=viewproblem2&cpid=206
[6]http://usaco.org/index.php?page=viewproblem2&cpid=207
[7]http://www.usaco.org/index.php?page=viewproblem2&cpid=223
[8]http://www.usaco.org/index.php?page=viewproblem2&cpid=224
[9]http://www.usaco.org/index.php?page=viewproblem2&cpid=225
[10]http://usaco.org/index.php?page=viewproblem2&cpid=241
[11]http://usaco.org/index.php?page=viewproblem2&cpid=242
[12]http://usaco.org/index.php?page=viewproblem2&cpid=243
[13]http://usaco.org/index.php?page=viewproblem2&cpid=259

2013 Mar Bronze 2 Breed Proximity[14]
2013 Mar Bronze 3 Breed Assignment[15]

2013 Open Bronze 1 Bovine Ballet[16]
2013 Open Bronze 2 Blink[17]
2013 Open Bronze 3 Photo[18]
2013 Open Bronze 4 Haywire[19]

2013-2014 Season

2013 Nov Bronze 1 Combination Lock[20]
2013 Nov Bronze 2 Goldilocks and the N cows[21]
2013 Nov Bronze 3 Farmer John has no Large Brown Cow[22]

2013 Dec Bronze 1 Record Keeping[23]
2013 Dec Bronze 2 Cow Baseball[24]
2013 Dec Bronze 3 Wormholes[25]

2014 Jan Bronze 1 Ski Course Design[26]
2014 Jan Bronze 2 Bessie Slows Down[27]
2014 Jan Bronze 3 Balanced Teams[28]

2014 Feb Bronze 1 Mirror Field[29]
2014 Feb Bronze 2 Auto-Complete[30]
2014 Feb Bronze 3 Secret Code[31]

2014 Mar Bronze 1 Reordering the Cows[32]
2014 Mar Bronze 2 The Lazy Cow[33]
2014 Mar Bronze 3 Cow Art[34]

---

[14] http://usaco.org/index.php?page=viewproblem2&cpid=260
[15] http://usaco.org/index.php?page=viewproblem2&cpid=261
[16] http://www.usaco.org/index.php?page=viewproblem2&cpid=278
[17] http://www.usaco.org/index.php?page=viewproblem2&cpid=279
[18] http://www.usaco.org/index.php?page=viewproblem2&cpid=280
[19] http://www.usaco.org/index.php?page=viewproblem2&cpid=281
[20] http://usaco.org/index.php?page=viewproblem2&cpid=340
[21] http://usaco.org/index.php?page=viewproblem2&cpid=341
[22] http://usaco.org/index.php?page=viewproblem2&cpid=342
[23] http://usaco.org/index.php?page=viewproblem2&cpid=358
[24] http://usaco.org/index.php?page=viewproblem2&cpid=359
[25] http://usaco.org/index.php?page=viewproblem2&cpid=360
[26] http://usaco.org/index.php?page=viewproblem2&cpid=376
[27] http://usaco.org/index.php?page=viewproblem2&cpid=377
[28] http://usaco.org/index.php?page=viewproblem2&cpid=378
[29] http://usaco.org/index.php?page=viewproblem2&cpid=394
[30] http://usaco.org/index.php?page=viewproblem2&cpid=395
[31] http://usaco.org/index.php?page=viewproblem2&cpid=396
[32] http://usaco.org/index.php?page=viewproblem2&cpid=412
[33] http://usaco.org/index.php?page=viewproblem2&cpid=413
[34] http://usaco.org/index.php?page=viewproblem2&cpid=414

2014 Open Bronze 1 Odometer[35]
2014 Open Bronze 2 Fair Photography[36]
2014 Open Bronze 3 Decorating the Pastures[37]

2014-2015 Season

2014 Dec Bronze 1 Marathon[38]
2014 Dec Bronze 2 Crosswords[39]
2014 Dec Bronze 3 Cow Jog[40]
2014 Dec Bronze 4 Learning by Example[41]

2015 Jan Bronze 1 Cow Routing[42]
2015 Jan Bronze 2 Cow Routing II[43]
2015 Jan Bronze 3 It's All About the Base[44]
2015 Jan Bronze 4 Meeting Time[45]

2015 Feb Bronze 1 Censoring[46]
2015 Feb Bronze 2 Cow[47]
2015 Feb Bronze 3 Cow Hopscotch[48]

2015 Open Bronze 1 Moocryption[49]
2015 Open Bronze 2 Bessie Gets Even[50]
2015 Open Bronze 3 Trapped in the Haybales[51]
2015 Open Bronze 4 Palindromic Paths[52]

2015-2016 Season

2015 Dec Bronze 1 Fence Painting[53]
2015 Dec Bronze 2 Speeding Ticket[54]
2015 Dec Bronze 3 Contaminated Milk[55]

---

[35] http://usaco.org/index.php?page=viewproblem2&cpid=430
[36] http://usaco.org/index.php?page=viewproblem2&cpid=431
[37] http://usaco.org/index.php?page=viewproblem2&cpid=432
[38] http://usaco.org/index.php?page=viewproblem2&cpid=487
[39] http://usaco.org/index.php?page=viewproblem2&cpid=488
[40] http://usaco.org/index.php?page=viewproblem2&cpid=489
[41] http://usaco.org/index.php?page=viewproblem2&cpid=490
[42] http://usaco.org/index.php?page=viewproblem2&cpid=507
[43] http://usaco.org/index.php?page=viewproblem2&cpid=508
[44] http://usaco.org/index.php?page=viewproblem2&cpid=509
[45] http://usaco.org/index.php?page=viewproblem2&cpid=510
[46] http://www.usaco.org/index.php?page=viewproblem2&cpid=526
[47] http://www.usaco.org/index.php?page=viewproblem2&cpid=527
[48] http://www.usaco.org/index.php?page=viewproblem2&cpid=528
[49] http://usaco.org/index.php?page=viewproblem2&cpid=545
[50] http://usaco.org/index.php?page=viewproblem2&cpid=546
[51] http://usaco.org/index.php?page=viewproblem2&cpid=547
[52] http://usaco.org/index.php?page=viewproblem2&cpid=548
[53] https://www.usaco.org/index.php?page=viewproblem2&cpid=567
[54] https://www.usaco.org/index.php?page=viewproblem2&cpid=568
[55] https://www.usaco.org/index.php?page=viewproblem2&cpid=569

2016 Jan Bronze 1 Promotion Counting[56]
2016 Jan Bronze 2 Angry Cows[57]
2016 Jan Bronze 3 Mowing the Field[58]

2016 Feb Bronze 1 Milk Pails[59]
2016 Feb Bronze 2 Circular Barn[60]
2016 Feb Bronze 3 Load Balancing[61]

2016 Open Bronze 1 Diamond Collector[62]
2016 Open Bronze 2 Bull in a China shop[63]
2016 Open Bronze 3 Field Reduction[64]

2016-2017 Season

2016 Dec Bronze 1 Square Pasture[65]
2016 Dec Bronze 2 Block Game[66]
2016 Dec Bronze 3 The Cow-Signal[67]

2017 Jan Bronze 1 Don't be Last![68]
2017 Jan Bronze 2 Hoof, Paper, Scissors[69]
2017 Jan Bronze 3 Cow Tipping[70]

2017 Feb Bronze 1 Why Did the Cow Cross the Road[71]
2017 Feb Bronze 2 Why Did the Cow Cross the Road II[72]
2017 Feb Bronze 3 Why Did the Cow Cross the Road III[73]

2017 Open Bronze 1 The Lost Cow[74]
2017 Open Bronze 2 Bovine Genomics[75]
2017 Open Bronze 3 Modern Art[76]

---

[56] http://usaco.org/index.php?page=viewproblem2&cpid=591
[57] http://usaco.org/index.php?page=viewproblem2&cpid=592
[58] http://usaco.org/index.php?page=viewproblem2&cpid=593
[59] http://usaco.org/index.php?page=viewproblem2&cpid=615
[60] http://usaco.org/index.php?page=viewproblem2&cpid=616
[61] http://usaco.org/index.php?page=viewproblem2&cpid=617
[62] http://usaco.org/index.php?page=viewproblem2&cpid=639
[63] http://usaco.org/index.php?page=viewproblem2&cpid=640
[64] http://usaco.org/index.php?page=viewproblem2&cpid=641
[65] http://usaco.org/index.php?page=viewproblem2&cpid=663
[66] http://usaco.org/index.php?page=viewproblem2&cpid=664
[67] http://usaco.org/index.php?page=viewproblem2&cpid=665
[68] http://usaco.org/index.php?page=viewproblem2&cpid=687
[69] http://usaco.org/index.php?page=viewproblem2&cpid=688
[70] http://usaco.org/index.php?page=viewproblem2&cpid=689
[71] http://usaco.org/index.php?page=viewproblem2&cpid=711
[72] http://usaco.org/index.php?page=viewproblem2&cpid=712
[73] http://usaco.org/index.php?page=viewproblem2&cpid=713
[74] http://usaco.org/index.php?page=viewproblem2&cpid=735
[75] http://usaco.org/index.php?page=viewproblem2&cpid=736
[76] http://usaco.org/index.php?page=viewproblem2&cpid=737

2017-2018 Season

2017 Dec Bronze 1 Blocked Billboard[77]
2017 Dec Bronze 2 The Bovine Shuffle[78]
2017 Dec Bronze 3 Milk Measurement[79]

2018 Jan Bronze 1 Blocked Billboard II[80]
2018 Jan Bronze 2 Lifeguards[81]
2018 Jan Bronze 3 Out of Place[82]

2018 Feb Bronze 1 Teleportation[83]
2018 Feb Bronze 2 Hoofball[84]
2018 Feb Bronze 3 Taming the Herd[85]

2018 Open Bronze 1 Team Tic Tac Toe[86]
2018 Open Bronze 2 Milking Order[87]
2018 Open Bronze 3 Family Tree[88]

2018-2019 Season

2018 Dec Bronze 1 Mixing Milk[89]
2018 Dec Bronze 2 The Bucket List[90]
2018 Dec Bronze 3 Back and Forth[91]

2019 Jan Bronze 1 Shell Game[92]
2019 Jan Bronze 2 Sleepy Cow Sorting[93]
2019 Jan Bronze 3 Guess the Animal[94]

2019 Feb Bronze 1 Sleepy Cow Herding[95]
2019 Feb Bronze 2 The Great Revegetation[96]
2019 Feb Bronze 3 Measuring Traffic[97]

[77] http://usaco.org/index.php?page=viewproblem2&cpid=759
[78] http://usaco.org/index.php?page=viewproblem2&cpid=760
[79] http://usaco.org/index.php?page=viewproblem2&cpid=761
[80] http://usaco.org/index.php?page=viewproblem2&cpid=783
[81] http://usaco.org/index.php?page=viewproblem2&cpid=784
[82] http://usaco.org/index.php?page=viewproblem2&cpid=785
[83] http://www.usaco.org/index.php?page=viewproblem2&cpid=807
[84] http://www.usaco.org/index.php?page=viewproblem2&cpid=808
[85] http://www.usaco.org/index.php?page=viewproblem2&cpid=809
[86] http://www.usaco.org/index.php?page=viewproblem2&cpid=831
[87] http://www.usaco.org/index.php?page=viewproblem2&cpid=832
[88] http://www.usaco.org/index.php?page=viewproblem2&cpid=833
[89] http://usaco.org/index.php?page=viewproblem2&cpid=855
[90] http://usaco.org/index.php?page=viewproblem2&cpid=856
[91] http://usaco.org/index.php?page=viewproblem2&cpid=857
[92] http://usaco.org/index.php?page=viewproblem2&cpid=891
[93] http://usaco.org/index.php?page=viewproblem2&cpid=892
[94] http://usaco.org/index.php?page=viewproblem2&cpid=893
[95] http://www.usaco.org/index.php?page=viewproblem2&cpid=915
[96] http://www.usaco.org/index.php?page=viewproblem2&cpid=916
[97] http://www.usaco.org/index.php?page=viewproblem2&cpid=917

2019 Open Bronze 1 Bucket Brigade[98]
2019 Open Bronze 2 Milk Factory[99]
2019 Open Bronze 3 Cow Evolution[100]

2019-2020 Season

2019 Dec Bronze 1 Cow Gymnastics[101]
2019 Dec Bronze 2 Where Am I?[102]
2019 Dec Bronze 3 Livestock Lineup[103]

2020 Jan Bronze 1 Word Processor[104]
2020 Jan Bronze 2 Photoshoot[105]
2020 Jan Bronze 3 Race[106]

2020 Feb Bronze 1 Triangles[107]
2020 Feb Bronze 2 Mad Scientist[108]
2020 Feb Bronze 3 Swapity Swap[109]
2020 Open Bronze 1 Social Distancing I[110]
2020 Open Bronze 2 Social Distancing II[111]
2020 Open Bronze 3 Cowntact Tracing[112]

2020-2021 Season

2020 Dec Bronze 1 Do You Know Your ABCs?[113]
2020 Dec Bronze 2 Daisy Chains[114]
2020 Dec Bronze 3 Stuck in a Rut[115]

2021 Jan Bronze 1 Uddered but not Herd[116]
2021 Jan Bronze 2 Even More Odd Photos[117]
2021 Jan Bronze 3 Just Stalling[118]

---

[98] http://usaco.org/index.php?page=viewproblem2&cpid=939
[99] http://usaco.org/index.php?page=viewproblem2&cpid=940
[100] http://usaco.org/index.php?page=viewproblem2&cpid=941
[101] http://usaco.org/index.php?page=viewproblem2&cpid=963
[102] http://usaco.org/index.php?page=viewproblem2&cpid=964
[103] http://usaco.org/index.php?page=viewproblem2&cpid=965
[104] http://www.usaco.org/index.php?page=viewproblem2&cpid=987
[105] http://www.usaco.org/index.php?page=viewproblem2&cpid=988
[106] http://www.usaco.org/index.php?page=viewproblem2&cpid=989
[107] http://usaco.org/index.php?page=viewproblem2&cpid=1011
[108] http://usaco.org/index.php?page=viewproblem2&cpid=1012
[109] http://usaco.org/index.php?page=viewproblem2&cpid=1013
[110] http://usaco.org/index.php?page=viewproblem2&cpid=1035
[111] http://usaco.org/index.php?page=viewproblem2&cpid=1036
[112] http://usaco.org/index.php?page=viewproblem2&cpid=1037
[113] http://usaco.org/index.php?page=viewproblem2&cpid=1059
[114] http://usaco.org/index.php?page=viewproblem2&cpid=1060
[115] http://usaco.org/index.php?page=viewproblem2&cpid=1061
[116] http://usaco.org/index.php?page=viewproblem2&cpid=1083
[117] http://usaco.org/index.php?page=viewproblem2&cpid=1084
[118] http://usaco.org/index.php?page=viewproblem2&cpid=1085

2021 Feb Bronze 1 Year of the Cow[119]
2021 Feb Bronze 2 Comfortable Cows[120]
2021 Feb Bronze 3 Clockwise Fence[121]

2021 Open Bronze 1 Acowdemia I[122]
2021 Open Bronze 2 Acowdemia II[123]
2021 Open Bronze 3 Acowdemia III[124]

2021-2022 Season

2021 Dec Bronze 1 Lonely Photo[125]
2021 Dec Bronze 2 Air Cowditioning[126]
2021 Dec Bronze 3 Walking Home[127]

2022 Jan Bronze 1 Herdle[128]
2022 Jan Bronze 2 Non-Transitive Dice[129]

2022 Jan Bronze 3 Drought[130]
2022 Feb Bronze 1 Sleeping in Class[131]
2022 Feb Bronze 2 Photoshoot 2[132]
2022 Feb Bronze 3 Blocks[133]

2022 Open Bronze 1 Photoshoot[134]
2022 Open Bronze 2 Counting Liars[135]
2022 Open Bronze 3 Alchemy[136]

2022-2023 Season

2022 Dec Bronze 1 Cow College[137]
2022 Dec Bronze 2 Feeding the Cows[138]
2022 Dec Bronze 3 Reverse Engineering[139]

---

[119] http://www.usaco.org/index.php?page=viewproblem2&cpid=1107
[120] http://www.usaco.org/index.php?page=viewproblem2&cpid=1108
[121] http://www.usaco.org/index.php?page=viewproblem2&cpid=1109
[122] http://usaco.org/index.php?page=viewproblem2&cpid=1131
[123] http://usaco.org/index.php?page=viewproblem2&cpid=1132
[124] http://usaco.org/index.php?page=viewproblem2&cpid=1133
[125] http://usaco.org/index.php?page=viewproblem2&cpid=1155
[126] http://usaco.org/index.php?page=viewproblem2&cpid=1156
[127] http://usaco.org/index.php?page=viewproblem2&cpid=1157
[128] http://usaco.org/index.php?page=viewproblem2&cpid=987
[129] http://usaco.org/index.php?page=viewproblem2&cpid=988
[130] http://usaco.org/index.php?page=viewproblem2&cpid=989
[131] http://usaco.org/index.php?page=viewproblem2&cpid=1203
[132] http://usaco.org/index.php?page=viewproblem2&cpid=1204
[133] http://usaco.org/index.php?page=viewproblem2&cpid=1205
[134] http://www.usaco.org/index.php?page=viewproblem2&cpid=1227
[135] http://www.usaco.org/index.php?page=viewproblem2&cpid=1228
[136] http://www.usaco.org/index.php?page=viewproblem2&cpid=1229
[137] http://usaco.org/index.php?page=viewproblem2&cpid=1251
[138] http://usaco.org/index.php?page=viewproblem2&cpid=1252
[139] http://usaco.org/index.php?page=viewproblem2&cpid=1253

2023 Jan Bronze 1 Leaders[140]
2023 Jan Bronze 2 Air Cownditioning II[141]
2023 Jan Bronze 3 Moo Operations[142]

2023 Feb Bronze 1 Hungry Cow[143]
2023 Feb Bronze 2 Stamp Grid[144]
2023 Feb Bronze 3 Watching Mooloo[145]

2023 Open Bronze 1 FEB[146]
2023 Open Bronze 2 Moo Language[147]
2023 Open Bronze 3 Rotate and Shift[148]

2023-2024 Season

2023 Dec Bronze 1 Candy Cane Feast[149]
2023 Dec Bronze 2 Cowntact Tracing 2[150]
2023 Dec Bronze 3 Farmer John Actually Farms[151]

2024 Jan Bronze 1 Majority Opinion[152]
2024 Jan Bronze 2 Cannonball[153]
2024 Jan Bronze 3 Balancing Bacteria[154]

2024 Feb Bronze 1 Palindrome Game[155]
2024 Feb Bronze 2 Milk Exchange[156]
2024 Feb Bronze 3 Maximizing Productivity[157]

2024 Open Bronze 1 Logical Moos[158]
2024 Open Bronze 2 Walking Along a Fence[159]
2024 Open Bronze 3 Farmer John's Favorite Permutation[160]

---

[140] http://usaco.org/index.php?page=viewproblem2&cpid=1275
[141] http://usaco.org/index.php?page=viewproblem2&cpid=1276
[142] http://usaco.org/index.php?page=viewproblem2&cpid=1277
[143] http://www.usaco.org/index.php?page=viewproblem2&cpid=1299
[144] http://www.usaco.org/index.php?page=viewproblem2&cpid=1300
[145] http://www.usaco.org/index.php?page=viewproblem2&cpid=1301
[146] http://www.usaco.org/index.php?page=viewproblem2&cpid=1323
[147] http://www.usaco.org/index.php?page=viewproblem2&cpid=1324
[148] http://www.usaco.org/index.php?page=viewproblem2&cpid=1325
[149] http://usaco.org/index.php?page=viewproblem2&cpid=1347
[150] http://usaco.org/index.php?page=viewproblem2&cpid=1348
[151] http://usaco.org/index.php?page=viewproblem2&cpid=1349
[152] http://usaco.org/index.php?page=viewproblem2&cpid=1371
[153] http://usaco.org/index.php?page=viewproblem2&cpid=1372
[154] http://usaco.org/index.php?page=viewproblem2&cpid=1373
[155] http://www.usaco.org/index.php?page=viewproblem2&cpid=1395
[156] http://www.usaco.org/index.php?page=viewproblem2&cpid=1396
[157] http://www.usaco.org/index.php?page=viewproblem2&cpid=1397
[158] http://www.usaco.org/index.php?page=viewproblem2&cpid=1419
[159] http://www.usaco.org/index.php?page=viewproblem2&cpid=1420
[160] http://www.usaco.org/index.php?page=viewproblem2&cpid=1421

Codeforces problems

https://codeforces.com/

- Round #839 (Div. 3) Problem A: A+B?[161] Introduction
- Round #587 (Div. 3) Problem B: Shooting[162] Search : Greedy
- Round #587 (Div. 3) Problem C: White Sheet[163] Geometry : Rectangles : Overlap

CSES Problems

https://www.cses.fi/

- Introductory problems: Weird Algorithm[164] 1.3: Introduction
- Sorting and Searching: Ferris Wheel[165] 5.5 Search : Greedy

---

[161]https://codeforces.com/problemset/problem/1772/A
[162]https://codeforces.com/contest/1216/problem/B
[163]https://codeforces.com/contest/1216/problem/C
[164]https://cses.fi/problemset/task/1068
[165]https://cses.fi/problemset/task/1090

Appendix B. Practice Beyond USACO

This appendix offers additional study and practice resources If you've worked your way through the chapters in this book, and you're looking for even more ways to ensure your success in the competitions, you're in the right place!

If you Google "USACO Bronze practice," you'll be inundated with a tsunami of topics, algorithms, graphs, data structures, and more. It can be overwhelming, even discouraging, to find yourself drowning in information.

Let's keep you afloat! To stay focused and simplify your approach, I recommend that you start with the resources here in this appendix, which are just right for a competitor working on the Bronze level and keeping an eye on Silver as well.

So, here are a few of my favorite resources, appropriate for a new competitor. Be sure to watch for the latest updates on the club's page, at http://www.usacoclub.com.

B.1. Online Guides and Live Coaching

1. USACO Guide - https://usaco.guide/ - The almost-official guide to USACO. Authored by a group of Gold and Platinum alumni, this is a very good resource., combining explanations, problems, and various communities, as well as classes. Because the guide organizes content according to the different levels, you can focus on Bronze subjects and problems if you wish, or try some of the Silver level material.

2. Sites that offer personal tutoring in private and group settings, synchronous and asynchronous:

   - Alpha Star Academy - https://alphastar.academy/
   - X-Camp academy - https://x-camp.academy/
   - VPlanet - https://www.vplanetcoding.com/- A site by Riya Arora, a previous USACO finalist who offers personal coaching.

3. Sites that allow you to search for a local tutor for in-person coaching:

   - Breakout Mentors - https://breakoutmentors.com/usaco-competitive-programming-academy/
   - Momentum Learning - https://www.momentumlearning.org/USACO
   - Recursive Dragon - https://www.recursivedragon.com/
   - Absolute Academy - https://www.absoluteacademy.net/

B.2. Online Practicing and Competing

In addition to the sites listed above that offer guides, the sites below also offer extensive opportunities to practice your skills.

1. USACO - http://usaco.org/ - The official site for the USACO competition, it also includes competition rules, related information, and solutions to all problems.
2. Codeforces - https://www.codeforces.com/ - This is a very well-known site, with an established system used to rate competitive programmers. It hosts competitions for various rating levels, with solutions and discussions available.
3. Kattis - https://open.kattis.com/ - Very similar to Codeforces, this site includes many problems, contests, and a ranking system.
4. DM::OJ - https://dmoj.ca/ - This site offers competitions and many problems, with automated judging available for your submissions. They run their own competitions and also host mirrors of competitions from countries such as Croatia (Croatian Open Competition in Informatics) and Canada (Canadian Computing Competition).
5. UVa - https://onlinejudge.org/ - This site offers a popular online judge for your submissions. It hosts the archive of questions from a college-level competition known as ICPC. These questions go far beyond the level of Bronze, so be sure not to get overwhelmed.
6. CSES (Code Submission Evaluation System) - https://cses.fi/ - It's not a competition system, but rather a well-curated list of problems, grouped by subject, which is especially beneficial for training.
7. A few sites gear themselves toward aspiring job seekers rather than competitive coders, but they still offer good practice:

   - Hacker Rank - https://www.hackerrank.com/
   - Top Coder - https://www.topcoder.com/

8. Code Chef - https://www.codechef.com/ - This site helps you learn new programming languages, practice, and compete.
9. These sites allow you to practice your skills in a different context:

   - Project Euler - https://projecteuler.net/ - The first 100 problems are excellent for Bronze.
   - Coding through fun exercises - https://codecombat.com/
   - Coding competitions in a game setting - https://www.codingame.com/

10. These sites focus more on learning to code. You can use these to improve your skills in your current programming language, or pick up a new language.

    - https://www.codecademy.com/
    - https://www.khanacademy.org/computing/computer-programming
    - https://www.whizkidzcc.com/

B.3. Books

The good news is that you've already read the only essential book you need for Bronze: this one! If you'd like to study from the additional books below, be sure to focus on just the first few chapters of each one, as these apply to Bronze.

1. "An Introduction to the USA Computing Olympiad" - https://darrenyao.com/usacobook/cpp.pdf - by Darren Yao. A great free resource, it covers mainly Bronze and Silver material.
2. "Guide to Competitive Programming" - https://link.springer.com/book/10.1007/978-3-319-72547-5 - by Antti Laaksonen.
3. "Competitive Programming" - https://cpbook.net/ - by Steven Halim and Felix Halim.
4. "Programming Challenges: The Programming Contest Training Manual" - https://link.springer.com/book/10.1007/b97559 - by Steven Skiena and Miguel Revilla. Select this book if you're ready to advance far beyond the Bronze level.
5. "CS Guide" - https://github.com/alwayswimmin/cs_guide/blob/master/guide.pdf - by Samuel Hsiang, Alexander Wei, and Yang Liu. This book, too, is more advanced than the Bronze level.
6. "Looking for a Challenge?" - http://www.lookingforachallengethebook.com/ - From the University of Warsaw, this book offers more advanced competitive programming.

TIP: If any resource or practice problem has you pulling your hair out or banging your head against your desk, just let it go! It's not the right resource or problem for you right now. As a beginner in the world of computer programming, you need to access appropriate challenges. Challenges that are too hard are likely to discourage you. When that happens, step back, assess the resource, and pick something geared more toward beginners. That way, you'll be challenged in a way that's fun and productive!

www.ingramcontent.com/pod-product-compliance
Lightning Source LLC
Chambersburg PA
CBHW060651060326
40690CB00020B/4595